The Invention of Craft

The Invention of Craft

Glenn Adamson

BLOOMSBURY

LONDON · NEW DELHI · NEW YORK · SYDNEY

Bloomsbury Academic

An imprint of Bloomsbury Publishing Plc

50 Bedford Square
London
WC1B 3DP
UK

175 Fifth Avenue
New York
NY 10010
USA

www.bloomsbury.com

Published in association with the Victoria and Albert Museum, London.

First published 2013

British Library Cataloguing-in-Publication Data
A catalogue record for this book is available from the British Library.

ISBN: HB: 978 0 85785 064 5
PB: 978 0 85785 066 9

Library of Congress Cataloging-in-Publication Data
A catalog record for this book is available from the Library of Congress.

Typeset by Apex CoVantage.
Printed and bound in the UK

CONTENTS

LIST OF ILLUSTRATIONS

Plates

Figures

ACKNOWLEDGMENTS

This book was written mainly in 2010 and 2011, when I probably should have been doing something else. At the time, I was hard at work on the *Postmodernism: Style and Subversion 1970 to 1990* exhibition held at the V&A. I suppose the two projects served as useful antitheses: a curatorial examination of the recent past, dwelling mainly on issues of self-referential image making; and this book, an exploration of a more distant history, which looks at a much more substantial material history. In any case, this book would never have been written without the practical and intellectual support I derived from my colleagues at the V&A, especially my co-curator Jane Pavitt and assistant curator Oliver Winchester, and exhibition officer Rosie Wanek. I would particularly like to acknowledge present and past members of the V&A/RCA Course in the History of Design: Marta Ajmar, Sarah Cheang, Richard Checketts, Christine Guth, Victoria Kelley, Ulrich Lehmann, Angela McShane, Viviana Narotzky, Ana Pereira, Katrina Royall, and Sarah Teasley. Among the many other friends and colleagues at the museum who provided assistance during this time, directly and indirectly, were Christopher Breward, Laurie Britton-Newell, Clare Browne, Julius Bryant, Lily Crowther, Alice Evans, Catherine Flood, Sarah Gage, Alun Graves, Loraine Long, Beth McKillop, Liz Miller, Sue Prichard, Alicia Robinson, Carolyn Sargentson, Jana Scholze, Greg Sullivan, Abraham Thomas, Marjorie Trusted, Carol Tulloch, Eric Turner, Zoe Whitley, Damien Whitmore, Christopher Wilk, Lucy Wood, Helen Woodfield, and Hilary Young. Research support for the book was provided by a series of wonderful interns, design historians of the future: Tiffany Jow, Hans Liu, Emily Sack, and Marilyn Zapf.

Tanya Harrod and Ned Cooke, my coeditors of the *Journal of Modern Craft,* continue to be my foremost intellectual partners in writing craft history. I am most grateful to them for their ongoing friendship and inspiration, as I am to the other contributing editors of the journal: Elissa Auther, Stephen Knott, Joseph McBrinn, Louisa Mazanti, Kevin Murray, and Catherine Whalen. For me, the journal has been, above all, a means of bringing them and other voices together. Sarah Archer, Julia Bryan-Wilson, Freyja Hartzell, Stephen Knott, Ethan Lasser, Patricia Ribault, Catharine Rossi, Ezra Shales, T'ai Smith, and Jenni Sorkin are among the new generation of craft theorists and historians who are reshaping this field. All have been in active dialogue with me as this book developed, and I hope they will find it interesting.

I would also like to acknowledge the help and friendship of Simon Cowell, Kathryn Earle, Tristan Palmer, and all their colleagues at Berg (now Bloomsbury); Elissa Auther, Luke Beckerdite, David Benedict, Dipti Bhagat, Raphaelle Bischoff and her colleagues at Bischoff Weiss Gallery, Andrew Bolton (Metropolitan Museum of Art), Alison Britton, Julia Bryan-

Wilson, Victor Buchli, Daniel Charny, Tony Cragg, Patrick Elliott (National Galleries of Scotland), Paul Ferguson, Ryan Gander, Charles Gant, David and Maggi Gordon, Aya Haidar, Greg Hilty (Lisson Gallery), Neil Hunter, Alice Kettle, Zoe Laughlin, Henrietta Lidchi (National Museums Scotland), Ben Lignel, Martina Margetts, Tatjana Marsden and the staff at Marsden Woo Gallery, Jennifer and Mike Mikulay, Alice Motard (Raven Row Gallery), Mark Nesbitt (Kew Economic Botany Collection), Simon Olding, PostlerFerguson, Jon Prown, Benjamin Schmidt, Ezra Shales, Zoe Sheehan Saldaña, Nancy Sazama, Sarah Fayen Scarlett, Tim Screech, Elaine Tierney, Louise Valentine, Jorunn Veiteberg, Alicia Volk, Namita Wiggers, and Anne Wilson. And to Nicola Probert for a week of writing in Wales, and many other wonderful times besides.

Finally, to my family—Arthur, David and Joyce, Petty Felice and Bruce, Judy and Fred, Kevin Megan and Cally, Peter Ursula Sophia and Johanna—much love.

INTRODUCTION

Craft's reputation is as something eternal. It has always been with us, it seems, since the first pots were made from clay dug out of riverbeds and the first simple baskets were plaited by hand. Seen from this perspective, craft is intrinsic to what it is to be human. In modern times, though, it seems to be under constant assault. Its steady disappearance, in the face of the more powerful and efficient forms of production that we call "industry," is therefore to be understood as a tide of depersonalization. We must try to turn the clock back, to revive craft's organic role in society, or at least slow the pace of its vanishing.

That is the usual way of looking at things. But this book is going to tell the story rather differently. Rather than treating craft as an ever-present aspect of human behavior increasingly threatened by technological advances, I argue that craft is itself a modern invention. It is customary to speak of the century from 1750 to 1850 as the time of the "industrial revolution," a phrase that conveys a sense of radical transformation. And rightly so: it is impossible to miss the novelty and importance of the mechanization, factory organization, mass production, and division of labor that characterized this period in history. Yet it is easy to overlook the fact that craft was taking shape at the same time. It emerged as a coherent idea, a defined terrain, only as industry's opposite number, or "other." Craft was not a static backdrop against which industry emerged like a figure from the ground. Rather, the two were created alongside one another, each defined against the other through constant juxtaposition.

What had been an undifferentiated world of making, in which artisans enjoyed relatively high status within a broader continuum of professional trades, was carved into two, with craftspeople usually relegated to a position of inferiority. This bifurcation divided the infinitely complex field of human production into a set of linked binaries: craft/industry, freedom/alienation, tacit/explicit, hand/machine, traditional/progressive. This book aims to describe the formation of these dialectical pairings, to establish their historical origins and also to deconstruct them, illustrating their ideological qualities. I chart the emergence of this oppositional model of modern craft, while also examining the effacements and elisions necessary to erect this binary structure. I therefore present artisans as drivers of change, as well as its opponents. And I discuss the ways that modern improvers and reformers depended on craftspeople—and sometimes held them up for praise—even as they devised new ways to manipulate them.

The Invention of Craft is intended as a sequel (or, given the earlier period under study, perhaps a "prequel") to my previous book, *Thinking through Craft*.[1] There the focus was principally upon modern and contemporary art. My objective was to demonstrate the important role craft plays in recent art history, precisely because of its constructed inferiority. I tried to show how various aspects of craft's non-art status could be productive as frictional constraints, and also asked what might happen if that vertical structure were done away with. In the intervening five years, many artists and designers have pursued postdisciplinary, nonhierarchical practice—to an extent that I certainly did not predict. In *The Invention of Craft*, I have tried to respond to these developments, continuing where I left off in some ways. But here the framework is much less art historical. Though I do look at contemporary artists at various points in the text, they no longer take center stage. Rather, I have tried to examine the broader question of craft's position within modern production—not just in studios, but in factories as well. If I am right that craft was invented principally as a counterpart to industry, this also complicates received ideas about the historical origins of its inferior (or supplementary) identity.

In this effort, I try to enlarge on the work of authors like Larry Shiner, who in his similarly titled book, *The Invention of Art* (2003), likewise argues for a differentiation of craft from fine art.[2] Shiner does not consider craft to be a novel conception in the modern period (he assumes it has always been with us), and his chronology is a bit more elastic than mine—he is concerned to locate the sources of craft's second-class status in the Renaissance. But my primary departure from his work is that he sees the craft object's opposite number not as the industrial commodity, but as the autonomous work of art. For Shiner, a divergence between art and craft first emerged in the Renaissance and culminated in an absolute institutional separation in the eighteenth century. While there is something to be said for this argument, my feeling is that it gets the chronology wrong, mainly because the opposition between craft and fine art (rather than industry) is drastically overemphasized in his account. The habit of defining craft principally in opposition to fine art is, in fact, a largely twentieth-century, even post-1945, tendency. It is an outgrowth of the fact that we tend to encounter craft in museums and galleries, because it is only in these rarefied circumstances that it can achieve economic viability. Authors like Shiner tend to project their own concerns about the relation between art and craft backward, as if that were the main consideration in craft history. But this is to put the cart a long way in advance of the horse. The domain of production as a whole was massively reshaped in the late eighteenth century, and fine art plays a very minor role indeed in that transformation. To understand the invention of craft, we must look at other spheres of thought and making.

In *The Invention of Craft*, then, I do sometimes touch on sculpture, painting, and contemporary art, but I do not accord these fields any preeminence. At the same time, I should be clear that the book is not intended as a substantive history of labor, industry, technology, or economy between 1750 and 1850. Nor does it attempt to systematically survey productive trades in the period or to provide a comprehensive political history of artisan communities—though I have cited many works by other scholars that aim to do all these things. Instead, the strategy I have employed is akin to intellectual history, in that I try to track the development of an idea over time—with the difference that this idea is not only formulated in period writings, but also inscribed into objects and their popular reception. Each of the book's four chapters analyzes an aspect of craft's differentiation as a discrete form of practice. These key traits are examined in detail through a series of thematically grouped case studies, each of which culminates in a leap forward to the present. Each chapter ends with a discussion of contemporary production that might be associated with the historical material just described. My coverage of this contemporary material tends not to dwell on the normative crafts media of ceramics, textiles, and so forth, but instead looks at other creative areas such as sculpture, fashion, design, material science, and amateur practice. This indiscriminate approach is a way of acknowledging today's climate of postdisciplinary flux. The stark dichotomies suggested by the pairing craft/industry no longer hold. I try to suggest some critical and theoretical paths through the resulting maze of possibilities.

Thus as a whole, *The Invention of Craft* is structured like a pair of parentheses. My aim is to bracket the story of modern craft, placing its long-ago moment of formation (its invention) in relation to its present-day transformation (and hence, the possibility of its reinvention).

* * *

The conventional narrative of craft in the period of the industrial revolution is one of decline followed by renewal. Artisans were drummed out of work by machines, with tragic consequences both for the experience of the makers themselves and the quality of the things they produced. Eventually the Arts and Crafts movement arose in response as a reclamation project. Because of its simplicity, this received story is deeply satisfying. It provides us with a noble but fallen victim (the craftsman in his picturesque shop), a cardboard-cutout villain (the capitalist lording over his belching factory), and a heroic savior (the high-minded craft reformer). It also comes with impressive intellectual backing. The ideas of William Morris, loosely based on the inspiring examples of John Ruskin and Karl Marx, were formative to an international craft revival that sought to undo the pernicious effects of industrialization. Morris and his many followers saw themselves as restoring craftspeople to their rightful historical place so that they would once again be masters of their own hands. They knew full well that handwork could only be marginal within a capitalist economy, and they drew various conclusions from that depressing fact. Morris became an avowed utopian, envisaging a total reform of society along socialist lines. Others adopted a model of retreat, advocating a withdrawal from modernity; or emphasized craft's ameliorative role, hoping it might soften the hard edges of the modern; or operated in symbolic terms, emulating the model of fine art. But until recently, there has been near unanimity on one point: craft is fundamentally antithetical to the processes of modernization. It can only be understood as a corrective or an escape hatch, never as a contributing factor. From the Arts and Crafts movement around the turn of the century through to the Studio Craft movement, the counterculture of the 1960s and 1970s, and today's fashionable DIY scene, the constant has been that craft is an antidote to modernity.

Yet this medicine has been delivered in absence of a proper diagnosis. An objective look at the late eighteenth and early nineteenth centuries suggests that John Ruskin and William Morris did not see the whole story. Consider the fact that in Europe in 1850 there were undoubtedly *more* skilled artisans, plying a far greater range of trades, than there had been in 1750. Far from being obsolete, manual skill was the primary way the workforce divided itself: a "labor aristocracy" of highly trained craftspeople maintained and defended their privileged position, just as guild-backed workshop masters had a century before. Craft revivalists like Ruskin and Morris also ignored the nuanced interdependencies of the hand and the machine: the variable rate and irregular manner in which automation was introduced to workshops; the many trades in which new tools extended the reach of hand skills, rather than replacing them; and the craftsmanship necessary to make machines and other industrial tools in the first place. If we broaden the scope to include the whole range of Victorian material culture, to include not only domestic crafts but also practices like bridge building, leatherwork, carriage making, tailoring, boot making, taxidermy, and the fabrication of scientific instruments, it becomes obvious that skills were not in decline in the mid-nineteenth century. On the contrary, craft was the order of the day.

If Morris and his adherents were disinclined to closely examine the craftsmanship of their own time, they also idealized the period prior to industrialization. It would be naïve to say that industrialism did not bring exploitation, especially in areas such as textile manufacturing that lent themselves to early and extensive mechanization. But craft revivalists regularly downplayed the fact that exploitative labor long predated the industrial revolution. They treated the arena of premodern production in ahistorical terms—as if it did not contain its own stories of institutional, technological, and commercial transformation. When I argue that craft was invented in late eighteenth- and early nineteenth-century Europe and America, clearly I do not mean that artisanal work had not been done before that, or was not being done elsewhere. But before the industrial revolution, and outside its sphere of influence, it was not possible to speak of craft as a separate field of endeavor—from what would it be separated? Even the most mundane, serial production (Adam Smith's proverbial example of pin making, for example) could only be done through the work of many hands. Of course skill played a key cultural role in the ancient, medieval, and Renaissance periods in Europe, and also in Asia, the Americas, Oceania, and Africa. But these chronological and geographical contexts have one thing in common: they lacked that distinctively modern discursive shift, particular to Europe and America, in which craft was marked out as something special. Indeed, even speaking of "craft" in these other contexts generally involves an imaginative projection in which certain forms of labor are isolated and interpreted in terms of a peculiarly modern, Eurocentric worldview.[3]

So strongly geographical is the opposition between industry and craft that it became a means of dividing the globe into contrasting productive spheres. Craft was a crucial prop in the theater of imperialism. In his book *The Bureaucracy of Beauty*, a study of British design interventions into colonial India, Arindam Dutta has noted, "As a figure of difference, the artisan does not disappear with the advent of industrialism. Rather, it appears within it...Had colonial officials found no artisanry in the vast territories under imperial control, it would have been necessary to *invent some*."[4] Within this coercive project, craft conditioned the relations between colonizer and colonized by framing the latter as static, trapped within tradition. British authors like James Mill described Indian artisans as slow and intuitive. Modern textile designers, by contrast, were presented as inventive, progressive, technological, efficient: in short, as pioneers in a developing realm of production. Never mind that in the mid-nineteenth century, Indian cottons were superior in quality and lower in unit cost than their mass-produced British equivalents. That problem would doubtless be conquered in time, just as colonial subjects themselves had been. Yet this was not simply a matter of disdain. Qualitative superiority was certainly assigned to the progressive manufacturing techniques of modern industry, but there was also a process of active valuation at work. Craft was invented as having positive qualities of creativity, rootedness, and authenticity. Sympathetic early ethnographers, for example, esteemed Native American culture even as they painted it in the colors of tragedy. They idealized the indigenous people's ways of living, even as they were being "reformed" in matters of religion, manufacturing, and everyday life, so as to better consign them to the scrap heap of history. Here is an uncomfortable truth: the ascription of authenticity to traditional culture may seem generous—we still do it all the time—but it is actually inseparable from long-established Eurocentric mechanisms of domination. For this reason, I concentrate throughout the book on case studies that are either set in Europe and America, or that show how people from that part of the globe understood "other" ways of making—for it was in this asymmetrical geographic formation that the invention of craft occurred. To assist me in the effort of deconstructing this dimension of modern craft, an ambition I shared with a wide range of postcolonial scholars, I enlist techniques borrowed from anthropologists, notably Alfred Gell.

Just as Euro-Americans positioned "exotic" craft at the far end of a newly created temporal axis, they applied the same discursive technique to their own premodern past, which in modern thinking is classically framed as a *longue durée* characterized by simplicity, cyclical rhythms, and localism. From this perspective, artisans are primarily important because they preserve knowledge of this past. To call something "craft," by the mid-nineteenth century, was to imply that it was rooted in precedent, or to use a more charged word, "tradition" (which is also a matter of projection from the outside, at least in its own moments of invention).[5] This is not to say that craft is devalued under modernity, exactly; rather, it is valued differently from other forms of cultural production. It is positioned as fundamentally conservative, both in the positive and negative senses of that word. Progress is always located elsewhere—in political radicalism, machinery and technology, organizational structures—but never in skilled hands themselves. This attitude puts strict limits on craft. In the nineteenth century, it was typically consigned either to a merely mechanical role, as the execution of designs, ideas, and imperatives, or given responsibility for static tradition. Artisans and their products, then, were understood in one of two ways: as in need of constant "improvement," or on the contrary, as fragile connections to the traditional past.[6]

This did accord artisans an unprecedented cultural responsibility, but though much was gained from this set of associations, today we have more to discover by departing from it.

So if the early nineteenth century can be described as an open parenthesis, which inaugurated a new, modern phase in the history of craft, then it is worth asking: what happens when the closed parenthesis arrives? That is, what will succeed modern craft? This is the question we need to confront now. Well into the flourishing of an undefined postdisciplinary condition in which categories of making are increasingly intermingled and hybridized, it is not surprising that the modern, oppositional way of thinking about production has lost its purchase on the creative imagination. The path forward is not at all clear. Craft-based institutions seem to lack direction, and innovative work—whether it inclines to the worlds of architecture, art, design, film, or elsewhere—is only thinly supported by critical theory when it comes to questions of manual skill. Yet a new generation of craft theorists has begun to engage with the possibilities arising from contemporary postdisciplinary practice.[7] *The Invention of Craft* draws from and hopefully extends their work, by proposing that a deeper understanding of craft in the period from 1750 to 1850, the developmental phase of modernity, may hold some lessons for our own uncertain present.

* * *

This book pursues this set of ideas through an elastic chronological structure. Each chapter examines developments in the eighteenth and nineteenth centuries, establishing a conceptual framework on the basis of that historical exercise, and then applies the framework to contemporary practice. Over the course of the book I move from the late eighteenth century, discussed chiefly in chapter one, through the early nineteenth, covered in chapters two and three, and finally, in chapter four, to the first explicit responses to modern craft's invention, in the shape of revivalism and finally the Arts and Crafts movement in the late nineteenth century. The period under discussion is marked at its beginning by the height of guild-based luxury craft production (the elaborate objects that we characterize today as rococo), and takes the Great Exhibition of 1851, the set-piece triumph of Victorian industry and empire, as its culminating moment. Many historians have positioned this event as the grand opening act in the development of modern design—and for good reason. Directly or indirectly, the Great Exhibition spawned many of the key institutions of design reform around the world, with the South Kensington Museum (now the V&A, my own workplace) as a notional center. It boosted design education. It was a giant showcase for innovators, from American engineers to Gothic Revival designer A.W.N. Pugin to "ornamentist" Owen Jones to architect-engineer Joseph Paxton, who designed the Crystal Palace of iron and glass in which the Great Exhibition was staged. In *The Invention of Craft*, however, this event is presented as the climactic outcome of a process, not the beginning of one. It was the confirmation of a widespread rethinking of skill, which is now being rethought yet again. So we need to look backward through the great globalizing optic of the Great

Exhibition. Studying pre-1850 modes of making gives us certain theoretical tools that might help to invert or undo the logic of modernization and hence point the way forward.

The first chapter, on the theme of *manipulation,* has to do with control. While the conventional narrative that pictures artisans shunted aside by machines is largely fictitious, modern systems of production did reposition skilled hands, consigning them to a secondary role. This was the formation of craft's supplementarity, which I examined in *Thinking Through Craft.* In that book, I defined this characteristic primarily in the formal terms of fine art. From the normative perspective of modernist art criticism, craft is a supplement to the work of art, even though it is through craft that the real work happens. That is, it is only through the application of know-how that artworks come into being, but that physical consideration has been consistently sidelined so that other qualities—opticality, transcendence, aesthetic resolution, conceptual depth—can take center stage. I compared craft to the frame around a painting, which is assigned a marginal position in order to support the painting's status as an object of autonomous aesthetic interest. My examination of modern regimes of workforce control parallels this discussion, but displaces the theme of supplementarity back in time to the decades before and after 1800, and into fields of production well outside the art world. I show how craft was invented by British capitalists, "improvers," and artisans themselves as that which tacitly supports other forms of making, including industry and architecture. This repositioning cannot be attributed to the effect of machines. In very few industries was mechanization able to replace hand skill. Indeed, images of artisans from the middle of the eighteenth century already captured the shift, even before the introduction of widespread automation had occurred. Of particular importance here are the division and specialization of labor, which originated not in British factories but in artisanal workshops on the Continent. These transformations did not, as is often claimed, de-skill workers. Rather, the modern invention of craft literally put artisans "in their place." In fact, it was precisely their workers' valuable skills that motivated capitalists to invent new techniques of controlling them. As craft technique was isolated as a subject of concern in its own right through division and explication, the person executing the technique was—in a countervailing move—made to seem inconsequential or generic.

Maxine Berg demonstrated some years ago that it was the process of subdivision, rather than the introduction of technology, that did most to affect established patterns of skilled work: "Machinery did not displace labor. Rather, it differentiated this labor by dismembering the old craft."[8] I enlarge on this claim, arguing that it was not only in mechanized factories that "dismemberment" occurred but also in the upper echelons of the luxury trades. Woodcarving is an exemplary case. This craft was impossible to mechanize, but was nonetheless thoroughly transformed in the late eighteenth and early nineteenth centuries. I examine that transformation, concentrating particularly on American carver and architect Samuel McIntire, who managed to exploit the new disciplinary framework that affected his career. McIntire invested his carvings with the "flat" logic of drawing. This is one instance of the habit of assigning to draftsmanship, itself a hand skill, a legislative function over all others. The chapter concludes with a theoretical consideration of tooling—the infrastructure of making in which various forms of control play out—and moves on to look at the contemporary phenomenon of outsourced labor. Far from being a settled issue, the control exercised over skilled hands has become an even more important political question over the last few decades, as the global displacement of labor has led to ever more sophisticated forms of control. Hopefully, by the conclusion of this first chapter the scope of the problem will become clear. The very word "manipulation" derives from the Latin for "hand." Craft is itself a powerful form of control, but precisely because of that potency, a telescoping system of larger forces seeks to control it. Craft's fate in modern times has been to manipulate and be manipulated in turn.

In chapter two, the book moves off the shop floor and into the field of discourse proper. Here the focus is not about what artisans do, but how they are talked about. I argue that the modern invention of craft involved the systematic revealing of its secrets. The veil of artisanal *mystery* was replaced with a self-serving form of explicit description. The accounts of making published in the nineteenth century far transcended the demands of utility; taken as a whole, they diminished the proprietary knowledge of artisans as far as possible. This argument will not surprise anyone who has spent much time with Victorian sources, which are famous for their thoroughly researched verbosity. I set the period's discourse on craft alongside other contexts exhibiting the same tendency, such as museum displays and early anthropological texts. In all of these cases a claim to transparency actually concealed a power play. By explaining artisanal potency, Victorian writers tried to explain it away. That effort betrays a further attempt to control the artisan, consistent with the manipulative structures explored in chapter one. Yet craft does not submit easily to explication. As anyone who has tried to describe a skilled process knows, it is not possible to thoroughly replace the actions of a craft with a linguistic equivalent.

Even as didactic texts flowed freely, craft retained something of its former mystery, a factor that persists to this day as an aspect of its appeal. I discuss magic as a signifier for this unruly element, one aspect of its cultural power. Inexplicable things formerly held great cultural status. But now they were seen as untrustworthy, to be dispelled through rational explanation. This was so whether the magic in question was associated with the skill of the artisan, the power of an object—usually a handmade one—or whole "primitive" cultures, themselves associated with craft (as the prevalence of the term "witchcraft" in early anthropology attests). Yet it is worth emphasizing that the moment of revelation promised by these explanatory structures was itself pleasurable. This meant that even as the Victorian culture of explanation marshaled its forces against craft secrecy, it also engaged in performative experiences of oscillating concealment and revelation. In this respect craft can be compared to sleight of hand, like the kind practiced on stage. I examine this dynamic both in narratives of skill in performance, and also in the case of materiality itself, by examining three media important at the time—cast iron, papier-mâché, and rubber. These were understood as completely plastic, subject to a designer's willpower. But this was a fantasy. Though these materials were tractable, their materiality remained to some degree outside a designer's control, and the craft knowledge required to manage that physical specificity did too. The chapter concludes with a discussion of our own culture of explanation, brought about by the seemingly all-pervasive information machine that is the Internet. I examine contemporary issues in intellectual property, asking how craft might play a part in difficult questions about knowledge ownership. The chapter closes with a few examples of art and design practice in which the skilled management of secrecy and explication becomes a subject matter in its own right.

Chapter three recasts the old division between the mind and the hand—a division that long predates the invention of craft, but certainly played a crucial role in its formation. Many discussions of craft then and since have revolved around this separation, which portrays craft as instinctive or unthinking, and other categories (design, art, engineering) as fundamentally intellectual. As mentioned previously, that opposition goes far back in European history, back to Renaissance and ancient distinctions between the liberal and *mechanical* arts.[9] The longevity of this opposition has led many to conclude that European culture has always observed a hierarchical arrangement that held artistic and scientific pursuits separate from and superior to craft. I depart from this interpretation. Recent scholarship on early modern European science, engineering, and fine art alike has shown that these fields were thoroughly shot through with artisanal elements, and that these were not separated out or consciously opposed to intellectual work. Chemistry, sculpture, and architecture were certainly accorded higher social status than apothecary work, ornamental carving, and building. But we should not therefore assume that the latter were distinguished as "crafts," or indeed that early modern people were unsympathetic to the artisanal aspect of higher-status activities. It was in the eighteenth and especially the early nineteenth century that these rigid distinctions came into play. This was the moment when the term "mechanical" acquired its modern sense. Once it had denoted the interaction between matter and motion (as in Newtonian physics) or practical as opposed to theoretical concerns. Now it came to mean rote execution that could be clearly distinguished and separated from intellectual work. Perhaps only with the advent of widespread automation could such an idea have gained currency. Factory system advocates frequently compared artisans to machines, with the crucial caveat that they were less efficient and consistent than their automated equivalents. In response, anti-factory reformers began to prize craft precisely for its instinctive, inefficient, and irregular qualities.

This value system has been sustained ever since, but few today seem aware that it has its roots in early nineteenth-century debates. I examine the application of new ideas about the mechanical in two contexts: first, the training of artisans, particularly at what were called "mechanics' institutes," which sought to impart knowledge to their audiences and thus improve them; and second, in cross-cultural encounters. British understandings of India, and the treatment of Native Americans in the United States, were conditioned by a growing association of craft with cultural difference. Once it had firmly been associated with tradition and opposed to modern progress, craft came to signify whole realms of making practiced by non-European cultures. Efforts to elevate "natives" from their position of inefficient alterity often targeted the crafts; if they could be sufficiently improved, then these people might be able to beat a broader path to civilization. This racist and imperialist attitude is surprisingly similar to the treatment of domestic artisans at the mechanics' institutes, and again has a powerful resonance that lasts to this day in uninspected notions about craft as a pleasurably inefficient "other" to modernity. The chapter also considers another aspect of mechanical work which was crucial in the nineteenth century, and continues to the present: the crafting of exact copies. I argue that this *analogue* practice—a word that I use in the double meaning of "material" and "imitative"—has been an intrinsic aspect of modern craft. Both in the historic production of replicas, such as plaster casts, and in the context of contemporary sculpture and design, I show how copying can be used as a route back to an undifferentiated attitude to the conception of the mechanical, in which jobs that might seem rote or uncreative are shown to be powerfully innovative in their own right.

The final chapter brings us past the crucial date of 1851 and to the reform movements of the late nineteenth century. My objective here is not to provide an overview of the reform-ist discourse—unlike the other topics covered in this book, it has been well documented already by craft historians—but rather to show how they responded directly to ideas about craft that had already been formulated. Ruskin, Morris, and their followers are typically seen as the originators of the narrative of modern craft. By showing them to be fundamentally reactive to earlier ideas, I hope to reposition them within a broader story about craft and modernity, and also to clarify the true nature of their contribution. *Memory* serves as the ordering principle for the chapter, because it is in forming a new relation to the past that craft proves most indispensable. Modernity, a word I use a lot in this book, has been defined and theorized in many ways since the late eighteenth century; I use it in a rather conventional way, to designate a new world, in the words of Miles Ogborn, "in which rational beings are caught within an iron cage of their own making, and one where all that is solid melts into the air of dramatic and disruptive transformation."[10] Many commentators have contested the idea of a fundamental rupture in history along these lines. According to Bruno Latour, for example, "we have never been modern," and the conceptual apparatus attached to the term is a marker of self-interest rather than real cultural change. Latour's skeptical perspective is consistent with my own, to some degree—I portray the various "improvers" of the nineteenth century as operating in bad faith more often than not. But it is doubtless the case that by the middle of the nineteenth century, there was a widely shared perception that a radical break had occurred. This feeling could be expressed in theory and text, but it was also a shift in bodily experience, the arena in which craft itself is active. As Elizabeth Wilson puts it, modernity "refers to things both intangible and undeniably material: the atmosphere and culture of a whole epoch, its smells, its sounds, its rhythms. While an economic analysis may ultimately explain our society more objectively than any other, the use of the term 'modernity' makes possible the exploration of our subjective experience of it."[11]

Karl Marx's famous phrase "all that is solid melts into air," quoted by Ogborn, is a remarkably concise summary of this modern feeling.[12] It is not surprising that craft, with its deep connection to materiality and cultural continuity, should have emerged as a remedy.

But there was as much willful blindness among the craft reformers as their opponents. Indeed, the distortions put forward by the two positions mirror one another with uncanny exactness. In the final chapter, I analyze the presumption of craft as a repository and signifier of collective memory, turning to the techniques of Freudian theory to do so. Craft has been embraced, above all, as a mitigating factor in modern life. While acknowledging the historical importance of this role, I try to show how limiting this view has been, and the symptomatic effacement such a view entails. I argue that craft needs to be liberated from this disengaged position, in which it stands in opposition to the disruptive forces of change. What role, then, should it play? That is a harder question to answer, and I approach it circumspectly, looking first at instances in which craft was seen as consistent with progress, such as the earliest large-scale union of artisans (the Amalgamated Society of Engineers). The chapter—and the book—ends with a discussion of the ways in which craft's claim to cultural memory can be retained, without fixing it as backward looking or conservative. It is no coincidence that in this concluding passage, feminist methodology comes to the fore. For any craft historian, feminism is an indispensable theoretical framework because of its thorough critique of patriarchal control. In their attempts to undo that pervasive subjugation, feminist writers have modeled numerous ways of rewriting social history and imagining a more just future (and many, including the late Rozsika Parker, have positioned craft in a central role).[13] I hope that this spirit pervades all my work, but it is perhaps most obvious here at the end of the book, as I examine a wide range of women's crafts across a spectrum from disempowerment to radicalism. In the lace industry of Ireland, starving girls were put to the grueling work of fashioning finery for self-congratulatory British patrons. Meanwhile, working-class women were making ends meet through painstaking, low-paid outwork and sweatshop labor. They were the ancestors of today's garment industry workers. Yet in the context of the suffragette movement, needle skills were put in the service of unprecedented claims for gender equality. Across this panoply of women's experience, craft emerges as a complex and contradictory form of self-reliance. A concluding set of case studies, again chosen from divergent points in a sociopolitical spectrum, shows how contemporary media culture continues to employ the heavily freighted materiality of craft to dramatically diverse ends. The cumulative effect of these examples once again demonstrates the core insight of feminist theory. Agency, including whatever agency can be claimed through craft, is always compromised, always performed, never totally authentic. That, in fact, is the secret of its power.

* * *

It might be useful, as a final introductory note, to clarify what I mean by the word "craft." This has been the central term in my work for well over a decade now, and I have always tried to use it in a commonsense fashion, though I do try to use it to designate a process or activity, rather than a category. The conventional designation of certain media, like pottery and weaving, as "crafts," and others, like welding and painting, as something else, has never had much appeal for me. For me, craft has always meant something like "making something well through hand skill," no more and no less. In the process of writing this book, though, I have come to realize that no such innocent usage of the term is possible. That is because craft is a modern artifact in its own right. For convenience, I use the terms "artisan" and "artisanal" when I want to talk about skilled people and skill-intensive practice in a less ideologically charged manner.[14] There is no way of talking about modern craft that is neutral. It was invented at a time of conflict between the ranks of the skillful and others involved in production, who recognized the unique potency of skill and therefore wanted to contain and control it. This book is about the history of that episode, its legacy, and the imminent possibility of its undoing. At that point the story of modern craft will have run its course. What happens next is for the makers to decide.

NOTES

1. Glenn Adamson, *Thinking through Craft* (Oxford: Berg Publishers, 2007). In the interval I also completed *The Craft Reader* (Oxford: Berg, 2010), an anthology of writings that provided much of the inspiration for this new book.
2. Larry Shiner, *The Invention of Art: A Cultural History* (Chicago: University of Chicago Press, 2003).
3. See Jean Baudrillard, "The Artisan," from *The Mirror of Production* (1973), reprinted in *The Journal of Modern Craft* 4/1 (March 2011): 87–91.
4. Arindam Dutta, *The Bureaucracy of Beauty: Design in the Age of its Global Reproducibility* (London: Routledge, 2007), pp. 31, 77. See also Bruno Latour, *We Have Never Been Modern* (Cambridge, MA: Harvard University Press, 1993 [orig. pub. 1991]).
5. Eric Hobsbawm and Terence Ranger, *The Invention of Tradition* (Cambridge: Cambridge University Press, 2002). See also John Roberts, "Labour, Emancipation and the Critique of Craft Skill," *Journal of Modern Craft* 5/2 (July 2012): 137–148.
6. David Gross, *Lost Time: On Remembering and Forgetting in Late Modern Culture* (Amherst: University of Massachusetts Press, 2000), p. 142.
7. Much of this work has appeared in the *Journal of Modern Craft,* which I coedit with Tanya Harrod and Edward S. Cooke, Jr.
8. Maxine Berg, *The Machinery Question and the Making of Political Economy* (Cambridge: Cambridge University Press, 1980), p. 33.
9. Here it is worth noting the erroneous tendency to associate the hierarchical opposition of liberal and mechanical arts with the philosophical position of mind/body dualism, associated particularly with Descartes. Debates stemming from Cartesian rationalism seek to address the question of whether the mind (or soul) is material—fundamentally a part of the body—or immaterial. Either way, there is no necessary implication that the mind should be *preferred* to the body; the philosophical problem is ontological, not social or cultural, in nature.
10. Miles Ogborn, *Spaces of Modernity: London's Geographies 1680–1780* (New York: Guilford Press, 1998), p. 2.

11. Elizabeth Wilson, "Fashion and Modernity," in *Fashion and Modernity,* eds. Christopher Breward and Caroline Evans (Oxford: Berg, 2005), p. 1.

12. The phrase appears in Karl Marx and Friedrich Engels's *Communist Manifesto* (1848). See Marshall Berman, *All That Is Solid Melts Into Air: The Experience of Modernity* (New York: Penguin, 1982).

13. Rozsika Parker, *The Subversive Stitch: Embroidery and the Making of the Feminine* (London: Women's Press, 1984).

14. This approach is ratified by continuing usage in other European languages, such as French and Italian, where there is no exact equivalent for "craft" and *artisanat* and *artigianato* are used generically to refer to skilled workers. In non-European languages, too, one seeks in vain for an equivalent to the clear separation between art, craft, and industry that exists in modern English.

I   MANIPULATION

In 1784, an engineer named Henry Maudslay designed a lock that he claimed was impervious to any thief. In 1801, it was mounted on the shop door of Bramah's Patent Lock Company, accompanied by a sign (Plate 1), which read:

> The artist who can make an instrument that will pick or open this lock shall receive 200 guineas the moment it is produced.

It took five decades, but in 1851, Alfred C. Hobbs managed the feat. It took him fifty-one hours, spread over sixteen days. His success was a press phenomenon, partly because it happened in London during the Great Exhibition then captivating the world's attention, and partly because Hobbs was an American. The manner in which he had opened the lock—the amount of time he took and the nature of the tools he used—became the subject of extensive argument, dubbed by one newspaper "The Great Lock Controversy." Should he receive the prize or not?

The story of the Bramah lock serves as an apt point of entry into the question of manual skill in this period, because it so clearly demonstrates the confusion that attended craft in the period of industrialization. In some ways, the narrative follows the script of modernity perfectly. Surely Hobbs's picking of the lock was progress made manifest: a victory of the latest know-how over a stubborn remnant of the eighteenth century, proof that the industrial revolution had left its stuttering early stages behind. But in other ways, as an allegory of modernity, this anecdote doesn't quite meet the minimum requirements. Hobbs was no captain of industry, nor an inventor who furthered the cause of science and knowledge. His route into the lock business had been through an early career as a cutter of glass doorknobs, a trade he left behind after discovering his talents as a lockpick.[1] After beating similar challenges in America to the one laid out by Bramah, he had come to London to sow doubt as to the security of any British lock, and not incidentally, to sell new and improved locks of his own design. Hobbs was a professional manipulator, equal parts traveling salesman, spectacle promoter, and stage magician. His talented fingers set back the triumphant narrative of the moment; his feat was not so much a victory of 1851 over 1784, but a suggestion that perhaps 1784 hadn't been so hot after all. This little story, then, is about one artisan (Maudslay) who embodied the forward march of progress, and another (Hobbs) who troubled that grand narrative. The subtext of the Great Lock Controversy is also the central theme of this chapter: skilled hands are manipulative, in both a positive and negative sense, but they can also be manipulated. Craft is both a necessity and a problem for modernity.

Back in the late eighteenth century, when he patented the lock, Joseph Bramah was also busy on many other fronts, setting new standards for ingenuity. He'd already invented the modern flush toilet, not to mention a hydraulic press, improvements on the steam engine, and a machine that printed serial bank notes.[2] His top technician, Henry Maudslay, was the man who fabricated the lock. Another of the great minds of the industrial revolution in Britain, Maudslay was particularly innovative in the field of machine tool design.[3] Bramah's public declaration that his company had developed an unpickable lock was an expression of faith in his associate's skills, and an assertion that secrets could still be made safe. There was nothing cagey about it. As the shop window challenge suggests, this was a very visible kind of secrecy, a public declaration that technology was advancing and making the world a better, more secure place. Not the age-old mysteries of the craft guild for Bramah and Company, but rather the impregnable realities of public proclamation and cold calculation. The odds of the lock's sliders aligning at every one point with the notched bars that prevented them from falling into place, and allowing the lock to open, were nearly 7 million trillion to one. Try arguing with that logic.

Of course, A. C. Hobbs didn't need to worry about the math; he had a trunk of tools instead. The record is not totally clear on the matter, but it seems that he proceeded as follows. After announcing that he would take up the sixty-five-year-old challenge, he was granted access to Bramah's celebrated lock. Then he set to work. Though Hobbs's exact procedure was never revealed, he seems to have first made a wax impression of the lock's interior. Then he used this casting to craft a specialized set of instruments, some of which he screwed to the wooden door on which the lock was mounted. Among his tools were a "small bent lever of steel" to turn the barrel of the lock, a "powerful reflector" to shine light into its interior, and two probes, "one like a small stiletto and the other like a lady's crochet needle"—not the tools of the engineer, one notes, but of the sneak thief and the domestic hobbyist.[4] One by one, he coaxed the sliders into position. Finally he was able to demonstrate success, raising the hasp of the lock and then reclosing it to the satisfaction of an impartial committee of judges.

The London *Times* and other papers tracked Hobbs's progress intently; this was something like a spectator sport. But when he succeeded, they pronounced themselves outraged. It was no ordinary trade whose honor had been defiled. Two years previously, *The Journal of Design* had described one of Bramah and Co.'s leading competitors, John Chubb, in the most reverential terms: "From year to year, from month to month, some new and ingenious device appears to issue from his manufactory, and every possible *tour de force* that the locksmith (proverbially the most skilful workman) can contrive is given to the world."[5] Now an upstart American was making these prodigies of modern workmanship look foolish (indeed, as a lead-up to the Bramah challenge, Hobbs had also picked a Chubb and Son lock at their shop and boasted of the feat).[6] The London press therefore took the part of Bramah and Co., and did so vociferously. The media protested that when the challenge had been laid down all those years ago, no one could have dreamed that an operator would be granted two weeks of uninterrupted access. Had the true key once been inserted into the lock and turned during that time, they pointed out, it would have undone all of Hobbs's work. So he had hardly prevailed under the conditions a normal thief would face. One writer put it succinctly: "it must be recollected that [Hobbs] was fifty one hours in accomplishing his task—so that the practical security of the lock was in no wise injured by his success."[7]

For their part, members of the British lock industry, forced into damage control mode, were not above indulging in a bit of nationalism to defend themselves, nor did they shy away from character assassination. In a letter to faraway Calcutta, a key market for exported locks, Chubb and Son wrote:

> You may perhaps have seen in some of the London newspapers that an American who has come to the Great Exhibition in order to sell some locks has been endeavouring to ruin the reputation of every English lock; and ours has had the honour of being the special object of his attacks. He has cunningly avoided bringing the real question to an issue, and the opinion now of impartial and competent men is that he dare not even attempt one of our Locks unless he has an opportunity of tampering with its works before trying it.[8]

Bramah and Co., meanwhile, resorted to legalistic pettifogging. They pointed out that the wording of the challenge had said that "The artist who can make *an* instrument that will pick or open this lock shall receive 200 guineas," and Hobbs had not produced any such instrument. He had used many different tools, and no one was sure which ones, or in what order, or just how they worked. This was no advance of knowledge; the lockpick's feat could not be duplicated. As the company bitterly put it, "Mr. Hobbs has increased his fame and reputation as a clever and skillful manipulator, and Messrs. Bramah will pay the 200 pounds. Beyond this, no practical end or purpose whatever has been obtained."[9] (The American press, of course delighted with Hobbs's achievement, was not above engaging in a bit of good-natured mockery on just this point. *The Living Age,* published in New York, after proclaiming that "Bramah, hindu diety, who distributes miraculous ironmongery to a British public, is vanquished," wondered whether "similarly Baconian industry might not bring the cognate sciences of pocketpicking, forgery, and smashing, to perfection."[10])

Bramah and Co. also rushed to defend the honor of their long-dead founder. "Upon opening the outer case of the lock," they wrote in an open letter to the judging panel, "the actual barrel enclosing the mechanism was found to be $2\frac{1}{4}$ inches in length, and $1\frac{1}{2}$ inches in diameter. The space in which the works was confined, and its snug, compact appearance, was a matter of astonishment to all present" (see Figures 1.1 and 1.2). The "best hands" then in the employ of the firm stood round the ravished lock, muttering appreciatively about the "character of the workmanship."[11] British technical know-how had taken a knock, but like a momentarily dazed boxer, it would regain its feet. As the company reported: "The old familiar board, with the same challenge, will, we were informed, occupy its old place in a few days, and one of the locks now manufactured by Messrs. Bramah, with such improvements as have been made in it up to the present time, will replace the original

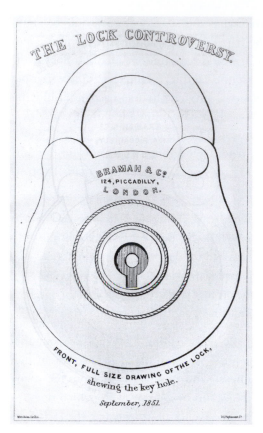

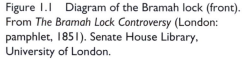

Figure 1.1   Diagram of the Bramah lock (front). From *The Bramah Lock Controversy* (London: pamphlet, 1851). Senate House Library, University of London.

one made 50 years since."[12] And there you have it: the tricks of an artisan, his subtle hand skills, could still win the day, but not the hearts and minds of the chattering classes.

What does this story tell us? First, it suggests that skill hadn't disappeared in the period from 1784 to 1851 as we are often told. Hobbs was evidently no less adept with his hands than Bramah or Maudslay. And he was not alone in this respect, or even unusual. Lock making was still an intensive handcraft in the middle of the nineteenth century, a mainstay of the light metals industry in and around Wolverhampton, and it would remain so for decades to come (Figure 1.3). As late as 1898, one writer noted, "owing to the amount of detail and intricacy in the trade, unskilled labour is useless."[13] What had changed was not the level of manual ability available in the trade; if anything, that had increased in both quantity and quality. It was, rather, the way people regarded skill and talked about it. And this is the second, more subtle lesson of the Great Lock Controversy. Bramah and Co. insisted that Hobbs's cleverness was "impractical" or unproductive. They shared in the very modern assumption that craft should always be in the service of some larger project. This is why the inner workings of the challenge lock were described as astounding to behold, while Hobbs's picking of it was merely clever and devious. Strange to say, even Hobbs himself participated in this belief system. So universal was the disapproval that rained down

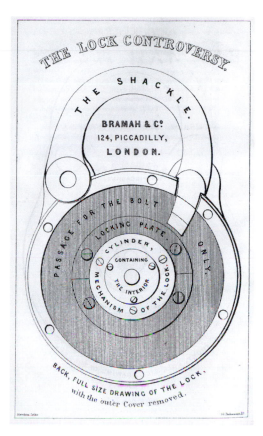

Figure 1.2   Diagram of the Bramah lock (rear). From *The Bramah Lock Controversy* (London: pamphlet, 1851). Senate House Library, University of London.

on the American's head that he felt compelled to defend himself in print, and when he did so, he adopted exactly the same rhetoric aimed against him. His critics, he wrote, "will hardly catch me 'tinkering,'—as it is elegantly expressed—'with my basket of instruments,' either upon their demand or that of any other man."[14] Even in the midst of a press campaign based on his own accomplishments in the field of lock picking, the last thing Hobbs wanted to be seen as was manipulative.

The Great Lock Controversy is an unusually entertaining anecdote from the key moment of nineteenth-century industrial history, the Great Exhibition of 1851. But it also has the virtue of encouraging us to see that big event much as it would have been seen at the time: the culmination of a historical process, not the beginning of one. We look back at 1851 with the benefit of hindsight and tend to see in the Crystal Palace the antecedents of modern industry (not to mention Parisian arcades, International Style architecture, and suburban shopping malls). But what really excited the public about the Great Exhibition, and the great engines and endless profusion of goods it contained, was not what it portended. For the Victorians, the Great Exhibition was not a great cathedral of the future, a mystery forever withheld, but rather a ringing endorsement of the present day. Like Bramah's lock writ large, the Crystal Palace stood for clarity and certainty: a secure faith in

Figure 1.3   Lock shop of Richard Cooper and Son, Wolverhampton. From
Wolverhampton and South Staffordshire Illustrated: Biographical and Commercial Sketches
(London: Robinson and Son, 1898). Wolverhampton Civic and Historical Society.

the progress wrought by industry. In this context, Hobbs's stunt of craftsmanship was only
a minor inconvenience, perhaps, but a telling one. It was a bothersome reminder of the fact
that no technology is certain, that ingenuity doesn't always travel in a straight line, and that
the machine age could still be shown up by the skills of a craftsman.

THE CENTER HOLDS

The invention of craft as a troublesome thing is inscribed deeply into modernity, and nowhere is this clearer than in the various attempts made to control it. As Michel Foucault
has shown, the characteristic modern technique for managing potentially disruptive social
elements is *discourse*. Foucault summarizes this development as follows:

> From the eighteenth century onwards there has been a specific reflection on the way in
> which these new procedures for training and exercising power over individuals could
> be extended, generalized, and improved...I constantly show the economic or political
> origin of these methods; but, while refraining from seeing power everywhere, I believe
> that the methods used, right down to the way of conditioning individuals' behavior,
> have a logic, obey a type of rationality, and are all based on one another to form a sort
> of specific stratum.[15]

Foucault has famously analyzed the control of sexuality, violence, and criminal behavior
by examining the formation of such institutions as schools, the military, and prisons. His
persistent theme is that it is the discursive elements of such institutions—not only words

(in speech or print) but also signification of other kinds, such as images—that are most effective in exercising power, partly because they are internalized by the individuals they seek to control. The classic example of this argument, from Foucault's book *Discipline and Punish,* is the circular prison, or "panopticon," proposed by Jeremy Bentham in 1785. In this building, a single guard is positioned centrally, so as to be able to see many hundreds of prisoners. Of course, he can only survey a few cells at a time, but each prisoner must behave *as if* he is under surveillance at all times. Discipline is absorbed into subjectivity, to the extent that it becomes constitutive of individual identity. The panopticon was never realized exactly according to Bentham's plans (though some recent buildings, frighteningly enough, come pretty close). But Foucault was not being literal. He argues that the panopticon was a conceptual template for real architecture during this period, and, moreover, a metaphor for disciplinary control at large.

Foucault's method can also be applied to the discursive institutional formations that surround modern craft. It is true that skilled hands were sometimes brought under control during the period of industrialization through brutal, direct means. This was especially true in areas where dramatic economies of scale could be achieved, as in the crucial sector of textiles, which led Britain's rise to international economic dominance and physically transformed the north of England. This is the industrial revolution of our imagination, depicted in paintings of belching, satanic factories and in the horrified texts of critics like Peter Gaskell, Friedrich Engels, and Karl Marx. As recent historians of the industrial revolution emphasize, however, the move to large-scale factories was slow in coming and limited to only a few places and trades. Much more wide-reaching and significant was a softer form of centralization in which skilled hands were brought under control through discursive and pictorial, rather than physical, means. An excellent example is afforded by Denis Diderot's *Encyclopedie, ou Dictionnaire Raisonné des Sciences, des Arts et des Métiers,* compiled in the 1750s for publisher Jean le Rond d'Alembert as a comprehensive description of all areas of art and science. Like many Enlightenment projects, the twin aim of the *Encyclopedie* was to subdivide and clarify, and it brought this impulse to the world of production in textual and visual form. In her thorough discussion of the publication, Celina Fox summarizes Diderot's aim in describing the mechanical arts: "to encompass tacit, physical and sometimes inefficient work practices within an elite literary format in order to make them rational and productive."[16] The effectiveness with which this massive exercise in representation brought craft into a new order is clear from the depictions of the Gobelins tapestry works in the *Encyclopedie,* which depict a grand processional space divided in a way that suggests the rhythms of mass production (Figure 1.4). While a mid-eighteenth-century genre painter might have individualized the figures in a scene of work, Diderot's vision is one of complete regularity, the weavers as interchangeable as warp threads.

The homogeneity of the workers behind their looms finds a correspondence elsewhere in Diderot's compendium, where tools of all sorts (whether hand tools like chisels and hammers, or large-scale equipment like looms, sawmills, and forges) are pinned to the page like an entomologist's insect specimens. There is also a profusion of finished goods,

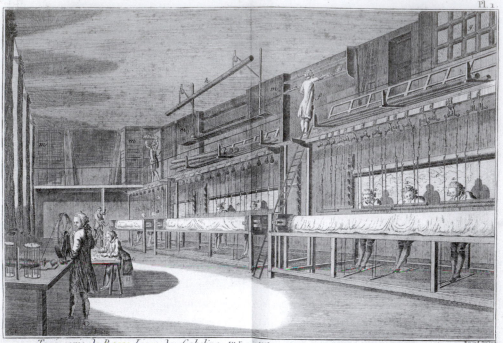

Figure 1.4   Gobelin workshops, from the *Encyclopedia* by Denis Diderot. The Stapleton Collection, Bridgeman Art Library.

arranged in grids as in a retail shop of the day, and many images of workspaces, based on site visits where Diderot's assistants conducted in-depth interviews with artisans. In the plates, many of the spaces are weirdly depopulated—in one image depicting the cross-section of a kiln, for example, it is as if the potters had just left the room, leaving the fire untended. Some processes are shown using depictions of busy, disembodied hands, cut off just above the elbow (Figure 1.5). In the plates that do feature whole bodies at work, the figures are depersonalized, mannequin-like, and rigorously productive, going about their business as if on a contemporary theatrical stage, or perhaps as if they were puppets controlled by unseen strings.

In the *Encyclopedie,* then, we see modern craft setting off on a bifurcated path toward abstraction and theatricality. This double trajectory would lead ultimately to its disappearance into engineering on one hand, and the nonproductive but captivating demonstrations of the art gallery and the fairground on the other. These two tendencies have in common a newly *explicit* positioning of craft.[17] Though Diderot was well aware of the difficulties of fully describing that which is stubbornly tacit, he sought to overcome the frictional, irregular quality of artisanal work through sheer quantity of description: "to reveal," as Fox writes, "what should no longer be hidden."[18] I return to this theme in the following chapter, but for now it is worth noticing that it was not in the factories of northern England

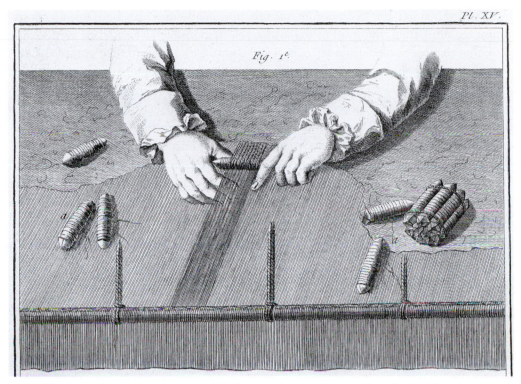

Figure 1.5 Basse-Lisse technique at the Gobelins tapestry manufactory, from the *Encyclopedia* by Denis Diderot, 1770. Giraudon, Bridgeman Art Library.

that this vision was first advanced, but rather in Paris—a center of luxury production. It is surprising, but true: it was in the seventeenth- and eighteenth-century furniture workshops of Paris, the tapestry ateliers of the Gobelins, and the silk weaving factories of Lyon that the division of labor was initially elaborated. What Diderot and his assistants did on the page, manufacturers did in real life, setting their highly skilled operatives into ever more specific roles. By the late eighteenth century, England had adopted this strategy of division, and had even overtaken its French neighbors. This way of manufacturing continued to require extensive hand skill, but it subjected artisans to increasing specialization. As a French industrial spy named Le Turc observed on his visit to England in 1786: "There is no country where labor is so divided as here. No worker can explain to you the chain of operations, being perpetually occupied with one small part: listen to him on anything outside that and you will be burdened with error. This division is well intentioned, resulting in inexpensive handwork, the perfection of the work, and the security of the property of the manufacturer."[19]

The division of labor is a preeminent consideration in any discussion of craft's relation to industry, and one to which I repeatedly return. From Adam Smith's *The Wealth of Nations* (1776) through the work of Karl Marx in the mid-nineteenth century, on to Harry Braverman in the 1960s and, most recently, the polemical writings of Matthew Crawford and Richard Sennett, the separation of one task into smaller parts has been taken as tantamount to "mutilating" the spirit of the worker. No responsible historian can overlook the alienation that has resulted from separation and specialization in countless workplaces; this process continues apace today in countries worldwide. As anthropologist Jane Collins has noted, skill has been redefined by multinational corporations to signify speed rather than quality—a phenomenon especially common in sectors dominated by female workers, such as the garment industry.[20] Such a conception of skill may seem simply exploitative, something to reject outright. But doing so would be to make a mistake in the opposite direction, idealizing skilled production and ignoring its real nature. In fact, speed, separation, and specialization were all driving factors in craft workshops of the eighteenth century. And the higher the echelon of the trade and the finer the work produced, the more true this was. To fully tabulate the production that went into a single elite interior at this date, we would have to make a list of many specialists—joiners, masons, plasterers, glaziers, decorative painters—each of whose trades were further divided according to level and expertise. And that is before the furniture was even brought in. This was division of labor of the highest order, not in the familiar, Fordist sense in which we might use the phrase, but division of labor nonetheless. And like all divided labor, it led eventually to an erosion of the artisan's autonomy and economic advantage, without necessarily involving a reduction in skill.

Some trades, like furniture making, were less easily divided than others, like textile manufacture, or the making of fans, clocks, and dresses. But even so, the sheer number of hands involved in the creation of a single high-quality piece of French cabinetwork was considerable. One might even say that multiplicity of skills and materials was the main design feature of the objects. They were showpieces not just of individual artisans' work, but for the corporate structure of the trade. Even a relatively simple piece of French court furniture (Figure 1.6) might require the contributions of a carcass maker, veneer specialists (who might be responsible for particular subspecialties such as marquetry or inlaid floral decoration), and leather workers. The bronze mounts on the furniture required further collaborative work: a carver to make the wood model, a *bronzier* to cast the metal, and chasers and gilders who embellished the mounts before turning the results over to the cabinetmaker for assembly. The making of furniture therefore required not only extensive managerial coordination, but also centralization of design agency.

Increasingly, such duties were handled not by artisans, but third parties. Teams of craftsmen with specialized skills had long been required to create lavish interiors, of course, and they were always organized in some way—through guilds and companies at first, then in the seventeenth century through the mediating figure of the upholsterer, who often stage managed the appointment of an entire house. The early eighteenth century saw the emergence of the Parisian *marchands merciers,* specialists in provision who marshaled the forces of many different trades (as well as the subdivisions within the trades), either by coordinating work for the decoration of a single house or by assembling parts made by different tradesmen into synthetic objects.[21] In Britain, similarly, highly capitalized companies such as Seddon or Gillows—early examples of what design historian Pat Kirkham

Figure 1.6 Gaspard Feilt, *bureau plat,* ca. 1750. Veneered with tulipwood, with marquetry of kingwood and gilt-bronze mounts. V&A: 1052:1 to 5–1882. © Victoria and Albert Museum, London.

calls the "comprehensive manufacturing firm"—were established in the 1760s.[22] This concentrated decision-making authority in a single company rather than a dispersed group of tradesmen.

Another form of centralization, still rare in the eighteenth century (though much studied by historians), occurred when sculptors and architects offered their services as professional designers. This phenomenon was again pioneered in France, but from the middle of the century figures such as William Kent and Robert Adam in England or Benjamin Henry Latrobe in America began to wield sole or primary design authority for interiors. As I noted in the introduction, it has often been argued that this period witnessed a separation of fine art from craft—with pride of place given to voices like Royal Academician Joshua Reynolds, who contended that while the artist might begin his studies with "the attainment of manual dexterity," the process of his maturation consisted in advancing to a trade in concepts: "The wish of the genuine painter must be more extensive: instead of endeavouring to amuse mankind with the minute neatness of his imitations, he must endeavour to improve them by the grandeur of his ideas."[23] Art, in his view, must be a matter of concept rather than facility. There were also certain aesthetic preferences in the eighteenth century that militated against the equation between artistic skill and craftsmanship. The best sculpture, for example, was thought to transcend its own weight and substance, hence its origins in the dirty, slow work of the stone shop. As Tomas Macsotay has recently argued, the extemporaneous sketch of the draftsman was embraced as a model in this regard, so that freshness and immediacy became the most desired of sculptural effects.[24]

Yet voices like Reynolds's were in the minority in the eighteenth century. It remained extremely common for sculptors and architects to design furniture and other decorative art; as David Irwin puts it, "pronouncements within the walls of the Royal Academy did not accurately reflect activities outside it."[25] In practice, the problem was the reverse of what one might expect: it was not that artists sneered at the prospect of designing decorative art, but rather that they were often not up to the task. They were often inexperienced at the job and had a difficult time managing the artisans hired to execute their ideas. The results ranged from the merely infelicitous, as in the case of the rather hideous designs of Kent—who knew a lot about Italian architecture and sculpture, but clearly very little about furniture, to judge from the awkward collisions of mismatched forms that he contrived— to chairs by Latrobe that had such poorly designed joints they were prone to catastrophic breakage just above the seat (as surviving examples attest; Figure 1.7).

A more subtle but perhaps more telling instance of the problems that attended early architects' attempts to wield design authority is a cabinet designed by Robert Adam, from Kimbolton Castle, England (Plate 2). This extraordinary object from the early 1770s was meant not for any strictly functional purpose; the only access to the shelved interior is through the doors on the canted sides. This inconvenient structure is due to the fact that the cabinet was made only for show—literally. Its primary purpose was to display its own façade, which is mounted with a collection of Italian *pietra dura* plaques. When the cabinet was new, the plaques were already antiques—they date to 1708. The unusual commission

Figure 1.7   Benjamin Henry Latrobe (designer), Thomas Wetherill (cabinetmaker) and possibly George Bridport (painter), *klismos* side chair, 1808. Oak, yellow poplar, white pine, plaster composition, paint, and gilding. Chipstone Foundation.

brought Adam together with two major craft firms: cabinetmakers Matthew and Ince, and the metalwork factory of Matthew Bolton. How did they do? In 1857, on the occasion of the Art Treasures exhibition in Manchester, a firm opinion was offered: the seventy-year-old Kimbolton cabinet was described as "a monument of labour and materials misapplied."[26] While this was perhaps meant only as a snide statement about style, there is something to the idea that the object bears the marks of "misapplication." Mayhew and Ince had acted in the synthetic coordinating role that might in Paris have been played by a *marchand mercier,* but they yielded the responsibility for the design of the object to an architect who, like Kent and Latrobe, had little practical knowledge of furniture making. Careful inspection of the cabinet shows how awkward it was for Mayhew and Ince to coordinate with Boulton in the execution of Adam's rigid design. The interlocked circles of the brass ornament had to be squeezed into oval shapes to fit neatly at the front of the projecting column bases on the façade; the runs of marquetry in the friezes are unevenly aligned with the ormolu capitals, creating a slight asymmetry most uncharacteristic of furniture of this level of formality and finish (Figure 1.8). And thanks to surviving correspondence, we know that there were other difficulties in coordination: the two firms were still arguing with one another about costs associated with the commission eight years later.[27]

Figure 1.8   Robert Adam (designer), Matthew Boulton (mount maker), and Mayhew and Ince (cabinetmakers), with earlier *pietra dura* plaques by Baccio Cappelli, the Kimbolton cabinet, 1771–1776. Mahogany and oak, with marquetry in satinwood and rosewood, *pietra dura* plaques and ormolu (gilt-bronze) mounts. W.43–1949. © Victoria and Albert Museum, London. Detail.

THE CARVED AND THE FLAT

The Kimbolton cabinet shows us that even the most accomplished British firms of the day sometimes struggled to meet the demands imposed by coordinated labor. What could be done in Paris, with its more advanced forms of design administration, was not easily mimicked elsewhere. Today, when craft is routinely described as an antidote to the homogenizing effects of corporate power (corporate, of course, meaning "a single body"), it is easy to forget how difficult it was to achieve that centralization in the first place. One historian of technology estimates that in the early nineteenth century, "only one worker in ten ever saw the inside of a factory; most labored in smaller shops or in the so-called traditional sectors, such as building, wool, and leather. These other activities, not the singular steam-powered cotton factories, contributed most of the country's manufacturing value, and experienced substantial growth themselves."[28] The specificity of workshop production, its internal routines and discrete character, had to be conquered one stage at a time. And because each craft was different, the prescription for change also varied widely. Some trades, like shoemaking, were industrialized in relatively short order. Weaving, often thought to be an archetypal case of industrialization, actually developed a two-tier system in which luxury manufacturers held tightly to craft-intensive processes while mass market producers introduced mechanization. Still other trades, like coopering, were not mechanized until well into the twentieth century.[29] Even within a single industry like the women's clothing trade, there could be a great disparity between small, flexible shops, like those that made tailored outerwear, and corset manufactories, which introduced extensive standardization.[30]

It might be helpful, therefore, to see how shifts in design agency affected a single trade. I will take the example of woodcarving, which like many long-established skills might initially be thought of as oppositional to modernity. The craft had a unique set of characteristics within late eighteenth-century furniture: a very high level of requisite skill; a complex and rapidly changing stylistic vocabulary; and an inherent insusceptibility to the techniques of centralized design. The craft was hugely transformed in the nineteenth century, but this was certainly not because of machines. With the technology available at the time, it simply was not possible to replace the hand skills of the carver through automation.[31] As Michael Ettema has written, while the first carving machine was patented in 1845, it was only capable of roughing out a form, which then needed to be detailed and finished by hand. Even today, the most high-tech computer-driven router cannot approximate the results achievable by a skilled craftsman. "In general," Ettema argues, "machinery allowed an increase in furniture production but failed to democratize style because machines could not produce inexpensive copies of expensive-looking ornament."[32] Certainly carved ornament in wood could be replaced in other materials through casting, as in ormolu (gilt bronze) furniture mounts, or plaster-based "composition," which was extensively used for interior embellishment. (Carvers were often employed in creating the models for these processes.)[33] But solid carved wood itself could not be replicated; nor could its production be easily divided among separate workers. Both to achieve stylistic integrity and because of the relatively small scale of the work, it was usual for the same carver to work on a piece from beginning to end.

No other branch of woodworking was so firmly connected to the skill of the individual maker. In 1802, the masters and journeymen of London's chair making industry finally managed to agree to a standard book of prices to prevent disputes over the value of certain tasks such as upholstery, joinery, and veneering. This was a typical case of the conceptual (rather than physical) division of labor, in which all the complicated processes of furniture making were "digested," set out in measurable, defined lists, and reduced to their "most diminutive parts."[34] In this exercise, ornamental carving was singled out as the only woodworking skill that was impossible to fix in price:

> on account of the great difference, which is frequently found in the quality of Ornamental-Carving, as performed by different Workmen, no precise value for the workmanship could be reasonably be affixed, previous to its execution: they have therefore considered it proper to omit it, and have confined themselves to the valuation of the more plain parts thereof, such as Moulding, Panneling, Fluting, Reeding, &c.... It is therefore intended to settle the Prices for such Ornamental-Carving, by precedent and mutual agreement.[35]

While standardized, open-ended runs of ornament-like cornice moldings or fluted legs could be priced by the inch, there was no way to accurately assess the cost of a given carver's rendition of a scroll or leaf. There was too much individuality, too much quality, too much "art" in it. This was one craft that seemed, by its very nature, to preserve its own autonomy.[36]

Yet the independence enjoyed by the carver was short-lived after all. In Britain, a first step toward management of the craft occurred in the late seventeenth century, when furniture was suddenly in great demand following the Great Fire of London. Chairs were made in large numbers through a piecework system in which carving, caning, and assembly were all handled by different specialists, often working in different shops.[37] But it was in the middle of the ensuing century, just as carvers were reaching the height of their artistic powers (thanks to the florid rococo ornament fashionable in the period), when the key mechanism of design control entered the scene: not machines, or even words, but rather images. Robert Campbell's 1747 guide to craft professions, *The London Tradesman,* is an early example of a text that insists on the importance of drawing to cabinetmakers and carvers alike, explaining that this was the only way they could keep up with fashion. So important was draftsmanship to the carver, wrote Campbell, that "the rest of their education may be as mean as they please."[38] In accordance with this newfound emphasis on delineation, the 1750s saw the introduction of "pattern books," initially published by prominent cabinetmaker-upholsterers such as Thomas Chippendale. Like other new techniques and media associated with design control, these publications presented considerable difficulties to their users. Chippendale opened *The Gentleman and Cabinet-maker's Director* (1754) on the defensive:

> Upon the whole, I have here given no design but what may be executed with advantage by the hands of a skillful workman, tho' some of the profession have been diligent enough to represent them (especially those after the Gothic and Chinese manner) as so many specious drawings, impossible to be work'd off by any mechanic whatsoever.

Though he claimed that his own shop was more than capable of realizing any of the designs in the book, he also equivocated on the degree to which they should actually be executed according to his plans, especially in the delicate matter of carving. Of some objects, he noted, "the carving may be lessened by an ingenious workman without detriment," while at other points he veered in the opposite direction, engaging in a bit of advertorial: "I had a particular pleasure in retouching and finishing this design, but should have much more in the execution of it, as I am confident I can make the work more beautiful and striking than the drawing." Perhaps he came closest to the truth in a caption for three richly ornamented stands: "intended for carving, and nothing of directions can be said concerning them, as their being well executed depends on the judgment of the workman."[39]

If one examines the drawings provided in another pattern book, the ambitiously titled *Universal System* (published serially from 1759 to 1763) by John Mayhew and William Ince, the same London cabinetmakers who contributed to the Kimbolton cabinet, and compares them to the real objects produced by their shop, it is abundantly evident how difficult it was to translate a rococo design into an actual object. The volumetric, curvaceous, and often asymmetrical style was completely dependent upon the nuances of execution, and of course those nuances were very different in pen-and-ink and chiseled wood. The text of the *Universal System* subtly reflected Mayhew and Ince's understanding of this problem of follow through, and suggested means to overcome it. In providing instructions for the rendering of an ornamental cartouche rendered by Matthew Darly after Ince's design (see Figure 1.9), for example, they counseled:

> The principal sweep or centre line is the foundation and basis of the whole order of ornament... [It] must be first drawn and made perfect (which can only be done by freedom of Hand) before you proceed any further; then form the other center lines, which must all spring with a natural freedom from the first or principal sweep, all of which must be perfectly correct before any other attempts are made... For young beginners it would be better to take any Part, and by degrees be able to manage the Whole.[40]

We can see in this seemingly innocuous passage a key tension of modern craft in its emergent phase. On one hand, Mayhew and Ince want to preserve the naturalness, the "freedom of Hand," that is the heart of any artisan's skill. On the other, they presume that learning a new technique—especially when copying an existing motif, like the cartouche—requires

Figure 1.9   Matthew Darly, *A Systimatical Order of Raffle Leaf from the Line of Beauty,* from John Mayhew and William Ince, *The Universal System of Household Furniture,* 1759–1763.

a process of dissection. As in the *Encyclopedie,* or indeed in any number of "how-to" books which have been printed since the middle of the eighteenth century, we see the urge to cut skill apart for ease of description and management. In an ingenious inversion of the more familiar phrase, Robert Cooper has described modernity as entailing a "labor of division," a process that "enables greater control over the social and material world through enhanced clarity, transparency, and visual certainty *at a distance.*"[41] Only when a task is seen clearly can it be controlled from afar. So techniques of visual representation, like drawing, were necessary for the development of systems of distributed agency.

As Cooper argues, the dissection of physical tasks into parts was part of a much broader cultural shift in which vision—long considered the most elevated of the senses—was accorded a legislative function. As Samuel Johnson wrote in his essay "The Need for General Knowledge":

> Wonder is a pause of reason, a sudden cessation of the mental progress, which lasts only while the understanding is fixed upon some single idea, and is at an end when it recovers force enough to divide the subject into its parts, or mark the intermediate gradations from the first agent to the last consequence.[42]

Here Johnson describes the acquisition of knowledge as requiring a process of constant division, until the parts are of a scale to be comprehensible. The wider picture of "general knowledge" is constantly being built from these fragments; wonder serves a useful purpose as an invitation to this process of discovery, but has no value in itself. Johnson's own principal contribution along these lines was of course his famous dictionary; in the entry for the word "wonder," he quoted the seventeenth-century bishop Robert South: "wonder is from surprise, and surprise ceases upon experience."[43] Thus the technique of dividing and defining could be achieved visually as well as textually. The modernization of medicine, architecture, navigation, the natural sciences, and exhibition making, to name only a few disciplines outside of the realm of manual craft, all depended upon improved methods of technical drawing.[44] Indeed, professionalization and draftsmanship were so closely linked in the eighteenth century that attitudes to the two changed in concert. In 1754, Robert Adam confided in a letter to his brother James that he was embarrassed to be seen at work, lest he be taken as a tradesman rather than a gentleman: "If I am known in Rome to be an Architect, if I am seen drawing or with a pencil in my hand, I cannot enter in to genteel company, who will not admit an Artist." Do not write "architect" on the envelopes of your letters, he continued; address me as "Robert Adam, *Gentilhomme Anglois.*"[45] Yet by the end of the century, Adam's profession ceased to be an obstacle to his status. Being an architect, and one known for his exquisite draftsmanship, was instead what cemented his fame, and he published lavish books of his hand renderings to charm his elite clientele.

Paralleling this change in the fortunes of draftsmanship was a change in the nature of drawing itself. The expressive flourishes of the rococo migrated to the domain of the hobbyist; professionals were expected to produce a much more precise sort of image. Similarly, images of craftspeople in the style of genre painting were displaced by other ways of representing skilled trades. "By the 1770s," Celina Fox notes, "the trend in treatises describing technical and industrial innovation was towards more mathematically based forms of description, eradicating figures of artisans at work in favour of strict projections ruled by geometry."[46] This shift went hand in hand with the emergence of a discrete profession of engineering, and with it "a gap of specialization developing between the research and development and the production aspects of manufacturing."[47] Artisans—those who made machine tools, prototypes, and patterns—were less likely to produce drawings themselves, and more and more frequently were called upon to fill the gap between sketch and product, placing them in a reactive mode negotiated through images.

There is a certain irony here, for those who initially produced and used design drawings considered them principally as aids to the artisan—a way of extending repertoire. In the seventeenth century (and to a lesser extent, even earlier) pattern books and ornamental prints had served as the primary means by which style was diffused from centers of decorative art production, such as Florence, Paris, and Antwerp, to less fashion forward places like London and the Americas.[48] By the 1740s and 1750s, as Anne Puetz has argued, the British were beginning to take draftsmanship much more seriously because it was a necessary weapon in the competitive market for luxury goods. This was the moment of elaborate rococo design in France and Germany, and great emphasis was laid on complex ornamental motifs, such as flowers and quasi-abstract raffle leaves. However, the penetration of drawing skills into the ranks of artisans was limited. Writers who instructed craftspeople in draftsmanship warned them not to attain to the "cerebral or conceptual" sort of drawing a fine artist might practice, but rather the more mechanical skill of direct copying.[49]

In the nineteenth century, drawing continued to be understood as an engine of prosperity for craftsmen, but now this was brokered through indirect workmanship and economies of scale. The *Journal of Design,* edited by Henry Cole and Richard Redgrave, would become an official instrument for this positive view, claiming on the first page of its inaugural issue (published in 1849) that a single high-quality rendering could generate ten thousand pounds of profit for a textile manufacturer or seven years of full-time work for eight potters.[50] Clearly such leveraging of a single design placed tight constraints on the free practice of skill and encouraged repetition (as those eight potters presumably would have swiftly realized). As the *Journal of Design* was at pains to point out, those who made the drawings and the artisans who executed them were rarely the same people, despite the many attempts made to remedy that division through private drawing schools and mechanics' institutes: "What the art workman does now is done by a sort of rule-of-thumb dexterity, with little knowledge of the principles of art, and in many cases without the ability of even making tolerably correct outlines."[51]

In her recent study *Grand Designs*, historian Lara Kriegel has shown how controversial the matter of drawing had become by this time. Those who wanted to improve British design and artisanship looked to draftsmanship as the answer. In her words, which distantly echo those of Mayhew and Ince, it seemed a "universal pursuit and a surefire way to improve industrial design."[52] Yet there was stark disagreement about how artisans could best benefit from learning draftsmanship. On one side were artistic reformers like Benjamin Robert Haydon, who favored a traditional academic approach premised on drawing from the nude figure. On the other were men like William Dyce, who took up the directorship of the government-sponsored School of Design (forerunner to today's Royal College of Art) in 1838, its second year of operation. Dyce thought that artisans would only be confused by figure study and should instead draw from geometric patterns and static objects, similar to the ones they might make in a workshop. (In the case of the textile sector, often a flashpoint for argument because of its economic value to the nation, the drawing was of course not much flatter than the design to be woven.) Haydon concentrated on "uplift" and improvement of taste, and left open the possibility that an artisan might discover an individual artistic genius, thus transcending the realm of the manual operative, to whom art was a closed mystery. Dyce's "conventional" approach, by contrast, emphasized vocational utility. It was consonant with the precept—soon to become an article of faith among the South Kensington reformers—that design was an objective, scientific pursuit, more analogous to botany than painting. Pioneering designer Christopher Dresser, who was educated within this system, recommended drawing the cross-sections of plants to such a degree of accuracy that "if a model of the plant was required, the drawings alone would be necessary"[53] (Plate 3). In practice, this exacting, dissection-like style of rendering usually involved a very boring regime of repetitive copying, especially for beginning students. But it was the method that carried the day in the School of Design and other British institutions of the mid-nineteenth century. The intention was to instill the values of "perseverance, care, and discipline."[54] From a psychological point of view, this is itself interesting, for boredom is a most effective means of discouraging creative autonomy.[55]

Kriegel shows how conscious reformers were about their own attempts to "improve" skilled artisans—a clear instance of craftspeople separated out as a special problem, distinct from others involved in making processes (with unskilled laborers beneath them and designers and architects above them). She also demonstrates without question that during this expansive phase of the industrial revolution, artisans were not disappearing from view—after all, it was precisely because their abilities were considered so vital to the progress of manufacturing that the matter of improving them was seen as a matter of great political import. However, we should not lose sight of the fact that this argument over artisans was fought at one remove, in the representational world of pencil and paper. In the debates that Kriegel documents, the notion that craft skill could be the means of its own improvement—which of course, had been the case for centuries under the system of apprenticeship—seems not even to have been considered. Reformers either sought to transform the most exceptional artisans into designers, or failing that, to maximize their operational efficiency. Throughout the modern era, these two objectives, the one implicitly condescending and the other explicitly manipulative, have remained the principal means of compromising craft autonomy.

Given the early nineteenth-century priority of draftsmanship over craftsmanship, it is no surprise that objects themselves began to reflect a preference for the flat over the volumetric. Certainly this transformation can be detected in ceramics. This was another medium of production in which hand craftsmanship was still the rule in the late eighteenth century. With the notable exception of ornamental lathe turning, few innovations in the ceramic industry (apart from the preparation of raw materials) involved machine technology. Yet a self-conscious process of modernization was under way nonetheless.[56] Ceramic designers in Stoke, Sèvres, and Dresden were engaged in a ceaseless quest for refinement and consistency. Factories and workforces were strictly subdivided according to discrete processes. From the consumer point of view, consistency across multiple identical forms (as in a dinner service, for example) became a principal mark of quality—a result achievable only when artisans could work reliably to a set design. Tellingly, a style of applied sprig ornament or painted motifs, clearly influenced by design drawings, became the default mode of decoration (Figure 1.10).[57] Motifs were applied to the clay like a graphic designer's clip art.

Further evidence of the predominance of line drawing can be found in the new prominence of silhouette in late eighteenth-century ceramics. After a vessel was thrown, operatives used hand lathes to shave the wall of the pot to a thin and very exact profile, using a stencil profile (essentially, a rigid drawing) to verify the correctness of the work. It is no coincidence that just as design renderings were entering this field of practice, classicism

Figure 1.10 Spode Ceramic Works, basket and cover, ca. 1810–1820. Stoneware with a smear glaze and white sprigged decoration. V&A: 2603&A-1901. © Victoria and Albert Museum, London.

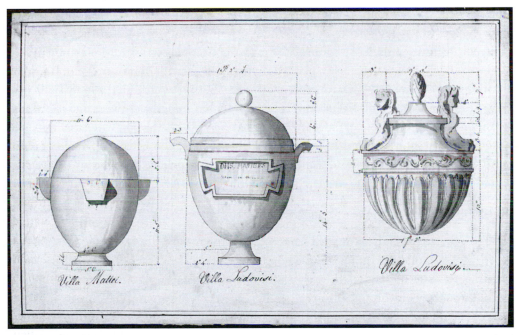

Villa Mattei.

Villa Ludovisi.

Villa Ludovisi.

Figure 1.11 Sir William Chambers, drawing of vases, n.d. Pen and ink, pencil and blue and gray washes. V&A: E.5004–1910. © Victoria and Albert Museum, London.

was in vogue. Antique red- and black-figure vases featured a lexicon of draftsmanship in their own right, which was propagated through carefully measured drawings by antiquarians, architects, collectors, and archaeologists (Figure 1.11). Once collected together and arranged across a mantelpiece, a garniture of vases, whether genuine Greek examples or contemporary variants, even formed a sort of line drawing in space. Finally, the primacy of form over materiality is also reflected in the diversity of media in which vases were made, with little concern for any original prototype (ceramic copies of glass antiquities, wood copies of ceramics, etc.).[58]

We should be careful, however, not to subscribe to a monolithic theory of modernization—as if designers and artisans were swept along unconsciously on a tide of inexorable change, with line drawings an unstoppable force controlling all their labor. Here is an example of the complexity of modern craft: makers themselves were among its most effective inventors, not its unwitting victims. As craft was invented, craftspeople reinvented themselves. While we might speak of a shift, in the broadest of terms, from the material to the visual, artisans were more than capable of manipulating their own skills in the service of that new visuality. The "labor of division," for all that it regulated the work of individual makers, could also be a prod to creativity for those able to manage the various degrees of separation. Thus far I have been using as examples the most obvious personnel of late eighteenth-century design history: Chippendale, Boulton, and Adam. But if we are looking for adaptive innovation at work, a model today's practitioners are more apt to follow, we are likely to find it among those practitioners who were *not* fully in control of these changes but were rather reacting to them. We might therefore look to the margins of eighteenth-century productive culture, to areas without intensive institutional presence: in rural towns, where artisans quickly adapted to new markets with improvement of transport links; or in colonies like North America and India—both of which were a long sea voyage away from the luxury production centers of Europe, but nonetheless were under pressure to emulate the products of a rapidly advancing system of divided labor. Colonial craftsmen lacked the state sponsorship that had nurtured that system, and usually operated in small shops with few hands. This meant simulating the technical achievements of a more sophisticated milieu through whatever means were available.

THE UNDISCIPLINED ARTISAN

How to achieve the ends of divided labor without the means? That was the question facing men like Samuel McIntire. In his day, which is to say the decades leading up to 1800, McIntire was the most modern designer in Salem, Massachusetts. Nevertheless, it was partly through his involvement in the "traditional" craft of carving that this Renaissance man of New England negotiated the opportunities and challenges of operating within a new style. He can be understood as a figure caught at the junction of two countervailing trends. On one hand, he was a skilled craftsman, and thus embodied a long-established manner of practice. On the other, he was that new thing in America—an architect—and in this respect a member of a growing class of professionals, most of whom (unlike McIntire) lacked craft knowledge but would nonetheless eventually come to dictate the production of everything from houses to teapots. McIntire, then, emblematizes modern craft's emergent phase. Working in paper and wood, line and volume, he inhabited a Janus-faced condition. On one hand he continued the tradition of the elite specialist artisan, but on the other he adopted the very form of authorship that rendered that craft model obsolete.

As mentioned earlier, with very few exceptions (such as London cabinetmaker John Linnell, who happened to have trained as a carver when he was young with his own father), drawings of ornaments were rendered by different people from the specialists who actually went on to carve them. McIntire, however, did both. His official obituary stressed this flexibility in no uncertain terms:

> Mr. M'Intire was originally bred to the occupation of a housewright, but his vigorous mind soon passed the ordinary limits of his profession, and aspired to the highest departments of the interesting and admirable science of architecture…He also made a profession in the kindred art of sculpture, in which he had arrived at a very distinguished rank. The uncommon native genius of Mr. M. displayed itself in many subjects not connected with his professional pursuits; and in the various objects to which his unerring taste directed him, he never failed of reaching a degree of excellence that would have been honorable to a professed artist.[59]

In 2007, the Peabody-Essex Museum in Salem continued this tradition, devoting an exhibition to McIntire's work in various fields of design—not only architecture, drawing, and decorative carving, but also the realization of sculptural ships' figureheads—describing him as "one of America's most versatile artists."[60] This insistence on the multiplicity of McIntire's talents seems to be telling us something beyond the standard hagiography of the heroic designer. As Abbott Lowell Cummings noted all the way back in 1957, there was both a steady increase of specialization in New England in the late eighteenth century and a penetration of specialization *downward* through the social spectrum. This was true of both the furniture and the building trades, so that, as Cummings put it, "by the time of the building of [McIntire's] Tucker house of 1808–9, bills show how thoroughly specialization had penetrated even the less ambitious houses of the period."[61] This was quite different from the situation that prevailed in Paris and London fifty years earlier—when specialism and divided labor was associated mainly with luxury production. Even in his own day McIntire's versatility made him seem the exponent of a dying breed. Prominent Salem minister and diarist William Bentley noted in his diary upon McIntire's death that "The late increase of workmen in wood has…added nothing to the character and reputation of the workman, so that upon the death of Mr. McIntire no man is left to be consulted upon a new plan of execution beyond his bare practice."[62]

Close reading of a typical McIntire chair attests to his skills as a generalist, but also the degree to which his work was premised upon an internalization of the dialectic between design control and artisanal freedom. It is as if he had purposefully tamed his own carving, bringing the unruly craft into the aesthetic register of an architect's flat rendering (Figure 1.12). The strong, taut silhouettes of his furniture suggest the importance of drawing to his design sensibility, and the linearity of his carved motifs—his tendency to ply his chisel as if he had a quill pen in his hand—confirms that affinity. Furthermore, he embellished the backgrounds surrounding his motifs with star-shaped, punched marks, lending the flatness of the ground a graphic, designerly effect. Unlike most rococo ornaments of a few decades earlier, in which the carving is physically carved into the object's surface, McIntire's ornaments are literally "applied art"—the bits of wood are glued on, not carved from the solid. In this respect they are not unlike the sprig moldings on Wedgwood's pots. But while the potter confined his own activities to the relatively hands-off processes of design and technical experiment, McIntire seems to have been determined to maintain a direct connection, and a lively and inventive approach, to his work. Yes, his ornaments are constrained within tablet-shaped frames and flat patterned panels, which function almost like sheets of paper for rendering an ornamental design. And yes, carving is subsumed within the overall compositional logic of this furniture, so that one feels one is looking at the work of someone who thinks primarily as an architect. The individual details, the bows and baskets and the rest, are pinned onto his furniture and walls much like the tools in the *Encylopedie*—butterflies on a board.

Yet one still gets a powerful sense of the craftsman's hand at work. McIntire's furniture was beautifully poised, a finely calibrated accommodation of a new style and a new profession, which threatened to make his artisanal specialism obsolete even as it offered him new possibilities to shape the material culture of his time. It is also worth noting that McIntire was not reluctant to outsource the fabrication of his designs or to employ replication alongside bespoke craftsmanship. He could not carve all the ornaments in a house, and was more than willing to place cast composition ornament or standard moldings right alongside his

Figure 1.12   Samuel McIntire, armchair, 1801. Mahogany, birch, white pine. Metropolitan Museum of Art, 45.105.

beautifully made hand-carved fireplaces. The fact that he was able to move across many fields and modes of operation, practicing an "undisciplinarity" that anticipates contemporary habits, makes him an instructive example. In his open-mindedness with respect to tactics of making, he resembles the postdisciplinary practitioner of the present.

POOR PLAIN AND PALTRY: THE DECLINE OF CARVING

If McIntire is an attractive figure today, this is not just because of the elegance of his work—after all, that is a matter of taste. Rather it is because he negotiated the means of his own production so adroitly. He conformed to the new standard of design (flat, directive, visual), while carving out his own space of invention. But it is important to note that McIntire was a rather singular figure, and his work was made possible only by a confluence of factors, ranging from the relatively small size of his milieu, the lack of competition from other professionals in his chosen fields, and above all the moment he inhabited. By the 1820s, McIntire's work would already have seemed fussy and antique. Up-to-date European furniture makers now avoided carving for the most part and instead focused on flat expanses of veneer. This was the so-called Biedermeier or "pillar and scroll" style, which dominated furniture production in these years in Austria, Germany, England, and America alike, and to a lesser extent in France, and broke all previous records for flatness (Figure 1.13). In 1839, Wardour Street cabinetmaker Robert Holme

Figure 1.13 Frantz Steindl, secretaire, 1814. Vienna. Mahogany, with gilt-bronze mounts. V&A: W.22–1981. © Victoria and Albert Museum, London.

Bowman complained about the prevailing lack of ornament, writing, "for the last 40 or 50 years instead of that gorgious [*sic*] splendid furniture of Queen Elizabeth's time we have had poor plain and paltry."[63]

Bowman's dates were a bit off, but his basic point was right. There was certainly highly skilled carving around in the early nineteenth century: in ambitious shops from that of Charles Honoré Lannuier to that of John Henry Belter, and in the burgeoning antique restoration and reproduction trade. Other parts of the world such as India and China exported carved furniture to Europe and America in quantity, though attitudes to such work were becoming mired in stereotype. But the general tide of furniture was undeniably away from the carved and toward the flat. Already in the late eighteenth century, the most fashionable neoclassical furniture featured curved marquetry façades, giving it the appearance of a design drawing unfurled into domestic space. In ensuing decades, larger furniture operations—Duncan Phyfe's factory in New York, for example, or the fancy chair makers of New England and Baltimore—were increasingly likely to avoid relief ornament, instead employing veneer or stencil painting as a form of embellishment.

This was the easiest way to diminish the autonomy of the carver: eliminate the carving itself, through the mechanism of stylistic preference. But there was another means available too. In 1986, Adrian Forty noted in his seminal book on design history, *Objects of Desire,* that the East End furniture jobber in London was the very type of the underpaid and overworked Victorian craftsman.[64] Specialized piecework was now the rule. As one London cabinetmaking guide lamented in 1830, "it is almost universally the case, that a workman in one branch is entirely ignorant of the methods used by another."[65] Even when a man did make a cabinet or a chair from start to finish, he was unable to dictate how much compensation he would receive, as prices were knocked down by large furnishing firms. As labor historian Bruce Laurie puts it, "more and more furnituremakers worked in garretlike shops on single lines of goods for wholesalers in a process best described as a nonmechanized assembly line."[66] We have here a familiar narrative in which capitalism breeds alienated labor—but not through a machine-induced process of deskilling. Somewhat counterintuitively, in fact, subdivided labor may even have *increased* the skill level of the individual maker, because it brought about increased specialization. (After all, repetition is not the opposite of craft skill, but rather the best way of attaining it.)

Though the historian can spend a great deal of time parsing the methods by which artisanal workers were brought to heel in various trades, in terms of workplace organization the process did conform to a general pattern. Below a skilled craftsman like a carver, the apprentice became a weak link. Rather than progressing to journeyman status, makers were increasingly kept at this putatively trainee level, and so became easy to exploit; the ratio of journeymen to better-paid, more autonomous masters also steadily increased. At all skill levels, precise timekeeping and piecework were instituted as a means of tracking each artisan's productivity, in anticipation of the fraudulent scientism of Frederick Taylor in the twentieth century.[67] Meanwhile, above the skilled craftsman's head, professionals of more general, less artisanal talents were installed—architects, entrepreneurs, and eventually industrial designers. These were the new types of worker against which the master craftsman came to be defined—not by his skills, but rather by his supposed limitations.

Carvers, like other craftspeople, felt obliged to defend themselves. One anonymous contributor to the *Mechanic's Magazine* explained that the trade had been subsisting on restoration work for some time, or otherwise working to the design of "modern architects," who were hardly the easiest of clients to serve:

> with very few exceptions, [they are the] most boisterous and overbearing individuals, to those over whom they can exert any influence, that it is possible to conceive... However erroneous the modern architect's ideas may be on any particular branch of art, he will never submit to be set right by the suggestions or the experience of the practical man. To deviate from an architect's drawing in the most trifling detail would be high treason. And, oh, those drawings! What a collection of hard wiry lines, copiously interlarded with sections and profiles, to make "discrimination indiscriminate"! Yet it is principally through men such as these that talent is suffered to rust for want of use, and the beautiful art of wood carving is supposed to be lost.[68]

This writer made it clear that the skill of carving had not declined, but merely suffered due to mistreatment and neglect. Fairly or not, when carving did return to fashion in the 1830s thanks to the popularity of revival styles (Gothic, Renaissance, rococo), it earned a reputation for deadness in relation to its historical precedents—this was the "age of ugliness," as a memorable exhibition title at the Rijksmuseum in Amsterdam had it.[69] A huge expansion in the scale of the furniture industry led to a situation in which (as one 1873 cabinetmaker's guide complained) "the demand everywhere is for quantity and cheapness."[70] Again, it was not the introduction of steam power or machine tools, but rather the emergence of a competitive market in which highly decorated furniture was available to middle-class consumers, that led to this tendency toward rote execution.

The pressure to maximize production and reduce costs had predictably deleterious results on quality. While excellent carving could still be found in the middle of the nineteenth century, it was typically consigned to showpieces, works of art presented as exceptions that proved the rule. Thus we see a craftsman named William Bryer praised in a 1858 issue of the London *Times* for his "very beautiful specimen of wood carving" showing a game cock poised over his adversary. Painting served as the relevant (and inevitably, superior) point of reference for this "wood picture":

> Each object of the present specimen is carved in a different degree of relief, thus showing the power of the artist to mould his subjects in any shape, and almost to give the effect of light and shade, and even of clouds, or morning and evening. The painter can do all this at will, but the wood carver has much difficulty with which to contend—a difficulty, however, which in this instance Mr. Bryer has surmounted with surprising effect.[71]

With supporters like these, carvers clearly needed no enemies, and it is no surprise to see the same newspaper, some two decades later, noting the formation of a national school dedicated to the revival of the "greatly neglected art of wood-carving in this country."[72] A Florentine artisan was brought in to teach the classes, attended mainly by amateurs, including women, rather than the "persons of the industrial classes" originally targeted by the school's sponsors.[73]

One index of the preference for the autonomous and exceptional showpiece is the nineteenth-century enthusiasm for the historical figure of Grinling Gibbons (1648–1721), who had been the greatest carver of his time. Gibbons had never been an anonymous artisan. He specialized in nonfunctional ornaments for elite clients and (like McIntire) was thought of as a sculptor as well as an ornamental carver. Some of his creations occupied an undefined zone between these two categories. Horace Walpole, the great eighteenth-century wit and collector, prized one of these—a *trompe l'oeil* lace cravat (Plate 4). (He even wore it at his collar to greet his guests to a dinner party on one occasion, as if in knowing satire of its pointlessness.) Appreciation of Grinling Gibbons was given an enormous boost with the publication of his biography in Allan Cunningham's *Lives of the Most Eminent British Painters and Sculptors* in 1830. Cunningham was hardly a partisan of carving as a medium—he pointed out that wood's relative ephemerality as a material, compared to stone or metal, meant that those who work it "commit their hopes of fame to a most deceitful foundation, and need not hope to survive in their works."[74] He also agreed with other period observers that the craft had fallen onto hard times since Gibbons's day:

> At this period, and for many centuries before, the art of architectural enrichment was much encouraged; and as men of genius were employed, it was every where bold, lavish, even magnificent…In those days the artist who embellished the interior of a mansion brought a painter's eye to the task: he was not afraid of erring against the rules of sober and severe decoration deduced from the Greek temples. It is otherwise now. All is at present bald, bare, and barren; flowers are etched, not carved—and birds can no longer build and bring forth, as of old, amid the flowers, festoons, and deep enrichments of the entablatures. Since the genius of Gibbons was withdrawn, the interior splendour of our churches and palaces has suffered an eclipse.[75]

Cunningham positioned Gibbons as an ideal craftsman of a sort that no longer existed. This rhetorical use of the historical artisan was to become an increasingly common conceit in the nineteenth century. John Ruskin would famously install the anonymous Gothic stone carvers of Venice as the brightest stars in his aesthetic firmament (more on this in chapter four). In ceramics the names of Bernard Palissy and Cipriano Piccolpasso, and in bronze casting eccentric genius Benvenuto Cellini, became emblems of past glory that would never be equaled again.[76] In one short item in the *Mechanics' Magazine,* an anonymous carpenter quoted Cellini's autobiography, misleadingly implying that in the Renaissance craftsmen were always treated as gentlemen: "this shows how much that wise and polished people the Florentines esteemed the 'arts.'"[77] The tacit message—that artisans in the writer's own day lacked such respect—was all too clear.

These exceptional historic figures served as templates for the modern craftsman, but only to an extent: they were not meant to be models for the rank-and-file artisan, but rather the equally exceptional talents whose genius would allow them to transcend the limits of their medium. One of the surest signs that an artistically endowed craftsman had reached this elite status, ironically, was his ability to make other people execute the more "mechanical" aspects of the work. Gibbons again provided a model here. Cunningham stressed the fact that the great carver did not execute all his work himself; he had directed the work of other hands, perhaps through the mediation of design drawings. In the architectural ornaments at Chatsworth House, for example, "the head, perhaps, more than the hand of Gibbons was employed." Enlarging on this point, Cunningham noted that Gibbons should be considered not just an artisan but a sculptor; and though sculptors may employ assistants they ought, like architects, to be seen as the sole authors of their work: "no one will think of attributing to them the just fame of the works thus produced, any more than of dividing the glory of St. Paul's between Sir Christopher Wren and his mason."[78]

Gibbons inspired not only praise, but also imitation. The best-known English carver of the nineteenth century, William Gibbs Rogers, explicitly patterned himself after his baroque predecessor (Figure 1.14). Joyce Stephenson, a historian and descendant of Rogers,

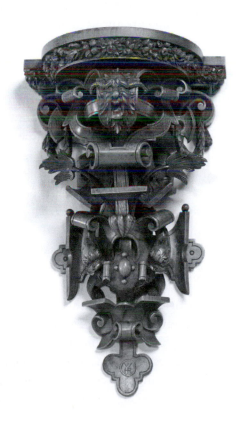

Figure 1.14 William Gibbs Rogers, bracket, ca. 1853. Carved boxwood. V&A: W.28–1972. © Victoria and Albert Museum, London.

describes his work accurately as meeting "the market for grandiose objects for ostentatious display [that] was increasing throughout the Victorian period."[79] Like other carvers of his era, much of his work consisted of restoring historical examples (including works attributed to Gibbons himself), but he also produced revivalist architectural carving, ecclesiastic commissions, and one-off objects like a cradle in boxwood for the royal family on the occasion of the first birthday of the Prince of Wales. Rogers exhibited this specimen of his work and no less than sixty others at the Great Exhibition of 1851, where they were taken as exceptional in every sense of the word.[80] Like William Bryer's "wood picture," the decorative carvings of Rogers were showpieces, as surely as Gibbons's cravat was when Horace Walpole hung it from his neck.

And so, over the course of a century, carving—despite its many advantages over other crafts from the point of view of autonomous workmanship—was systematically transformed. It could either be cheaply bought off the peg, or conversely, time-consuming and "artistic," and hence relegated to the realm of the artist or the amateur.[81] As we have seen, this gradual process had little to do with industrialization as that term is typically understood. It is very tempting to explain the "decline" of craft autonomy through recourse to technological determinism—that is, by drawing an invisible line of advancement through objects, showing how they illustrate the onward march of machines and the displacement of handwork. And there are some ways in which such an account might help us to understand the change in the status of carvers. The pillar and scroll style, for example, could be read as the result of improved veneer manufacturing (made possible by the introduction of circular saws in the first decade of the nineteenth century, initially by engineer Marc Isambard Brunel), which made expanses of flat, figured wood attractive to makers, especially when compared to the costs of hired skilled carvers. However, such economies were much less important in setting the course of furniture manufacture than new organizational tactics. And it is striking how diverse these tactics were: piecework systems, the increasing dependence upon design drawings, hierarchical professionalization, consolidation of manufacture under one roof, and finally the separation of the highest-quality carving out of the professional ranks of the trade altogether, to the status of a fine art or hobby.

Since the time of Alfred Chandler's influential book *The Visible Hand* (1977), it has been products of considerably less refinement than hand-carved furniture that have been associated with modernization in woodworking: the inexpensive clocks of Yankee tinkerers like Eli Terry, for example, or mass-produced carriage parts, or sewing machine cases.[82] But even, and perhaps especially, in the upper echelons of the carving trade, we can see an important and neglected aspect of this story—one all the more compelling to us today because of its aesthetic and individualist dimensions. As we have seen, far from destroying the integrity of craft outright, the pressures of modernity could prompt individual artisans to creativity of the highest order. We need to understand craft's transformation under the conditions of modernity as a creative as well as a destructive process.

THE CUTTING EDGE

In any attempt to draw a parallel between the historical and the contemporary—within craft practice or any other context—it is necessary to involve a degree of abstraction. Obviously, there are innumerable differences between the experience of craftspeople prior to 1850 (an age without electricity, much less the Internet) and those working today. Yet there are also certain instructive correspondences. Here, and at the end of subsequent chapters, I introduce a theoretical structure that aims to draw lessons from the foregoing historical discussion, and then apply that set of ideas to a series of contemporary case studies. I begin with the concept of "tooling"—a fashionable term at the moment in art schools, design consultancies, and architectural firms. Tooling can be defined as the making of objects that go on to make other objects. It is best understood as an ongoing process—not the supply of actual physical tools, lying ready to hand, but rather the whole system by which an infrastructure of making is brought into being and subsequently transformed to suit various tasks. Tooling is thus a distinctive form of research and discovery, one that operates only indirectly on the finished product, whether that is an object, a building, or a digital artifact.

In some cases, there may be quite a direct relation between a single tool and the result (as in the stone axe of prehistory, which was used for many different purposes and rarely in conjunction with other tools).[83] More commonly, however, making takes place within an extensive tooling chain. One object makes another which makes another which makes another *ad infinitum,* before the maker or manufacturer arrives at a final product. At each stage within this "linear" progression, there is also a "horizontal" connectivity between the tooling strategy and other variables, such as space, materiality, supply, labor, and skill, all of which interact in complex and often unpredictable ways. The generation and application of a tooling system always has potency inscribed into it. Remember Hobbs the lockpick, who did not produce a single instrument that could open Bramah's impregnable lock (as the company was at pains to point out) but was able to open it nonetheless, through a complex system of tools known only to himself. It was precisely this adaptive multiplicity of means that made him seem so threatening.

Tooling is a complicated matter, but we can bring it into focus by concentrating on one idea: the cutting edge. I use this phrase both in a literal and allegorical sense—edge tools physically cut, but they are also a metaphor for innovation. In both these senses, the concrete and the abstract, the edge is a site at which systemic forces converge. A cutting tool may be quite a simple thing, like a carving chisel. It might be a huge piece of apparatus made up of many parts, like an industrial replicating lathe with cutting attachments. Or it could be simple in form yet complex in fabrication, like a Japanese sword. But in any case, the tool is designed around the single line or point of contact with the thing to be cut. The logic of any cutting tool—the way it is made and operated—flows forward to this edge, and then turns back into the body of the tool. More indirectly, that logic extends along the productive chains that make the tool possible. Improvements can be made locally, as it were, by physically altering the tool itself. The chisel's handle can be reshaped or made out of rubber instead of wood, and thus made more comfortable in the hand. A machine tool can be made heavier and thus more stable, or powered using electricity rather than a leather belt. A sword's blade can be flattened out and folded many hundreds of times to increase the strength and flexibility of its metal. Even in these cases, tooling is adaptive and self-directed, operating through the principle of feedback to achieve constant improvement. It is also objective, in that it can be proven: a cut is either accurate enough for a given job, or it isn't.

The same test will apply if the tool is "improved" by a change not to its own physical makeup, but rather the broader context in which it is made and used: the mining of different metals to make better chisel blades, the establishment of a power grid to run factories, the maintenance of traditional apprenticeships for sword makers (and the support of those traditional practices through government funding). Even in this expansive, multivariable environment, the cutting edge remains a double horizon. It is the site at which the whole tooling system is tested, and potentially informs any subsequent change to that system. One might even say that a cutting edge is a line at which spatial and temporal concerns meet: certain physical effects are either transformed over time through innovation, or retained through tradition, and tooling is the principal matrix in which both change and stasis happen.

The cutting edge is also a helpful metaphor in trying to understand the dynamic of control in craft. When we ask about questions of power, as I have been doing in this chapter, the ownership of tools is a cardinal concern. In any form of making, control is determined mainly by "the means of production," who guides their working (through both direct and indirect means), and how this field of agency is structured. An investigation of tooling, in this expanded sense of the term, is therefore intrinsic to any politically aware investigation of craft—all the more so in a postdisciplinary environment where the relationship between people and tools is highly unstable. When assessing the expanded field of contemporary making, it can be very difficult to localize judgment. Every act of making is relative, embedded in a complex system of production. If we want to adopt an ethical standpoint, though, we must draw a line somewhere. I propose that the cutting edge, where tool meets work, is just where that line should be drawn. It is the site at which all the concerns of making converge, from the aesthetic to the ethical. It may seem counterintuitive, but it is in closely examining the action of tools that we will be able to look outside the work itself, to the conditions (the tooling systems) that impinge on it, that make it possible in the first place—because the relation between the work and the productive context is by nature recursive.

We can further particularize this idea by introducing to the discussion the concept of *friction*. At the cutting edge, at least two things are needed in order to ensure effective work: sufficient tooling, and sufficient skill to apply that tooling. Bringing those conditions about is difficult because of the physical and social frictions imposed within the making process: the variability of material, the margin for error allowed by the tool, as well as the absolute limits of strength, scale, and time. Various means can be brought to bear in order to overcome these forms of resistance, reducing that friction but never doing away with it entirely. And all of these will have both a material and a sociocultural footprint.

In our case study of carving between 1750 and 1850, we have seen how the techniques of visualization (drawings), organization (large-scale shops and outsourcing), and replacement technologies and styles (the use of casting instead of carving, or veneer instead of ornament) were employed in this way in an attempt to diminish the literal and figurative friction imposed by the carver's autonomy. We have also seen how, in moments of transformation, craftspeople like Samuel McIntire could creatively exploit this expanded tooling system to their own advantage. Yet we can also see what is lost in the process: not skill itself, but rather independence and integration.

The metaphor of friction is also helpful in examining contemporary postdisciplinary practice. In this undefined arena, it is still the case that the tool's edge is where the "work"—fixed and subject to critical judgment—meets the productive context, the system necessary for the making to happen. Clearly this is a charged metaphor, for the concept of the "cutting edge" closely resembles the idea of the avant garde, the great bugbear of twentieth-century art theory. Without getting too deep into these waters, it is worth saying that modernist and postmodernist theorists concerned with the radical, political "efficacy" of art have almost always concentrated their attention on finished works. For the most part, conversation about an artwork's avant garde status began in the gallery (or wherever else the work might be installed), not the studio, much less the factories where an artist's equipment and raw materials might have been manufactured. This is not universally true, of course; the manner in which an object was brought into being might be considered relevant if, for example, it involved ready-mades—as in the case of a Dada collage or Robert Rauschenberg's combines. But even in such a scenario, making was not considered primarily a matter of practical necessity. It was assumed that if an artist or designer wanted to create a certain effect or form, she or he would simply find a way to do it. In retrospect, and in the face of the spectacular, highly capitalized works that now dominate art and design fairs across the globe, such confidence seems amazingly naïve. But the tooling required to make a work—that is, the whole palette of skills and material infrastructure lying behind its fabrication—was simply not treated as a central issue in art theory until very recently.[84] When we do redirect our attention in this way, the theoretical legerdemain that besets discussion of the avant garde is forestalled, and possibly set aside entirely, replaced by a more pragmatic conversation about who does what and how.

THE HANDS OF OTHERS

Innovation, these days, is often not a matter of creating a work; rather, it is a matter of inventing a whole new way of working. This is a signature feature of the postdisciplinary condition: the free movement of makers in relation to their own practices, and the ensuing discovery of new forms of friction, from the physical to the political. British art theorist John Roberts has discussed this momentous turn in his important book *The Intangibilities of Form* (2007). His argument is too complex to reprise here in its entirety, but briefly, he argues that the inception of apparently antimaterialist conceptual tactics, such as Marcel

Duchamp's ready-mades or the abstract "Telephone Paintings," enamel on steel, that László Moholy-Nagy reputedly ordered up from metal fabrication shops, involve not only the stripping away of traditional artisanship—deskilling—but also necessitate the invention of new artistic processes, which Roberts terms "reskilling."[85] Postdisciplinary practitioners do not necessarily make things by hand (though they might). They are more likely to function as "producers," in the sense that the word is used in the film industry. They bring about the specific conditions that make the work happen. In effect, they create tooling systems, whose edges are always on the move. In some cases, Roberts points out, multiple productive modes can exist within a single artwork: artisanal making (skill), appropriation (deskilling), and strategic reinventions of the artistic profession itself (reskilling). Duchamp himself could be seen as operating in this tripartite fashion, as in his "assisted readymades," which incorporated both handmade and found objects, and also were presented and re-presented through photography, text, and other forms of mediation.

It is not only in Duchamp's idiosyncratic gamesmanship and Moholy's early experiment in outsourcing that one can see modernist experimentation within the skill/deskilling/reskilling triangle.[86] Among the other important touchstones are the Constructivists' attempts to bind together craft, art, and industry; the late, artisanally inflected architecture of Le Corbusier; and minimalist sculptures by the likes of Donald Judd, which were made by uncredited shop fabricators. As different as these various art historical landmarks are from McIntire's neoclassical carved chairs made in late eighteenth-century Salem, it is striking how structurally similar they are. In both cases (in the past, responses to the restrictions of emerging disciplinarity; today, responses to the emergent possibilities of postdisciplinarity) there is a looseness of approach to the task of production. Skill is combined inventively with management in a single authorial structure. Frictional craft is applied alongside techniques that control or replace that friction. Contemporary practitioners are exploring this terrain by outsourcing labor halfway across the globe, transforming art galleries into miniature factories, staging impromptu collaborative craft projects, or constructing elaborate mash-ups of the handmade and the ready-made. Examples range from the austerely conceptual to the giddily stylized.

We will encounter many of these in this book, but for the moment let's begin with late fashion designer Alexander McQueen, who just before his death designed a line of shoes in tribute to none other than Grinling Gibbons. The project is a perfect example of craft reinvented in the image of its own past; according to *Vogue* magazine, the shoes are "sculpted, exceptionally high-crafted and artful, embracing arcane and modern techniques"[87] (Plate 5). To realize these objects of high fashion, McQueen turned to his frequent collaborator, wood carver Paul Ferguson, who has operated a shop in Bedfordshire, England, since 1978. Ferguson, like most professional carvers working today, has attained his skills mainly as a restorer and replicator. He first trained as a frame maker and then branched into architectural renovation work, often repairing an existing bit of ornament or perhaps creating one or more duplicates of an object so a client will have a pair or set. (Such tasks required him to match the skill level of centuries-old work, arguably the best way for a contemporary maker to train in that it simulates the copying techniques common in premodern apprenticeship, albeit at a great temporal distance.) Among his commissions from McQueen was a pair of mannequins for use in the designer's retail spaces, which were based on a life-cast from a model, and feature historicist leaf carving on the décolletage; and perhaps most extraordinarily, a pair of prosthetic legs for disabled supermodel Aimee Mullins. To realize this project, McQueen worked not only with Ferguson but with medical technicians at the University of Roehampton, who shaped the tops of the legs where they would fit precisely onto Mullins's knees. These were joined to simple blocks of wood and sent to Ferguson for carving—a textbook example of the division of labor according to specialist skills, not unlike the making of an elaborate rococo chair in a large workshop, despite the very different nature of the project.

In determining the patterns of all his work for McQueen, including the Gibbons-inspired shoes, Ferguson feels that the designer was "pretty specific about he wanted—I wasn't left to my own devices." He first drew the ornament for approval, conforming to the long-established authorial hierarchy with a process of making. (As he notes, "I draw what I need to know; I don't draw a pretty picture first unless I need to impress a client.") The single pattern of the shoe Ferguson carved was then used to make a high-quality casting mold, so that the fine detail of his original could be replicated innumerable times. The project is absolutely typical of one style of contemporary luxury production—whether encountered in the form of art, fashion, or design doesn't much matter. The buyer of the finished commodity, or indeed the browsing reader of *Vogue* magazine, can appreciate the traces of craftsmanship, but only at a remove. This physical separation echoes the authorial separation dividing Ferguson from the products of his own work. Nowhere in the pages of *Vogue,* or indeed in any other public presentation of McQueen's work, will you see him credited. Nor, for that matter, will you find the names of any of the other fabricators working for the designer. This is so despite the fact that, in Ferguson's opinion anyway, McQueen was deeply respectful of his collaborators' skills—he wasn't like some other people who "look upon craftsmen as something on the bottom of their shoe." Ferguson views his removal from the public eye with equanimity: "Personally, I feel if someone brings me a design and I make it for them it's still their design; I don't really feel that it's morally my copyright." So would he have liked to be recognized, say, in the wall text of the recent, spectacular exhibition of McQueen's work at the Metropolitan Museum of Art in New York City? "It would have been nice to have my name up there, but it's wasn't my decision."[88]

McQueen was first among equals in contemporary fashion design, unrivalled in his commitment to the well-crafted spectacular, but otherwise typical in his use of other people's hands to realize his fantastical conceptions. This is the standard operating procedure of contemporary couture. On one hand, it embraces the sturdiest of craft values—complex pattern cutting, bespoke tailoring, and the traditional leather-working skills that go into high-end handbags and shoes. On the other hand, this artisanal content is intermixed with new technology, and wrapped in a thick, gauzy shroud of celebrity-anchored brand management. The quick-moving world of fashion may present itself as an exception, but in these fundamentals, it is not very different from other areas of contemporary art and design practice. No matter how it is packaged, postdisciplinary production tends to involve the distribution of authorship, just as Roberts says. Indeed, given that fashion ever looks toward the next thing, it seems quite likely to be the shape of things to come. Increasingly this means that practitioners of all kinds are adopting the methods of haute couture, in which deep craft and superficial image are bound up in a single, potent gesture.

I have argued for understanding such forms of practice by thinking in terms of tooling, a frictional frontier that localizes judgment in relation to a broader system. Sometimes we can find that edge easily—each of Ferguson's chisels has one, and you can bet he keeps them sharp. But at other times, it can be very difficult to know where to fix this mobile edge in our minds. This is as true for institutions as for individual practitioners. Postdisciplinarity easily slips into exploitative labor, and also can be used to justify the abandonment of an established craft infrastructure. A colleague has sardonically observed to me that the Social Practice Workshop recently established at The California College of the Arts (CCA) is above all an ingenious financial maneuver. While the program legitimately constitutes an innovative, off-site expansion of the art school's activities—it encourages students to create "urban interventions, utopian proposals, guerrilla architecture, 'new genre' public art, social sculpture, project-based community practice, interactive media, service dispersals, and street performance"—from an administrative perspective, it is also a whole new department with no overhead costs except for the utility bills. Not coincidentally, as many craft partisans have noted, CCA was until recently CCAC—the California College of Arts and Crafts. A mordantly funny T-shirt made by the students a couple of years back read "CCA[C]: The C is Silent." It is a condition that one young artist in the fiber program, Lacey Jane Roberts, sought to redress through guerilla action, reinstating the letters "& CRAFTS" in orange fabric on the college's façade during alumni week, to the embarrassment of the school's leadership.[89] Such protests against the erasure of craft (so redolent of the transformations of the late eighteenth century) could be considered an ideal outcome. It is only when craft is banished that enthusiasts rush forward to claim it—a dynamic that is endemic to modern craft history, as we see in this book's final chapter. Maybe it was worth losing the words from the façade for that one shining moment when Roberts restored them. At CCA, certainly, discourse around craft spiked noticeably when the word disappeared from the school's letterhead. On the other hand, one can imagine the situation that would prevail if this tendency were generalized: art schools could maximize both their profits and their claims to progressive practice by eliminating studios entirely, instead training their students in spaces resembling open-plan offices, as is already the case in most architecture, design, and engineering programs. As one craft department after another closes in order to save the costs of materials, staff, and even fuel (sorry, glass makers), one is struck by the likelihood that soon an art student will be able to make his or her work out of almost anything, as long as it's not a material identified with the crafts like wood or clay. Clearly, neither CCA nor any other art school wants to see this happen, and it is both instructive and salutary to note that as the Social Practice Workshop has matured since its founding, it has both lived up to the last word in its name—encouraging a genuinely intensive exchange between the faculty and students in the department—and importantly, has forged strong ties with the established craft-based departments at the school. Collaborations between "relational" and material practices turn out to be the most effective way to realize the promise of this new initiative. The demands placed on traditional studio equipment are heightened, not lessened, by postdisciplinary activity.

Art school provisioning is just one example of the greatest dilemma for postdisciplinary practice: not just the question of tooling, but *access* to tooling—another overdetermined phrase. In 1968, American activist and publisher Stewart Brand famously adopted "access to tools" as the motto of his countercultural listings guide, *The Whole Earth Catalog*. His ambition was to change the world ecologically, economically, socially, and drastically. Brand—like other design thinkers of his era such as Buckminster Fuller and Victor Papanek—was emphatic in describing the creation and distribution of tooling as the key to cultural transformation. This was no left-wing fantasy in which the "people" or the "movement" or the "freaks" would simply take hold of the means of production. For all their visionary tendencies, Brand, Fuller, Papanek, and their contemporaries were more pragmatic than that; they saw that change would require finding the right (perhaps old) tool for the (new) job. This sort of invention might involve intentional misuse of tools— turning a hammer or paintbrush round the other way, for example. It might involve creating interactions between tools from radically different spheres of production. Artists are empowered through tooling; no tool is too simple to disregard, and none is too complex to be off limits.

This all sounds well and good, perhaps, but access to tools (as Brand well knew) can never be taken for granted. Charles Jencks and Nathan Silver made this point a few years later in their book *Adhocism: The Case for Improvisation* (1972), a bible of adaptive bricolage entirely in tune with Brand's ideas. *Adhocism* featured on its cover a snappy red chair designed by Silver for his own house—a witty pop art conflation of a tractor seat, wheelchair parts, gas pipe, and insulation foam. Inside the book, readers found a welter of examples of adaptation: using the front of a car as a planter, crucifying a mannequin at a feminist protest march. But one of the key examples was a bit harder to celebrate: a shantytown in Casablanca, Morocco. This desperately poor neighborhood bristled with ad hoc design solutions: crate sides employed as wall materials, with printed exhortations not to break the glass in place of the windows inhabitants couldn't afford; solid walls of motor oil packaging that might have made Andy Warhol proud; and above all, an accidental sculptural aesthetic born out of sheer necessity. Silver and Jencks tried not to be idealistic about the living conditions in this slum: "totally scavenged environments can have a breathtaking beauty," they wrote, "but the adhocism of poverty…has no romantic attraction for those who are forced to suffer it."[90] In one sense, they were not looking down on the bricoleurs of the shantytown. They had good cause to be sympathetic, because, in common with most radical designers of the 1970s, they themselves had few means at their disposal. This was after all the age of paper architecture: of proposals so radical, so important, so groundbreaking, they had zero chance of getting built. (The message of *Adhocism* was: build it anyway.) Even taking into account such notional fellow feeling, however, there is no question that Jencks and Silver, two prosperous white architects who met at Cambridge University, could only have a distant relation to the inventive builders of Casablanca. They were conscious of that problem, and so too have been many writers since who have addressed recycled and scavenged work from around the world.[91] Yet it is perhaps all too easy to admire, or take pride in, the ad hoc transformation of unpromising resources. The urgent challenge is to retain an ethical (as well as aesthetic) compass within the rough-and-tumble situation of displaced production.

If moral considerations concerning production are tough in a poor Moroccan town, they are even more difficult to navigate in the case of highly capitalized labor, a context in which skill and ingenuity are typically not set in the foreground (as in ad hoc making) but entirely effaced behind a screen of branding, marketing, and spectacular imagery. If one had to choose a single arena of production that emblematizes this problem, the game of football might be a good choice. Called *soccer* in America and Australia, *fútbol* in Spanish, *calcio* in Italian, *zuqiu* in Chinese, and *sakka* (an approximation of the American term) in Japan, football is truly a global commodity. It is played worldwide and commands the highest television audience of any sport. Of course football is in itself a theater of skills—those of the athlete instead of the artisan—but the labor that makes the sport possible is almost entirely invisible. As it happens, the sport was one of the first identified as an engine of exploitative labor. In 1996, journalist Sydney Schamberg traveled to Pakistan to see how footballs were made. His article, entitled "Six Cents an Hour," showed that the workforce of manufacturers like Nike and Adidas was composed largely of children, living in conditions tantamount to slavery. It was a textbook case of displacing labor in order to hide it. "The words Hand Made are printed clearly on every ball," Schamberg noted; "not printed is any explanation of whose hands made them."[92] Following Schamberg's exposé, the image of children sewing footballs for starvation wages became a kind of shorthand for exploitative labor conditions. Activists and NGO officials heaped scorn on sporting goods companies. Free market proponents rushed to argue that sweatshops were an unfortunate but necessary by-product of developing economies. Economic theorists posited a breakdown in the established relations between national and private interests, so that labor became "a naked commodity, no longer embedded in relations of reciprocity rooted in social and political communities."[93] There was only one point of agreement. Everyone concurred that globalism was radically changing the reality of production.

Amidst the debate, people kept making footballs. And while arguments continue over the plight of laborers in Pakistan, another thing has become clear. Manufacturers are highly aware of the politicized nature of their products, and they have gone to considerable lengths to change the narrative. Nike, by many accounts the worst offender in the industry, signed up to a "Global Compact" to protect human rights, and Adidas promised to exert pressure on its Indonesian suppliers.[94] More important, they have employed tooling systems themselves as a way of dealing with the ethical implications of their own industry. Even here though, it is important to distinguish rhetoric from reality. The *Jabulani* (a word meaning

Figure 1.15   Jabulani football by Adidas, 2010.

"to celebrate" in the Zulu language) was developed by Adidas specifically for use in the 2010 World Cup (Figure 1.15). Assembled using a minimum number of seams achieved through a novel design of interlocking curved panels, covered in slick polyurethane, and light in weight, the ball was meant to be a technical marvel, but the Jabulani's flight proved unpredictable, and players dismissed it as a "beachball," "appalling," a "supermarket ball," a "disaster." Coaches called it "impossible." Goalkeepers suspected a conspiracy; as Claudio Bravo from Chile put it, "they created it to make life difficult for keepers, so they make more mistakes and there are more goals."[95]

Inevitably, the furor over the Jabulani's playability drew attention to the details of its production. Where was this strange thing from? Certainly not South Africa, where the World Cup was being played.[96] Like so many other global commodities, it was manufactured in China, partly from components made elsewhere.[97] As a short promotional film released by Adidas reveals, it was made in the manner that has led to Chinese domination of many industries: a combination of highly skilled (if repetitive) handwork and full automation.[98] Much of the labor of making the Jabulani goes into its assembly, as might be expected, but a great deal of the work involves applying decals to the surface: logos, trademarking, and a pattern of multicolored rings that evoke both African decorative patterning and the Olympic insignia. Compared to the roadside sheds Schamberg saw in Pakistan, crowded with underage pieceworkers, the factory where the Jabulanis were fabricated is quite high tech, clean, and impressive. But one still wonders about the experience of working there. It may be significant that not a single operative's face is included in the Adidas footage—only adept hands going about their tasks at incredible speed. The means by which the footballs are made are brand new, but like modern craftspeople for two centuries, the makers find themselves working at the intersection of two fields of manipulation: they masterfully shape their materials but are themselves controlled within a larger system of mastery.

The real story of the Jabulani, then, is not that it is difficult to kick or catch. Rather, it is the way the ball marks a typical displacement within globalism: from one site of outsourcing to another—which is perhaps less exploitative, but more likely just more efficient. Pakistan has seen its share in the global football market slip from a high of eighty-five percent to something below forty percent in the past few years, thanks to inroads made by their Far Eastern competitors. The loss of the World Cup contract must have hurt (though workers in the Punjab were still kept busy making low-quality Jabulani knockoffs).[99] Part of the reason for this shift is the sensitivity mentioned previously; companies like Adidas have a financial stake in keeping their names clean, and once established, the image of the Pakistani sweatshop is hard to dispel. But it also has to do with the ongoing cycle of global production, in which different patterns of work, most of them exploitative in one way or another, displace one another at a bewildering pace. How can we adequately formulate a politics of production when our understanding of laboring conditions changes more slowly than the conditions themselves do? This difficulty is exacerbated by the fact that the (perhaps deceptive) image projected by even a single object can become so important. The Jabulani ball may have been a failure from a design point of view, but it was still seen in action by nearly 30 billion people in the summer of 2010. Paradoxically this means that investigating the means of production, at the most basic and physical level, has never been more important.

One lesson to take from the story of the Jabulani ball is that the attention paid to the ethical burden of tooling tends to diminish rather than increase as the stakes get higher. We might even take it as a general rule: unfortunately, the more capitalized the system of production the more likely it is to obscure its own workings. This is as true in the world of art and design practice as it is in the economy at large. Anish Kapoor and Richard Serra, two of the chief exponents of outsourced industrial-scale sculpture, recently put on a sort of clinic of disingenuousness in this regard, insisting in a press interview that, against all appearances to the contrary, their practice was centered in manual craft. "I'm very much studio-based," said Kapoor. "I employ a few people, because you can't do it all yourself, but the studio is all; every problem, every issue is here. I can't solve them in a plane or in my head and I don't believe that intellectual practice is enough." Serra concurred: "I'm a little cottage modelmaker. I use a hammer and nails!"[100] In a limited sense, this is true: both artists no doubt are extensively involved in prototyping and other small-scale, studio-based activities. But to pretend that the value of their monumental works derives entirely, or even mainly, from their artistic ideas (as encapsulated in preparatory studies) would be the sheerest folly. Their careers, however inventive, depend on elaborate projects involving the labor of hundreds of people and the investment of millions of dollars. Needless to say, that investment has to pay off. This is one aspect of what Johanna Drucker describes, memorably, as the "contingency" of contemporary art—its thorough engagement with the culture industry, the terrain the avant garde once assigned itself the task of attacking.[101] Artists and art galleries now compete on more or less equal terms with Hollywood films, shopping malls, amusement parks, and fashion houses. (That artists also place their work in all those contexts is no coincidence.) Despite the very real worries brought about by the decline of studio-based teaching in art schools, for the moment there is no shortage of astounding feats of making. Bespoke craft is no longer abjured (as was the case for much of the twentieth century), but on the contrary is the mechanism that drives competitive display.

This sort of outsourcing reproduces the modern hierarchical structure that has kept craft in a subordinate position for centuries. Should we regret this state of affairs? Yes and no. The point is not to call for a retreat to a more confined conception of art, in which it is considered an autonomous critical instrument—a cutting edge of a more familiar kind. We cannot roll back the years to a time before mammoth art and design fairs, inflated secondary markets, and the transformation of artists into celebrity entrepreneurs. We can, however, insist that all forms of practice should reveal and even reflect on the conditions that bring them about. In this respect, early modern artisans who navigated changing circumstances through a flexible repertoire of skilling, deskilling, and reskilling, might still serve as a model for production in general.[102] Another way of putting this is that our critical judgments about art and design should always involve, and even prioritize, the relation

Figure 1.16   Wim Delvoye, Cement Truck no. 1, 1990–1999, as shown at the Venice Biennale, 1999. Carved wood. Courtesy of the artist.

between a work and its production. In conclusion let us return to the example of carving, the craft I have been analyzing throughout this chapter, to see how this particular trade can perform in a postdisciplinary context.

In the early 1990s, Belgian artist Wim Delvoye began self-consciously "exploiting" woodcarvers as human tools within his own practice. The procedure was a simple one, though the results were elaborate in the extreme. The artist would select a given object—typically an unlovely industrial artifact like a concrete mixer or a dump truck—and ask his carvers to create a sculpture of the object from solid wood, festooned with historical Flemish ornament typical of his own geographical origin (Figure 1.16). For Delvoye, despite the fact that this was an act of triple appropriation—industrial form, "local" décor, and outsourced labor—the results nonetheless were the opposite of ready-mades ("because they are so crafty," he explained).[103] They were a way of reflecting on his own implication in global production. Given his own position in place and time where things are *not* made skillfully, Delvoye's project has an aspect of willful overcompensation. It is postmodern and nihilistic, taking for granted that an artist's relations to the craftspeople who serve him can only ever be asymmetrical. Not for nothing did he follow this body of work with the infamous installation work *Cloaca,* a transparent mechanical digestive system that transforms organic material into synthetic feces. As Birgit Sonna notes, this work did for self-reproducing consumption what the carved work did for outsourced production: "we have arrived in the inner world of the post-industrial society, in which machines are engaged in a compulsive ritual, endlessly producing goods, without sense or purpose."[104]

Delightfully, though, the story does not end here, in the customary impasse of postmodern commodity critique. For there was a fourth, unanticipated layer of appropriation to come. According to one of the artist's critical supporters, on a visit to Indonesia to see how one of his teams of carvers was getting on with a full-scale sculpture of a carved dump, "Delvoye found to his horror that local workshops had taken to reproducing ornamental sized versions of the truck for the Western tourist market."[105] I think it is impossible not to feel that the Indonesian artisans not only took the upper hand in this exchange, but also made the more provocative objects. Delvoye is fond of saying, "the Yellow Pages are my studio," a self-conscious nod back to the tradition of reskilling established by Moholy-Nagy. But his sculptures aren't made in a telephone directory. They are made, as he knows full well, by people working with real tools in real space. (The series that began with the carved teak objects, and which has continued with full-scale and miniature construction equipment made in Gothic styled laser-cut metal, is entitled *Chantier,* or "workshop.") Delvoye's gambit was to control the three-way interface between skill, deskilling, and reskilling: to manipulate that whole tooling system within a single gesture of art production. The rejoinder of the Indonesian carvers, though motivated by pragmatic rather than theoretical concerns, effectively deconstructed this circuit—picking the complicated lock of the system with seeming ease. Their "ornamental" miniatures of Delvoye's artwork may occupy the unauthorized milieu of the tourist souvenir, or curio, rather than the authorial realm of gallery-bound sculpture. Delvoye was apparently displeased about the knockoffs, just as a fashion brand would be dismayed by inferior copies of its garments. But perhaps he might have come to a different conclusion. In the Indonesian carvers' "unauthorized" copy (a word whose double meaning in this case is evident) he could easily have seen the completion of his own work, or if that is asking too much, at least another link in the tooling chain he had set in motion.

In any case, the artisans' ability to reframe their own work in their own terms, compromised and marginal as they may be, reminds us of the frictional power of craft. Whenever artists depend on the hands of others to make their work, those hands become part of the meaning of the work, like it or not, as surely as the specific resistances of wood or stone or clay limit the possible forms of a carving. More and more artists are beginning to realize this, and moreover, to make that fact of interdependency into the primary content of their work. The inevitable example here is Ai Weiwei's recent installation *Sunflower Seeds* (2010), in which the Tate Modern's Turbine Hall was filled with over 100 million handmade ceramic seeds fashioned by ceramic artisans in Jingdezhen, China. This work is the *ne plus ultra* of outsourcing in contemporary art, at least so far; its conceptual and even its aesthetic impact is entirely premised on the horrifying fact of the labor that went into its making. Ai restages the sublime scale of global outsourcing, and even its dynamics, in an art gallery. Recall the point mentioned at the beginning of this chapter, that in the contemporary economy skill is often defined in terms of speed rather than quality—especially when female workers are involved. Sure enough, when asked about the hundreds of workers who laboriously painted the black stripes on each side of each seed to give it verisimilitude, most of whom were women, Ai explained that the skilled ones could achieve a satisfactory result with three strokes of a brush; less skilled workers needed four.[106]

Perhaps the most sobering fact about the seeds, though, is that the Chinese workers who created it were sorry to see the project come to an end. It had provided two years of much-needed employment in a city whose principal industry has fallen on hard times.[107] It is useful to juxtapose Ai Weiwei's hard-headed confrontation with the reality of production in such an environment with the concept of "relational aesthetics"—a coinage of French theorist Nicolas Bourriaud.[108] A relational artwork, in Bourriaud's terms, includes its viewers in its own form; or to put it another way, the work could not exist as such without its viewers' active participation. Relational aesthetics is an unfortunate term because it has a slackness built into it, a presumption that all forms of relation within the work are more or less equal, or at least, all charged with the possibility of social transformation. This is a dangerous assumption. As Clare Bishop points out, an open relational structure, because of its tacit enclosure of its audience, may simply extend the authority of the curator or artist over the public, producing an effect of dominance. (Bourriaud's own career, arguably marked by cliquishness and a penchant for sweeping declarations of new zeitgeists, would seem to confirm her view.[109])

One of the cornerstones of Bourriaud's thinking is that relational aesthetics is an appropriate artistic response to our postindustrial condition, in which knowledge and service, rather than making, are the primary drivers of the economy. Yet perhaps it is no coincidence that relational artworks often gravitate to craft-like effects, without actually involving the application of skill on the part of artist or viewer. A particularly powerful example is Felix Gonzales-Torres's sculpture *Untitled (Portrait of Ross in L.A.)*, 1991, an early example of audience involvement in the form of the work. The physical makeup of the work is simple enough: a pile of store-bought hard candies, each in a brightly colored wrapper. Each viewer is invited to take and eat a single candy. It is a tactic used extensively in Gonzales-Torres's work—not only candies, but also printed pieces of paper and other giveaways—but in the case of *Portrait of Ross in L.A.*, the work is freighted with an unusual emotional burden. Ross was the artist's lover, and was at the time dying of AIDS in Los Angeles. The sculpture functions as a living portrait in the sense that it was installed at Ross's healthy body weight. As visitors remove each candy, they inexorably reduce the pile, mimetically reprising the wasting away of his body. (The fact that Gonzales-Torres himself died of AIDS in 1996 makes the work even more poignant.) There is of course nothing handmade about the sculpture—it consists entirely of ready-mades—yet in its attention to detail, color, and the incorporation of the work of many hands (which place and then remove the candies), it has the intimacy and material nuance we often associate with craft.

And indeed, since relational practice was established as an artistic strategy, it has often been grounded in the skill of the maker, which is offered up to the viewer as a sort of gift.[110] Rirkrit Tiravanija has prepared Thai cuisine for gallery goers; Lee Mingwei has crafted immaculate, ritualistic spaces for everyday activities like letter writing, sleeping, and (again) eating; Liam Gillick's varied relational works have often involved handmade architectural environments so precise that they recall the minimalist sculptures of Donald Judd. Given that relational aesthetics is the latest turn in the history of conceptual art, it may seem strange that artists working in this vein should so regularly depend on craft. In large part this is simply a matter of sentimental affect. It's all well and good to operate relationally, but how do you draw the audience in? When an artist needs to create a rhetoric of available openness to the public, the pliancy and populism associated with craft are obviously useful.

Yet there is a deeper sense in which craft is relevant here: it is an indispensable element in all artistic relations, whether those occur within making, consumption, or a relational construct in which making and consumption are one. (Even when an artwork requires no skill, as in the Gonzales-Torres, it is conspicuous by its absence.) As this chapter has explored, any gesture that absents an artist or manufacturer from production tends to bring about exploitation or at least effacement of making. To the degree that such abdication occurs in a relational artwork, the artist is literally making his or her audience into tools. It is helpful to contrast Bourriaud's ideas to those of Italian political philosopher Paolo Virno, who is also reacting to the widespread economic shift from making to service and knowledge, but founds his theoretical writings on "virtuosity" rather than relationships. For Virno, virtuosity in the contemporary workplace is no longer a matter of technical specialization, but rather adaptability and socialization. "Nowadays," he writes, "workers learn [their] abilities by living in a big city, by gaining aesthetic experiences, having social relationships, creating networks: all things workers learn specifically outside the workplace."[111]

Virno would want us to see any engagement with a relational work as part of an ongoing continuum of acculturating experiences—an idea that resonates with the previous discussion of extended chains of tooling. In this case, the question is not just what is given to us through the work but also what we give it in return.

This brings us back finally to the question of skill. As Bishop notes, Bourriaud is notably indifferent to the means by which relational art is brought about: "*what* Tiravanija cooks, *how* and *for whom,* are less important to Bourriaud than the fact that he gives away the results of his cooking for free."[112] But when a work makes no demands on its audience beyond enjoyable participation, it comes perilously close to other phenomena that treat their viewers as more or less passive consumers. As a comparison, think of a promotional party thrown by Pabst Blue Ribbon, in which its product is freely distributed. The company's hope is that there will be a quick passage from a miniature gift economy to a more profitable state of affairs. This suggests how thinly generosity can disguise self-interest. Thai curry and beer, art and commerce are not fundamentally different in this regard. Despite the critical and neo-utopian intentions that lay behind relational aesthetics, they are worryingly compatible with other forms of cultural manipulation.

Craft skill changes this calculus. For all that exploitation is at the heart of many art projects, and even though the relation of artist to maker remains hierarchical in these examples, skilled hands (like those of the Indonesian carvers working with Delvoye) might just reclaim a degree of agency. If the audience must be *trained* to make the work, or alternatively, must bring their existing skills to the project, then the relationship between artist and audience is no longer abstractly manipulative. Rather, the artist and the audience will be mutually dependent, just as Delvoye and Ai need their workforce of carvers and potters and vice versa, and that relation will have to be included as part of the content of the work. Equally, there is a largely untapped potential in ways of working that integrate the fabricators of an art or design work into the narrative of authorship. It may sound like a fairy tale in which a puppet comes to life and cuts its own strings. But it does happen, and in a postdisciplinary condition it will inevitably happen more and more. The result will be a thorough dissolution of the binary relation between author and fabricator, and the creation of new structures of making. Power structures we will always have with us. But there is one thing we can count on: as sophisticated as the means brought to bear on its control may be, craft skill will always retain the possibility of its own reinvention.

NOTES

1. "Hobbs, the American Artisan," *The Morning Post [London]* (Oct. 24, 1851), p. 7.
2. Ian McNeil, *Joseph Bramah: A Century of Invention, 1749–1851* (New York: A.M. Kelley, 1968).
3. John Cantrell and Gillian Cookson, eds., *Henry Maudslay and the Pioneers of the Machine Age* (Stroud: Tempus Publishing, 2002).
4. *The Bramah Lock Controversy: Excerpts From the Press* (London: T. Brettell, 1851), p. 16.
5. "Metals: Ornamental Keys," *Journal of Design* (1849): 138.

6. A. C. Hobbs, "The Lock Controversy," Letter to the Editor, *The London Times* (Wed., June 11, 1851), p. 6.

7. *The Bramah Lock Controversy: Excerpts From the Press*, p. 63.

8. Chubb and Son to T. E. Thomson, Calcutta, August 19, 1851. Wolverhampton City Archives, DB/24/B/465. Previously, the firm had both taken advantage of and suffered from the publicity afforded by lockpicking challenges. In 1823, it claimed to have set a prison ship convict, formerly a lockmaker and renowned for his skill at picking, the task of breaking into one of its new locks. The firm proudly advertised his failure in doing so. Conversely, in 1832, the company's founder, Charles Chubb, had to defend one of the company's patent lock designs against a similar assault by a former Chubb and Son employee: "it may be necessary for me to state that the said THOS. HART was sometime since a journeyman in my employ, but now (or very lately) in the employ of a Lock Maker in Wolverhampton of the name of Richards—that Hart has *by any fair means* picked any of my locks *I totally deny.*" *Mechanics Magazine* no. 13 (Nov. 22, 1823), p. 193–195; *Wolverhampton Chronicle*, March 14, 1832, n. p.

9. Letter from Bramah and Co. to George Rennie, reprinted in *The Bramah Lock Controversy*, p. 22.

10. "News of the Week: Locks Ruined," *The Living Age* 31/387 (Oct. 18, 1851): 142.

11. Letter from Bramah and Co. to George Rennie, reprinted in *The Bramah Lock Controversy*, pp. 20–21.

12. Ibid., p. 22.

13. *Wolverhampton and South Staffordshire Illustrated: Biographical and Commercial Sketches* (London: Robinson and Son, 1898), p. 79.

14. A. C. Hobbs, "The Lock Question," Letter to the Editor, *The Times* (July 15, 1853), p. 5.

15. Michel Foucault interviewed in *L'Express Magazine*, reprinted in Lawrence Kritzman, ed., *Michel Foucault: Politics, Philosophy, Culture* (London: Routledge, 1988).

16. Celina Fox, *The Arts of Industry in the Age of Enlightenment* (New Haven, CT: Yale University Press, 2009), p. 263.

17. For an extensive discussion of modernity as an ongoing process of "explicitization," see Michael McKeon, *The Secret History of Domesticity: Public, Private and the Division of Knowledge* (Baltimore, MD: Johns Hopkins University Press, 2005). For a consideration of the cult of craft demonstration in the interwar period, see Victoria Cain, "The Craftsmanship Aesthetic: Showing Making at the American Museum of Natural History," *Journal of Modern Craft* 5/1 (March 2012): 25–50.

18. Fox, *The Arts of Industry in the Age of Enlightenment*, p. 271.

19. Quoted in Larry Stewart, "A Meaning for Machines: Modernity, Utility, and the Eighteenth-Century British Public," *Journal of Modern History* 70.2 (June 1998): 259–294, 263.

20. Jane L. Collins, "Mapping a Global Labor Market: Gender and Skill in the Globalizing Garment Industry," *Gender and Society* 16/6 (2002): 921–940.

21. Carolyn Sargentson, *Merchants and Luxury Markets: The Marchands Merciers of Eighteenth-Century Paris* (London: V&A Publications in association with the J. Paul Getty Museum, 1996).

22. Pat Kirkham, *The London Furniture Trade, 1700–1870* (London: Furniture History Society, 1989).

23. Joshua Reynolds, *Seven Discourses on Art: Discourse III* (delivered to the Royal Academy, 1770). See also Larry Shiner, *The Invention of Art: A Cultural History* (Chicago: University of Chicago Press, 2003), esp. pp. 99–120.

24. Tomas Macsotay, "The Tortoise and the Hare: Extempore Performance and Sculptural Practice in Eighteenth-century France," *Journal of Modern Craft* 3/3 (Nov. 2010): 293–308.

25. David Irwin, "Art versus Design: The Debate 1760–1860," *Journal of Design History* 4/4 (1991): 219–232, 221.

26. Quoted in Nicholas Goodison, *Matthew Boulton: Ormolu* (London: Christie's, 2002), p. 249.

27. Lindsay Boynton, "An Ince and Mayhew Correspondence," *Furniture History* 2 (1966): 23–36.

28. Thomas J. Misa, *Leonardo to the Internet: Technology and Culture from the Renaissance to the Present* (Baltimore, MD: Johns Hopkins University Press, 2004), p. 60.

29. Richard Stott, "Artisans and Capitalist Development," *Journal of the Early Republic* 16/2 (Summer, 1996): 257–271, 263. For two influential overviews that emphasize diversity in the transformation of skilled trades, see Raphael Samuel, "Workshop of the World: Steam Power and Hand Technology in Mid-Victorian Britain," *History Workshop* 3 (Spring 1977): 27–32 (partially reprinted in Adamson, *The Craft Reader*); Charles Sabel and Theodore Zeitlin, "Historical Alternatives to Mass Production: Politics, Markets, and Technology in Nineteenth-Century Industrialization," *Past and Present* 108 (Aug. 1985): 133–176.

30. Bernard Smith, "Market Development, Industrial Development: The Case of the American Corset Trade, 1860–1920," *Business History Review* 65/1 (Spring 1991): 91–129.

31. Carving is notably absent from the following 1862 list of automated woodworking processes, most of which are preparatory: "Planing, dowelling, dovetailing, grooving, tenoning, molding, rebating and other carpentering processes, are in the present day effected very rapidly by machines specially invented for those purposes, and with greater accuracy than by hand." George Dodd, "Saw Mills and Wood Working," in *Where Do We Get It and How Is It Made?* (London, 1862), p. 130.

32. Michael Ettema, "Technological Innovation and Design Economics in Furniture Manufacture," *Winterthur Portfolio* 16/2-3 (Summer/Autumn 1981): 197–223.

33. On the history of composition, see Mark Reinberger, *Utility and Beauty: Robert Wellford and Composition Ornament in America* (Newark: University of Delaware Press, 2003). For an experiment in making "artificial wood" by molding a composite of glue and sawdust, see "The Art of Imitating Wood," in James Smith, ed., *The Mechanic, or, Compendium of Practical Inventions* (Liverpool: Caxton Press, 1816), pp. 202–206.

34. *Supplement to the London Chair-makers and Carvers' Book of Prices for Workmanship* (London: T. Sorrell, 1808), p. vi.

35. *The London Chair-makers and Carvers' Book of Prices for Workmanship* (London: T. Sorrell, 1802), p. xii.

36. Luke Beckerdite and Alan Miller, "A Table's Tale: Craft, Art, and Opportunity in Eighteenth-Century Philadelphia," in *American Furniture 2004,* ed. Luke Beckerdite (Milwaukee, WI: Chipstone Foundation, 2004).

37. Glenn Adamson, "The Politics of the Caned Chair," in *American Furniture 2002,* ed. Luke Beckerdite (Milwaukee WI: Chipstone Foundation, 2002).

38. Robert Campbell, *The London Tradesman: Being a compendious view of all the trades, professions, arts, both liberal and mechanic, now practised in the cities of London and Westminster* (London, 1747), p. 172.

39. Thomas Chippendale, *The Gentleman and Cabinet-maker's Director* (London, 1754), pp. vi, 8, 22, 24.

40. William Ince and John Mayhew, *The Universal System of Household Furniture* (London: 1762), plate II.

41. Robert Cooper, "The Visibility of Social Systems," in *Ideas of Difference,* ed. Kevin Hetherington and Rolland Munro (Oxford: Blackwell, 1997), p. 33. Emphasis in original. See also my own essay "The Labor of Division: Cabinetmaking and the Production of Knowledge," in *Ways of Making and Knowing: The Material Culture of Empirical Knowledge,* eds. Pamela Smith, Harold Cook, and Amy Meyers (Ann Arbor: University of Michigan Press/Bard Graduate Center, 2012).

42. Samuel Johnson, "The Need for General Knowledge," *The Rambler* 137 (July 9, 1751); reprinted in *Major Works* (Oxford: Oxford University Press, 1984), p. 222.

43. Samuel Johnson, *A Dictionary of the English Language,* vol. 2 (London: W. Strahan, 1755), p. 2293.

44. See Fox, *The Arts of Industry in the Age of Enlightenment,* p. 449ff.

45. Quoted in Richard Tames, *Robert Adam* (London: Shire, 2004), p. 13.

46. Fox, *The Arts of Industry in the Age of Enlightenment,* p. 286. See also Deanna Petherbridge, *The Primacy of Drawing: Histories and Theories of Practice* (New Haven, CT: Yale University Press, 2010).

47. Henry Petrovsky, *The Pencil: A History of Design and Circumstance* (New York: Alfred A. Knopf, 1989), p. 126.

48. Anthony Wells-Cole, *The Art of Decoration in Elizabethan and Jacobean England: The Influence of Continental Prints, 1558–1625* (New Haven, CT: Yale University Press, 1997).

49. Anne Puetz, "Design Instruction for Artisans in Eighteenth-Century Britain," *Journal of Design History* 12/3 (1999): 217–239, 233.

50. "Address," *Journal of Design and Manufactures* 1/1 (Mar. 1949): 1.

51. Ibid., p. 2.

52. Lara Kriegel, *Grand Designs: Labor, Empire, and the Museum in Victorian Culture* (Durham, NC: Duke University Press, 2007), p. 24.

53. Christopher Dresser, *Botany as Adapted* (1857–1858), quoted in David Brett, "Design Reform and the Laws of Nature," *Design Issues* 11/3 (Autumn 1995): 37–49, 40. On Dresser and botanical principles of design, see also Stephen Eisenman, *Design in the Age of Darwin* (Chicago: Northwestern University Press, 2008).

54. Kriegel, *Grand Designs,* p. 28.

55. See Patricia Meyer Spacks, *Boredom: The Literary History of a State of Mind* (Chicago: University of Chicago Press, 1996), ch. 3 and 4, passim.

56. On the use of lathes to partially automate production in ceramics, see Donald Carpentier and Jonathan Rickard, *Slip Decoration in the Age of Industrialization, Ceramics in America 2001* (Milwaukee, WI: Chipstone Foundation, 2001).

57. Kate Esther Smith, "The Potter's Skill: Perceptions of Workmanship in the English Ceramic Industries, 1760–1800" (PhD thesis, University of Warwick, 2010).

58. Stefanie Walker, ed., *Vasemania: Form and Ornament in Neoclassical Europe* (New York: Bard Center for Studies in the Decorative Arts, 2004).

59. Obituary in the *Salem Gazette* (February 12, 1811), quoted in Fiske Kimball, *Samuel McIntire, Carver: The Architect of Salem* (Portland, ME: The Southworh-Anthoensen Press/Essex Institute of Salem, 1940), p. 22.

60. Dean Lahikainen, *Samuel McIntire: Carving an American Style* (Salem, MA: Peabody Essex Museum, 2007).

61. Abbott Lowell Cummings, "Samuel McIntire and His Sources," in *Samuel McIntire: A Bicentennial Symposium,* ed. Benjamin W. Labaree (Salem, MA: Essex Institute, 1957), p. 49.

62. Quoted in Kimball, *Samuel McIntire,* p. 21.

63. Robert Holme Bowman papers, National Art Library MSL. 1986/10.

64. Adrian Forty, *Objects of Desire: Design and Society 1750–1980* (London: Thames and Hudson, 1986).

65. G. A. Siddons, *The Cabinet-Maker's Guide, or Rules and Instructions in the Art of Varnishing, Dying, Staining, Japanning, Polishing, Lackering, and Beautifying Wood, Ivory, Tortoiseshell and Metal…* (London: Sherwood, Gilbert and Piper, 1830), p. ix.

66. Bruce Laurie, *Artisans Into Workers: Labor in Nineteenth-century America* (New York: Hill and Wang, 1989), p. 42.

67. Jonathan Zeitlin, "Engineers and Compositors: A Comparison," in *Divisions of Labour: Skilled Workers and Technological Change in Nineteenth-Century England,* ed. Royden Harrison and Jonathan Zeitlin (Sussex: Harvester Press, 1985), pp. 202–203.

68. R. P., "Wood Carving," *Mechanic's Magazine, Museum, Register, Journal and Gazette* (Sept. 14, 1833): 428. On the relationship between architects and builders more generally in the mid-nineteenth century, see Catharine Bishir, "Jacob W. Holt: An American Builder," *Winterthur Portfolio* 16/1 (Spring 1981): 1–31.

69. *The Age of Ugliness: Showpieces of Dutch Interior Design 1835–1895* (Amsterdam: Rijksmuseum, 1995).

70. Richard Bitmead, *London Cabinet-Maker's Guide* (London, 1873), quoted in L.O.J. Boynton, "High Victorian Furniture: The Example of Marsh and Jones of Leeds," *Furniture History* 3 (1967): 55.

71. "Wood Carving," *The London Times* (March 19, 1858), p. 8.

72. "National School of Art Wood-carving," *The London Times* (September 17, 1879), p. 8.

73. "School of Art Wood-Carving, South Kensington," *The London Times* (July 9, 1885), p. 6.

74. Allan Cunningham, *The Lives of the Most Eminent British Painters and Sculptors,* vol. 3 (London: John Murray, 1830), pp. 4–5.

75. Cunningham, *Lives,* p. 5. The same point is made two decades later in "Wood Sculpture," *Journal of Design and Manufactures* (September 1, 1850): 106–110, 137–141; the anonymous author of this text goes so far as to argue that the flatter works of Chippendale anticipate "today's machine carving" (p. 138). For more on Cunningham and the reception of Gibbons,

see Frederick Oughton, *Grinling Gibbons and the English Woodcarving Tradition* (London: Stobart, 1979).

76. See "Bernard Palissy," *Penny Magazine* 773 (April 20, 1844) and 774 (April 27, 1844); Henry Morley, *Palissy the Potter* (London: Chapman and Hall, 1852); Steve Wharton, "Ordinary Pots: The Inventory of Francesco di Luca, *Orciolaio,* and Cipriano Piccolpasso's 'Three Books of the Art of the Potter,'" in *Everyday Objects: Early Modern Material Culture and its Meaning,* eds. Tara J. Hamling and Catherine Richardson (Burlington, VT: Ashgate, 2010).

77. A Carpenter, "Rank of Artizans Among the Florentines," *Mechanic's Magazine* no. 37 (May 8, 1824): 135.

78. Cunningham, *Lives,* pp. 10, 12.

79. Joyce A. Stephenson, *The Wood Carvings by William Gibbs Rogers for St. Michael's Church, Cornhill* (Oakville, Ontario: Author, 2009), p. 8.

80. Ibid., p. 10.

81. On amateur carving at the end of the nineteenth century, much of it practiced by women, see Jennifer L. Howe, ed., *Cincinnati Art-Carved Furniture and Interiors* (Athens: Ohio University Press/Cincinnati Art Museum, 2003).

82. Alfred D. Chandler, Jr., *The Visible Hand: The Managerial Revolution in American Business* (Cambridge, MA: Harvard University Press, 1977); David A. Hounshell, *From the American System to Mass Production, 1800–1932* (Baltimore, MD: Johns Hopkins University Press, 1984).

83. For an expansive discussion of the stone axe, and other tools' impact on art, see David Summers, *Real Spaces: World Art History and the Rise of Western Modernism* (New York: Phaidon, 2003).

84. Though explicit discussion of this matter in art history is still rare, several authors have considered the issue particularly in relation to the minimalist and postminimalist art of the 1960s. See Caroline Jones, *The Machine in the Studio: Constructing the Postwar American Artist* (Chicago: University of Chicago Press, 1997); John Roberts, *The Intangibilities of Form: Skill and Deskilling in Art After the Readymade* (London: Verso, 2007); Anna C. Chave, "*Minimalism* and the *Rhetoric* of Power," *Arts* 64 (January 1990): 44–63; Michelle Kuo, "Industrial Revolution: The History of Fabrication," *Artforum* 46/2 (October 2007): 306–315; and Julia Bryan-Wilson, *Art Workers: Radical Practice in the Vietnam War Era* (Berkeley: University of California Press, 2009).

85. John Roberts, *The Intangibilities of Form.* See also Louis Kaplan, "The Telephone Paintings: Hanging Up Moholy," *Leonardo* 26/2 (1993): 165–168; and Joan Key, "Readymade or Handmade?," in *Craft* (Cambridge: Kettle's Yard, 1997), reprinted in *The Journal of Modern Craft* 4/2 (July 2011): 203–214. Key writes: "When positioning a 'work of craft,' identified with its specific demand, as a 'work of art,' there are two considerations: in the first instance the object itself is placed in the gallery in a gesture close to that of the unassisted readymade; in the second instance, which 'craft' investigates, the object relates to the artist's gesture not only though installation, but through how it has been made, even if the artists did not directly make the object."

86. For an intriguing parallel to Roberts's theories in the world of economic analysis, see Paul S. Adler, ed., *Technology and the Future of Work* (Oxford: Oxford University Press, 1992). In this edited volume, Adler and his colleagues optimistically describe "upskilling," the extension

of a workforce's capabilities, as the inevitable result of competition, and "reskilling" as the natural consequence of any instance of "deskilling."

87. Jess Cartner-Morely, "Brought to Heel," *Vogue* (Nov. 2010): pp. 229–230, 281; 230.

88. All quotes from Paul Ferguson are from a phone interview conducted on May 17, 2011.

89. See Lacey Jane Roberts, "Put Your Thing Down, Flip It, and Reverse It: Reimagining Craft Identities Using Tactics of Queer Theory," in Maria Elena Buszek, *Extra/Ordinary: Craft Culture and Contemporary Art* (Durham, NC: Duke University Press, 2011).

90. Charles Jencks and Nathan Silver, *Adhocism: The Case for Improvisation* (Garden City, NY: Doubleday, 1972), p. 159.

91. See Charlene Cerny and Suzanne Seriff, eds., *Recycled/Re-seen: Folk Art from the Global Scrap Heap* (New York: Harry N. Abrams, 1996), and David Doris, "Destiny World: Textile Casualties in Southern Nigeria," *African Arts* 39/2 (2006): 36–47, 86–88.

92. Sydney Schamberg, "Six Cents an Hour," *Life* (June 1996). See also Bob Herbert, "Brutality in Vietnam," *New York Times (*March 28, 1997); Bill Bigelow, "The Human Lives behind the Labels: The Global Sweatshop, Nike, and the Race to the Bottom," *Phi Delta Kappan,* 79/2 (1997): 112–119.

93. William I. Robinson, "Social Theory and Globalization: 'The Rise of a Transnational State,'" *Theory and Society* 30/2 (2001): 170 and 171.

94. Gary Gereffi et al., "The NGO-Industrial Complex," *Foreign Policy* 125 (July–August 2001): 56–65; Jason Burke, "Child Labour Scandal Hits Adidas," *The Observer* (November 19, 2000).

95. "World Cup's Jabulani is a Rotten Ball, Says Casillas," *Agence France-Presse,* May 31, 2010.

96. On Africa's inability to participate in global commodity production, see Y. Z. Ya'u, "The New Imperialism & Africa in the Global Electronic Village," *Review of African Political Economy* 31/99 (2004): 11–29.

97. The glue, ink, and fabric in the ball were all produced in China, but the polyurethane coating is from Taiwan and the inner latex bladder is from India.

98. "Production process of the official 2010 FIFA World Cup match ball Jabulani," http://www.youtube.com/watch?v=zbLjk4OTRdI. On contemporary Chinese manufacturing, see also Edward Burtynsky's film *Manufactured Landscapes* (2006).

99. Zofeen Ebrahim, "The Other Side of World Cup Footballs," *Asia Times* (July 9, 2010).

100. Ossian Ward, "Size Matters," *TimeOut London* (Oct. 16–22, 2008): 53–54.

101. Johanna Drucker, *Sweet Dreams: Contemporary Art and Complicity* (Chicago: University of Chicago Press, 2005).

102. Pascal Gielen and Paul de Bruyne, eds., *Being an Artist in Post-Fordist Times* (Rotterdam: NAi Publishers, 2009).

103. Robert Enright, "Vim and Vigour: An Interview with Wim Delvoye," *Border Crossings* 96 (November 1, 2005): 20–35.

104. Birgit Sonna, "When A Concrete Mixer Cross-Breeds with a Baroque Pulpit in a Thai Boudoir: On the Baroque in Wim Delvoye's Work," in *Wim Delvoye: Gothic Works* (Manchester: Manchester City Galleries, 2002), p. 115.

105. David Gilmour, "Wim Delvoye," *Catalogue of the Venice Biennale* (June 1999): 251.

106. This comment, and footage of the largely female workforce for the project, appeared in a video commissioned by the Tate Modern and shown alongside the work.

107. On the decline of the Jingdezhen ceramics industry, which parallels that in Stoke, England, but is of much greater extent, see the documentary film *Broken Pots Broken Dreams* (dir. Maris Gillette, 2009).

108. Nicolas Bourriaud, *Relational Aesthetics* (Paris: Les Presses du Réel, 1998).

109. Clare Bishop, "Antagonism and Relational Aesthetics," *October* 110 (Fall 2004): 51–79. Bishop beautifully dissects Bourriaud's work in the seminal show *Traffic* (1993), which put relational aesthetics on the contemporary art map, and at the Palais de Tokyo in 2002. This did not prevent him from approaching the exhibition *Altermodern* (London: Tate, 2008) in a similar vein—a promotion of artists with whom he is personally friendly. There is nothing wrong with this curatorial tactic necessarily (it has long been practiced and sometimes results in wonderful exhibitions), but Bourriaud disguised his real operation with the vague, sweeping categorical claim of the exhibition's title and supporting literature. He also presided over the event, in the form of a video centrally located in the display.

110. This connects relational aesthetics to thinking about gift giving as an economic and expressive form, pioneered by early twentieth-century anthropologist Marcel Mauss and furthered by Lewis Hyde in *The Gift* (London: Vintage, 1999).

111. Sonia Lavaert and Pascal Gielen, "The Dismeasure of Art: An Interview with Paolo Virno," in *Being an Artist in Post-Fordist Times,* ed. Pascal Gielen and Paul de Bruyne (Rotterdam: NAi Publishers, 2009). See also Paolo Virno, "Virtuosity and Revolution: The Political Theory of Exodus," in *Radical Thought in Italy* (Minneapolis: University of Minnesota Press, 1996).

112. Bishop, "Antagonism and Relational Aesthetics," p. 64.

2   MYSTERY

An 1893 issue of *Pearson's Monthly Magazine* (put out by Cyril Pearson, who would go on to be the first British publisher of H. G. Wells and, in 1922, of a new invention called the crossword puzzle) presented its readers with a terrific little story about trickery, automata, and the game of chess.[1] The narrative is set in Paris, during the occupation of the city at the end of the Franco-Prussian war, and is told from the (fictional) perspective of an American named Edward Smith. An aspiring painter, Smith fights a duel with the city's leading art critic. He figures he's had it in the art business, and while drowning his sorrows at the local café, he meets a mysterious prestidigitator named Robert-Houdin, whose reputation precedes him: "beyond a doubt the most talented miracle-monger that ever stood upon a stage." The two men play chess, a game at which Smith has quite a bit of skill. In fact, he defeats the French magician handily, though commenting that Robert-Houdin's "manner of playing chess was very peculiar. His eyes were seldom upon the board, nearly always fixed upon those of his adversary."

Robert-Houdin, impressed, tells Smith that he ought to have a match with Helmuth von Moltke—a real historical figure, the commander of the Prussian army then occupying Paris. A meeting is duly arranged. Smith and Von Moltke play, and the American wins, though only with difficulty. Robert-Houdin, now doubly impressed, takes Smith aside and tells him, "your play recalled to me the inerrancy, the sluggish persistence, the sledgehammer invincibility of my own mechanical chess-monitor... It was prodigious! In every way worthy of my marvelous mechanical monitor." Smith is astonished. A mechanical chess player? Such a thing doesn't seem possible. He had heard of the automaton of Wolfgang van Kempelen, made at the end of the eighteenth century. But everyone knows that was a hoax: a puppet in the turban and clothing of a Turk, sitting atop a box that concealed the operator (Figure 2.1). Reports varied as to whether the secret chess player inside the automaton was a dwarf or a double amputee. But while details were uncertain, the thing had been exposed as a fraud, not a genuine mechanical marvel at all.[2]

Robert-Houdin scoffs at Smith's protestations, however. "All who had attempted the problem before me," he says, "labored under the idea that the construction of a chess automaton must be as complex as the mind of the human being with whom he was to contend. Thus viewed, it is a wonder that the problem was ever attempted at all. Imagine the absurdity of file and hammer, steel and brass, as factors in the construction of mechanical equivalents for [thought]... The man moves by will, a capacity variable and capricious;

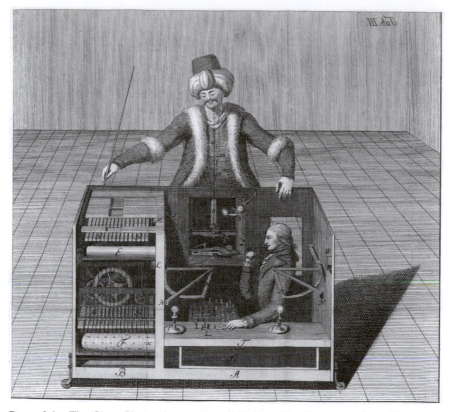

Figure 2.1   The Chess Playing Automaton of Wolfgang Van Kempelen. From *Uber den Schachspieler des Herrn von Kempelen und dessen Nachbildung* (Leipzig und Dresden: Joh. Gottl. Breitkopf, 1789). Colored engraving. Humboldt-Universität, Berlin. © Humboldt-Universitaet zu Berlin / The Bridgeman Art Library.

the automaton by necessity, the stern and inexorable law which guides the stars." No, says Robert-Houdin, he didn't need to make a mechanical man; only a mathematical machine, something like the difference engine of Charles Babbage (often celebrated as the world's first computer, which had been based on the general principles of the jacquard loom). As in the execution of a math problem or a woven pattern, Robert-Houdin says, in chess "there can be but one correct reply to each move; there may be a million moves possible, but only one can be correct...My work was mere routine."

And so Robert-Houdin unveils his automaton. Unlike Van Kempelen's, it is not in the form of an exotic Turk. In fact, it has no obvious complicated machinery, nor even any visible moving parts. It is a simple chessboard, only a bit thicker than usual. "It is not intended to play the game, but only to guide the player," explains Robert-Houdin. "Your opponent has no sooner moved than one of the small squares is replaced by another, whereupon are two figures, which indicate thereon the proper piece to move in reply, the other the square upon which it should be placed. So that after every move your opponent, disconcerted by the quickness and accuracy of your game, grows flurried, makes errors, and falls an easy victim, while you reap all the glory of victory without the toil of battle." Smith, armed with the automaton, eagerly plays his rematch with Von Moltke. It is an epic game. "The automaton prompts me," says Smith, "and I confront him with a new combination, another skirmish ensuing which requires the utmost nicety of management on his part to avert a crushing overthrow."

Robert-Houdin, incidentally, was quite real too. His full name was Jean Eugène Robert-Houdin, and most historians consider him the first great modern stage magician. He had gotten his start as a clockmaker and was indeed best known for his automata, which included a mechanical tightrope dancer, a bush that would sprout oranges at a command, and an artificial juggler that could perform various tricks with balls and cups. He also made a clock whose hand seemed to turn independently of any visible works and yet struck the hour accurately. He was a master of stage performance, too. He would place four harps on stage that could produce music of their own accord after being given a quick spin and would stop immediately if spun again. In one routine, he played a sword-wielding Indian who stuffed a young prince into a basket and appeared to stab him to death, only for the prince to reappear unharmed, waving to the audience from high up in the theater. His "heavy chest" trick was so effective he was purportedly sent to Algeria in the service of the French government to intimidate the local Arabs with the act. Robert-Houdin would first present on stage a metal-bound box and lift it easily. He then challenged all comers to try to bear its weight—and it was suddenly impossible to budge it from the floor, even for a group of adult men. Then, with a snap of the fingers, Robert-Houdin would raise it aloft again. He was also able to summon a bust of Socrates, which could, in the words of one period account, "issue [from its mouth] learned replies to the questions of the Athenian sage, who is anxious to discover how Socrates likes it as far as he has got."[3]

Robert-Houdin was so important in the history of magic that Harry Houdini named himself after the Frenchman, and then, in 1909, wrote a book revealing his secrets. But Houdini was far from the first to try that. Indeed, Robert-Houdin is intriguing partly because nineteenth-century writings about him consist almost entirely of *explanations* of his effects; his reputation was premised upon the revelations of his secrets. I have read some of these, so I can tell you that his famous clock had not two but three glass disks mounted in it, the middle one of which was attached to a worm screw in the bezel rim; this revolving glass plate was turned by a mechanism in the base. It has the metal clock hand fixed to it, so that it appears to turn rather than the glass. The sounds of the automaton harps were actually produced by musicians hidden beneath the stage. The harps' stands continued through the floor and carried signals on their poles so that Robert-Houdin could give the musicians the high sign to play or stop playing by giving each harp a spin. The boy prince escaped his death by dropping out of a false bottom in the stage basket, a process disguised by a mirror mounted on the front of a table. The boy then ran out the back of the theater, through a side entrance, and to his new seat, while Robert-Houdin distracted the audience by miming the unspeakable murder. The heavy box routine was initially performed using a powerful electromagnet. By turning the current on and off, Robert-Houdin could affix it immovably to the stage. Later, he became concerned that the principle of magnetism was becoming too well known to his audience, so he varied the trick, lifting the chest using a pulley. He himself could raise the box easily with one hand; but again, six strong men were not able to do it. The secret lay in a false pulley. The rope passed through it and up through the ceiling, where it was attached to a large second wheel, allowing Robert-Houdin to lift the box easily; when an assistant shifted the rope to a smaller wheel, it was impossible for volunteers from the audience to do the same. The bust of Socrates, finally, was actually a magician's assistant whose head protruded through a large mirror. The ceiling of the stage, hidden from view but reflected in the mirror, was decked out in curtains, producing a reflection that looked like the back of the stage.

The revelation of these secrets may perhaps give the sense of an aesthetic; the Victorian love of wondrous disturbance being set to rights. Of course many people saw Robert-Houdin perform and were simply baffled. But many more experienced his trickery much as you have just experienced it: in books that described his tricks, which were initially puzzling but then reassuringly restored to rational comprehension. This was also the pleasure of his automata, which conformed to E.T.A. Hoffmann's contemporaneous description of such animate machines as the products of "remarkable acuteness—or, I might say, systematic craftiness—in overlooking nothing in the process of deceiving us."[4] Through his staging of mysteries in the light of day, Robert-Houdin the magician became something quite different from A. C. Hobbs the lockpick, who we encountered in chapter one. Robert-Houdin was deceptive and dextrous, to be sure, capable of numerous feats of sleight of hand. His "quickness of hand was so wonderful," we read, "his flow of small talk so unceasing, that he could force your attention in any direction he chose."[5] But those skills were merely a serviceable distraction from the main event, his power of public invention.

Now, when we left Smith and Von Moltke, they were playing a furiously paced chess match in a Paris café, with the American's every move directed by Robert-Houdin's chess-playing machine. Much to Smith's surprise, though, he is not able to defeat the Prussian general, even with the aid of the automaton. After hours of play, they finally declare it a draw. In the meantime, the "crafty, catlike" Robert-Houdin has slipped away, never to be seen again, at least not by Smith. But many years later, he does encounter Von Moltke, who is now quite old. After they share a drink, talk turns to their match in 1871. The stately Prussian gathers himself to make a confession. He was not playing fair. The chessboard, he admits, had been an automaton, which secretly told Von Moltke every move he should make. Smith can only sputter, "We have both been duped! Imbeciles we have been; noodlepates; lay figures in a harlequinade of fools! [Robert-Houdin] prepared this game before we came; had marked it upon two cylinders which were concealed in the board, one on each side; and after we were seated he simply turned a crank prompting each of us in turn." Immediately the two men run to fetch an old, well-known encyclopedia of renowned chess matches, and sure enough: they discover there the very game that they played, or were made to play, move for move. Von Moltke looks up from the book and says, "Son, that game was not drawn; we were both checkmated." So the chessboard wasn't the real automaton in this story. Von Moltke and Smith were the ones controlled by an unseen hand.

THE AGE OF THE REVEAL

In the story of the chess-playing machine, French magician Robert-Houdin is presented as an unlikely modern hero. Unlikely because he was skilled with his hands and traded in deception—two traits systematically subjected to skepticism in his lifetime. For this reason, it is notable that, at least in the anecdote related earlier, Robert-Houdin's real power lies in indirect technological and psychological manipulation, rather than the direct manipulation of materials (his fabrication of the chessboard, for example, is little remarked); and also that his magical secrets were unveiled through narrative, in a carefully controlled and highly staged manner. The theatricalization of knowledge, in which it is shown emerging from obscurity step by inexorable step, was a quintessential nineteenth-century pleasure. The Victorian era was entranced by trickery, but also by explanation, the one providing the necessary antidote for the other. Wordiness was one of the period's most obvious characteristics, and writing on craft was no exception. Authors bestowed their works with emphatically comprehensive titles—a long-standing practice in European publishing, but no less striking when you are faced with a book called *The Artist's and Mechanic's Encyclopædia, or, a Complete Exposition of the Arts and Sciences, As Applicable to Practical Purposes, Containing Facts and Principles Useful and Indispensable*—and then described the workings of a given trade (or, as in this case, many different trades) at mind-numbing length, often providing readers with hundreds of pages of detailed explication.[6] These texts seemed to be engaged in an all-out war against secrecy. For centuries, making had been cloaked in a self-protective mantle aptly summarized by the common phrase "art, trade and mystery." But in the nineteenth century, craft expertise was to be a public matter. No longer would it be exchanged tacitly, bit by bit behind the closed doors of a workshop, but exhaustively, in the wide open arena of the marketplace. This process was itself described just as explicitly at the time, in a manner that suggested its inevitability. Though it was a discursive and social, rather than a mechanical transformation, the explication of what was now called "handicraft" was infused with the triumphal logic of modern technology—rather like Van Kempelen's Turk-shaped automaton which, in the words of Walter Benjamin, "was so constructed that it could counter any move of a chess-player with a counter-move, and thereby assure itself of victory in the match."[7] Like Robert-Houdin's later automata, making now exerted its hold on the public imagination mainly through acts of explanation, which had all the more force because they banished mystery. Production had entered the age of the reveal.

What did it mean for artisanal knowledge, long guarded by a guild-enforced culture of secrecy, to be opened up and made public in this way? In the last chapter, we saw how dissecting a craft and laying it out for examination allowed it to be subjected to various forms of control. But the same division into parts also offered pleasure: the thrill of discovery, the satisfaction of a trick explained. Aside from publications, the most important mechanisms for the delivery of this modern form of gratification were international expositions, culminating in the Great Exhibition of 1851. These events were above all celebrations of making, both industrial and artisanal, and placed the productive achievements of various nations in explicit competition with one another (a displacement of warlike rivalries into "the bloodless contention of skilled labour," as a reviewer of the 1853 Irish Industrial Exposition nicely put it).[8] Given the amount of political and economic capital invested in these events, it is not surprising that they were veritable cathedrals of explanation—it was crucial that the massive audiences who attended should get the right message. All the same, it is impressive how fully the technology of clarification was realized in the Crystal Palace. The deep-perspective glass and steel structure provided an experience of gradual revelation for the proto-*flâneurs* who came to see it. As they walked the long halls, visitors were presented with a seemingly endless series of distant spectacles, which were inexorably revealed to them as they approached each in turn (Figure 2.2).

Between the perceiver and the object of wonder there might be a veil of mystery, perhaps one having to do with production—how were all these things made, and by whom?

Figure 2.2   T. J. & J. Mayer, commemorative pot lid showing the interior of the Crystal Palace, 1851. Transfer-printed earthenware. V&A: CIRC.789–1969. © Victoria and Albert Museum, London.

But that veil would always be penetrated. There was a strong sense of inevitability built into this modern way of looking at the world—a near certainty that each generation would be more ingenious than the last, and ever closer to banishing ignorance. One contributor to an 1863 number of the *Continental Monthly* summed up this attitude beautifully. After mocking his contemporaries' obsession with curiosities—for example, their tendency, if they visited an agricultural fair, to "be found examining the 'mammoth squashes' and various products of prodigious growth"—he went on to define wonder simply as "the effect of novelty upon ignorance." "Most objects which excite wonder," he wrote, "are magnified by the distance or the point of view, and their proportions diminish and shrink as we approach them."[9] Knowledge was sure to be gained through the simple act of forward movement. As one popular bit of doggerel had it:

> The small enlarged, the distant nearer brought to sight
> Made marvels in a denser age
> But science turns with every year a page
> In the enchanted volume of her thought
> The wizard's wand no longer now is sought.[10]

The progressive spirit that animates this poem, which recalls the understanding of knowledge voiced by Samuel Johnson (see chapter one), can also be found in the how-to books of the time, which explained the procedures of crafts in explicit detail. This type of literature was not entirely new. Books of trades had been popular since the seventeenth century, but they had been aimed mainly at professionals with a craft, and, generally speaking, were much less forthcoming, containing mainly formulas difficult to put to use without extensive practical experience. But Diderot's *Encyclopedia* had marked the onset of a drastic increase in informative content. By the early nineteenth century, any literate soul could read all about the "mysteries" of any trade he or she liked. The pleasures of this how-to literature can be compared to those of other genres new at the time, such as the mystery novel and the tell-all memoir. Books of revealed craft secrets did of course have a practical interest, but they must have been read mostly for their sheer entertainment value, rather than to actually learn how to make something (much as how-to books tend to be used today).

The full explication of any skilled trade makes it clear just how much there is to be comprehended. One can well imagine the reaction of the nonspecialist reader faced with the reams of technical information in the typical nineteenth-century craft treatise or a volume aimed at a younger audience like *The Book of Trades, or, Circle of the Useful Arts,* which after discouragingly informing its readers that "the imaginative has given place to the useful," insisted that "all knowledge may be said to be a circle. We can never understand any branch of it thoroughly, without attending to its connexion with the whole."[11] Given their extensive mapping of many trades, such books certainly placed artisanal specialism within an overarching structure, much like the organizational regimes of the workplace at the same time. But in the very act of revealing craft knowledge, these texts made it seem like a vast terrain that could be traversed only with great difficulty. The tacit nature of craft results in one of the curious inversions that marks its invention: it was precisely the wide publication of technical secrets that yielded the insight that artisanal skill is fundamentally incommensurable with discourse. Like a conjurer's trick, even when seen up close, craft process doesn't reveal itself entirely, nor can it easily be repeated. So one counterintuitive message of the nineteenth-century technical manuals, for all their expansive detail, is that to really teach a given process requires repeated demonstration, and then (crucially) handing over the tools. The only way to really learn a craft is to do it yourself, over and over; not only reading about it, but even seeing it enacted at close range, is a mere spectator sport.

This was another idea about craft that was forged in the period of the industrial revolution: though it could be described, it could never be fully accounted for in words. Nor is it universally consistent. According to the terms of its modern invention, craft does involve knowledge that can be set down, but this is always a matter of incomplete approximation, because artisanal skill is personal, intuitive, and capricious (in the sense that its results will be different in each set of hands, and from one piece of raw material to another). You can put craft knowledge in a book, but it will still be tricky to put it into practice. Within this modern framework, craft is opposed to other, more explicit and objective categories of knowledge: science and engineering. This division is itself a cultural artifact, but so powerfully have our own intuitions about craft been shaped by the modern idea that it is nonverbal and intuitive that we cannot imagine any other way of seeing it. Yet this understanding of practical know-how had certainly not been prevalent prior to the eighteenth century—prior to the differentiation of craft from other ways of making and knowing. Within the early modern field of production—that is, from the Renaissance up until the eighteenth century—tacit and explicit knowledge were not distinguished from one another. As historians of science Ursula Klein and E. C. Spary have noted in their recent volume on early modern technical expertise, research into materials and their properties was not limited to "a closed space of scholarly, or scientific, investigation of nature distinguished by an 'epistemic rupture' from other forms of inquiry in the arts and crafts and everyday life. They were investigated using methods and concepts belonging to the scholarly world, but were never severed from the world of artisanal production."[12]

A good example of this lack of differentiation is the fact that even the most objective and detailed information about techniques, of the sort we now associate with engineering, was exchanged largely through implicit means. Historian of science Stephan Epstein notes that "the technical knowledge of premodern craftsmen and engineers was largely experience-based. Thus, practically all premodern technical knowledge...had to be transferred in the flesh."[13] Despite this natural safeguard against widespread dissemination of secrets, however, artisans protected their processes with all the vigilance of modern corporations, on the assumption that knowledge was all too easily transmitted. Apprenticeship was a key means of exerting such control. It did instill knowledge into a young artisan, but was also important in safeguarding that knowledge. Because of the apprenticeship system's inflexibility and duration, its regulation through guild rules, and the close social bonds that linked most apprentices to their masters, the more highly skilled members of a workshop knew exactly to whom they were imparting their secrets. Conversely, any slippage of information (the recipe for a metallic alloy, for example, or the process of constructing a given machine) was eagerly seized and put into practice by rivals. These "knowledge transfers" were worked out by skilled professionals over many centuries. They took place in workshops, on building sites, and in shipyards, guildhalls, and coffeehouses.[14] Such exchanges, both intended and illicit, were the basis for the whole organizational structure of premodern craft. Artisans believed that talking about a trade could be an adequate way of giving a useful account of it—all too adequate—and so they took extensive precautions.

Just as early modern artisanal workshops were hotbeds of technical research, artisanal skill was the empirical basis for science itself. In the alchemical laboratories of the seventeenth and eighteenth centuries, the fabrication of equipment—glass vessels, ceramic crucibles, metal instruments, and brick furnaces—was necessary to the conduct of precise experiments. Historians have recently undertaken a thorough reevaluation of alchemy, abandoning the older view of it as fanciful hocus-pocus (which, as we will see, was a prejudice against craft-based knowledge formed in the early nineteenth century). Pamela Smith has taken a leading role in this revisionist literature, describing early modern natural philosophy as "active rather than contemplative," a "practice, rather than a set of theories, [which] flourished in such places as laboratories, theatres of nature, and cabinets of curiosities."[15] All along this continuum of activity, not only were different types of making intermixed freely, but things made by people—*artificialia*—were juxtaposed and sometimes blended with natural specimens—*naturalia*. A nautilus shell, for example, might be engraved or carved in shallow relief, highlighting the delicate translucency of the material, and then mounted in an elaborate gold stand. A "curiosity" like this was valued because it displayed not just the mysterious workings of nature, but also the equally wondrous workings of the maker's hands, and the harmonious conjunction of the two.[16] Such objects may seem merely decorative to us, but in the seventeenth century they would have been understood as concrete manifestations of knowledge, the product of an investigation into art and nature alike (Figure 2.3).

The state of affairs leading up to 1750, then, was that there was an undifferentiated field of making, in which what we latterly choose to call science was inseparable from the artisanal trades. It was a very different matter, however, when the curtain that had hidden craft processes from view was drawn aside. This happened via means both formal (the how-to publications and books of trades described earlier, as well as popular lectures and demonstrations) and informal (the breakdown of guilds, leading to an itinerant or "tramping" workforce, and improvements in transport, which placed artisans in increasing competition with one another).[17] Previously, knowledge had been a scarce commodity in its own right, preciously guarded and stintingly imparted. In the nineteenth century, by contrast, the problem was the surplus of information—and the sheer difficulty of deploying it.

Perhaps the most influential mechanism of change, within this broad shift toward the codification of craft knowledge and its distribution, was patent legislation. This was the

Figure 2.3 Cup and cover, sixteenth century, Nuremberg. Nautilus shell in silver-gilt mount. V&A: 863:1, 2–1882. © Victoria and Albert Museum, London.

means by which new forms of knowledge were controlled, and a crucial instrument in separating craft from industry and science. Patents are a social rather than a mechanical technology, but were nonetheless regarded as a crucial means of opening up the secrets of nature to view. Already in 1776, the sentiment could be expressed in remarkably totalizing terms, as in this popular verse:

> The time may come when nothing will succeed
> But what a previous Patent hath decreed
> And we must open on some future day
> The door of Nature with a patent key.[18]

Patents were not new in the eighteenth century. They had been awarded by the English government since Elizabethan times, and even earlier on the Continent.[19] They had always involved a tradeoff: an inventor disclosed information about an idea to the public, in exchange for which a temporary exclusive right of use was granted. Yet important changes in these laws occurred over the course of the eighteenth century. As patents became increasingly common, they also grew more detailed, often accompanied by lengthy written descriptions. A turning point was reached in 1788, when a British judge ruled that a "specification should be sufficiently full and detailed to enable anyone, skilled in the art or trade to which the invention pertained, to understand it and apply it without further experiment."[20] From this point onward, the patent became an explicit means of distinguishing the small-scale, everyday improvements of the workshop—the little tricks of the trade a machinist might undertake in the course of doing a job—from the innovations of the professional "improver." As historian Moureen Coulter puts it, "the patent system...conferred upon the inventor a status separate from and superior to that of the artisan or mechanic: the status of an original thinker, a man who could make a living with his mind rather than his hands."[21] It was the way that an innovation was described, rather than any absolute distinction in its nature, that made the difference between a craft technique and an invention.[22]

In 1962, conservative cultural theorist Michael Oakeshott introduced terminology that is helpful in understanding this division. He distinguished between *technical* and *practical* knowledge, with the former being "susceptible of formulation in rules, principles, directions, maxims—comprehensively, in propositions." "Technical knowledge can be learned from a book; it can be learned from a correspondence course," he wrote. "On the other hand, practical knowledge can neither be taught nor learned, but only imparted and acquired. It exists only in practice, and the only way to acquire it is by apprenticeship to a master—not because he can teach it (he cannot), but because it can be acquired only by continuous contact with one who is perpetually practicing it."[23] Oakeshott saw clearly that the rise of modern "rationalism" involved a preference for technical knowledge over its practical counterpart:

> Rationalism is the assertion that what I have called practical knowledge is not knowledge at all, the assertion that, properly speaking, there is no knowledge that is not technical knowledge. The Rationalist holds that...what I have called practical knowledge is really only a sort of nescience [i.e., ignorance] which would be negligible if it were not positively mischievous. The sovereignty of "reason," for the Rationalist, means the sovereignty of technique.[24]

Oakeshott did not do much to ground his arguments about practice historically. He saw the origins of modern rationalism in a diversity of sources: the "mechanical" scientific method of Francis Bacon, the philosophy of René Descartes, and the realpolitik of Niccolò Machiavelli; and his phrase "sovereignty of reason" perhaps refers to the eighteenth-century Enlightenment.[25] But his principal targets were the self-conscious political modernizers of his own day, the 1960s. In any case, he did not concern himself particularly with craft and industry.

Had Oakeshott wanted to locate a historical source to bear out his claims, however, he could have done worse than to focus on the early nineteenth-century doctor, chemist, and polemicist Andrew Ure. A product of the impulse toward social improvement that would bring the new Mechanics' Institute to London and other cities across Britain (see chapter three), Ure had trained in medicine in Glasgow, and in 1804 had succeeded George Birkbeck as a lecturer for artisans attending the Andersonian Institution. He was a man of definite opinions. Though best remembered for his absurdly optimistic apologia for the factory system *The Philosophy of Manufactures* (1835), which earned him the particular enmity of Karl Marx, Ure was also well known for his explanatory texts about modern industry.[26] In these descriptive writings, Ure aligned himself with what Oakeshott would have called technical knowledge, insisting on the adequacy of his own descriptions and aspiring to scientific standards of detail, objectivity, and universality. He undertook this project in an evangelistic spirit, heaping scorn on anyone who tried to stand in its way. For Ure, mystery was not only a sign of backwardness and economic counterproductivity; it was also a moral failing. Fortunately, he wrote, secretiveness was also rare in the modern day, and would become rarer still because it was inherently self-destructive:

> The few individuals who betray jealousy of intelligent inspection are usually vain persons, who, having purloined a few hints from ingenious neighbours, work upon them in secret, shut out every stranger from their mill, get consequently insulated and excluded in return, and thus, receiving no external illumination, become progressively adumbrated... Mystifiers of this stamp are guilty of the silly blunder of estimating their own intrinsic resources above those of all the world beside.[27]

As the slighting reference to "intrinsic resources" here suggests, Ure was deeply suspicious of any form of introversion—not only the keeping of secrets, but any form of self-reliance. It is not surprising that he saw craft as the paradigm of such asystematic, blinkered production. He could not have been more explicit in relegating "handicraft operations" to a separate sphere, describing them as "multiform, capricious, and hardly susceptible of scientific investigation."[28] So accustomed are we to thinking of craft in this way—albeit usually using more positive terms, such as flexible, individualistic, and tacit—that it is perhaps easy to miss the novelty of the distinction Ure was drawing here. It is another example of inventing craft in a spirit of antagonism: defining it as the opposite of progress. In the same passage just quoted, which appears in the preface to a dictionary of manufacturing he published in 1839, Ure continues: "had such topics been introduced into the volume, it would have presented a miscellaneous farrago of incongruous articles, too numerous of their being expounded in a manner either interesting or instructive to the manufacturer and the metallurgist." As Ure well knew, earlier books of trades had just that kind of breadth. They were packed with technical information about all types of production, hand or machine driven, and had been popular for more than two centuries. He was consciously overturning precedent.

For Oakeshott, the mindset of rationalist explicators like Ure was not only wrongheaded, in that it mistook the nature of knowledge (which he saw as adaptive and provisional, rather than objective and certain), but also disastrous: "the life of a society loses its rhythm and continuity and resolves into a succession of problems and crises."[29] Whether or not one is inclined to share Oakeshott's pessimism, he was certainly right to say that the modern discourse that emerged in the nineteenth century valued technical knowledge far more than its practical equivalent. Ure was not alone in this regard. A widespread attitude toward skill that gained ground in the late eighteenth century and culminated in the scientism of the nineteenth understood it as the happenstance emanation of a preexisting and constant body of knowledge.[30] In 1855, on the occasion of his appointment as the first British university chair in technology (he felt it necessary to explain the word, "so unfamiliar to English ears," to his audiences), George Wilson located craft at the animal level:

> The bird is an exquisite architect; the beaver a most skilful bridge-builder; the silk-worm the most beautiful of weavers; the spider the best of net-makers. Each is a perfect crafts-man, and each has his tools always at hand. Those wise creatures, I believe, have minds like our own, to the extent that they have minds, and are not mere living machines, swayed by a blind instinct.[31]

In a sense, craft did not even count as knowledge per se for the Victorians. It was simply natural—the secondhand, physical manifestation of principles that could be written down and taught. This is one sense of the term "applied arts," which means not only design put to a functional purpose, but rather technical understanding put to work by a maker.

PORCELAIN: A MODERN ARCANUM

Thus far, I have been describing the nineteenth-century shift from secrecy to public knowl-edge in broad terms. Like the manipulation of skilled artisans by outside authorities dis-cussed in chapter one, however, the change in attitudes to knowledge played out in very different ways and at different times, depending on the trade. Areas of production that had a strong basis in what we might call formulae or recipes had a particularly vexed relation-ship to proprietary knowledge, and it was a matter of particular public import to resolve questions about the ownership of this information. Taxile Doat, a great Sèvres pottery designer from the turn of the twentieth century, once observed that "whether a ceramicist is a painter or a sculptor, architect or simply a technician, to obtain a successful result he must also be a chemist."[32] British ceramic manufacturers of the eighteenth century would certainly have concurred. In this context, knowledge of materials and techniques was quite literally the difference between success and failure. Moreover, ceramic technicians or "arcanists" often sought to imitate clay bodies that had heretofore been imported—with Chinese porcelain the holy grail.

The British were relative latecomers to the project of reinventing porcelain; they were repeating the experiences of the Japanese, the Italians, the Germans, and the French before them. Though European arcanists, from the court of Francesco de' Medici onward, had been able to formulate a "fake" soft-paste porcelain with a white, glassy body, the true material—a compound of two materials, china clay and china stone (in Chinese, *kaolin* and *petuntse*) eluded them. In 1709, success finally came to Johann Friedrich Böttger, paving the way for the opening of the Meissen factory in Dresden.[33] Böttger was a professional alchemist—not a scholar, necessarily, but a talented practitioner in the laboratory and, like many alchemists, a man willing to engage in outright charlatanism when it seemed expedient to do so. When imprisoned by the elector of Saxony, Augustus II ("the Strong"), under orders to repeat a transmutation of base metal into gold that he had fraudulently effected, Böttger managed to produce first a fine red stoneware reminiscent of Chinese Yixing ware and then a hard-paste white porcelain (Figure 2.4). Understandably, given that an early defection led to the creation of a competing factory at Vienna, Böttger's formula was immediately placed under the strictest security measures. Secrecy at Meissen was a near obsession. British merchant Jonas Hanway, visiting in the 1750s, described the factory as something like a prison:

> Our author had an opportunity of being convinced of the secrecy with which this manu-factory is conducted; for there is no admittance into the works without an order from the Governor of Dresden; nor are the workmen ever seen without the gates; for they are all confined as prisoners and subject to be arrested, if they go without the walls: for this reason a chapel, and every thing necessary is provided within.[34]

Figure 2.4   Tankard, ca. 1715. Meissen. Hard-paste porcelain (Böttger porcelain) with applied reliefs. V&A: C.136–1945. © Victoria and Albert Museum, London.

The secrecy that encircled the successful production of porcelain was not simply an inconvenient obstacle. It was fundamental to the value placed on the enterprise in the first place. Throughout the eighteenth century, even after accurate accounts of the Chinese porcelain industry had been published by the Jesuit missionary Père d'Entrecolles and then widely paraphrased by other authors, porcelain retained its reputation as an arcanum: "the real true and full art mystery and secret," as the founders of the English porcelain factory at Worcester put it.[35] Hardness, whiteness, and translucency may have made porcelain an attractive commodity, but secrecy made it a cipher of courtly, and later national, ambition.

A good example of the continuing premium placed on "mysteries" by British porcelain manufacturers is found in the 1750 patent of Thomas Frye, the Dublin-born principal of the factory at Bow (Plate 6). Apart from its subject, the language of the patent could have been lifted directly from an alchemical text of a century earlier:

> As there is nothing in nature but by calcination, grinding and washing will produce a fixed indissoluble matter, distinguished by the same name of virgin earth, the properties of which [are] strictly the same whether produced from animals, vegetables, or ... all fossils of the calcerous kind, such as chalk, limestone, etc.; take therefore any of these classes, calcine it until it smokes no more, which is an indication that all the volatile sulpherous parts are dissipated, and the saline are sett loose; then grind and wash in many waters to discharge the salts and filth, reiterate the process twice more, then the ashes or virgin earth will be fit for use.[36]

Frye's wording is intentionally vague. His allusion to "fossils of the calcerous kind," for example, was probably as close as he was willing to come to naming bone ash as a crucial component in his porcelain paste. This ingredient distinguished Bow from the other earliest porcelain manufacturers (Chelsea, Worcester, Derby, and Bristol), so it is not surprising that Frye would have wanted to keep it secret, just as Böttger and other alchemists always kept their techniques closely guarded.[37] A more explicit resonance with alchemy in the patent is found in Frye's choice of the phrase "virgin earth," which recalls the *prima materia* made in the initial stage of alchemical work. Frye's descriptions of "volatile sulpherous parts" and discharged "saline" parts are also taken from the lexicon of the alchemical tradition, in which volatility itself was traditionally described as embodied by sulfur, whereas static and waste materials were generically referred to as salts. Of course these terms had little relation to the actual chemical properties involved, as today's scientists would understand and describe them, nor did they refer with any particularity to the materials Frye was using—but that was of little consequence. Like an alchemist, he found it expedient to talk of transmutation in terms of abstract properties rather than concrete descriptions.

When Philadelphia entrepreneurs Gousse Bonnin and George Anthony Morris undertook their own "invention" of porcelain, the substance had already been invented several times, by men increasingly inclined to see the challenge of doing so in terms of chemistry. Though it was short-lived, lasting only from 1770 to 1772, Bonnin and Morris's enterprise was not only the first porcelain manufactory in America, but preceded the next successful effort by several decades (Tucker Porcelain, also made in Philadelphia beginning in 1826). Bonnin and Morris seem to have borrowed many of their forms and technology from British soft-paste porcelain manufacturers like Bow, who were by this time well established. Yet, like so many before them, they insisted that porcelain was just as much an arcanum as ever—in Bonnin's words, a "mysterious system" "no body could unravel."[38] This was so despite the fact that their porcelain was very much in line with the soft-paste recipes that had been manufactured in England for some thirty years (Figure 2.5). Why did Bonnin and Morris employ the rhetoric of unveiling an ancient secret? Unlike Böttger, they were no alchemists. They were businessmen, and their formula did not come from an arcanist (as had been the case at Chelsea, for example, where the founder, goldsmith Nicholas Sprimont, was given a recipe by a mysterious unnamed "chymist"), but from some direct knowledge of the Bow porcelain factory.[39] Their achievement might be better framed not as invention, but rather a successful instance of industrial espionage. No longer was the penetration of nature's mysteries a worthy goal in itself, a matter of individual and courtly pride. Now, any scientific enterprise—including the making of porcelain—was seen by entrepreneurs (at the time, the terminology would have been "improvers" or "projectors"), experimentalists, and governments alike as a public achievement. With Bonnin and Morris's "invention" of porcelain, we see not an actual technological advancement, but instead a breakthrough in cultural terms: a suggestion that porcelain was not the creation of an inspired individual, but rather the work of a like-minded community.

Throughout the short two-year run of their American Porcelain Manufactory, Bonnin and Morris conducted themselves in a remarkably public manner—turning on its head the secrecy that had always attended manufactories like theirs. Their 1770 *Pennsylvania Gazette* advertisement offered prices for bones—to be turned into ash, one of the ingredients of their paste formula—and also advertised for other crucial ingredients, such as "zaffer" (cobalt oxide) and broken pieces of flint glass. Meanwhile, their self-promotional writings were shot through with distinct streaks of American exceptionalism, which contrast sharply with the defensive, competitive stance of British porcelain manufacturers of the time: "the Manufacture of China Ware in this Province, certainly deserves the serious Attention of every Man, who prays for the Happiness of his Fellow-subjects, or that the very Semblance of Liberty may be handed down to Posterity."[40] In short, Bonnin and Morris asserted that their own time and place, Philadelphia on the eve of revolution, held special significance for the history of science, and they had no hesitation in placing themselves in that context.

In 1798, another Philadelphian, Thomas P. Smith, would make this point quite emphatically while speaking before the city's Chemical Society. Extended the honor of giving the annual oration to the group, he elected to present a "Sketch of the Revolutions in Chemistry." His brief history typifies the almost hysterical attack on alchemical empiricism and secrecy that became commonplace in the late eighteenth century. From the days of the ancient Egyptians onward, Smith claimed, there had been men who possessed only practical knowledge—"confined to the forge of the *smith* and the work-shop of the

Figure 2.5   Gousse Bonnin and George Anthony Morris, pickle stand, 1770–1772. Soft-paste porcelain. Metropolitan Museum of Art.

lapidary"—but no understanding of "general principles." Insofar as they pretended to a larger conception of the workings of science, "their object was merely to gain an ascendancy over weak minds . . . hence arose the idea that these priests, who perhaps understood little more than how to delude a superstitious, ignorant people, were possessed of a knowledge of all the arcana of nature." Smith characterized the search for the Philosopher's Stone as a "mania" in which "immense fortunes were dissipated by men who would not have advanced the smallest sum for the discovery of any truth whatever from which they could not hope to derive some pecuniary advantage. Thus was avarice enlisted in the cause of science." Predictably, Smith was as triumphant in proclaiming the successes of modern chemistry as he had been in dismissing "the dark gathering clouds of ignorance and superstition" of the past. He portrayed the development of contemporary science as inevitable—"nor need we be afraid that any false theory, however specious it may appear, will be permanent; for, *whatever system is not founded in truth must fall!*"[41]

This caricatured view of the history of science, in which the falsehoods and greed of alchemical practice were gradually displaced by the democratic objectivity and openness of modern technical thought, was widely accepted by the end of the eighteenth century.[42] Indeed, this narrative still forms the basis of the popular understanding of scientific history today. This is to a great extent the legacy of attacks on secrecy led by self-promoting scientists and entrepreneurs, men like Bonnin and Morris, Thomas Smith, or for that matter Josiah Wedgwood. In 1775, only a few years after the failure of the Philadelphia factory, Wedgwood issued his own public critique of secrecy, challenging a patent for the making of porcelain held by arcanist William Cookworthy and his partner Richard Champion. "In a Case like this," Wedgwood wrote:

> where *no new Art is taught to the Public;* where the *Result* of all the Experiments with Re-spect to the Practice of this Art, the Proportions in which the Materials are to be mixed, and the Manner in which the Ware is to be painted and burnt, are all (contrary to the very first Principle and Condition of a Patent) kept profound Secrets from the Public, would be a Precedent of the most dangerous Nature, contrary to good Policy, and of general Inconvenience.[43]

We see here a familiar side of Wedgwood, who (whether digging canals or marketing his own wares) was never shy about identifying his own private advantage with that of the public. He casts "secrets" as a dirty word and himself as a champion for public knowledge—an identity he often adopted as part of his relentless claim of self-promotion.[44]

As in so many other aspects of his career, Wedgwood's embrace of public knowledge reflects his skill at gaining personal advantage by anticipating broader currents within the ceramic industry. As we have seen in the example of Bonnin and Morris, the late eighteenth century witnessed a great shift in the ceramic industry: from an alchemical, secretive, and arcane art to a self-consciously modern, scientific industry based on such new social tech-nologies as patenting.[45] It was not until many years later, however, that the first full-fledged manifesto for this new way of doing business appeared. The author was Simeon Shaw. Born in Lancaster, he had come to the Staffordshire area to work as a printer and gradually acquired a profile as a scholarly author, opening a commercial gallery and publishing both scientific and historic works. He is best known today for his indispensable *History of the Staffordshire Potteries* (1829), but in the present context the most interesting of his writings is rather his later, less frequently read scientific treatise *The Chemistry of the Several Natural and Artificial Heterogeneous Compounds Used in Manufacturing Porcelain, Glass and Pottery* (1837). As its title implies, the book was a very detailed account of the ceramics and glass industry of the day—a comprehensive unveiling of secrets, in the manner of a stage magician exposing all the tricks of the trade. Shaw applied all his rhetorical fervor to a defense of his actions:

> In reference to the Potter's Art, perplexity and incertitude have generally predominated. Little comparison of theory with experiment, and its immediate consequences, has been attempted . . . Selfishness, which is always shortsighted, has hitherto governed its destinies; and disastrous has been its sway, alike to its own interests, and those of the community.[46]

Against this inefficient, secretive state of affairs, Shaw juxtaposed the new science of chemis-try, a discipline that "now promulgates Facts in the universal language of experiment."[47] He railed against the concept of the inherited recipe ("kept in the privacy of the manufacturer's office, or mixing room") as a basis for ceramic production, instead insisting that all elements of a ceramic body or glaze formula should be considered separately and understood completely, both with respect to their own properties and their interaction with other elements.[48] The logical result of this "heterogeneous" scientific understanding, Shaw thought, would be a long overdue separation of ceramics from the realm of alchemy—that "notorious fraternity," as he put it—and its habits of artisanal secrecy.[49] Parallel ideas about manufacturing were circulating in the 1820s and 1830s in many industries, and Shaw's ideas about "the universal language of experiment," in which every component of ceramic technology was conceptually isolated and considered in relation to all other components, is a good example of the general principle of the systematization of knowledge, as well as labor, that was circulating at the time. With a culture of public-minded experimentalism in place, the potteries would join the modern world.

SLEIGHTS OF HAND

We can see this putatively public-minded, but actually self-serving and commercial attitude to knowledge running right through the lineage of heroic figures of the industrial revolution. This idea was firmly grasped by the "improvers," promoters of industry who claimed to be great lovers of truth but whose rhetoric, in its combination of partial truths, misdirection, and disguise, often recalls the stage patter of a magician. One might have expected that industrialists like Wedgwood would have wanted to retain sole ownership of their technical know-how, but instead they acted like the conjurer Robert-Houdin. Living as they did in a culture that considered explanation an important and morally upright public activity, they recognized that this could be a protective screen that permitted them to advance their own interests. They also knew very well that the most pleasurable (and hence profitable) aspect of a revealed truth was the moment when the veil was whisked aside. Theatricality was therefore central to their methods of self-presentation. As historians such as Larry Stewart, Jan Golinski, and Barbara Maria Stafford have shown, the late eighteenth century saw the rise of a culture of public performance around science and technology, so that (in Stewart's words) "to be able to show why some machines worked, and why some others simply could not, was potentially a ticket to fame and modest fortune that was anxiously exploited by scientific lecturers."[50] Those who sought to derive benefits from invention, but also to reveal the processes they or others had invented, invariably argued that the public good was best served by this system of controlled disclosure. Tacit craft knowledge, which could not be described in satisfyingly revealing terms, was sidelined in this performance of (half) truths—not necessarily absent, but always given second billing.

For example, inventor Charles Babbage wrote in the preface to the second edition of his book *On the Economy of Machines and Manufactures* (1832): "It has been objected to me, that I have exposed too freely the secrets of trade. The only real secrets of trade are industry, integrity, and knowledge: to the possessors of these no exposure can be injurious; and they never fail to produce respect and wealth." Easy enough to say, but behind this forthright declaration lay a complicated personal history, in which Babbage came frequently into conflict with artisans and their principles of secrecy. As Simon Schaffer has written, this story began when Babbage was just a young boy and became enthralled by an automaton on display at John Merlin's Mechanical Museum in London—a female dancer executed in silver. As he later recalled, "the lady attitudinized in a most fascinating manner."[51] It was the beginning of a lifelong interest in automata; in the 1840s, he even tried to make a chess-playing automaton like the ones in the story of Robert-Houdin related earlier. He felt that such a device, if properly constructed, could best any human player thanks to its superior powers of calculation. (He was right about that, but it took a century and a half to finally prove the point.)[52] By that time he had been able to buy the silver dancer that so enchanted him in his youth, putting it on display in his own Marylebone salon alongside the calculating engines and other machines he himself had invented. As Schaffer suggests, this contrast was intended to show how technology of the sort that lay behind the automaton could be put to more useful purposes: "Throughout Babbage's career he felt it necessary to explain to what he saw as an irredeemably puerile public how to spot the difference between the engines which could make them rich and intelligent and those which deluded them into the gaudy fantasies of tricksy parlour games and theatrical delights."[53] Of course, he ignored the fact that he had been attracted to the automaton as a boy, presumably for reasons less than wholly scientific.

Babbage's position as an arch explicator put him into awkward positions from time to time, for he routinely exploited the knowledge of others for his own purposes. In the late 1820s, he had extensively studied the machinery of other entrepreneurs both in England and on the Continent—effectively engaging in industrial espionage. He was also reliant on instrument makers and machinists, such as Francis Watkins and Joseph Clement, and got into a bitter dispute with the latter over the patent rights to his famous difference engine—often described as the first computer. Despite the many contributions the artisan had made to the project, Babbage was awarded clear and exclusive patent rights in court, a decision that reflected the widespread opinion that thinking, not making, constituted the work of the inventor. The exception, as usual, was the directive medium of drawing—in the case of the difference engine, enough drawings "to cover a space of 1,000 square feet."[54] As might be expected of a man who saw factory production as a corrective to the inevitable errors of handwork, Babbage was dismissive of craftsmen's rights, and even comprehension, in the matter of invention: "Convinced as I am…that the prosperity and success of the master manufacturer is essential to the workman, I am compelled to admit that this connexion is, in many cases, too remote to be understood by the latter."[55] As Sadie Plant has written, Babbage's repression of his own dependencies was multiple. The contribution of Ada Lovelace, a brilliant mathematician who contributed in important ways to the development of the analytical engine (successor to the difference engine), was relegated to the position of a commentator, author of a set of notes that functioned literally as a "supplement" to Babbage's act of invention; similarly, Babbage underplayed the importance of the Jacquard loom as a precedent to his calculating machines.[56]

We see the same tendency to take the mechanical for granted in the figure of Thomas Edison, who put his name to more patentable designs than any other inventor (1,093 in all), but whose most effective innovation was arguably the organization of his own machine shop. In 1876, he began assembling a team of skilled technicians, organizing them according to the template of "a work culture that stretched back to the craftsmen of Europe and their guilds and apprenticeships," as Andre Millard has written.[57] Within five years, he had over eighty men working in this "invention factory." While this artisanal milieu was relatively egalitarian and could even be playful on occasion, Edison also worked his men hard and then took sole credit for every invention that emerged from the collaborative environment. He was even more effective at promoting himself than Wedgwood, Babbage, or Robert-Houdin, grasping the levers of modern celebrity culture whenever possible.

All of these examples—canonical within the history of design—show how mystery, once firmly associated with craft's professional identity, was extracted from narratives of making and equated instead with deception. It was something to stamp out. Edison may have been nicknamed the "wizard of Menlo Park," but of course that ironic title only made his difference from the alchemist of old that much more stark. In chapter one, we saw how Hobbs the lockpick was seen as suspect because he yielded no replicable set of tools and refused to explain his methods; earlier in this chapter, we saw how Robert-Houdin's fame as a magician was premised on the publication of secrets rather than the safeguarding of them. These are just two instances of the modern treatment of mystery as a problem, something to be explained away if possible.

Even P. T. Barnum, the quintessential wonder merchant of the nineteenth century and all-time champion of the improbable hoax, got in on the act. In 1866, he published a bestseller entitled *The Humbugs of the World: An Account of Humbugs, Delusions, Impositions, Quackeries, Deceits and Deceivers Generally, in all Ages.* It took as its epigram the Latin phrase "omne ignotum pro mirifico," a well-traveled citation taken from the Roman author Tacitus, translated in this context as "wonderful, because mysterious." In rendering the translation Barnum took advantage of the flexibility of Latin, reversing the usual meaning of the phrase. While it had classically been used to refer to the wondrous infinity of creation—"all that is unknown is marvelous"—in Barnum's new-model book of revealed truths, wonder was equated simply with trickery. Mystery was the weapon of the humbug. It was demoted from its traditional position as an invitation to knowledge; now it was nothing more than a tease, or at best, the quizzical speculation that comes before understanding. Barnum promised to set the record straight, engaging in a theater of explanation historian Neil Harris has called an "operational aesthetic," which involved both lavish descriptions of technical processes and the insistent revealing of tricksters' deceptive practices.[58] It is no surprise that when it came to his attitude to his own workmen, the ones who manned his spectacles, Barnum sounded the familiar theme, describing them as instruments in service to a higher authority (himself). In his disarmingly titled book *The Art of Money-Getting* (1880), he wrote: "Men in engaging employees should be careful to get the best. Understand, you cannot have too good tools to work with, and there is no tool you should be so particular about as living tools."[59]

Wedgwood, Babbage, Edison, and Barnum all felt confident that, provided they could separate themselves definitively from the echelon of artisans, their status as innovators would allow them to work profitably at the intersection of private invention and public knowledge. Furthermore, all shared a parallel belief that the hands that put their schemes into practice were just that—hired hands, not equal partners (in fact, not partners in any sense) in the process of innovation. This sidelining of artisanal forms of research was of a piece with a broader attitude to invention. Another Victorian explicator, Charles Tomlinson, noted in the preface to his enormous and comprehensively researched *Cyclopaedia,* published in the wake of the Great Exhibition, that he was concerned only with "Useful Arts and Manufactures which depend on the application of scientific principles," rather than with "Trades which depend chiefly on manual skill and dexterity." Like Andrew Ure, he criticized the secrecy that had once surrounded "the *mystery* of the trade," which was only "gradually revealed to the young mechanic in the course of his apprenticeship," and praised the modern tendency to put technical knowledge into the public sphere.[60] Clearly his own book was intended as a monumental contribution to this effort. For Tomlinson, invention was the critical driver of modern industry, and for the second edition of the book (published in 1862) he included an essay trying to puzzle out its true nature. After a long, typically detailed discussion of the life and work of one exemplary inventor, Johannes Gutenberg (a revealing choice, given that the printing press had made possible the project of modern explication itself), Tomlinson went on to define invention in exclusively intellectual and religious terms, as a matter of the mind alone that was guided not by human hands, but providence. "The materials for a great invention," he wrote, are "all at hand, but men's eyes are so holden that they cannot seize and appropriate the idea, and the reason is that the time has not yet arrived. They talk about the thing and declare it impossible, the thing is done, and then they say it is so simple a child may have found it out."[61] These words (which, interestingly, anticipate Thomas Kuhn's analysis of scientific progress as marked by quantum paradigm shifts) present invention as an optic, a way of seeing.[62] From this perspective, the frictional aspects of craft, by which innovations are actually brought into being, are merely child's play.

AN ELASTIC AGE

The erasure of craft from the story of modern invention attests to the close relationship between the modern assault on craft agency, discussed in chapter one, and the parallel assault on craft secrecy. Though one of these attacks was more direct than the other, both were ways of diminishing the autonomy afforded by skill. The nineteenth-century desire to have everything explained was a constant challenge for improvers. The successful among them were able to exploit the impulse, partly by fully explaining the details of their inventions (newspaper and magazine editors of the time were astonishingly confident in the appetite of their readership for technical information), but also simply by creating the impression that they were forthcoming, with nothing to hide. In this literally overstated culture, hard and fast technical knowledge was routinely prioritized, leaving the adaptable, manual basis of inventing to one side. That strategy was outstandingly successful. It has continued to this day, in fact, in the form of advertisements—which routinely claim to reveal the technical advantages of products, but almost never give insight into the practical realities of their manufacture.

The ideal of public knowledge was on unusually explicit display in the introduction of new substances—an occurrence that in an earlier age would have been described in terms of magic. The invention of materials was a common enough occurrence in the nineteenth century, and one that had particular implications for the discourse of craft. It was one thing to explain a machine while ignoring the skills that went into its making. In such a case, it made a certain kind of sense to take the crafts involved—ceramics, metalsmithing, woodworking, and the like—for granted. They were well known to most readers anyway, and relatively constant from one innovation to another. No matter how significant the contributions of artisans might have been, it was possible to pretend they were simply the backdrop against which the real inventing took place. But it was quite another matter to present novel substances to the public without emphasizing the physical processes of working them. Here I would like to take the three examples of cast iron, papier-mâché, and rubber, which all shared a remarkable property: they seemed to be moldable into any form desired. Though all three of these materials placed evident demands on the capabilities of the manufacturer—including both machinery and skills—they tended to be described as if they were brought into being effortlessly, rather like the rabbit brought out of the hat of a conjurer. Indeed, these new materials seemed to prove the infinite potency of scientific know-how itself. Yet, as in the case of Robert-Houdin's amazing performances, it was crucial that this seemingly magical, elastic relation to form be thoroughly explicated.

There was a problem here, though. The manufacturers of cast iron, papier-mâché, and rubber were typically artisanal experimenters, not metallurgists or professional chemists. To recall Oakeshott's terminology, they were in possession of practical knowledge, but wanted to present it as technical knowledge. This was not unprecedented; in the course of the industrial revolution, from steam engines to sawmills, much of the innovation had been done by empirical trial and error.[63] In these mechanical cases, technical knowledge had tended to come quickly; explication could be retrofitted to each invention, as it were, and thus could displace artisanal knowledge in fairly short order (a diagram of the machine, which presented it in linear forms rather than worked materials, was the preferred means of doing this). The wondrous action of new substances, however, operated on a molecular level, out of sight. How did improvers in these areas of manufacture describe their work? Their responses might be seen as occupying a middle ground between long-established and newly emerging ways of thinking about materiality. To some extent, improvers presented their amazing products in alchemical terms. They ascribed them quasi-magical, animate powers, reserving for them the mystery that had once attended all transmutable materials. At the same time, they subjected them to the usual welter of explication we have seen in the case of ceramics; and went further still, beginning to articulate what we might call scientific formalism, which treated materiality as purely a matter of calculation and ideation. Insofar as cast iron, papier-mâché, and rubber could be made to assume any form, they provided a seemingly unmediated route from intention to object. Explanation could therefore focus on the underlying science of the materials, which made that leap possible; and design, which directed the aesthetics of the result. The practical basis of manufacture, by which individual objects were actually fabricated, was taken for granted.

We can easily spot the future inheritance of this critical turn in attitudes to materiality if we describe it using the term *plasticity*. That word was often used to describe other materials in the nineteenth century, notably clay, but in retrospect it seems to have been particularly apt in the case of cast iron, papier-mâché, and rubber. These materials were for the nineteenth century what plastic was for the twentieth.[64] Roland Barthes memorably wrote in *Mythologies* (1957) that plastic seems miraculous, "the very idea of its infinite transformation ... it is less a thing than the trace of a movement." Yet it is also thoroughly inhuman in its qualities, resilient but textureless, without the grain of wood, the tractability of metal, or even the cold brilliance of glass: "it must be content with a 'substantial' attribute which is neutral in spite of its utilitarian advantages: *resistance,* a state which merely means an absence of yielding."[65] To some degree, these ideas belong to Barthes's own time, when artificial materials had made much greater encroachments into the realm of everyday life. Yet a century earlier, cast iron, papier-mâché, and rubber too seemed virtually infinite in their elasticity and equally lacking in the qualities of human touch.

It may be difficult to recover the strangeness and novelty of such materials today, but we can start by considering a cast iron stove made about 1780 (Figure 2.6). The manufacturer was the Carron Company in Falkirk, Scotland, a frequent collaborator of Robert Adam, who designed the Kimbolton cabinet discussed in the previous chapter.[66] Certainly the academic neoclassicism of this stove suggests his involvement, but it is not authorship that concerns us here—nor would the identity of the designer have incited curiosity at the time. For this was the very latest in modern domestic equipment, not only in stylistic terms, but also because of its functionality and materiality. Cast iron was not a new technology at the end of the eighteenth century. It had been used for centuries in making shallow castings, such as the decorated fireback plates used in hearths. From the mid-seventeenth century, similarly fabricated cast iron plates were used as the sides of box-like stoves for heating. (Benjamin Franklin invented a version of this design in 1741.) But a freestanding cast iron stove like the one made by Carron would have been a remarkable novelty.[67] Its manufacture was possible because of two recent innovations in the iron smelting process: first, the use of coke—a hot-burning, processed form of coal introduced by Abraham Darby in 1707—and second, the introduction of steam engines to pump air powerfully and steadily through the furnace.[68] These improvements produced a casting iron free of impurities, which could be molded in sand into highly detailed, volumetric forms. Andrew Ure exclaimed over its extraordinary plasticity:

> it is capable of being cast into moulds of any form...of being sharpened, or hardened, or softened at pleasure. Iron accommodates itself to all our wants and desires, even to our caprices; it is equally serviceable to the arts, the sciences, to agriculture, and war; the same ore furnishes the sword, the ploughshare, the scythe, the pruning-hook, the needle, the graver, the spring of the watch or of a carriage, the chisel, the chain, the anchor, the compass, the cannon, the bomb.[69]

Though it is certainly possible to overplay the ease of working this newly improved material (as Ure arguably did), it was indeed essential to the industrial revolution, playing a key role in engineering projects, the manufacture of machines, decorative art, and architecture.

The smelting and molding of cast iron required many skilled hands. In fact, the early story of the Carron works (founded in 1759) is essentially that of a drafting campaign to lure artisans up to Scotland from the established works at Coalbrookdale in Shropshire, to build the necessary blast furnaces and associated equipment: "masons and bricklayers and millwrights and bellows makers," as one of the founding partners wrote to another.[70] Pattern makers were also required to make wooden models for every casting (more on that in chapter three). As Ellen Marie Snyder has noted in her study of Victorian iron

Figure 2.6   Robert Adam, designer (attributed to), stove, ca. 1780. Made at Carron Iron Co., Falkirk, Scotland. Cast iron. V&A: M.3–1920. © Victoria and Albert Museum, London.

furniture, "some of the most highly trained workers in American industry were found in iron casting."[71] Even so, there is no doubt that the material played an important role in sidelining craft within the narrative of modern progress. It is the now familiar story in which artisans remained vital to production but were nonetheless effaced. The simple fact that iron could be molded at large scale led to heroic narratives in which a single engineer, rather than a team of skilled contributors, was assigned sole authorship for huge public projects like bridges and tunnels. And iron also engendered an extreme form of identification between prominent improvers and technology (Henry Maudslay—the maker of the Bramah and Co. lock described at the beginning of chapter one—went so far as to be buried under an iron tomb monument).[72] Unlike wrought iron, cast iron cannot subsequently be worked by hand by a blacksmith, so the "movement" of casting, to use Barthes's term, seemed to contain the entire making process. This was one kind of making where artisanal processes were displaced directly by an industrial one, as Samuel Smiles noted in the 1860s:

> since the invention of cast-iron, and the manufacture of wrought-iron in large masses, the art of hammer-working has almost become lost; and great artists...no longer think it worth their while to expend time and skill in working on so humble a material as wrought-iron. It is evident from the marks of care and elaborate design which many of these early works exhibit, that the workman's heart was in his work, and that his object was not merely to get it out of hand, but to execute it in first-rate artistic style.[73]

Almost a century before Smiles wrote, the Carron stove already exemplified the shift he described. Not only is it "plastic" in its surface quality, with no evident marks of the hand anywhere on it, but it freely imitates other materials that would have been worked by hand at the time, rendering them all in one undifferentiated black mass. There is the central vase form of the stove, drawn from pottery (or perhaps stone, given its size); the moldings that run along the edges of the supporting plinth, which emulate woodwork; the decorative swags and rams' heads, which imitate ormolu mounts; and the vent that centers the base, which seems to echo the furnace in which the stove itself was made. This indiscriminate quality, in which any form could be achieved regardless of that form's origin in another material, was both striking and (as we will see) ultimately concerning to observers. Over the course of the nineteenth century, it only became more evident, as iron was used to imitate other crafts, even lace (Figure 2.7), as well as a diversity of natural forms from snakes to branches to clusters of grapes. As one historian cogently puts it, "the euphoric enthusiasm felt in the nineteenth century for cast iron which was being produced in ever better ways and ever greater quantities led to a desire to make everything, absolutely everything, in that material and using that technique."[74] Though this kind of substitution may seem like other early modern *trompe l'oeil* objects, in which one material was substituted for another (a particularly common practice in ceramics), in fact the two types of imitation are antithetical. Despite the name, *trompe l'oeil* does not so much deceive the eye as engage it, inviting the viewer to inspect the mastery expended on a feat of imitation.[75] In the case of the iron stove, by contrast, one look is enough to tell the viewer that the cast iron could be made into any form the mold maker pleased. A handmade *trompe l'oeil* object is a triumph of craft over material; cast iron was a triumph of material over craft.

Because cast iron manufacture was a particularly dramatic case of technology exceeding the capabilities of the traditional artisan, it led immediately to the idea of the blacksmith as a figure rooted in the past, or at best the pastoral scenery of the countryside. This is one of the earliest and clearest instances in which the craftsman was increasingly distinguished from the industrial worker. In the early 1770s, Joseph Wright of Derby had created a series of five paintings in which he showcased his talent for light effects by focusing on the process of metal forging. In each canvas, the focus is provided by a glowing ingot of iron, which illuminates a group of figures gathered round (Figures 2.8 and 2.9). Three of these images are set in a blacksmith's shop, and two in a "modern" forge, but the treatment is virtually identical, down to the details of the architectural surroundings. Also unchanged is the glowing ingot at the center of the picture, an icon of raw potential, matter yet to take form. (A similar painting of Wright's shows a medieval alchemist in his shop, dramatically underlining this theme.) So similar are the dominant figures in these paintings—strong, poised men in worker's shirtsleeves—that they could be the same person, with only a slight change of costume. Yet there is one important difference: while the blacksmith still plies his trade with concentrated effort, hammer in hand, the forge man is free to fold his arms and direct his glance sideways toward his family, as the powered drop hammer does the work. As David Solkin has pointed out, though both workers are ennobled through their bearing and dress, which have "the free-flowing grace of classical draperies," there is a suggestion here of the moral benefit to be reaped from the introduction of industrial processes.[76] We see here an early visualization of the theme that would become more and more common over succeeding decades. The artisan, while never despised, was increasingly located in the

Figure 2.7   Edward Schott, fan, ca. 1862. Made at Ilsenburg-am-Harz, Germany. Cast iron. V&A: 5369–1901. © Victoria and Albert Museum, London.

past. The blacksmith was now to be "ye olde blacksmith," no less virtuous (indeed, even more so) but increasingly detached from progressive sensibilities.[77]

The blacksmith continued to be an emblematic figure in this discursive shift, no doubt precisely because of the unusually vivid contrast (which Wright was among the first to notice) between forging by hand and large-scale casting. John Holland, writing in the 1830s on *The Progressive Improvement and Present State of the Manufactures in Metal,* devoted many pages to industrial work and little space to hand forging. He did note, however, that the natural habitat of the "modern blacksmith" was in "villages remote from the large towns," where he "may be seen to assume not merely his real importance as a mechanic, but his relative consequence as a member of society, by presenting that *factotum* character, which not only indicates that he is an indispensable artificer in iron and even steel, but which has led to his figuring in poetry, romance, and even music."[78] And indeed, Henry Wadsworth Longfellow's poem "The Village Blacksmith" (1841), certainly the best-known description of an artisan in Romantic literature, would famously position him as a completely self-reliant figure detached from any compromising ties to the external world:

> Under a spreading chestnut-tree
> The village smithy stands;
> The smith, a mighty man is he,
> With large and sinewy hands;
> And the muscles of his brawny arms
> Are strong as iron bands.
> His hair is crisp, and black, and long,
> His face is like the tan;
> His brow is wet with honest sweat,
> He earns whate'er he can,
> And looks the whole world in the face,
> For he owes not any man.

Almost needless to say, such idealistic images bore little relation to the actual lives of rural blacksmiths of the eighteenth or nineteenth century—they were no doubt physically strong, but they were certainly not independent of market forces. Most worked as smiths only part of the year, often trading their services in kind with other agricultural laborers; like any independent business owner they were enmeshed in involved financial relationships with those both inside and outside their communities. They were in conscious and active competition with goods brought in from urban manufactories, and often engaged in piecework, serving distant markets as a way to supplement their income.[79] The fantasy of the blacksmith as a heroic character who "owes not any man" was a modern production, every bit as much an invention as the cast iron foundry that served as his conceptual opposite. So rapidly and thoroughly did this way of thinking penetrate thinking around the craft that it formed the basis of blacksmiths' own self-perception, at least to judge from a portrait of Philadelphia blacksmith Pat Lyon, painted in 1826–1827 by John Neagle.

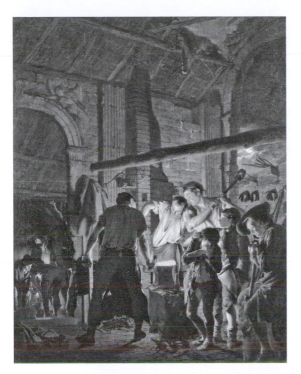

Figure 2.8   Joseph Wright of Derby, *The Blacksmith's Shop*, 1771. Oil on canvas. Yale Center for British Art.

Figure 2.9   Joseph Wright of Derby, *The Iron Forge*, 1772. Oil on canvas. Broadlands trust, Hampshire. Bridgeman Art Library.

In this case, the artisan stage managed the terms of his own romanticization, explicitly directing the artist to paint his own garments and tools:

> I wish you, sir, to paint me at full length, the size of life, representing me at the smithery, with my bellows blower, hammers, and all the etceteras of the shop around me. . . . I wish you to understand clearly, Mr. Neagle, that I do not desire to be represented in the picture as a gentleman—to which character I have no pretension. I want you to paint me at work at my anvil, with my sleeves rolled up and a leather apron on.[80]

In actual fact, Lyon may not have been a gentleman, but he was certainly an entrepreneur with a profitable lock making business; he also supervised the construction of fire engines and attained a prominent position as a Philadelphia businessman. But most important to him, in the years just before his death, was that he be presented as an autonomous, idealized figure, hammer in hand.

A slightly different story is that of papier-mâché, a material that also substituted for other media (notably carving) but had no obvious correlate within the world of traditional crafts. The medium had first come into use in 1740s Paris as an inexpensive replacement for architectural plasterwork; as a cheap, light building material (in the form of thin

Figure 2.10   John Neagle, *Pat Lyon at the Forge,* 1826–1827. Oil on canvas. Museum of Fine Arts, Boston.

boards, useful in coach building, for example); and as a casting material for making frames for pictures and mirrors, as well as small domestic articles such as trays and boxes. In this latter context, it was often decorated with "japanning" (a surface treatment that imitated Asian lacquer, which also had a contemporary vogue in tinware and furniture), and could be further enlivened with mother-of-pearl inlay. The medium would have remained a rather minor decorative art had it not been completely transformed by the introduction of steam-powered presses in the 1830s. The addition of heat and pressure allowed manufacturers like Charles Frederick Bielefeld to cast a slurry of paper, glue, and china clay into permanent and detailed sculptural forms. Previously, papier-mâché objects had to be constructed from multiple layers, which considerably reduced strength and plasticity. But with these improvements, a large mass could be cast in a single mold, rather like plaster.[81] Bielefeld's promotional treatise on the new process stressed its modernity. The result of his process was:

> alike only in name to the *papier mâché* of the last century; its hard compactness, its strength, its imperishable nature, its tractability...and the facility with which it may be prepared and fixed, and finally its cheapness, are qualities which eminently distinguish it, but which cannot perhaps be fully appreciated but by those who have had extensive experience in its use.[82]

In one sense, papier-mâché was typical of the new materials of the nineteenth century, in that its production was dependent on machinery but it also required extensive hand finishing. "It is to be cut with the saw and chisel," Bielefeld instructed, "and may be bent by steam or heat, planed and cleaned up with sand paper to the smoothest face."[83] On the other hand, the very fact that he felt it necessary to explain this process indicates that, to untrained eyes, it was very difficult to work out how papier-mâché was made. And this, of course, was its attraction. A chair made by Bielefeld's principal competitors, the Birmingham firm Jennens and Bettridge, might initially seem more or less indistinguishable from other domestic "fancy goods" of the day[84] (Plate 7). At the time, though, the deep curvature of the chair's back qualified not only as high design, but as advanced technology. The wooden legs of the chair, cartoonishly sinuous as the carver had managed to make them, cannot compete with the plasticity of the open-work papier-mâché back, which is further enlivened with inlaid mother-of-pearl and japanned decoration. The ballooning shapes and lack of joints in such objects would otherwise have been impossible to achieve and they were amazing to behold.

Making a chair like this certainly wasn't easy. Rag paper had to be laid by hand over a mold, burnished smooth, then fired in an oven (somewhat like a clay body), before final treatment of the surface with paint, inlay, and varnish. Yet the extraordinary elasticity of papier-mâché prompted the thought that it could assume absolutely any form, for the shape of such a chair was not at all constrained by the material itself, as would have been the case when using timber. It is hard to reconstruct how astounding this idea must have been in the 1840s. Previously, every known material had imposed obvious limitations due to its dimensions, workability, or internal structure.[85] As Bielefeld put it:

> whatever the genius of Grinling Gibbons himself has attempted in wood, may be executed in *papier mâché* with no less sharpness, no less relief, no less lightness, and *much less* liability to injury; for *papier mâché* has this great advantage over wood, that, although as hard, it is tougher, and is wholly without the *grain* of wood, which gives it a bias or tendency to chip off in one direction…there is no possible enrichment, in any style, however complicated or elaborate, that may not be readily executed in it.[86]

By invoking the name of Gibbons, who (as we saw in chapter one) was a byword of craft mastery in the nineteenth century, Bielefeld framed papier-mâché as an improvement on the skills of even the best carver.

In 1847, the *Art-Union* extolled the virtues of papier-mâché articles in similar terms, refuting those who characterized them as poor replacements for objects in richer materials. On the contrary:

> [They] have been designated by some as substitutes for art; but such they by no means are, being, in truth, happy facilities, exhibiting as much the essence of the art as the clay from the hand of the sculptor; the art is there, and the quality of the art is not improved either by the subsequent marble, gold, or silver.

When a writer calling himself Philoponos quoted this passage a few years later, he added the further comment: "admirably expressed. A question of art is not a question of material, but the latter becomes a question of cost, according to its own value and the difficulty of elaboration."[87] The implication is that materiality is irrelevant to the quality of the "art" of the product, except insofar as it inconveniences the designer; and the advantage of papier-mâché was that it posed so little inconvenience. Unlike other carving materials like wood and stone, which were limited in regard to dimension and internal structure, papier-mâché could be made into anything the designer pleased.

A similar enthusiasm accompanied vulcanized "India rubber" products when they began appearing on the market in the 1840s.[88] Natural latex or *caoutchouc* (the French term was often used in English), harvested from trees in Brazil and India, had been imported to Europe in the eighteenth century, but it was not good for much besides erasing pencil marks. Brittle, easily cracked, hard and inflexible at low temperatures but prone to stickiness on hot days, it was not very satisfactory even in the few other uses found for it over succeeding decades (though Scottish entrepreneur Charles Macintosh had success in making rubber-lined raincoats, hence our present-day term).[89] By the 1830s, there was already considerable importation into England and widespread interest in its "peculiar and remarkable properties."[90] But just as it took technology to completely alter the material qualities of papier-mâché, it required the process of vulcanization—in which sulfur is added to the rubber under heat, a technique first discovered by American Charles

Goodyear in 1839 and then separately by British inventor Thomas Hancock, who patented the process in 1843—to turn rubber into a permanently elastic super commodity capable of being made into seemingly anything. Once the natural latex was "masticated" (torn to shreds) with rotary knives and vulcanized, it could be worked at varying levels of solidity: machined on a lathe, cast in molds, drawn into thread, or rendered in liquid form as a varnish. It was resistant to heat and cold and waterproof; it could be colored or polished. As Tomlinson wrote, "it is also capable of being moulded into the most intricate ornaments," adding (in a telling phrase) that "its characteristic elasticity remov[es] all embarrassment in relieving the undercut parts."[91]

This eminently modern chemical transmutation made rubber seem wonderful proof of the infinite possibilities of modern science. Along with gutta-percha, a similar plant material imported largely from Singapore and Malaysia that could also be used for a broad range of applications, India rubber was often described using extremely precise technical language (the fastidious Tomlinson provided its melting temperature, carbon content, and even its specific gravity).[92] When it was displayed at the Great Exhibition of 1851, it was presented in the manner of an exhibit at a science fair. The material was shown in its raw state, partly processed in block, sheet, and thread form, and in finished articles. Though other raw materials such as exotic woods were showcased in a similar fashion as a way of demonstrating the riches of Britain's colonies and the expertise of European manufacturers in transforming them, rubber made an unusually dramatic display because it could be put to a seemingly endless list of uses. Indeed, written lists of such applications frequently accompanied published descriptions of rubber. Here is Thomas Hancock enumerating some of its states and uses:

> Whether adhesive or unadhesive, vulcanized or unvulcanized, possessing elongated elasticity or rendered rigid by hard vulcanizing, plain, coloured, printed, embossed, moulded portraits, medallions, tablets, stick and umbrella handles, mechanical applications, toys...cloaks, capes of double and single textures, air-beds, pillows, cushions, life-preservers, model pontoons, diving dresses, gas-bags, &c., &c.[93]

Gas-bags indeed. In that "&c., &c." is contained the promise of infinite plasticity. To "these remarkable substances," as the official Great Exhibition catalogue put it, all conceivable purposes were "subservient."[94] Illustrated trade catalogues showed rubber and gutta-percha assuming one form after another in a dizzying array: inkstands and ear trumpets, gas lamps and loom parts, fire buckets and chamberpots. As was the case with papier-mâché, these products often copied the forms and even the surface characteristics of more familiar materials—a notable example being "ebonite," a hard, black rubber that mimicked the valuable wood ebony. But rubber was clearly something radically new. Manufacturers understood this, and they launched into explanation of its potential with gusto.

A particularly remarkable instance is a rubber tablet made by Charles Macintosh for display at the Great Exhibition, which describes itself in a closed loop of explanation and exemplification. The plaque presents itself as a self-sufficient object, "susceptible of delicate embossing." Materiality and explanatory language map onto one another completely, without residuum or remainder, or any evident dependency on the hands of an artisan. Like one of Robert-Houdin's revealed magic tricks, Macintosh's tablet amazes and informs all at once. There is no need for secrecy, it seems to say; this modern material will meet every eventuality, and will even narrate itself while doing so. Yet rubber only required such self-conscious explanation because it seemed so magical. It was, after all, a strange new substance. Who knew what it might be capable of? A semi-humorous essay published in 1853 described rubber as a master metaphor for the expansive adaptability of modern culture:

> What with our elasticity and our impermeability, we are certainly becoming a redoubtable race in this nineteenth-century…We certainly live in an elastic age. If we cannot break that which opposes us, we bounce away from it with great agility and feel not much the worse for the encounter. There is a fair amount of caoutchouc in the human mind.[95]

Despite the self-satisfied optimism of this passage—a tone struck again and again in discussions of rubber—the author's belligerence toward "that which opposes us" suggests a

Figure 2.11   "Useful Articles in Gutta Percha," from *Illustrated List of Ornamental and Useful Applications of Gutta Percha* (London: Gutta Percha Company, 1851), p. 15.

certain enmity between people and materials, one people might be losing. This is a peculiarly modern worry: that artificial substances might take on a life of their own, like a genie let out of a bottle. Today, with a century and a half's hindsight, we feel that anxiety much more keenly. Modern materials do seem to impose their own characteristics upon us—and the idea that we might have minds made of caoutchouc is much less appealing than it was in the 1850s.

It is no coincidence that the dissenters who identified a creeping dehumanization in these modern materials are a virtual role call of the progenitors of the Arts and Crafts movement: John Ruskin, Gottfried Semper, and Gothic Revival architect A.W.N. Pugin, who lambasted "the mechanical contrivances and inventions of the day, such as plastering, composition, *papier-mâché,* and a host of other deceptions," which "only serve to degrade design, by abolishing the variety of ornament and ideas, as well as the boldness of execution, so admirable and beautiful in ancient carved works."[96] Ruskin, who cultivated a vivid dislike for imitative processes in general, had particularly harsh words for cast iron, writing in *Fors Clavigera* that "every poor flourish of [Sheffield] cast iron, every bead moulding on a shop front, is borrowed from Greece or Venice," and arguing that cast iron was a typical (i.e., lamentable) example of contemporary work in that it had nothing to do with the

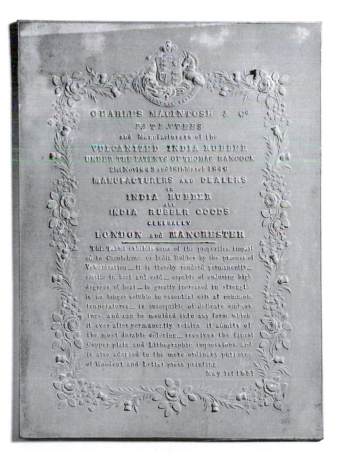

Figure 2.12   Charles Macintosh &
Co., exhibition plaque, 1851.
Vulcanized rubber. Kew Economic
Botany Collection.

inherent qualities of the metal as it existed in the ground—"which, like nearly all other right principles in art, we moderns delight in contradicting as directly and specially as may be."[97] This latter idea, that plasticity was fundamentally unprincipled, had a strong moral charge in an age when design and the public good were seen as strongly linked. It was a theme examined in greater depth by influential German design theorist Semper, resident in London during the Great Exhibition. Semper pointed to rubber as an instance of the "superfluity of means" that had arisen as a result of too much technology arriving too fast:

> We can accomplish the most intractable and laborious things with playful ease by the application of technical means borrowed from science; the hardest porphyry and granite can be cut like chalk and polished like wax, ivory can be softened and pressed into shapes, India rubber and gutta-percha can be vulcanized and used to produce deceptive imitations of carvings in wood, metal and stone, in ways which far transcend the natural domain of fabricated materials...Machines now sew, knit, engrave, cut and paint, thereby deeply intervening in the realm of human art and exposing every human skill to scorn...How will we be able to prevent this universal devaluation from spreading to the genuinely hand-crafted and traditionally produced works? And how then will we avoid regarding such things as nothing but an expression of affectation, of antiquarian curiosity, of esoteric interest and eccentricity?[98]

Semper presciently positions the advent of plasticity as a great divide, a rift in the continuum of stylistic progress. Previously, he argues, form had always arisen through the logic of craft—the interaction of material, tools, and function—rather than through conscious imposition. Now those various forms of resistance were banished. Subsequent theorists in this "formalist" tradition, mostly writing in France and Germany, would continue to regard materials as animate, elevating them, in the words of Dario Gamboni, "from the status of inert matter to that of agents in the creative process."[99] Few of these writers, though, were so alive to the consequences for craftsmanship as Semper was. For him, if materials imposed no friction upon makers—if they merely preserved, to recall Barthes's words, "the trace of a movement"—then skill itself would come to seem irrelevant, a mere anachronism.

Today this sounds like a familiar worry, and indeed, in the early reaction to plastic materials, we begin to see the first stirrings of a new, dominant narrative about modern craft, one that casts it in the role not of a silent partner for industry (albeit one that must be strictly controlled), as we have seen so far, but rather that of a remnant of earlier times, whose loss might well be disastrous. By the late nineteenth century, it had become common wisdom that (in the words of one industrial historian) "the slow and laborious process of making things by hand" was gradually superseded by an efficient and automatic "copying principle" in which the forms of (mass) production were more and more "contained within the machine itself."[100] Actually, this was only true in the case of a few materials—notably the three I have discussed here—and a few tools, such as replicating lathes. But this did not prevent Semper, as well as figures like Pugin, Ruskin, and Morris, from absorbing the triumphalist industrial narrative and turning it into an alarmist one in which the forming powers of the artisan were seen as being directly supplanted by the twin powers of automation and plasticity. I return to this matter of anxiety in chapter four. For now, I want simply to underline the fact that it was in reference to materials themselves that the specter of craft's displacement seems to have loomed most clearly into view. It is another of the ironies that accompanied the invention of craft: artisans first seemed to drift back around the bend of history at exactly the moment when the means at their disposal were expanding fastest.

EXPLAINED AWAY: CRAFT AND CULTURAL IMPROVEMENT

In cast iron, papier-mâché, and rubber, we see a transference of the Victorian impulse to explicate into the very substance of materials themselves. Plasticity seemed to short-circuit traditional understandings of making. For the first time, "technique" was formulated as something that could operate on its own, independently from the work of human hands. The artifacts made from these new materials, accordingly, seemed to close the yawning gap between principle and practice. In this sense, they perfectly matched the cultural program of the South Kensington system, which sought to infuse all production with the uplifting powers of draftsmanship and principle and disregarded artisanal skill in the process. Though no Victorian improver would have seen it this way, this was in fact another kind of magical thinking. Substances were treated as if they were subject to any purpose humans desired—the pure emanation of design. This fantasy of control over materiality is one of the signature elements of modernity.[101] But though it pretended to address issues of pure form, this set of ideas was implicitly grounded in a narrative of cultural improvement. According to this logic, if the specific, frictional, and hard-won realities of craft were being gradually supplanted by technology, then this also marked a great step forward in the ongoing progress of civilization itself. That feeling of progress was powerfully generative, leading ultimately to the modernists' thrilling embrace with technology beginning in the 1910s. But it was also harmful on many fronts. As we have already seen, it entailed a distortion of the actuality of production—leading to misperceptions about the real relations between skill and industry that have lasted to this day. A much more destructive consequence of this progressive thinking occurred in another context: the encounter with societies that seemed to lie outside the sphere of modernity itself.

If artisanal production was seen as in need of improvement in Europe and America—with explication and technology the principal mechanisms for doing so—then that same logic was applied with far greater force to artisans in other parts of the world. When Europeans made contact with supposedly "primitive" populations, they asked themselves two questions: how might we gain advantage from these people? And how might we improve them, bringing them within the pale of civilization? Taken together, this meant treating people much like raw materials. The techniques of imperialism mirrored those of industrialization, aiming to banish resistance and achieve total plasticity. As it happens (and as its name implies), the extraction of India rubber was an instance in which a people and a material were exploited at one and the same time. Rubber was harvested and prepared not only in India, but also in South America and Indonesia, before being imported to the modern factory. Making the bottle-shaped lumps of rubber was by no means easy. First, latex had to be sapped from the rubber tree. The milky fluid was allowed to dry in layers over a wooden bat, which was held over a fire to speed the process. As the industry increased in scale, the existing artisanal knowledge of the Native Americans was thoroughly commandeered. Large plantations were set up, tended by workers who were for all practical purposes enslaved. Often, the industry displaced not only former ways of gathering and using rubber, but also the land itself—previously the mainstay of indigenous agricultural economies. The replacement of crop farming with rubber harvesting exposed populations to progressively more brutal exploitation, as they became increasingly dependent upon the plantation system.[102] This was a continuation of the colonialist policies previously established as a way of securing other commodities, such as sugar and precious metals. But we can also see the exploitation of Native American rubber workers as an intensified version of the treatment of skilled labor in Europe. Once again, the "secrets" of a workforce were ferreted out and systematized, allowing for their progressive subjugation.

As one of the primary operations of nineteenth-century imperialism, the imperative to extract materials and knowledge has drawn extensive attention from postcolonial theorists. Most of these scholars tend to focus on matters of domination and agency, which revolve around the degree to which the subaltern can be seen to "speak."[103] But colonized people also asserted their agency by remaining silent: by refusing to yield their mysteries. Just as in discussions of European artisans, though with a heavy overlay of racist antipathy, European writers expressed their exasperation at the secretiveness of indigenous populations in the Pacific, Africa, and the Americas. Charles Tomlinson complained that these traditional methods of "inspissating and indurating" (that is, making the rubber thicker and harder) were still "kept secret" by the indigenous populations in Brazil, who had traditionally used rubber to waterproof boats and to prepare weapons and other necessities.[104] Physician Thomas Winterbottom similarly commented on the "great unwillingness which [Africans] shew to disclose the secrets of their medical art," preventing Europeans from adding to the known *materia medica*.[105] Even as writers like these tried to gain a purchase on this local knowledge, they also tended to treat it as mere superstition. In eighteenth- and nineteenth-century narratives of encounter, magic served as a convenient catch-all concept to explain "primitive" belief systems (cosmology, medicine, conceptions of the afterlife) that did not open themselves to "rational" exchange. For Europeans, these forms of knowledge were legible only as sorcery or idolatry. Here is another parallel with attitudes to knowledge in Europe: at the very moment entrenched belief systems (such as alchemy) were being dismissed as a hindrance to the superior explanatory power of science, the same logic was applied to exotic cultures. Magic became a means of conceptualizing the knowledge of non-European peoples and craft-based knowledge in Europe alike as static, rooted in a primordial past.

Handmade objects were central to this discourse—as is suggested by the period use of the term "fetish" (from the Portuguese *feitico,* meaning "to fabricate") to describe artifacts used in native rituals, especially in Africa.[106] Henry Meredith, writing about the Gold Coast in 1812, interpreted the fetish as purposefully obfuscatory, describing it as "an indefinite object" used by Africans with the aim "of concealing the mysteries of their superstition."[107] The European response to such potent artifacts was to explain them away. Exotic craft objects played a starring role in eighteenth-century didactic mechanisms, including publications and public collections, where these items were displayed as "specimens" alongside natural items that were equally susceptible to classification and explication. Just before opening his museum-cum-emporium in London (the "Holophusicon") in 1775, for example, aristocratic collector Ashton Lever released a broadside advertising his interest in objects of seemingly any type: fossils, plants, "beasts entire, or their skins, horns, or limbs," and also "every production of Art that is rare or curious, either from its Antiquity, fine Workmanship, or the extraordinary Materials of which it is composed…of all Nations, and of all Ages."[108] This seemingly indiscriminate appetite—descended from earlier cabinets of curiosities—was brought into control through a systematic approach to display, based on the layout and construction of library bookcases, which departed radically from the inspired jumble of objects that typified earlier cabinets.[109] Lever's museum was a place of entertainment, but also of clarification, a visual catalogue of artifacts laid out in an absolutely regular grid. Artist Sarah Stone pictured it as a series of proscenium arches receding into space, an anticipation of the optic of discovery that would be deployed in the Crystal Palace. A celebrated album of illustrations by Stone depicts various artifacts from Lever's collection, including both natural objects like stones and shells as well as historical European artifacts and Pacific Northwest and Polynesian material culture collected by explorer James Cook on his voyages in the 1760s and 1770s.[110] Each object is rendered in a definite, concrete style that attests to her careful looking. The emphasis on explication is underlined by Stone's decision to transcribe the handwritten labels Lever had affixed to his curiosities—and even the red wax he used to do so. The assumed neutrality of her depictions both exploited and contained the strangeness of exotic curiosities.

The same dichotomy is evident in period accounts of the Holophusicon. "The wandering eye looks round with astonishment," wrote one visitor, and "sighs to recollect the prevalent power of fear and superstition over the human mind when he views the rude deformity of an idol carved with flint, by a hand incapable of imitating the outline of nature, and that works only that it may worship."[111] This double-faced attitude to non-European craft, in which its potency is conceded, but then dispelled by a more powerful framework of explanation, has remained at the core of treatments of non-European craft ever since. Over the course of the nineteenth century, it was extrapolated into professional anthropology and museology. As these fields developed, they proceeded from explaining away craft magic to transforming knowledge into a weapon of acculturation. No longer content to present (or represent) the handmade artifact as a sign of otherness,

Figure 2.13   Sarah Stone (after), Interior of the Leverian Museum, 1835 copy of a ca. 1786 original. Watercolor on paper. British Museum Am2006,Drg.54.

Figure 2.14   Sarah Stone, drawing from an album of objects from the Leverian Museum, 1780. Watercolor on paper. British Museum Am2006,Drg.53.

nineteenth-century scholars and reformers gradually repurposed the fusion of craft and explication into a technique of control.

This narrative unfolds in particularly appalling detail in the case of Native American culture. By the early nineteenth century, Europeans had already gone through several phases in their attitude to the "savages" they were displacing. These responses ranged widely, from admiration to enmity, but were in any case charted along a path of increasingly detailed investigation. Handmade objects played an important role in this gradual process. Europeans found it extremely difficult to gain an understanding of Native Americans through language alone, a difficulty they chalked up to the fundamentally irrational nature of Indian society. As Anthony Pagden writes in his classic study *The Fall of Natural Man,* "If language was not an adequate, or even a proper vehicle with which to describe the unfamiliar, then language would have to be replaced by some specimen of the unfamiliar itself."[112] Gradually, "curiosities" came into focus as evidence. An encounter that had been shot through with wonder was replaced by the calm confidence of science. Native Americans were now viewed as vestiges of an earlier stage of human development, which could be described in satisfyingly material terms (as progressing from the Stone Age to the Bronze Age to the Iron Age).[113] For those who believed in this progressive model, intuitive craft was evidence of a preliminary stage of development, a lower rung on the ladder of civilization. Even the most sympathetic early observers of Native American culture, such as pioneering ethnographer Lewis Henry Morgan, thought in these terms. Morgan was an indefatigable champion of Indian rights. Nevertheless, he believed that "mankind commenced their career at the bottom of the scale and worked their way up from savagery to civilization through the slow accumulations of experimental knowledge," and positioned Indians at an early phase of this development.[114] What he called their "artisan intellect" was proof of this, and so too was the fact that they could be improved through the introduction of new goods, technology, and ways of life. He pointed to certain products of a "mixed character," like baskets, pipes, and pottery, which "contrast strangely with those of their ancestors." Morgan was inclined to view such change positively, writing that these objects "furnish no slight indication of artisan capacity, and will serve as a species of substitute for those articles they have displaced, and those inventions which they have hurried into forgetfulness."[115]

Anthropologists like Morgan, who worked closely with, and even lived among, their objects of study, were horrified by the idea that white people might feel free to enslave or simply kill Native Americans. They argued instead for improvement of indigenous peoples—as if they were children requiring a good education. In practice, this meant assimilating them into the white population. And again, objects were seen as important tools for achieving this end. Reformers thought that if Native Americans could be induced to use manufactured European goods, for example, they would inevitably become more civilized. In 1838, the first head of the Bureau of Indian Affairs, Thomas McKenney, together with author James Hall and artist Charles Bird King, published the first volume of their monumental study *A History of the Indian Tribes of North America: With Biographical Sketches and Anecdotes of the Principle Chiefs.* Like Morgan, they were well meaning (indeed, one motivation for compiling the book was to advocate for a more humane government policy). Yet Hall wrote flatly that the Native Americans were in the grip of "shadowy superstitions" and had no productive capacity whatsoever: "they made nothing, they erected nothing, they established nothing, which might vindicate to succeeding generations their character as rational beings." His solution was to send to the tribes knowledge and objects of explication—"schoolmasters, artisans, teachers of husbandry and the mechanic arts, tools," and more generally, to "introduce the habits and arts of social life among them."[116]

Given this strategy, it is unsurprising that of all the Native Americans portrayed in the volume, McKenney and Hall reserved their greatest praise for Sequoyah, a half-German, half-Cherokee born about 1770 and famous for devising an alphabet to write his own native language. While it is difficult to separate fact from fiction in their account of Sequoyah (and indeed all subsequent biographies, which are based on theirs), he certainly seems to have conformed to the wildest expectations of the assimilationist. Indeed, he comes across as a Native American equivalent to the British improver. Described by McKenney and Hall as "of a pacific disposition, and of a mind elevated above the sphere in which he was placed," and with "an innate propensity for the imitative arts," Sequoyah reputedly occupied himself with various mechanical tasks as a child and as soon as he was able, taught himself the skills of drawing, blacksmithing, and finally silversmithing. He earned his living in these metalwork trades, and, though illiterate, even went so far as to make a die of his own name (as transcribed for him by another half-white, half-Indian who could read and write) so that he could mark his silver articles. Along the way, he apparently was tempted by the attentions of women and the drinking of "ardent spirits"—a habit that routinely drew the ire of Euro American reformers in their discussions of Native Americans—but ultimately resolved to avoid them, having seen them as promoting "the evil tendencies of idleness and dissipation." Eventually, Sequoyah made the breakthrough that would make him renowned. Curious about the way the whites inscribed their words onto "talking leaves," he devised his own system of writing with eighty-five phonetic characters, one for each sound in the Cherokee language. McKenney and Hall concluded the story rhapsodically: "Without advice, assistance, or encouragement—ignorant alike of books and of the various arts by which knowledge is disseminated—with no prompter but his own genius, and no guide but the light of reason, he had formed an alphabet for a rude dialect, which, until then, had been an unwritten tongue!" The portrait Charles Bird King furnished to accompany their text portrayed Sequoyah in the pose of an explicator, his finger directing attention to a tablet that could almost be biblical in origin.[117]

At least in McKenney and Hall's treatment, Sequoyah's bibliography replicates in miniature two other narratives that loomed large in the early nineteenth-century mind: the improvement of the artisan through drawing, technique, and textual knowledge; and the parallel progression of humanity at large from its primitive origins to the modern day, as described by Lewis Henry Morgan and other early anthropologists. Indeed, Morgan identified the phonetic alphabet as the dividing line that separated barbarians from subsequent phases of development: "here civilization begins."[118] As might well be imagined,

Figure 2.15 Henry Inman (after Charles Bird King), *Portrait of Sequoyah*, ca. 1830. Oil on canvas. National Portrait Gallery, Smithsonian Institution, NPG.79.174.

period observers were enthralled with Sequoyah. Though some, like early eugenicist Josiah Clark Nott (a particularly vile man) concluded that his achievements must be attributable to his Caucasian blood—"mental cultivation cannot elevate an inferior to the level of a superior race"—more typical was the view of William Cooke Taylor, the British factory system promoter, who paraphrased McKenney and Hall's narrative in his book on "the origin and course of human improvement," describing Sequoyah's story as "a pleasant one" that demonstrated the capability of Native Americans to change for the better.[119] Subsequent views have been equally positive. Sequoyah's script was indeed adopted as the basis of written Cherokee, and the man himself became an icon of Cherokee culture—his name has been given to a league for Indian reform, countless baseball teams, and a particularly upright tree. In more recent years, his likeness has appeared on a stamp, and the cabin where he lived has been made a historic landmark. And in 2009, amazingly enough, a set of petroglyphs was discovered in Kentucky that he may even have carved himself, occasioning a small bout of Sequoyah-mania.[120]

As warranted as such hagiography may be, it is nonetheless the case that Sequoyah was very much an exception who proved the rule. During the mid-nineteenth century, the tide of racism against Native Americans was rising steadily, and their supposed inability to improve themselves through industry was taken as the key problem to be solved.[121] This was not a universal. In the eighteenth century, French *philosophes* had been entranced by the Indians' evident freedom, and well into the nineteenth century, writers (including Alexis de Tocqueville) continued to see them as natural aristocrats, enviably free of the trappings of bourgeois culture.[122] Missionary John Heckewelder propounded the same view in 1818.

While the Indians acknowledged the ingenuity of the whites in making things like axes, guns, kettles, and shirts, to which they themselves had become accustomed:

> "Yet," they say, "our forefathers did without all these things, and we have never heard, nor has any tradition informed us that they were at a loss for the want of them; therefore we must conclude that they also were ingenious; and, indeed, we know that they were; for they made axes of stone to cut with, and bows and arrows to kill the game: they made knives and arrows' points with sharp flint stones and bones, hoes and shovels from the shoulder blade of the elk and buffaloe; they made pots of clay, garments of skins, and ornaments with the feathers of the turkey, goose and other birds. They were not in want of anything...we had therefore everything that we could reasonably require; we lived happy!"[123]

That singularly open-minded sentiment, however, could not withstand the more prejudicial ideas associated with the civilizing process. It is important that we remember the close association between assimilation and genocide, its even uglier counterpart. Charles Dickens, not a name one normally associates with blind hatred, wrote in 1853, "I call a savage a something highly desirable to be civilised off the face of the earth ... [he is] cruel, false, thievish, murderous; addicted more or less to grease, entrails, and beastly customs; a wild animal with the questionable gift of boasting; a conceited, tiresome, bloodthirsty, monotonous humbug."[124] And a member of the London-based Anthropological Society, speaking in 1869, offered this chilling opinion about bringing technology to Native Americans: "We are disposed to consider it as extremely likely that the juxtaposition of the unquestionably artificial civilization of Europe and the uncivilized native life of savagedom ... may frighten the 'noble savage,' first out of his wits, and then out of existence altogether."[125]

In the politics of Indian reform, these malevolent strands intertwine with more charitable impulses, to the extent that it is impossible to pull them apart. And as the nineteenth century progressed, craft increasingly acted as a binding agent between the two. We saw the association between artisanal skill and self-improvement in the life of Sequoyah, and it occurs again in the figure of Richard Henry Pratt, a former coppersmith and Civil War officer (fighting on the Union side) who went on to form the Carlisle Industrial School in Pennsylvania in 1879. This was the first and most well known of several vocational schools set up for Native American children in the late nineteenth century, both in America and Canada.[126] These institutions were directly descended from the British Mechanics' Institutes I discuss in chapter three, in that they had moral uplift as their objective and looked to craft reform as the best means to achieve that end. If a large measure of class condescension was detectable in the British case, though, it is nothing compared to the jaw-dropping racism of the Indian industrial schools. In Pratt's memoirs (which he related verbally to his daughter at the end of his life), he compared the United States government's policy of separating Native Americans on reservations to the treatment African Americans had received prior to their emancipation. To him it seemed that slavery had been the more benevolent of the two systems. "The Negro," he said, "was now a citizen. The fitness for that high place he had gained by the training he was given during slavery, which made him individual, English speaking, and capable industrially. This was a lesson which in some way should be applied to the Indian."[127] In accordance with this dismaying attitude, he set up a school in which students would be acculturated through craft training. Complete with facilities for Pratt's own craft of coppersmithing, as well as shoemaking, carpentry, tinsmithing, harness making, tailoring, blacksmithing, and, for the girls—this being a strictly sexist institution as well—laundry, sewing, and cookery. There was a system of "outing" in which the Indian children, already forcibly removed from their families, would be placed with white households during the summertime. This policy Pratt described as Carlisle's "right arm...It enforced participation, the supreme Americanizer."[128] But otherwise, rather like the roughly contemporaneous Arts and Crafts colonies it eerily resembled, the Carlisle Industrial School was devoted to the principle of self-sufficiency. Students made their own uniforms, wares for cooking and eating, and furniture, as well as items for sale outside. Despite its name, the school upheld the virtues of craftsmanship rather than industry: "In all the shops as little machinery as possible is used, in order that each pupil may learn his trade in a way that will make him most skillful with his hands."[129]

In 1893, for the World's Columbian Exposition in Chicago, Pratt led a parade of students, who bore both the tools and the products of their craftsmanship aloft on long poles. It was one of numerous occasions on which he displayed his students, often having them perform craft skills such as printing, shoemaking, carpentry, wagon making, and best of all, blacksmithing, "with forge and red hot iron," as he proudly recalled, "making the sparks fly." One of his students, a Sioux boy named Luther Standing Bear, looked back on the experience with relative equanimity—"Captain Pratt was always very proud to show us off and let the white people see how we were progressing"—and indeed took up a career as a performer of his own ethnicity, joining Buffalo Bill Cody's touring Wild West show in 1898.[130] This was ironic, given that Pratt looked down on such popular entertainments as lowbrow, and yet strangely appropriate too, for Pratt was indeed making theater out of his own pedagogical approach. At the Chicago fair and other expositions of the late nineteenth and early twentieth century, craftspeople from the world over—India, Japan, and Africa, as well as Native Americans and traditional European and American craftspeople—were placed on stage, no longer kept out of sight.[131] The artisan was once again in the limelight, just as Joseph Wright of Darby had painted his blacksmiths, but with a crucial difference. For now, craft served not as a sign of present-day autonomy, but as a specimen of the past. So thoroughly explained was it that it no longer served any purpose but to demonstrate itself.

THE TASK OF RE-ENCHANTMENT

As disturbing as the "living exhibits" of the late nineteenth century may be in retrospect, the modern practice that did the most to explicate craft in this period was not live demonstration, but museum display. Like Pratt, the curators and anthropologists at institutions like the British Museum, the Smithsonian Institute, and the Musée de L'Homme had benevolent intentions. Yet in classifying handmade objects and presenting them didactically to their public, they created aesthetic regimes perfectly in harmony with the bureaucratic systems of empire.[132] They drained the life out of the objects they loved so well, positioning them firmly in a static past. A sure sign of this is the fact that curators of this generation became incensed when they detected any sign of modernity creeping into a traditional design. Smithsonian curator Otis T. Mason, for example—a man fully committed to the idea that civilization could be mapped as a steady progression "from naturalism to artificialism"—mourned the loss of "old time purity" in any Native American basket that incorporated new motifs or tools, or worse, "uncanny machinery." "It is a matter of profound regret," he wrote, "that already over much of the United States the art has degenerated, or at least has been modified. In methods, forms, and colours truly, all things have passed away, and, behold, all things have become new."[133] This lament— the cry of the antimodernist—was not new in Mason's time, but it was gaining ground. Today it has found general acceptance. So habituated are museum curators and visitors to the idea that change is "a matter of a profound regret," that they willfully blind themselves to the fact that craft has always and will always be dynamic. Adaptability, indeed, is one of the most admirable features of artisans. The desire to freeze them in place and time, to pin them down (much as Diderot did to the tools and disembodied hands in his *Encyclopedia*) so that their works can be properly explained, is quite simply a repressive instinct. Fortunately, like the other operations of modern craft I describe in this book, the deep-seated belief that museums are intrinsically about containment and didacticism, and the related conviction that craft is valuable because it preserves the past in a fixed state, are both giving way. Not coincidentally, it was specialists in African and Native American art who were among the first to embrace the idea that artifacts should not just be collected and explained, but rather should be treated as nearly living things, replete, impossible to fully explain.

Anthropologist Alfred Gell was one of the first observers to notice this potential and its consequences for postdisciplinary museum practice. He had been deeply impressed by the exhibition *Art/Artifact,* curated by Susan Vogel for the Museum for African Art in New York, and particularly her decision to display a hunting net (made by the Zande people of central Africa) tightly baled and set in the middle of a white cube gallery, looking for all the world as if it were a piece of contemporary art. Gell's response to this gesture was an article entitled "Vogel's Net: Traps as Artworks and Artworks as Traps," which argued for an ecumenical approach in which objects are shown not according to a preexisting category (fine art, craft, ethnographic material), but rather their potential to ensnare the audience in a web of interpretative implication. All objects that are "vehicles of complicated ideas," he wrote, including things like hunting nets that are ostensibly "pragmatic and technical" in nature, could be equally regarded as suitable objects for aesthetic and conceptual interpretation: "I would define as a candidate artwork any object or performance that potentially rewards such scrutiny because it embodies intentionalities that are complex, demanding of attention and perhaps difficult to reconstruct fully."[134] This idea of the difficult but entrancing object now runs rampant through museums of all kinds. The premodern cabinet of curiosities—which lacked the systematic qualities of Lever's Holophusicon and other museums of the Enlightenment and later years—has become a common point of reference for curators. Objects, especially if they are handmade, are increasingly presented in a way that emphasizes their potential to enchant.[135] This does not necessarily mean doing away with explanation entirely (though it may entail something as radical as that), but it does mean that curators are thinking about the affect of their displays on other registers. Their own craft of exhibition making is more akin to the performance of a magician than the detailed report of an anthropologist.

As the influence of cabinets of curiosity indicates, such currents in museology may be the latest thing, but they are also a return to older ways of thinking. In English, this is clear in the etymology. Our word "craft" derives from the German word *Kraft,* meaning power or potency, and its archaic bond with sorcery is preserved in terms such as "witchcraft." We also say "crafty," meaning deceptive or wily (a term often applied to Native Americans in the nineteenth century). Gell, in another important essay entitled "The Enchantment of Technology and the Technology of Enchantment," provided a persuasive theoretical account of this complex relationship between skill, potency, transfixion, and deception:

> The enchantment of technology is the power that technical processes have of casting a spell over us so that we see the real world in an enchanted form. Art, as a separate kind

Figure 2.16 "New Designs Obtruding Themselves Upon the Old in Coiled Basketry," in Otis Tufton Mason, *Indian Basketry: Studies in a Textile Art Without Machinery, vol. 1* (London: W. Heinemann, 1905). Photograph by A. C. Vroman.

of technical activity, only carries further, through a kind of involution, the enchantment which is immanent in all kinds of technical activity...It is the way an art object is construed as having come into the world which is the source of the power such objects have over us—their becoming rather than their being.[136]

Gell's account of artistic skill emphasizes the fact that it brings about an asymmetrical situation—the crafted object is inherently unreadable by those who lack the skill to make it. But this is not an absolute; in fact, it is crucial that the object be sufficiently legible that its astounding qualities of facture can be understood. Gell uses the amusing example of a trip he took to Salisbury Cathedral as a boy, which completely bored him. The visit was enlivened only by an encounter with a matchstick model of the building put on display in a side chapel: "certainly a virtuoso example of the matchstick modeller's art, if no great masterpiece according to the criteria of the salon, and calculated to strike a profound chord in the heart of any eleven-year-old."[137] At that young age, Gell had some experience of working in the limited materials of matchsticks and glue, so he was amazed by the model. The much larger and more impressive edifice in which it was housed made no impression on him, because he could not imagine himself into the position of the workers who had made it. An adult might well find enchantment in the whole of Salisbury Cathedral, shaped by long-ago hands, but this leap of imagination was impossible for the young Gell.

The lesson he draws from this modest example is that a crafted object is enchanting because we understand it in *relative* terms—relative, that is, to what we could achieve with our own hands. Craft stages an asymmetry between maker and viewer, articulated by a difference in practical knowledge. This explains why handmade objects, in general, are more likely to produce an effect of enchantment than mass-produced ones. Unless we happen to have professional expertise in plastic injection molding, electronics, and software development, for example, we have no means of understanding the creation or internal workings of a mobile phone. This has obvious drawbacks (most contemporary technology cannot be repaired by its users, for example), and it also limits our affective relations with the phone. What Oakeshott called technical knowledge may have a kind of power over us—anyone who organizes his or her life according to a mobile phone knows this—and it may even be designed to respond intimately with our bodies. But it will always lack the kind of enchantment Gell describes, in which the superior skill of another person is visibly invested into the object.

Gell's discussion of enchantment gives us the tool kit we need to undo a certain conceptual paralysis that attends modern craft. As we have seen, the late eighteenth century witnessed the onset of a powerful drive to explicate the mysteries of practical knowledge. But craft has remained stubbornly recalcitrant in the face of this effort, keeping its secrets to itself, thanks to its nondiscursive character. Often, this quality of unspokenness is simply celebrated for its own sake. The literature on craft is littered with paeans to "tacit knowledge," and the fingerprints of a maker (whether literal or figurative) are routinely fetishized as signs of genuine experience. As Danish craft theorist Louise Mazanti puts it, "the 'handmade' and the 'human imprint' are central characteristics in a search for authenticity that meets the needs of the alienated consumer in our industrial age."[138] Yet this simple juxtaposition of technical (explicit) and practical (tacit) knowledge, with the latter acting as a bulwark against the pervasive domination of the former, amounts only to a stalemate. Within the modern conception of craft, it can only ever stage a holding action. By contrast, Gell's relativist model introduces the variable of subjectivity into the situation. Nobody, not even a child, comes to a handmade object with a completely empty mind. The aesthetic experience one has in handling a work of craft is entirely dependent on prior knowledge, and—a key point—the enchantment of the object actually *increases* as one's own skill level rises. This was true for the young Gell, who had played about with matches but lacked masonry skills, and so could appreciate the cathedral model but not the cathedral itself. The same is true for a person handling a crafted ceramic bowl. If this act of appreciation is carried out in a state of complete ignorance by someone who has never touched wet clay, it will be quite a thin experience. Moderate levels of knowledge, like those of an amateur potter, will yield greater pleasure, while deep mastery (say, of a Japanese tea ceremony practitioner) will open the way to exquisitely nuanced pleasure, though an asymmetry between understanding and capability may well remain.

All along this continuum, the process of appreciation is sustained, vicarious, and haptic.[139] Our valuation of the craft objects centers on matters of touch, which we sometimes loosely describe as a form of "reading," but is in fact nonlinguistic in character. For a novice faced with a ceramic bowl, this might mean the extraordinary thinness of an expertly thrown shape; for an initiate, a glaze fired to just the right thickness; for a connoisseur, a subtle and easily overlooked pressure of a fingertip into the clay at the bowl's lip or foot. But in any case, the source of enchantment is the same—the user's ability to imaginatively approximate the knowledge of the maker. This is the same dynamic of partial revelation we have seen in nineteenth-century conceptions of magic. Anthropologist Michael Taussig has written:

> The real skill of the practitioner lies not in skilled concealment but in the skilled revelation of skilled concealment. Magic is efficacious not despite the trick but on account of its exposure.[140]

And Marina Warner puts it even more concisely: "Magical thinking involves deciphering enigmas."[141] Like these authors, Gell encourages us to experience craft not as something that can be explained, and hence explained away, through technical language, but rather as a mystery that only *increases* with practical understanding.

Putting Gell's theory into practice fully would demand nothing less than a re-enchantment of the world of craft production. Rather than treating craft as a static affair, an absolute and antimodern virtue, or conversely, as a body of knowledge that can be satisfactorily explained through language, we need to understand it as an active process of mystification. The sense of magic engendered by craft is not automatic, but rather achieved through the application of advanced skill. The more adept the maker, the more difficult it will be to follow the tracks of his or her making. This precept flies right in the face of the preference for self-evident technique prevalent in the Arts and Crafts movement and its later emanations: thick-walled pots with pronounced throwing rings; textiles with a coarse, nubbly weave; metalwork with a surface pattern achieved through innumerable hammer blows. These indexical traces of craft process were motivated by an honest desire to draw attention to the qualities of the handmade. Yet in retrospect, such self-explicating objects seem entirely in tune with the modern imperative for craft to operate in the open, making itself immediately available to external understanding. Indeed, there is an obvious correlation between the overstated workmanship of the Arts and Craft movement and the preference for evident manufacture one finds in modernist design and architecture.

Though clothed in the language of transparency, clarity, and directness (principles that were, again, no doubt strongly felt by the people involved), the modern taste for undisguised construction was also a power play. It left to craft only the job of mechanical execution that declared itself as such. Which is more difficult to make: the "Star of Brunswick" table, made by an upholsterer and carver named Henry Eyles for display at the Great Exhibition, the internal structure of which is deftly hidden with a heavy load of carved historicist ornament? Or a Gustav Stickley table made of squared, undecorated oak timber, held together with simple wedged through-tenons? The answer is all too obvious. The fact that late nineteenth-century craft reformers disdained the expertly crafted table and championed the barebones one, or indeed the fact that Stickley's rough and ready table still

Figure 2.17   Henry Eyles, the Star of Brunswick table. Carved walnut with pollard oak inlay and Chamberlain & Co. porcelain plaque. V&A: W.40–1952. © Victoria and Albert Museum, London.

Figure 2.18　Gustav Stickley for Craftsman Workshops, library table, 1906. Oak, leather. Metropolitan Museum of Art 1976.389.1.

speaks to us more loudly of craft aesthetics today than the "Star of Brunswick" does, even though the latter required much more skill to make, amply demonstrates the modern antipathy to the mysteries of making. If we want to undo this prejudice, with the objective of re-enchanting the world of craft, then the first step is to reevaluate the deceptive elements within skill, as well as its powers of revelation.

THE NEW ARCANISTS

Put this way, the task of re-enchantment sounds almost straightforward—it might be simply a matter of returning to traditional ways of making and letting them rip, encouraging astounding feats of craftsmanship that will dazzle us with skillful artifice. But it's not quite that simple. Many questions arise from any configuration of authorship and skill. As we saw in chapter one, some of these questions are political in nature. Even in the relatively marginal spheres of art and design, to say nothing of the massive production systems of global industry, craft is tightly bound up with power structures. Indeed, craft's magical properties are already embraced wholeheartedly by the luxury trades, which tend to be disguised behind a glossy veil of promotion and distortion. As attractive as these structures may be on the surface, they lend themselves all too easily to exploitation of various kinds, and tend to be carried out in a spirit of blithe self-promotion completely detached from critical engagement. There are other, less obviously vexed issues to consider too, of which the most pressing is that of technology. This chapter has been mainly concerned with the relations between information and physical form, and the way narratives of making are constructed through moments of concealment and revelation. Today, because of digital structures of knowledge making and sharing, this dynamic is more powerful than ever. On one hand, it is easy to think that we have reached and far surpassed the saturation point when it comes to information. The days when artisanal knowledge was consistently secreted could not seem more distant, given the range of technical and descriptive explanation available on any Web browser at a moment's notice. On the other hand, intellectual property is among the new millennium's most contentious topics of debate and competition. The very idea that knowledge can be owned has been persuasively attacked by such authors as Lawrence Lessig.[142] He has adopted the principle of "copy-left" (as opposed to copyright), which seeks to creatively put knowledge into the hands of people who can use it, rather than walling it off as a form of intangible capital. In some ways, ironically, Lessig's writings are descended from the improvement rhetoric of the nineteenth century. Like a latter-day Charles Babbage or Thomas Edison, he holds that the more generally available knowledge is, the better off everyone will be. The big difference, of course, is that the tools Babbage and Edison depended on to derive profit from their inventions (notably patents) seem completely inadequate to the reality of a twenty-first century economy, in which illicit duplication of products is rapidly becoming the norm rather than the exception. We now live in a culture in which unauthorized copies—both material and immaterial, knockoffs and downloads—are pervasive.[143] No wonder governmental and corporate power structures have become obsessed with means of ensuring secrecy, from digital encryption to legal action.

What role can craft play against this complex and contested backdrop? Very little, one might reasonably think. In comparison to a pharmaceutical researcher in a well-financed laboratory, an architectural engineer armed with the latest digital tools, or a military supplier capable of turning out fearsome laser-guided weapons of mass destruction, the capabilities of one individual, no matter how skilled, might seem very limited. But as Gell reminds us, craft is the origin and ultimate signifier of material potency. That pharmaceutical lab, that engineer's office, that weapons factory—all would grind to a halt without the skills of experimental technicians, model makers and prototypers. We need to insist on the fact that these workers are artisans. Craft exists within even the most high-tech situations. Just as important, we should consider craft-based knowledge as an alternative to the intractable binaries imposed by the concept of intellectual property. As Gell also says, craft is unusual in that it can be both open to view and secret, all at once. It can be placed right before your eyes, as in the context of live demonstration, without fully unveiling itself. Craft infuses the material world with enchantment not by revealing knowledge, nor by concealing it, but rather by rendering knowledge into material form, thus producing a moment of wonder.

Whatever may be said for or against intellectual property, it is not active and imaginative in this way. Instead, as Lessig argues, it is prescriptive. Exercising property rights over knowledge is a fundamentally constraining act. While it may help to motivate innovation and creativity by securing profits, in the end it "works" precisely by prohibiting work, by limiting innovation and creativity. Intellectual property operates by preventing others from integrating knowledge into their lives. You cannot subject craft to this logic. It secures value not through legislation or regulation, but through the more direct means of its own physical difficulty. Skill cannot be owned as such, but neither is it for the taking. This frictional quality sets the handmade object apart from a world in which information and importance are too often conflated. Craft slows down the movement of knowledge and embeds it in a matrix of the mysterious.

Perhaps this is why it feels so vital now. In a climate that suffers from a profusion of information, far more than the Victorian era, knowledge is available instantaneously and transparently. In fact, the information that passes through our lives is often less important than the manner of its passage. But a craft process is neither a black-box technology, impenetrable to understanding, nor can it be easily replicated. It is not quite obscure and not quite self-evident. Rather than policing the realm of knowledge, like intellectual property law, craft shapes and stages knowledge through its power of enchantment. So craft is regaining its old magic. This is especially evident in practices that involve the intensive investigation of materials. At its most ambitious, this sort of making recalls the premodern alchemist's quest for transmutation, a return to the *arcane,* a term that suggests both complexity and secretiveness. To suggest that contemporary making should orient itself to such a discredited intellectual tradition may seem perverse, but recall the work of historians of science like Pamela Smith, who argues that the alchemists laid down the experimental basis for modern science by developing an extensive repertoire of laboratory techniques. From this perspective, alchemy stands in historical relation to scientific method much as craft continues to stand in relation to technology: it is the oft-maligned but crucially necessary basis on which innovations occur. The arcanist operates in an imaginative register, working on what might be rather than exploiting what already exists.

You can find examples of this sort of materials-based thinking all over art and design practice. Intriguingly, some of them revisit the "plastic" materials of the nineteenth century and subject them to emphatically craft-intensive processes: Joris Laarman's scrolling *Heatwave* radiator, the product of a material experimentation that led the designer to replace the standard cast iron with fiber-reinforced concrete (Plate 8); Tomáš Libertiny's vases in paper and glue, in which the papier-mâché process is slowed down to a crawl, as hundreds of sheet of patterned paper are carefully glued into stacks before being turned on a lathe; or Hella Jongerius's research with chicle, a rubber-like material harvested in Mexican rainforests (Plate 9).[144] These projects reclaim the properties of infinite form that were so striking to Victorian observers of cast iron, papier-mâché, and rubber, but return them to the human scale of artisanal practice. Not coincidentally, all three also adopt stylistic cues of the eighteenth century—rococo flourishes, classical vase forms, and Delft blue and white. This matter of stylistic historicism suggests how powerfully premodern craft serves as inspiration for contemporary designers. Those long-ago, now thoroughly arcane practices continue to inspire wonder—the puzzling but stimulating amazement that Gell sees as the archetypal response to craftsmanship.

Makers who operate in this hermetic manner are hard to categorize. Are they artists? Scientists? Designers? Artisans? No: they are truly postdisciplinary. They not only combine known methods, but dedicate themselves to inventing entirely new ways of making. The arcanist's indifference to existing categories is matched only by a commitment to achieving a wondrous result. I'll give just three further examples here, selected to indicate the aesthetic range the arcane might take today. First is Zoe Laughlin, who, along with Mark Miodnowik, Martin Conreen, and other colleagues at Kings College, London, has founded the Institute of Making. Some four decades ago, materials scientist James Edward Gordon predicted that changes in his field would lead inevitably back to artisanal values:

> it now seems very possible that the coming new engineering materials will resemble much improved versions of wood and bone more closely than they will the metals with which most contemporary engineers are familiar. This does not mean that we shall go back to a William Morris world of woodcarvers and village carpenters...Although the new techniques will be very sophisticated in many ways perhaps we may be able to get back to the patient humility of the craftsman in the face of his material which has got lost somewhere in our arrogant factories.[145]

That promise is being realized today at the Institute of Making. It is not quite a science museum (though it has a collection of materials at its heart), nor a laboratory (for its equipage is slight), nor an artist's studio (Laughlin makes no "work" in a conventional sense). It is more like a twenty-first-century cabinet of curiosities—a flexible space for investigations into wondrous materials, both old and new. When you visit, Laughlin will immediately put something into your hands: a thread that feels for all the world like cotton, but responds to a small magnet by leaping through the air—the thread is actually made of superfine strands of steel. Or a little block that can be felt, but is barely visible to the eye (and that only because it has been handled by other people before you, whose hands deposited oil on its surface). This is Aerogel, a silica foam invented by NASA that is 98.8 percent air and only 0.2 percent matter, the lightest solid material on earth. It is ever so slightly blue, Laughlin says, "for the same reason that the sky is blue."[146] Or a short, stubby ingot of standard issue tin, which crackles audibly as you bend it in your hands (until it warms up thanks to your body heat, changing its ductility). Next, Laughlin might direct your attention to a row of cubes on a nearby shelf: metals, woods, foams, wax. They are identical in dimension, except for one made of white chocolate, which was nibbled by a mouse who broke into the Institute. It went for the edges only, the "mechanical weak points" of the cube, and left to its own devices would have eventually turned the block into a sphere. The mouse is an intuitive "materials interrogator," as Laughlin says, and so is she. Despite their similarity, these "swatches" of material (as she calls them) had to be made in a whole variety of processes. The wood was cut, the metals cast, the wax deposited in thin layers. The serial forms may resemble minimalist sculptures, but they are actually self-demonstrative, somewhat like the rubber plaque Charles Goodyear showed at the Great Exhibition—except that they are anything but explicit. Rather than explicating the logic behind their making and use, these sets of cubes offer intrigue, a suggestive palette of tactile and visual characteristics put to no particular purpose.

Laughlin summarizes her interest as "the performativity of matter," a principle she demonstrates not only through the "material encounters" that happen within the Institute's Materials Library, but also in a series of lectures she gives, and indeed in her tactics of making. Her preferred technique is that used in the cubes—rendering a single form in many substances, so as to underline the specific qualities of each material. As she puts it, this permits her audience to "recognize the multifaceted nature of materials and understand that which is, and is not, represented by the form and its relationship to materials properties."[147] She has serially produced not only cubes, but also tuning forks, bugles, and bells, demonstrating variation in auditory quality among different metals, as well as woods and plastics. A set of spoons similarly demonstrates variation in the taste of these non-food materials. In many respects, Laughlin operates in the opposite manner to a nineteenth-century improver. She has no defined objective in sight. Though she knows plenty about mechanical and chemical engineering, she is not that interested in explanations. Rather, she wants to incite a moment of curiosity, a moment of cognitive dissonance that reminds one immediately of Gell's conception of enchantment: "I think there's wonder in transformation, when the material's performed for you." While the manufacturers of objects in cast iron, papier-mâché, and rubber showed how one material could be made to assume any form they liked, Laughlin chooses one form and renders it in many materials. If Wilkinson, Bielefeld, and Goodyear thought of their materials as frictionless, in some sense without any content beyond the intention to which they were subjected, then Laughlin operates in a world of willful materials, and she delights in interacting with their most nuanced traits. That makes her sound like an artisan, and that is a final big difference between her and the Victorian improvers. Laughlin considers craft absolutely central to her practice, no less (though also no more) important than other methods of working. As she puts it, "it's all about knowing stuff in as many ways as possible."

The series of bells she made amply demonstrate this principle. There were at one time five in all, which (probably coincidentally) traverse the whole range of productive styles one finds in fine art, from appropriation to direct making to strategic outsourcing. Two are found objects: a bronze bell issued to her grandfather during World War II when he was a volunteer Air Raid Patrol warden, and a virtually identical brass school bell. She cast a version in lead, based on a lathe-turned wooden model. She commissioned Raymond Tribe, the technical director at a chemical glass fabricator, to create a hand blown and lamp worked copy of the bell. And finally, she worked with a professor of chemistry at the University of London to realize a bell in frozen mercury. This last one, which Laughlin describes as "an object for the imagination" given the impossibility of using it for any practical purpose, is sadly no longer extant.[148] (As anyone who has broken a thermometer knows, mercury is a liquid at room temperature—though an unusual one, in that it's not wet—and indeed at any temperature above $-38.83°$ Celsius, and there was a problem with

Figure 2.19   Zoe Laughlin, bells in bronze (a), brass (b), lead (c) and glass (d), 2009.

the freezer where the object was kept.) You can still try ringing four identically shaped bells in four different materials, though, feeling their weights, hearing their different sounds—the alarming clang of bronze, the sweeter, clearer tone of brass, the high ping of glass, the dull thud of lead. As Laughlin notes, this range might remind us of bells we hear in our everyday experience, without realizing we are hearing the music of materials: "from the deep authoritative tolling of Big Ben to the polite but firm tinkle of the passing cyclist."[149] And you don't need a PhD from a mechanical engineering program (which is what Laughlin got for her experiments) to feel, in your ears and hands, the marvelous material complexities that lead to these variations. For this contemporary arcanist, craft is a means rather than an end. But you'll never find someone who values the multifarious possibilities of making more than Laughlin. "When you encounter someone with a skill and see the processes of making performed," she says, "it allows you to imagine completely new objects."

At the other end of the aesthetic spectrum, we find Zoe Sheehan Saldaña, who also conducts materials-based collaborative research, but is as deadpan as Laughlin is performative. Sheehan is a political artist first and foremost. Through her practice she seeks to gain an understanding of the large-scale productive systems that condition our lives, whose inner workings are usually veiled by layer upon layer of technology. Her method is simple to describe, though extremely difficult to actually execute: she selects an everyday commodity and then retro-engineers it, making a functional equivalent. In this process, she relies entirely upon her own personal resources, though she does often confer with chemical engineers and other specialists to help her along. Among her projects so far are a friction match (entitled *Strike Anywhere*), bottles of hand sanitizer, a blaze orange life jacket, and a bottle of lamp black. None of these choices are innocent. *Strike Anywhere*, for example, refers both in its title and its materiality to the tradition of labor activism. Like Adam Smith's pins, matches are nearly valueless individually; they are always made and sold en masse. For this reason it was highly desirable that their production be mechanized. As a children's book with short lessons about different types of manufacturing noted in 1916, "it seems like a very simple matter to cut a splinter of wood, dip it into some chemicals, and pack it into a box for sale; and it would be simple if it were all done by hand, but the matches would also be irregular and extremely expensive. The way to make anything cheap and uniform is to manufacture it by machinery."[150] But this was difficult to achieve in practice, and only a few decades before matches had indeed been made by hand, in sweatshop conditions made horrendous because of the poisonous phosphorous involved in the manufacturing process. The poverty-stricken "little match girl" was a stock sentimental figure for the Victorians, at least until an industrial action in 1888, at which point she became a feminist icon in the history of labor unrest.[151]

Sheehan's handmade matches call this long-ago episode to mind, and because of their own potential to burst into flame at any moment, suggest an ongoing possibility for the revival of such activism. All of her projects offer the possibility for interpretation along similar lines. The bottles of self-brewed sanitizer speak to contemporary concern (not to say paranoia) about the spread of communicable disease, and a more general sense of alarm

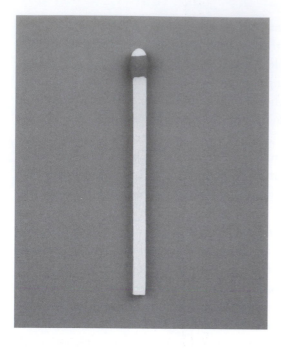

Figure 2.20   Zoe Sheehan Saldaña, *Strike Anywhere,* 2007–2008. Aspen wood, wax, gelatin, pigment, ground glass, chemicals. Created in collaboration with Dr. Glen Kowach, Chemistry Department, CUNY/City College.

about security issues. The life jacket seems an equally appropriate icon for a culture perpetually on "orange alert" against terrorism and other threats. The lamp black, traditionally a primary ingredient in ink making, is a carbon residue and so clearly suggests pollution; the modern use of the material in fabricating automotive tires only underlines this association. Like Laughlin (but in a different way) she positions herself as the opposite of an improver: she is a specialist in making things *less* efficiently. Nor is she interested in didacticism. Even the points of reference I have just named—labor politics, environmentalism, and so forth—are not warranted by the artist, strictly speaking.[152] Her works are allusive rather than informative, and the symbolic function of each work is far outweighed by the time, effort, and knowledge that went into making it.

Alongside her exhibitable works, Sheehan conducts a parallel project she calls "shop-dropping," in which she buys a garment from a big-box store, takes it home, and replicates it by hand.[153] She then "returns" her crafted copy to the retailer, introducing it as an alien agent into the commodity chain. Her carefully made replicas, resold to unsuspecting consumers at Wal-Mart for less than ten dollars apiece, are at once gifts to their unwitting recipients and tacit rebukes to a system in which Sheehan's own artistic labor is held to be many times the value of an anonymous garment industry worker's. Similarly, she donated her handmade bottles of sanitizer to a charitable organization that distributes goods to American soldiers serving in Afghanistan and Iraq—another instance in which critique and generosity are bound up with one another. All of her undertakings share a similarly arcane intent. By intermixing elements of revelation and deception within her practice—up to several years' worth of research and development, and many hours of skilled labor, all leading to objects that masquerade as standard-issue commodities—Sheehan creates a little eddy, a pause, or perhaps even a rupture, in the ceaseless flow of manufactured commodities. Nothing is really clarified through this undertaking. On the contrary, she encourages us to consider just how obscure the seemingly transparent sphere of contemporary production really is, and shows that penetrating it to any depth at all requires all the craft skill one can muster.

Laughlin and Sheehan's relationships to materials are marked by intensive focus, in which the process of research is so protracted that it accumulates meaning in its own right. This is one way that the artisanal values of alchemy can be reinvented for the present, but by no means the only one. Breadth is just as viable an option as depth. My final example of a "new arcanist," Ryan Gander, could be seen as the living embodiment of this fact. Though it is possible to encounter one of Gander's devious, clever works in isolation—in a museum group show, an international fair, a public space, or wherever art tends to congregate these days—it has been truly written of him that "seeing just one or two of [his works] does not do justice to the diversity of his oeuvre."[154] His studio is literally wallpapered with ideas for the future, and a recent publication on the artist lists hundreds and hundreds of works already realized: five nonfunctional television monitors, one hung at eye level and four somewhat higher (*Monitor*, 2001); a chaotic reconstruction of a Gerrit Rietveld chair, executed "in consultation" with an eleven-year-old girl named Grace, which is placed into sculptural dialogue with a sealed bag full of randomly purchased paperback books (*Rietveld Construction—Grace*, 2006); a tumble of inked blocks that can be used to print an alphabet invented by Gander (*The New New Alphabet*, 2008); a pile of brass chimes which, if hung in the proper order and played, will sound the tune of a standard-issue Nokia phone ringtone (2008; the title in this case consists of musical notation); and my personal favorite, *Linus Van Pelt and a World of Endeavour, Ambition and Optimism* (2008). The catalogue description of this work reads:

> A baby blue crocheted blanket with a blue silk edging hangs on a wall-mounted coat hook above a brown grocery bag which has been rolled closed and left on the floor. Around the entire exhibition space runs a waist high horizontal line made up of every shape of the mouth of the cartoon character Linus Van Pelt in sequential order, made during his high school president election speech, from the episode of *Peanuts* entitled *You're Not Elected* (1969).[155]

An erratum page mock-apologizes for the omission of a further hundred-odd works from the book, and even the punning title of the publication, *Ryan Gander: Catalogue Raisonnable*, with its pointed addendum—*Vol. 1*—promises endless wonders to come.

This profusion is not just meant to demonstrate the extent of Gander's creative energies; it is also a method of evading the conventional means by which art might be judged. There is no signature style here, certainly; nor is there ever a takeaway message, or even an element of clear expressive content. In each work, we are given ample evidence of an imaginative chain of associations, initiated by the artist, but no clear indication as to how we should respond. At best the viewers might continue the process, perhaps by conducting extensive research into the same topics that inspired Gander in the first place, or perhaps they will simply experience a pleasurable, stimulating and very particular kind of bemusement. In a recent interview with the artist, curator Christophe Gallois associated the desire to produce "effects" rather than definite meanings with the concept of alchemy, which he sees as "an alternative to the production of discursive meanings." Gander concurs: "There's nothing like a surprise, right? Not knowing, and desperately attempting to decipher a work, is the pinnacle for me."[156]

A series of related works called the *Alchemy Boxes* operates on this principle, even exaggerates it. In each case, a "vessel" of some kind is used to contain a large collection of disparate "ingredients," which are listed on a label nearby. (Actually, we have no proof of this claim; to find out what is inside we would need to break into the work, destroying it.) As usual with Gander the "ingredients" are diverse, initially bewilderingly so. *Alchemy Box No. 13 (Describe the Effect of Watching),* for example, includes thirty-two ounces of polypellets for stuffing soft toys, an unscratched lottery card that might be worth up to £10,000, a Christmas cracker with a joke inside, a black rubdown transfer of seven phases of the moon, and many other objects.[157] Upon reflection one might conclude that there is a theme here, perhaps one teasingly suggested by the title—something about containment and suspense? Yet any attempt at interpretation will inevitably feel like a personal choice rather than a discovery. The openness of the work is also conveyed by the forms of the "vessels" Gander uses, which are again extremely varied, though he says that all of them are "things you would expect to find in a gallery."[158] *Alchemy Box no. 3* (2008), actually the second one he made (more subterfuge), is subtitled *She Spoke in Images like some New Language* and assumes the form of a Donald Judd-like wall sculpture, which Gander adopted as a neutral guise for his inquiry into trust and secrecy. It is an object that looks like art, a cartoonist's denotation of a sculpture. In other cases he has occupied plinths for other artists' work as "vessels," or even things that don't look like containers at all, like a pile of art magazines or notebooks, or a fire extinguisher.

In the case of *Having Done More Work (Alchemy Box No. 11),* he retained a neighborhood master artisan named Pedro da Costa Felgueiras to make a beautifully fabricated mahogany box with an inset leather writing surface. Gander's decision to turn to a cabinetmaker, within a series of otherwise non-artisanal sculptures, is typical of his attitude to other people's skills. Though he acts the part of a sorcerer, forever conjuring new forms and ideas, he is also quite capable of taking on the role of an enthusiastic apprentice, deriving both knowledge and enjoyment from the specialists who make his works. (As he says of Felguerias's workshop, "You have to see it—the amount of powders and concoctions he has—talk about alchemy!") Gander sometimes produces such knowledge for himself, conducting what he calls "investigations—works that don't have the depth of meaning of the other works, but are about trying to understand what a making device is. They're exercises in learning about something, like refraction in a prism, or blowing eggs." So Gander is a perpetual student of process. Despite his frantic authoring of things of all kinds, he has a

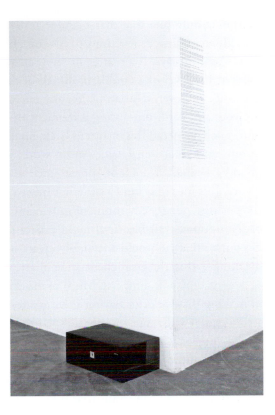

Figure 2.21   Ryan Gander, *Having done more work than most ten men (Alchemy box # 11)*, 2009. © Ryan Gander, Courtesy the artist and GB Agency. Image Aurelien Mole.

very fluid relationship with authorship itself. Each of Gander's ideas is materialized through a bespoke production process, which involves turning over the making to someone else.

Given the diversity of his output, the process of making the work is rarely repeated exactly. To realize one body of work, he asked a range of professional designers to create graphics for fictitious bands, films, a circus, and a video game; in other cases he has turned to skilled metal or plastic fabricators.[159] At all times, he relies on a project management team of three studio assistants, who in turn manage this constantly shifting galaxy of producers. Though Gander is the idea generator, and describes each work in detail to his assistants at the beginning of the process, he relies on them completely to get the work made. And if some artists are coy about their use of outsourced labor and skills, Gander is at the opposite extreme. He has documented many of the processes by which the artworks that bear his name came into being—even to the extent of reprinting e-mail exchanges. He is also interested in the reception of his work as a form of subsequent cultural production, republishing criticism of his work, both good and bad. An example of the latter, included in *Catalogue Raisonnable*, reads: "One of the striking things about his cleverish yet characterless conceptualism is that he conveniently makes things for, and about, art fairs…I think Gander has subsumed his artistic personality into a vast act of networking. 'Ironic' networking, of course."[160] He does not so much seek to defeat such potential criticism as absorb it into an ever-expanding discursive terrain that he claims through and around the work.

This is only one way that Gander anticipates an audience's reactions to his art, and indeed, an audience's reactions to his reactions to an audience's reactions. Conceptual art these days, he says, is a matter of "how many layers you can think," a game that already starts at the level of a double bluff. All of this, no doubt, sounds like it can be quite exhausting, and even infuriating. Yet any one of Gander's works has a good chance of catching you off guard, prompting a moment of puzzlement, intrigue, hilarity, or even—why not?—enchantment. This brings us back, finally, to the question of craft. He does not by any means espouse artisanal values in his work; yet he still finds a place for them, appropriating others' skills "as I might appropriate theatre or literature, or like a painter would use a color." This idea of craft as a swatch, ready to be put to purpose, is of course consistent with the postdisciplinary environment in which Gander thrives. It is no more, or less, than one of the options available. You might expect that by creating so much work, and so much discourse, that he would inevitably create a relativistic flux. If each move only takes its meaning within the great chess game of art, then what difference can craft make?

A great deal, as it turns out. Much of the effect of Gander's work resides in the care he takes in making his works, or having them made. That may seem an odd claim to make about a conceptual artist, but for what it's worth the artist agrees: "The production value of the work, whether it's a low value or a high value, is 90% of the work. It determines the ownership and authorship of the work." It is in the process of materialization that an artwork, like any artificial object, acquires its meaning: "you can tell more about something from the way it's made than from what it is." The cheapness or refinement of a making process (injection molding, goldsmithing) locates the value of the resulting object (a plastic cup, a bejeweled goblet) much more specifically than its function (drinking). And despite his lightness of touch, Gander relies constantly on these concrete details of production. As his *Alchemy Boxes* attests, he is always interested in this making as a form of concealment, a way to fashion a mystery. By putting an inexplicable object into the viewer's way, he invites open-ended speculation, rather than a singular moment of clarity. You can't determine the quality of a work, he says, by how long you're inclined to stand in front of it. "That's a stupid measurement. It's whether you are still thinking of it three weeks later … how many times you return to it." So for all of the talk surrounding his work, by himself and others, Gander is not interested in explanations. Like any good artist—or alchemist, magician, or artisan—he knows that when there is no secret, there's really nothing worth keeping.

NOTES

1. "A Fool's Mate," *Pearson's Monthly Magazine* (1893): 317–322.
2. On the chess-playing automaton, see Tom Standage, *The Turk: The Life and Times of the Famous Eighteenth-Century Chess-Playing Machine* (New York: Walker, 2002); and Simon Schaffer, "Enlightened Automata," in *The Sciences in Enlightened Europe*, ed. William Clark, Jan Golinski, and Simon Schaffer (Chicago: The University of Chicago Press, 1999).
3. "King of the Conjurors," *Harper's Magazine* 55 (1877): 817–31: 823.

4. E.T.A. Hoffman, "Die Automate" (1814), first published in Hoffmann, Serapions-Brüder vol. 2 (1819).

5. "King of the Conjurors," p. 824.

6. This particular example from 1830, a two-volume encyclopedia over 800 pages in length, was published by Edward James Wilson in Newcastle upon Tyne.

7. Walter Benjamin, "On the Concept of History" (1940), in *Selected Writings, Vol. 4: 1938–1940* (Cambridge: Harvard University Press, 2003). Benjamin famously used the automaton as a metaphor for a materialist account of history in which the economy seems to drive events but is actually the mere tool of a guiding transcendental spirit: "The puppet called 'historical materialism' is always supposed to win. It can do this with no further ado against any opponent, so long as it employs the services of theology, which as everyone knows is small and ugly and must be kept out of sight."

8. "The Irish Industrial Exhibition," *The Illustrated Magazine of Art* 2/9 (1853): 135–143; 135.

9. Perth Granton, "A Chapter on Wonders," *Continental Monthly* 3/4 (Apr. 1863): 461–464; 462, 463.

10. C. P. Cranch, "Seven Wonders of the World," *Atlantic Monthly* 43/259 (1879): 616–619; 618.

11. *The Book of Trades, or, Circle of the Useful Arts* (Glasgow: Richard Griffin, 1835), pp. 1, 2.

12. Ursula Klein and E. C. Spary, "Introduction: Why Materials?" in *Materials and Expertise in Early Modern Europe,* ed. Ursula Klein and E. C. Spary (Chicago: University of Chicago Press, 2010), pp. 9–10.

13. Stephan Epstein, "Transferring Technical Knowledge and Innovating in Europe, 1200–1800," paper presented at the Economic History Seminar, Department of Economics, Tokyo, December 18, 2006, p. 2.

14. On coffeehouses and the exchange of technical knowledge, see Rob Iliffe, "Material Doubts: Hooke, Artisan Culture and the Exchange of Information in 1670s," *The British Journal for the History of Science* 28/3 (Sept. 1995): 285–318.

15. Pamela H. Smith, *The Business of Alchemy: Science and Culture in the Holy Roman Empire* (Princeton, NJ: Princeton University Press, 1994), p. 4. See also Pamela H. Smith, "Vermilion, Mercury, Blood and Lizards: Matter and Meaning in Metalworking," in *Materials and Expertise in Early Modern Europe,* ed. Ursula Klein and E. C. Spary (op cit.); William R. Newman and Lawrence M. Principe, *Alchemy Tried in the Fire: Starkey, Boyle, and the Fate of Helmontian Chemistry* (Chicago: University of Chicago Press, 2002); William Eamon, *Science and the Secrets of Nature: Books of Secrets in Medieval and Early Modern Culture* (Princeton, NJ: Princeton University Press, 1994); and, well ahead of this recent scholarly turn, Arthur Clegg, "Craftsmen and the Origin of Science," *Science and Society* 43 (1979): 186–201.

16. Lorraine Daston and Katherine Park, *Wonders and the Order of Nature 1150–1750* (New York: Zone Book, 1998), pp. 277–280.

17. Richard Stott, "Artisans and Capitalist Development," *Journal of the Early Republic* 16/2 (Summer 1996): 257–271; 261.

18. Quoted in Peter Burke and Asa Briggs, *A Social History of the Media: From Gutenberg to the Internet* (Cambridge, UK: Polity Press, 2009), p. 91.

19. See Luca Mola, "States and Crafts: Relocating Technical Skills in Renaissance Italy," in *The Material Renaissance*, ed. Evelyn Welch and Michelle O'Malley (Manchester: Manchester University Press, 2007).

20. Christine MacLeod, *Inventing the Industrial Revolution: The English Patent System 1660–1800* (Cambridge: Cambridge University Press, 1988), p. 49. See also Harold Irvin Dutton, *The Patent System and Inventive Activity during the Industrial Revolution 1750–1852* (Manchester: Manchester University Press, 1984).

21. Moureen Coulter, *Property in Ideas: The Patent Question in Mid-Victorian Britain* (Kirksville, MO: Thomas Jefferson University Press, 1991), p. 62.

22. Stephan Epstein usefully distinguishes between modern scientific knowledge and the artisanal knowledge it sought to codify: "scientists' main epistemological objective is to identify and codify regularities, for codification is essential both to communicate, convince, and establish credentials, and to establish a shared base for further advance. Technicians, by contrast, identify and codify regularities only as a means to an end, the end being to make things work reliably and well...They do not avoid codification in principle, but they generate it less systematically than scientists and they do so largely in interaction with, rather than independently of, the production process itself." Epstein, "Transferring Technical Knowledge," p. 3. See also Pamela O. Long, *Openness, Secrecy, Authorship: Technical Arts and the Culture of Knowledge from Antiquity to the Renaissance* (Baltimore, MD: Johns Hopkins University Press, 2001).

23. Michael Oakeshott, "Rationalism in Politics," in *Rationalism in Politics and Other Essays* (London: Methuen and Co., 1962), pp. 10–11. My thanks to Tanya Harrod for this reference.

24. Oakeshott, "Rationalism in Politics," p. 11.

25. In the history of British science, Bacon was indeed the crucial figure in the erection of a rationalist scientific program; already at the beginning of the seventeenth century he was decrying "the vain and abusing promises of Alchemists and Magicians, and such like light, idle, ignorant, credulous, and fantastical wits and sects." *Valerius Terminus*, 1603; quoted in Peter Harrison, "Curiosity, Forbidden Knowledge, and the Reformation of Natural Philosophy in Early Modern England," *Isis* 92: 2 (June 2001): 265–290; 275. This anti-alchemical attitude was slow to gain ground, though, and only in the eighteenth century did a "scientific method" inspired partly by Bacon become general practice. For a helpful introduction, see Lawrence H. Principe and William R. Newman, "Some Problems with the Historiography of Alchemy," in *Secrets of Nature: Astrology and Alchemy in Early Modern Europe*, ed. William R. Newman and Anthony Grafton (Cambridge, MA: MIT Press, 2001).

26. Andrew Ure, *The Philosophy of Manufactures, or, An Exposition of the Scientific, Moral, and Commercial Economy of the Factory System of Great Britain* (London: Charles Knight, 1835). For an example of Marx's critique, see *Capital*, 1.15, excerpted in Glenn Adamson, *The Craft Reader* (Oxford: Berg Publishers, 2010).

27. Ure, *The Philosophy of Manufactures*, p. x.

28. Andrew Ure, *A Dictionary of Arts, Manufactures, and Mines, Containing a Clear Exposition of their Principles and Practice* (London: Longman, Orme, Brown, Green and Longmans, 1839), p. iv.

29. Oakeshott, "Rationalism in Politics," pp. 22–23.

30. David Spadafora notes that while Diderot had distinguished between art and science, the former involving action and the latter reflection, late eighteenth-century writers tended to view the two in concert, with art an application of scientific principles. It would take some decades, however, for "practical skills and techniques" to be separated out from the "arts and sciences" as a general category. Spadafora, *The Idea of Progress in Eighteenth-Century Britain* (New Haven, CT: Yale University Press, 1990), pp. 30–31, 34.

31. George Wilson, *What is Technology? An Inaugural Lecture* (Edinburgh: Sutherland and Knox, 1855), pp. 3, 8. A sort of Scottish analogue to Henry Cole at South Kensington, Wilson was the animating spirit behind the Royal Museum in Edinburgh—forerunner to today's National Museum of Scotland. My thanks to Henrietta Lidchi for this reference.

32. Quoted in Edmund de Waal, *Twentieth-Century Ceramics* (London: Thames and Hudson, 2003), p. 12.

33. On Meissen's early production, see Ingelore Menzhausen, *Early Meissen Porcelain in Dresden* (London: Thames and Hudson, 1988).

34. "The Travels of Jonas Hanway, through Russia into Persia," in *The World Displayed, or, a Curious Collection of Voyages and Travels, Selected from the Writers of All Nations* (London: T. Carnan and F. Newberry, 1759–1761), p. 49.

35. Hilary Young, *English Porcelain, 1745–95: Its Makers, Design, Marketing and Consumption* (London: Victoria and Albert Publications, 1999), p. 46.

36. Frye's patent is transcribed in Elizabeth Adams and David Redstone, *Bow Porcelain* (London: Faber and Faber, 1981), p. 70.

37. George Savage first noted the indirection concerning bone ash in the patent in his *18th-Century English Porcelain* (London: Spring Books, 1952), p. 125.

38. This and other quotes from Bonnin and Morris are taken from Graham Hood, "Bonnin and Morris of Philadelphia" (1972), reprinted in *Ceramics in America 2007,* ed. Robert Hunter (Milwaukee, WI: Chipstone Foundation, 2007). Material in this section is based on my own essay "The American Arcanum: Porcelain and the Alchemical Tradition," which appeared in the same volume; it was republished with some additional material as "Rethinking the Arcanum: Porcelain, Secrecy, and the Eighteenth-Century Culture of Invention," in *The Cultural Aesthetics of Eighteenth-Century Porcelain,* eds. Alden Cavanaugh and Michael Yonan, (Burlington, VT: Ashgate, 2010).

39. Young, *English Porcelain 1745–95,* p. 35.

40. Untitled essay, *The Pennsylvania Gazette* (August 1, 1771).

41. Thomas P. Smith, *A Sketch of the Revolutions in Chemistry* (Philadelphia, 1798), pp. 12, 13, 16, 24, 30, 35. See also Edgar F. Smith, *Chemistry in America: Chapters from the History of the Science in the United States* (New York: D. Appleton and Co., 1914).

42. For another attack on alchemy, see the first ever chemical dictionary, written by Pierre Joseph Macquer, the superintendent of the Sèvres porcelain factory, and translated by James Keir, a close associate of Josiah Wedgwood. Pierre Joseph Macquer, *A Dictionary of Chemistry: Containing the Theory and Practice of That Science,* trans. by James Keir (London: T. Cadell and P. Elmsly, 1777), pp. iv–xii. See also Wilda Anderson, *Between the Library and the*

Laboratory: The Language of Chemistry in Eighteenth-Century France (Baltimore, MD: Johns Hopkins University Press, 1984), pp. 26–30.

43. *Papers relative to Mr. Champion's application to Parliament, for the extension of the term of a patent.* [London], 1775, p. 14.

44. He resorted to similar tactics, for example, when placing the Portland Vase before the public in the form of his own copies and when promoting his newly invented pyrometer, which he published in *Philosophical Transactions* in 1782 and formally presented to King George III in 1786. Jo Dahn, "Mrs. Delany and Ceramics in the Objectscape," *Interpreting Ceramics* [online journal], no. 1 (2000); Gordon Elliott, *The Design Process in British Ceramic Manufacture, 1750–1850* (Stoke: Staffordshire University Press, 2002), pp. 169–172.

45. On the general prevalence of "trade secrets" in the eighteenth century ceramic industry, see Young, *English Porcelain,* chapter 4, passim.

46. Simeon Shaw, *The Chemistry of the Several Natural and Artificial Heterogeneous Compounds Used in Manufacturing Porcelain, Glass and Pottery* (London: Lewis & Son, Finch-Lane, 1837; reprinted London: Scott, Greenwood & Son, 1900), p. xv.

47. Ibid., p. xxii.

48. Ibid., p. xxxv.

49. Ibid., p. 5.

50. Larry Stewart, "A Meaning for Machines: Modernity, Utility, and the Eighteenth-Century British Public," *Journal of Modern History* 70.2 (June 1998): 259–294; 268. See also Jan Golinski, *Science as Public Culture* (Cambridge: Cambridge University Press, 1992); Barbara Maria Stafford, *Artful Science: Enlightenment, Entertainment, and the Eclipse of Visual Education* (Cambridge, MA: MIT Press, 1996).

51. Quoted in Simon Schaffer, "Babbage's Dancer and the Impresarios of Mechanism," in *Cultural Babbage: Technology, Time, and Invention,* ed. Francis Spufford and Jenny Uglow (New York: Faber and Faber, 1996), p. 55.

52. Feng-Hsiung Hsu, *Deep Blue: Building the Computer that Defeated the World Chess Champion* (Princeton, NJ: Princeton University Press, 2002).

53. Schaffer, "Babbage's Dancer," p. 59.

54. Charles Tomlinson, *Cyclopaedia of Useful Arts, Mechanical and Chemical,* vol. 1 (London: Virtue and Co., 1868; orig. pub. 1852), p. 270.

55. Charles Babbage, *Economy of Machines and Manufactures* (London: Charles Knight, 1832), pp. 250–251. For a discussion of this passage, and Babbage's attitudes to the working class more generally, see Anthony Hyman, *Charles Babbage: Pioneer of the Computer* (Oxford: Oxford University Press, 1982), pp. 110–116.

56. Sadie Plant, *Zeroes and Ones: Digital Women and the New Technoculture* (New York: Doubleday, 1997).

57. Andre Millard, "Machine Shop Culture and Menlo Park," in *Thomas A. Edison and the Menlo Park Experience,* ed. William S. Pretzer (Baltimore, MD: Henry Ford Museum and Greenfield Village/Johns Hopkins University Press, 1989), p. 49.

58. Neil Harris, *Humbug: The Art of P.T. Barnum* (Chicago: University of Chicago Press, 1981).

59. P. T. Barnum, *The Art of Money-Getting, or, Golden Rules for Making Money* (London: Ward, Lock & Co., 1883 [orig. pub. 1880]), ch. 7.

60. Charles Tomlinson, *Cyclopaedia of Useful Arts, Mechanical and Chemical,* vol. 1 (London: Richard Clay, 1852), p. vii.

61. Charles Tomlinson, *Cyclopaedia of Useful Arts,* 1862, p. xiv.

62. Thomas Kuhn, *Structure of Scientific Revolutions* (Chicago: University of Chicago Press, 1962).

63. Jennifer Karnes Alexander gives the example of millwrights, who were "taught to reason qualitatively, often considered analysis 'foolish and fruitless' and pursued technical advance through empirical testing." Alexander, *The Mantra of Efficiency: From Waterwheel to Social Control* (Baltimore, MD: Johns Hopkins University Press, 2008), p. 27.

64. On the early history of plastic, see Susan Mossman, *Early Plastics: Perspectives, 1850–1950* (Leicester: Leicester University Press/Science Museum, 1997); Jeffrey Meikle, *American Plastic: A Cultural History* (New Brunswick, NJ: Rutgers University Press, 1997). For typical usage of "plastic" as applied to clay and other materials, see Ure, *A Dictionary of Arts, Manufactures, and Mines.*

65. Roland Barthes, *Mythologies,* trans. Jonathan Cape (Paris: Editions de Seuil, 1957; trans. 1972), pp. 97, 98.

66. For a history of the company, see *Carron: Crucible of Scotland* (Falkirk: Falkirk Museums, 1998).

67. Another ambitious early stove, patterned along the lines of rococo furniture, is the "warming machine" produced in London in 1770 for the Virginia House of Burgesses, now at Colonial Williamsburg. See Samuel Y. Edgerton, "Eighteenth-Century House Warming by Stoves," *Journal of the Society of Architectural Historians* 20/1 (Mar. 1961): 20–26; 24. See also Priscilla J. Brewer, "'We Have Got a Very Good Cooking Stove': Advertising, Design, and Consumer Response to the Cookstove, 1815–1880," *Winterthur Portfolio* 25/1 (Spring 1990): 35–54.

68. For a period discussion of steam engine use in iron casting, see Arthur Young, ed., *Annals of Agriculture and Other Useful Arts,* vol. 8 (Bury St. Edmunds: J. Rackham, 1790). A third innovation, the heating of the air before it is blown into the furnace (the so-called hot blast) was patented in 1828. On its inventor, James Beaumont Neilson, see Samuel Smiles, *Industrial Biography: Iron Workers and Tool Makers* (London: Murray, 1863), ch. 9.

69. Quoted in William Fairbairn, *Iron: Its History, Properties, and Processes of Manufacture* (Edinburgh: Adam and Charles Black, 1851), p. 1.

70. Letter from Samuel Garbett to William Cadell, June 30, 1759, quoted in Henry Hamilton, "The Founding of Carron Ironworks," *Scottish Historical Review* 25/99 (Apr. 1928): 185–193; 190.

71. Ellen Marie Snyder, "Victory over Nature: Victorian Cast-Iron Seating Furniture," *Winterthur Portfolio* 20/4 (Winter 1985): 221–242; 224.

72. The monument was installed at St. Mary Magdalene in Woolwich in 1831. The earliest instance of such a gesture was probably the cast iron coffin that another improver, John "Iron Mad" Wilkinson, requested for his own interment in 1808.

73. Smiles, *Industrial Biography,* p. 283.

74. Georg Himmelheber, *Cast-iron Furniture* (London: Philip Wilson, 1996), p. 21. See also Elisabeth Schmuttermeier, et al., *Cast Iron from Central Europe 1800–1850* (New York/ Vienna: Bard Graduate Center/MAK, 1994).

75. For further discussion of this point, see Glenn Adamson, "The Real in the Rococo," in *Rethinking the Baroque,* ed. Helen Hills (Burlington, VT: Ashgate, 2011).

76. David H. Solkin, "Joseph Wright of Derby and the Sublime Art of Labor," *Representations* 83/1 (Summer 2003): 167–194; 170. Solkin also discusses Wright's practical, craftsmanlike approach to his work, including the use of a bit of gold leaf to enhance the glow of the ingot in the first blacksmith painting, as a riposte to the more mannered styles promoted by Joshua Reynolds at the Royal Academy (pp. 188ff).

77. For examples of the blacksmith as simple paragon of virtue, see "The Village Blacksmith, part II," *Sunday at Home: A Family Magazine for Sabbath Reading* (Jan. 17, 1861): 35–37, or more famously, the kindly Joe Gargery in Charles Dickens's *Great Expectations* (1861). The blacksmith was prominently positioned in opposition to contemporary technology in early film, from Edison's *Blacksmithing Scene* (1893) to Buster Keaton's *The Blacksmith* (1922), which knowingly juxtaposes horses and newfangled automobiles. Edison's early short film was shot on location at the metal shop of his own laboratory. As one film historian notes, "perhaps the ultimate center for modern, innovative technology [was] humorously transfigured into ye old fashioned blacksmith shoppe." Charles Musser, "At the Beginning: Motion Picture Production, Representation and Ideology at the Edison and Lumiere Companies," in *The Silent Cinema Reader,* ed. Lee Grieveson and Peter Krämer (Abingdon: Routledge, 2004), p. 17.

78. John Holland, *A Treatise on the Progressive Improvement and Present State of the Manufactures in Metal* (London: Longman, Brown, Green, Longmans, 1853; orig. pub. 1831–1834), p. 159.

79. For a well-researched account of blacksmithing as an occupation in the period, see Christine Daniels, "'Wanted: A Blacksmith who Understands Plantation Work': Artisans in Maryland, 1700–1810," *The William and Mary Quarterly* 50/4 (Oct. 1993): 743–767.

80. Quoted in Brigitte Weinsteiger, "Pat Lyon at the Forge: Portrait of an American Blacksmith," in *Building Community: Medieval Technology and American History,* online at www.engr.psu.edu/mtah/articles/pat_lyon.htm (accessed October 7, 2011).

81. An extensive description of the process, describing it as a matter of "practical skill rather than scientific knowledge," can be found in Robert Hunt, "Papier-Mâché Manufacture," *Art Journal* (November 1851): 277–278.

82. Charles Frederick Bielefeld, *On the Use of the Improved Papier-Mache in Furniture, in the Interior Decorations of Buildings, and in Works of Art* (London: J. Rickerby, ca. 1842), p. 5.

83. Ibid., p. 6.

84. For the story of the tray's design and manufacture, see Frances Collard, "Richard Redgrave and the Summerly Art-Manufactures," *The Burlington Magazine* 136/1094 (May 1994): 314–316.

85. Clay has these qualities when wet, but not when subjected to the heat of a kiln, which imposes strict limitations of size and form.

86. Bielefeld, *On the Use of the Improved Papier-Mache,* pp. 7, 9. The material continued to be used enthusiastically through the late nineteenth century, with one American magazine exclaiming

as late as 1889 that "there are no forms, however intricate, to which it is unequal." James Carruthers, "Papier Mache," *The Decorator and Furnisher* 15/1 (October 1889): 10.

87. Philoponos, *The Great Exhibition of 1851, or, The wealth of the world in its workshops: comparing the relative skill of the manufacturers, designers, and artisans of England with that of France, Belgium, Prussia, and other continental states* (London: Edward Churton, 1850), pp. 83, 84.

88. My thanks to Mark Nesbitt and Luke Stempien of the Kew Gardens Economic Botany Collection, who generously shared their research materials on India rubber and gutta-percha.

89. Macintosh's method, patented in 1823, was to dissolve the rubber in coal tar naptha and laminate it between two layers of cloth.

90. "India-Rubber, or, Caoutchouc," *Penny Magazine* (September 22, 1832): 242–243; 243.

91. Tomlinson, *Cyclopaedia of Useful Arts* (1862 ed.), p. 303.

92. Ibid., p. 298.

93. Thomas Hancock, *Origin and Progress of Caoutchouc or India-Rubber Manufacture in England* (London: Longman, Brown, Green, Longmans, and Roberts, 1857), p. 129.

94. *Great Exhibition of the Works of Industry of All Nations: Official Descriptive and Illustrated Catalogue,* vol. 2 (London, 1851), p. 778.

95. George Dodd, "India Rubber," *Household Words* (March 12, 1853); quoted in Adela Pinch, "Rubber Bands and Old Ladies," in *In Near Ruins: Cultural Theory at the End of the Century,* ed. Nicholas B. Dirks (Minneapolis: University of Minnesota Press, 1998), p. 160. Pinch comments that rubber was "the apotheosis of the commodity, living endlessly, stretching to accommodate the entire commodity system in its image" (p. 161).

96. A.W.N. Pugin, *Contrasts: A Parallel between the Noble Edifices of the Fourteenth and Fifteenth Centuries, and Similar Buildings of the Present Day, Shewing the Present Decay of Taste* (London: Author, 1836), p. 35. See also Pugin's attack on "the absurdities of modern metal-workers" in *The True Principles of Pointed or Christian Architecture* (London: J. Weale, 1853), reprinted in *The Theory of Decorative Art: An Anthology of European and American Writings 1750–1940,* ed. Isabelle Frank (New Haven, CT: Yale University Press, 2000), pp. 35–41.

97. John Ruskin, *Fors Clavigera: Letters to the Workmen and Labourers of Great Britain,* vol. 7 (1871–1874), p. 153; Ruskin, "The Work of Iron, in Nature, Art and Policy" (1858), in *The Two Paths* (London: Smith, Elder and Co., 1859), part 5, section 2.

98. Gottfried Semper, "Science, Industry and Art: Some Suggestions towards Encouraging the National Feeling for Art" (1852), as translated and excerpted in Charles Harrison, Paul Wood, and Jason Gaiger, *Art in Theory 1815–1900: An Anthology of Changing Ideas* (Oxford: Blackwell, 1998), pp. 332, 335.

99. Dario Gamboni, "'Fabrication of Accidents': Factura and Chance in Nineteenth-Century Art," *Res* 36 (Autumn 1999): 205–225; 220. Within the historiography of craft, Alois Riegl and Henri Focillon are particularly significant. See Richard Woodfield, ed., *Framing Formalism: Riegl's Work* (London: Routledge, 2001); and Henri Focillon, *The Life of Forms* (1934), excerpted in Glenn Adamson, *The Craft Reader* (Oxford; Berg Publishers, 2010).

100. Robert Routledge, *Discoveries and Inventions of the Nineteenth Century* (London: G. Routledge, 1891), p. 52.

101. For a classic discussion of this dynamic, drawing on Marx's analysis of bourgeois production as "constantly revolutionizing," see Marshall Berman, *All That Is Solid Melts Into Air: The Experience of Modernity* (New York: Penguin, 1982).

102. Robin Leslie Anderson, *Colonization as Exploitation in the Amazon Rain Forest, 1758–1911* (Gainesville: University Press of Florida, 1999), p. 74ff.

103. Gayatri Spivak, "Can the Subaltern Speak?," in *Marxism and the Interpretation of Culture*, ed. Cary Nelson and Larry Grossberg (Chicago: University of Illinois Press, 1988). See also Rosalind C. Morris, *Can the Subaltern Speak? Reflections on the History of an Idea* (New York: Columbia University Press, 2010).

104. Tomlinson, *Cyclopaedia of Useful Arts* (1862 ed.), p. 297.

105. Thomas Winterbottom, *An Account of the Native Africans in the Neighbourhood of Sierra Leone* (London: C. Whittingham, 1803), p. 2.

106. Yvonne Chireau, *Black Magic: Religion and the African-American Conjuring Tradition* (Berkeley: University of California Press, 2003), p. 40; William Pietz, "The Fetish of Civilization," in *Colonial Subjects: Essays on the Practical History of Anthropology*, ed. Oscar Salemink and Peter Pels (Ann Arbor: University of Michigan Press, 1999), p. 58.

107. Meredith provides the etymology from Portuguese ("*fetischo*"), but defines the term as "witch-craft." Henry Meredith, *An Account of the Gold Coast of Africa, with a Brief History of the African Company* (London: Longman, Hurst, Rees, Orme and Brown, 1812), p. 34.

108. Anton Lever, Broadside, 1773. British Museum EPH-AOA, B1.7.

109. For more on this shift in display techniques, see Glenn Adamson, "The Labor of Division: Cabinetmaking and the Production of Knowledge," in *Ways of Making and Knowing: The Material Culture of Empirical Knowledge,* ed. Harold Cook, Amy Meyers, and Pamela Smith (Ann Arbor: University of Michigan Press/Bard Graduate Center, 2011).

110. On Stone's drawings of Native American craft objects, see Jonathan King, "Woodlands Art as depicted by Sarah Stone in the Collection of Sir Ashton Lever," *American Indian Art Magazine* 18/2 (1993): 32–45. A similarly truth-obsessed visual exercise is the *Museum Brittanicum* assembled by John and Andrew Von Rymsdyk (London: J. Moore, 1788), who declared themselves enemies "of Nature-Menders, Mannerists, &c." See Nicholas Thomas, *In Oceania: Visions, Artifacts, Histories* (Durham, NC: Duke University Press, 1997), p. 114ff.

111. *European Magazine* (Jan. 1782), quoted in Troy Bickham, "A Conviction of the Reality of Things: Material Culture, North American Indians and Empire in Eighteenth-Century Britain," *Eighteenth-Century Studies,* 39/1 (Fall 2005): 29–47; 37.

112. Anthony Pagden, *The Fall of Natural Man* (Cambridge: Cambridge University Press, 1986), p. 12.

113. This historical model, based on early archaeology, was devised by Danish scholar Christian Jürgensen Thomsen in the 1820s. On professional anthropologists' treatment of non-European peoples as inhabiting a different time as well as a different space, see Johannes Fabian, *Time and the Other: How Anthropology Makes Its Object* (New York: Columbia University Press, 1983).

114. Lewis Henry Morgan, *Ancient Society* (New York: Henry Holt, 1877), p. 3. For an early statement of this view, see Edmund Burke, *An Account of the European Settlements in America* (London: 1808 [orig. pub. 1757]), p. 127: "Whoever considers the Americans of this day, not

only studies the manners of a remote present nation, but he studies, in some measure, the antiquities of all nations."

115. Lewis Henry Morgan, *League of the Ho-de-no-saunee, or Iroquois* (Rochester: Sage and Brother, 1851), pp. 353–354.

116. James Hall, "An Essay on the History of The North American Indians," in Thomas McKenney and James Hall, *The History of the Indian Tribes of North America: With Biographical Sketches and Anecdotes of the Principle Chiefs* (Edinburgh: John Grant, 1934 [orig. pub. 1838]).

117. Ibid., pp. 38–44. King's picture was destroyed by fire in 1865.

118. Morgan, *Ancient Society*, p. 12.

119. Josiah Clark Nott, *Two Lectures on the Connection between the Biblical and Physical History of Man* (New York: Bartlett and Welford, 1849), p. 35; William Cooke Taylor, *The Natural History of Society in the Barbarous and Civilized State: An Essay Towards Discovering the Origin and Course of Human Improvement* (London: 1840), p. 259.

120. John Noble Wilford, "Carvings from Cherokee Script's Dawn," *New York Times* (June 22, 2009).

121. On increasing institutional racism in the nineteenth century—directed not only against Native Americans, but also Africans and Asians—see Nicholas Thomas, *Colonialism's Culture: Anthropology, Travel and Government* (Cambridge, UK: Polity Press, 1994).

122. Harry Liebersohn, *Aristocratic Encounters: European Travelers and North American Indians* (Cambridge: Cambridge University Press, 1998). It is worth noting that the French Enlightenment's adoption of the "noble savage" is largely a fake, the fabrication of later racists who invented the story in order to attack it. Ter Ellingson, *The Myth of the Noble Savage* (Berkeley: University of California Press, 2001).

123. John Heckewelder, *Account of the History, Manners and Customs of the Indian Nations who Once Inhabited Pennsylvania and the Neighboring States*(Philadelphia: Historical Society of Pennsylvania, 1876 [orig. pub. 1818]), pp. 191–192. See also p. 202–203 for his detailed account of Native American women fabricating feather blankets.

124. Charles Dickens, "The Noble Savage," *Household Words* (June 11, 1853): 337. Grace Moore has argued that this "unprecedented public rant" should be contextualized as a response to contemporary developments in imperial India, and that the author had a more complex engagement with questions of race than this text implies. Moore, *Dickens and Empire: Discourses of Class, Race and Colonialism in the Works of Charles Dickens* (Burlington, VT: Ashgate, 2004), p. 4, ch. 3 passim.

125. Kenneth R. H. MacKenzie, quoted in Ellingson, *The Myth of the Noble Savage*, p. 298.

126. On the Canadian extension of the program, see Derek G. Smith, "The 'Policy of Aggressive Civilization' and Projects of Governance in Roman Catholic Industrial Schools for Native Peoples in Canada, 1870–95," *Anthropologica* 43 (2001): 253–271; Mark Francis, "The 'Civilizing' of Indigenous People in Nineteenth-Century Canada," *Journal of World History* 9/1 (Spring 1998): 51–87.

127. Richard Henry Pratt, *Battlefield and Classroom: Four Decades with the American Indian, 1867–1904* (New Haven, CT: Yale University Press, 1964), p. 214. See also pp. 311–312, which records Pratt praising slavery for integrating "primitive black people" to "our temperate

national family" while the reservation system, an "exactly opposite scheme," separated Indians from participation in white society.

128. Pratt, *Battlefield and Classroom,* p. 311. See also Hayes Peter Mauro, *The Art of Americanization at the Carlisle Industrial School* (Albuquerque: University of New Mexico Press, 2011).

129. *United States Indian School, Carlisle* (pamphlet, 1895), p. 39.

130. Lucy Maddox, *Citizen Indians: Native American Intellectuals, Race and Reform* (Ithaca, NY: Cornell University Press, 2005), p. 24.

131. For an overview, see Edward S. Cooke, Jr., "Rural Industry, Village Craft: The Politics of Modern Globalized Craft," the 12th Annual Peter Dormer Lecture, Royal College of Art. Online at: www.rca.ac.uk/Docs/1Peter_Dormer_Lecture.pdf. *On Native Americans and craft demonstration, see* Elizabeth Hutchinson, *The Indian Craze: Primitivism, Modernism, and Transculturation in American Art, 1890–1915* (Durham, NC: Duke University Press, 2009); Robert A. Trennet, "Selling Indian Education at World's Fairs and Expositions," *American Indian Quarterly* 11/3 (Summer 1987): 203–220.

132. Annie Coombes's work has been indispensable for understanding this phenomena from the Victorian age to the present day; see, for example, "Blinded By Science: Ethnography at the British Museum," in *Art Apart: Artifacts, Institutions and Ideology in England and North America From 1800 to the Present,* ed. Marcia Pointon (Manchester: Manchester University Press, 1994), pp. 102–119; and "Inventing the Post-Colonial: Hybridity and Constituency in Contemporary Curating," *New Formations* (December1992): 39–52. See also the excellent anthology edited by Donald Preziosi and Clare Farago, *Grasping the World: The Idea of the Museum* (Aldershot: Ashgate, 2004).

133. Otis T. Mason, *The Origins of Invention: A Study of Industry Among Primitive Peoples* (London: Walter Scott Publishing, 1902), p. 8; Otis T. Mason, *Indian Basketry: Studies in a Textile Art Without Machinery* (London: William Heinemann, 1905), pp. 8, 9. For an overview of Native American collecting in this period, see Rebecca J. Dobkins, "Art," in *A Companion to the Anthropology of American Indians,* ed. Thomas Biolsi (Oxford: Blackwell, 2004), p. 215.

134. Alfred Gell, "Vogel's Net: Traps as Artworks and Artworks as Traps," *Journal of Material Culture* 1/1 (1996): 36, 37.

135. Among the many recent exhibitions motivated by this way of thinking, which run right across disciplinary boundaries, are *Power of Making* (V&A, 2011), curated by Daniel Charny; *Alexander McQueen: Savage Beauty* (Metropolitan Museum of Art, 2011), curated by Andrew Bolton; *The Uncanny Room* (Pitzhanger Manor, 2002), curated by Tessa Peters and Janice West; and *Devices of Wonder: From the World in a Box to Images on a Screen* (J. Paul Getty Museum, 2001), curated by Frances Terpak and Barbara Maria Stafford. See also Joshua Landy and Michael Saler, eds., *The Re-enchantment of the World: Secular Magic in a Rational Age* (Palo Alto, CA: Stanford University Press, 2009); Simon During, *Modern Enchantments: The Cultural Power of Secular Magic* (Cambridge, MA: Harvard University Press, 2002).

136. Alfred Gell, "The Enchantment of Technology and the Technology of Enchantment," in *Anthropology, Art, and Aesthetics,* ed. J. Coote (Oxford: Oxford University Press, 1992); as reprinted in Adamson, *The Craft Reader,* p. 471.

137   Gell, "The Enchantment of Technology and the Technology of Enchantment," p. 471.

138. Louise Mazanti, "Super-Objects: Craft as an Aesthetic Position," in *Extra/Ordinary: Craft and Contemporary Art,* ed. Maria Elena Buszek (Durham, NC: Duke University Press, 2011), p. 60.

139. This gradualist model of aesthetic appreciation can be opposed to the optical, "all in one shot" experience of an artwork described by modern art theorist par excellence Clement Greenberg. See Adamson, *Thinking Through Craft,* ch. 2; Caroline Jones, *Eyesight Alone: Clement Greenberg's Modernism and the Bureaucratization of the Senses* (Chicago: University of Chicago Press, 2006). On Greenberg's antipathy to the decorative, and by extension the slowly crafted, see Elissa Auther, "The Decorative, Abstraction, and the Hierarchy of Art and Craft in the Art Criticism of Clement Greenberg," *Oxford Art Journal* 27/3 (2004): pp. 339–364.

140. Michael Taussig, "Viscerality, Faith, and Skepticism: Another Theory of Magic," in *In Near Ruins: Cultural Theory at the End of the Century,* ed. Nicholas B. Dirks (Minneapolis: University of Minnesota Press, 1998), p. 222.

141. Marina Warner, "Time Signatures: The Writing of Stones and the Logic of the Imagination," in *Dark Monarch: Magic and Modernism in British Art,* ed. Michael Bracewell, Martin Clark, and Alun Rowlands (St. Ives: Tate Publishing, 2009), p. 129.

142. Lawrence Lessig, *The Future of Ideas: The Fate of the Commons in a Connected World* (New York: Random House, 2001).

143. For a thoughtful consideration of black market knockoffs, see Marcus Boon, *In Praise of Copying* (Cambridge, MA: Harvard University Press, 2010).

144. Another example of such experimentation is the work of Studio FormaFantasma (Simone Farresin and Andrea Trimarchi), who have researched several "animal and plant polymers discovered by scientists in the eighteenth and nineteenth centuries" including *bois durci* (a mix of animal blood and sawdust) and dammar (a tropical tree resin). Riya Patel, "FormaFantasma," *Icon* 99 (September 2011): 36–37.

145. J. E. Gordon, *The New Science of Strong Materials, or, Why You Don't Fall Through the Floor* (London: Pelican Books, 1968), p. 3.

146. Unless otherwise noted, all quotations from Laughlin are from an interview conducted at the Institute of Making on July 6, 2011.

147. Zoe Laughlin, *Beyond the Swatch: How Can the Science of Materials Be Represented by the Materials Themselves in a Materials Library?* (PhD thesis, King's College London, University of London, 2010), p. 72.

148. Ibid., p. 162.

149. Ibid., p. 154.

150. Eva March Tappan, *Makers of Many Things* (Boston: Houghton Mifflin, 1916), p. 2.

151. The strike was partly initiated by an early example of muckraking journalism by Fabian writer Annie Besant: "White Slavery in London," *The Link* no. 21 (June 23, 1888).

152. When I invited Saldaña to contribute a statement about her practice to *The Journal of Modern Craft,* she provided only a set of how-to instructions, declining the opportunity to gloss her work with a specific interpretation. Zoe Sheehan Saldaña, "Statement of Practice," *Journal of Modern Craft* 5/1 (March 2012): 215–224.

153. For a discussion of *Shopdropping* in relation to other politically oriented textile works, see *Julia Bryan-Wilson*, "Sewing Notions," *Artforum* 49/6 (Feb. 2011): 73–74.

154. Douglas Vogle, "Denied Parole," *Artforum* (Feb. 2007): 257–258; 257.

155. *Ryan Gander: Catalogue Raissonable Vol. 1* (Zurich: Haus Konstruktiv/Christoph Keller Editions, 2010), p. xlviii.

156. Christophe Gallois, "The Klingon Frowns and Simply Replies, 'Sorry I Didn't Understand You': Interview with Ryan Gander," in *The Space of Words* (Luxembourg: Mudam, 2010), pp. 178–183; 180–181.

157. *Ryan Gander: Catalogue Raissonable Vol. 1*, p. 5.

158. Unless otherwise cited, all quotes from Ryan Gander are from an interview conducted by the author, August 5, 2011.

159. These works are documented in Ryan Gander, *Appendix* (Amsterdam: Artimo, 2003).

160. Jonathan Jones, "How Chris Ofili Saved Frieze Art Fair For Me," *Guardian* blog October 20, 2009 (online at: www.guardian.co.uk/artanddesign/jonathanjonesblog/2009/oct/20/chris-ofili-frieze-art-fair-ryan-gander), reprinted in *Ryan Gander: Catalogue Raissonable, Vol. 1,* p. 101.

3   MECHANICAL

On a Tuesday evening in November 1823, a whitesmith named John Johnson stood to speak. His listeners were more than two thousand in number, nearly all of them artisans. The venue was the Crown and Anchor Tavern, opposite St. Clement Danes Church in the Strand—hardly your usual tavern. This was one of London's preeminent meeting halls, with an enormous banqueting room that had seen many political gatherings in the past. On this occasion, the crowd had gathered to vote into existence a new organization called the London Mechanics' Institute. Preceding Johnson on the bill had been several of the country's most prominent men, among whom doctor and professor of natural history George Birkbeck was first and foremost. Back at the turn of the century, then only about twenty-five years old, Birkbeck had pioneered the practice of lecturing to audiences of mechanics. These talks, offered for free at the Andersonian Institution, had their origin in an encounter he'd had with some workshop operatives who were making a scientific instrument to his design.[1] As he recalled the event in his address to the London artisans, he had found himself encircled by a group of these craftsmen, who wanted to understand the purpose of the device they themselves had built. On the basis of "observing the intelligent curiosity of the 'unwashed artificers,' to whose mechanical skill I was often obliged to have recourse," he resolved to begin a lecture series for their edification in the principles of mechanics. It was an immediate sensation. In his words, "they came, they listened, they conquered—conquered that prejudice which would have consigned them to the dominion of interminable ignorance, and would have shut the gates of knowledge against a large and intelligent portion of mankind for ever."[2]

On the strength of this success in Glasgow, Birkbeck was confident enough to instigate Britain's first mechanics' institute in London. He gathered the support of a group of like-minded men, including Irish barrister and journalist John Sidney Taylor, civil engineer Benjamin Bevan, Sherriff of London (and future lord mayor) Peter Laurie, and Henry Brougham, who would a decade later become lord chancellor.[3] The proposed organization would host lectures, form a library and a school of design, and amass a collection of instructive working models. Above all, it would serve as a means to keep artisans out of the pubs and in a self-improving frame of mind. Artisans themselves would be entrusted with the operation of the institution. The twin mottos of the organization and its publishing organ, the *Mechanics Magazine, Register, Journal and Gazette,* were "Knowledge is Power" and "Ours and For Us." Autonomy was prized above all. Artisans could not depend on the government to train them; that would only be "the mere discipline of the hunting dog, which, by dint of severity, is made to forego the strongest impulse of his nature, and instead of devouring his prey, to hasten with it to the feet of his master."[4]

It was presumably with these convictions in mind that whitesmith John Johnson had been invited to take the stage. He was not unqualified as a speaker. As secretary to the Benevolent Institution of Smiths, he had some experience of collective action amongst skilled workers, and he was enough of a skilled engineer to propose (in an early issue of the *Mechanics Magazine*) a plan to excavate a tunnel under the Thames.[5] By the time Johnson addressed this meeting of men "resolved both to think and act for themselves," Birkbeck, Laurie, and Taylor had already addressed the crowd. To the embarrassment of the organizers, a few attendees had been so inebriated that they were ejected. But Birkbeck, in particular, had presented an idealized view of the enlightened mechanic, quoting Scottish philosopher Dugald Stewart: "when theoretical knowledge and practical skill are happily combined in one person, the intellectual power of man appears in its full perfection."[6] Expectations must have been high for Johnson's speech—here was a man who offered just such a combination of mental and manual facility. Yet he began, in the customary manner of a nineteenth-century orator, with protestations of his own inadequacy: "Permit an unlettered son of Vulcan, just emerging from the smoke of a forge, to address you." He had hard words for the class of operatives in which he himself was a member. Wasting their time and money in drink, games of chance, and prizefighting, they might spend their working hours "bringing to perfection some production of the vegetable kingdom," but lamentably, "the kingdom of mind is totally neglected by them." He even thought to mention the plight of women workers, who were "moping at home" instead of feeding their intellects. Throughout, Johnson stuck to the script: "we live to improve, or we live in vain."[7]

Though this rather self-effacing speech was warmly applauded, there was a less welcome response too. As the *Mechanics Magazine* noted in its coverage of the event, "Mr. Johnson's mode of pronouncing some words occasionally excited symptoms of risibility." The following speaker, an itinerant lecturer named Mr. Crook, felt compelled to defend the man who had just left the podium. Johnson, he said, was a wonderful example of a mechanic intent on self-education—properly deferent to other speakers, and yet "more pertinent to the business of the evening than any other which he had heard." To further applause, Crook continued:

> And if a smile was occasionally observed to arise in consequence of Mr. Johnson's pronunciation, the cause of it was only a still further proof of the necessity of such an Institution as the present, as it would enable men of powerful minds to express properly what they so forcibly felt.[8]

From a distance of nearly two centuries, it is impossible to say whether Johnson provoked the audience's derision as a result of some speech impediment, or if it was instead his working-class diction. Yet this moment of humiliating condescension, directed toward an artisan attempting to speak for himself, was of a piece with the more official attitudes prevalent at the founding of the London Mechanics' Institute. Time and time again, the artisan was framed as incapable of unaided rational discourse. If only mechanics could be guided to the realm of proper language through the agency of the new organization, however, their lot would improve dramatically—not only intellectually, but also morally and economically. An anonymous contributor to the *Mechanics Magazine,* writing under the name Tom Telltruth, put the matter unusually bluntly. The purpose of the proposed Mechanics' Institute, he observed, was "to effect nearly an entire change in the habits and character of the community; they are to be no longer mere machines; they are to be taught *principles;* they are to be elevated into the class of *thinking beings.*" He insisted that any conception of the British mechanic as intrinsically inventive was mere claptrap:

> The mechanics of Britain can claim no merit as mere workmen, which every machine in the country may not claim almost as well. The truth is, that here as well as every where else, the race of Mechanics have been hitherto looked upon as little better than mere machines, and have, as it appears to me, been *systematically* denied the means of becoming otherwise. Of "power of mind," alas! The working mechanics in all countries shown but little…Where are the great discoveries in art or science, that can be fairly traced to the observations of the *workshop?* I am afraid, that were we to ransack the whole volume of human knowledge, from the earliest periods down to the present, the laurels which the class of working mechanics might claim as their own, would be few indeed…From the ignorance in which the working classes have been kept, they have been nearly as passive and unobservant instruments as those of wood and metal, with which it has been their lot to co-operate.[9]

The idea that artisans were profoundly ignorant, the intellectual equals of the machines they operated, and indeed much like these artificial constructions in their movements and lack of mental activity, may seem surprising to us. We are used to the idea that artisan and machine are opposed. But the analogy between the two was widely current in the early nineteenth century, and indeed was one of the few points on which critics and advocates of industrialization agreed. Radical Manchester agitator and educator Rowland Detroisier, for example, described the workers of that city as "uncivilised, degraded and inhuman…machines for the creation of wealth."[10] John Sydney Taylor, one of the prime sponsors of the London Mechanics' Institute, argued that if a worker "is to be a moral agent, and not a *machine* or *mere animal,* you must have some consideration for [his] moral character."[11] The *Mechanics Magazine* ran a feature in which the comparison was spun out at length: "we almost doubt when we are told, that the human frame is a combination of wedges, levers, pulleys, pillars, props, cross-beams, fences, coverings, axes, cords, presses, or bellows, sieves, sprainers, pipes, conduits, valves, and receivers, all the actions of which are performed by *mechanical laws,* and by them only are intelligible."[12] And Thomas Carlyle, in his reformist 1829 text *Signs of the Times,* famously bemoaned the fact that "Men are grown mechanical in head and in heart, as well as in hand." As the century progressed, the metaphor did not lose its power. To an "artizan" speaking at the

London Mechanics' Institute in 1843, it seemed that "machinery goes on from day to day pulling man by man out of the ranks of independence, and reduces his being down to a mere broken spirited automaton."[13]

On the other side of the political spectrum, British factory system apologists like Andrew Ure and William Cooke Taylor (both of whom we encountered in chapter two) and Edward Baines extended this metaphor historically, arguing that it was the *preindustrial* artisan who was like an automaton, but that the industrial worker had a unique opportunity to escape that condition.[14] Prior to the onset of automation, they wrote, workers were trapped in routine, tedious handicraft. They had been little more than machines in the bad old days—albeit machines that made mistakes, as Ure took pains to point out—and it was machines that would liberate them by literally taking their place as surrogates. In France, too, this argument had currency. It was prominently espoused by Gérard-Joseph Christian, the director of the Conservatoire des Arts et Métiers, a state-sponsored analogue to the mechanical institutes in England. According to historian Jennifer Karnes Alexander, Christian believed that "the most perfect machine produced the most, the most rapidly, and with the greatest economy; it also contributed to the intellectual and physical well-being of the worker," by relieving them from repetitive tasks.[15] Interesting, even some critics of the factory system who were less inclined to idealize historical working conditions—including Karl Marx himself—were happy to concede this point, with the crucial corrective that the potential freedoms offered by the machine had not been realized, and could not without drastic political upheaval.

Those who were optimistic about industrialization tended to extrapolate from the idea that the mechanic was indeed mechanical and to describe the factory as a whole as functioning like a healthy body (with labor unions sometimes imagined as a disease that needed curing). As Baines put it in his *History of the Cotton Manufactures of Great Britain* (1835), "The steam-engine stands in the same relation to the spinning machines, as the heart does to the arms, hands, and fingers, in the human frame; the latter perform every task of dexterity and labour, the former supplies them with all their vital energy."[16] Occasionally, voices were raised in protest against this dehumanizing metaphor. Robert Owen, the early socialist reformer, turned the figure of speech against itself:

> Since the general introduction of inanimate mechanism into British manufactories, man, with few exceptions, has been treated as a secondary and inferior machine; and far more attention has been given to perfect the raw material of wood and metal than those of body and mind.[17]

But for the most part, there was a surprising convergence of opinion around the body of the artisan as being like an unthinking machine. Again, for us today, this may be hard to comprehend. We are used to the idea that skills, especially those based in handwork, are a form of creative, tacit knowledge—the opposite of automation. But in the early nineteenth century, a time when machines were not yet fundamentally distinguished from other kinds of tools, there was another, much more important opposition that superseded this one: the difference between practice and principle. From this perspective, the artisan did not possess knowledge as such, only habits and routines, as regularized as the workings of steam engines. Unlike the artist, who was animated by feeling, or the scientist, who was animated by the intellect, the artisan was merely mechanical, capable only of execution.[18] It was a commonplace of the time, and one saturated with class condescension: "if a gentleman employs a mechanic for any purpose at all of the daily routine of his business, he must, in general, not only superintend him, but think for him."[19]

For reformers, the solution was to lay a superstructure of dynamic theory atop the static edifice of mechanical expertise. This ambition was hardly new in the early nineteenth century. Thomas Sprat, the secretary of the Royal Society, wrote in 1667 that "Philosophy [will] attain to perfection when either the Mechanick Laborers shall have Philosophical heads; or the Philosophers shall have Mechanical hands."[20] As we saw in the previous chapter, alchemical research and other forms of early modern science made no firm distinction between artisanal and learned forms of knowledge (there was an active interchange between the two) but self-conscious modernizers like Sprat were already beginning to see artisans who lacked theoretical understanding as badly in need of improvement. The mechanics' institute movement set this principle squarely at the center of their reform project. In 1828, a Mechanics' Institute similar to Edinburgh's and London's was set up in Manchester, and like its predecessors, it announced a devotion to the imparting of knowledge rather than skill: "It is not intended to teach the trade of the Machine-maker, the Dyer, the Carpenter, the Mason, or any other particular business, but there is no Art which does not depend, more or less, on scientific principles, and to teach what these are, and to point out their practical application, will form the chief objects of this Institution."[21] This preference was absolutely typical of the times. By the 1830s, hundreds of institutes were being set up for the edification of artisans (though many of these were of relatively short duration), and though there was considerable variation in the curriculum offered by these organizations, the general tendency was to take specialized craft skill for granted. It was considered the one thing the audience could be presumed to possess already. Instead the focus was on the abstract principles that lay behind manufacturing processes. The first issue of the London journal *The Apprentice,* published in 1844 and aimed at the "young artificers of England," put the point with unusual force:

> It is a very prevalent fault of workmen, in the present day, that they value no information except that which bears upon some practical difficulty in their own particular art. Now, such a predilection is symptomatic of a narrow and perverted heart, and shows very clearly that while the *workman* is much considered, nothing is thought of the *man*... The aspiration upwards stops at a certain point, and does not extend so wide as it ought, to things of a higher concern.[22]

The one manual skill journals like *The Apprentice* consistently featured, alongside articles on general science, geometry, architecture, engineering, and lists of patentable inventions, was drawing—which, as we saw in chapter one, was a technique of abstraction by which artisanal skills could be brought into control. Though aimed at rank-and-file mechanics, these publications consistently propounded the view that only through "higher" branches of knowledge would the artisan find moral and professional satisfaction.[23]

At the end of the 1840s, in the run-up to the Great Exhibition, we find this attitude reaching its zenith. The editors of the *Journal of Design* lauded the improbably named Bookbinders' Finishers' Association—an organization of eighty artisans who sought through a program of collective self-education to "raise the character of their labours, from those of a mere blindly traditional handicraft to a really artistlike and tasteful pursuit"— in now familiar terms: "Nothing can be better calculated to raise the workman from the machine condition in which he is reduced from an excessive development of the division of the labour system."[24] Thus the mechanics' institute movement and its associated publications were premised on the idea that manual and mental skills were separate, and to a degree even oppositional.[25] One was specialist, the other general; one merely mechanical, the other improving (in a moral as well as practical sense). In this context, the artisan who garnered praise was the "weaver [who] studied with a book upon his loom."[26] Yet the same movement was devoted to synthesizing this dialectical opposition. No matter how knowledgeable craftsmen might be in the tools, tricks, and materials of a trade, if they lacked an understanding of theory, they were as good as ignorant.

ALL THINGS BUT A SELF

Just two years before Johnson's speech to the nascent London Mechanics' Institute, critic William Hazlitt published an essay entitled "The Indian Jugglers" in the magazine *Table-Talk*. Hazlitt too had taken a turn at the Crown and Anchor's podium, but in this piece of writing he reflected on an experience he'd had as an audience member elsewhere in London. He describes watching the performance of a man named Ramo Samee, whom he identifies as the "chief of the Indian jugglers, [in] white dress and tightened turban." Seated on the ground, the juggler commences with two balls, which as Hazlitt comments, "is what any of us could do"; but he then progresses to three balls, and then four, weaving an intricate pattern in the air, "like the planets in their spheres...like ribbons or like serpents" (Figure 3.1). Dazzled as he was by the juggler's amazing facility, Hazlitt was not quite sure how to react. Was this the apex of art he had witnessed—human ingenuity at its highest level? He considered this possibility, but decided against it. For Samee's performance was not art at all. It was something else, something lower. Yes, the Indian juggler had given his audience a wondrous spectacle, and there was, doubtless, an aesthetic pleasure in seeing his skill on display. Yet the more Hazlitt thought about Samee's ease and grace, the less impressed he became: "Man, thou canst do strange things, but thou turnest them to little account!"[27] Like Hobbs the lockpick (whom we encountered in chapter one), Samee was undoubtedly skilled, but was directing his talent to no particularly useful end. When he visited Boston in 1819, a local newspaper ran a brief notice dripping with

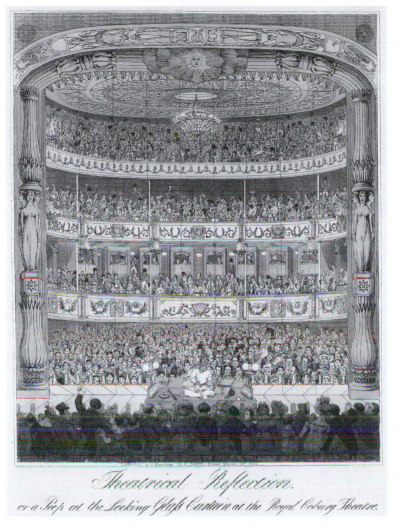

Theatrical Reflection.

or a Peep at the Looking Glass Curtain at the Royal Coburg Theatre.

Figure 3.1 *Theatrical Reflection* (Ramo Samee performing at the Royal Coburg Theatre), 1822. Print published by G. Humphrey, London.

ironical disregard: "Ramo Samee seems to be the only man that has any profitable business to attend to. His distinguished skill is rewarded as it merits."[28] This was a running theme in critical discussions of "jugglers"—a term that, in the eighteenth and nineteenth centuries, referred to any performer who "for the sake of money, by quick and artful motions of their hands…delude[s] the sense in an agreeable manner."[29] Thus juggling, in this period, included not only entertainers like Samee who kept balls or clubs aloft, but also magicians, rope dancers, acrobats, strong men, and even nonhuman automata. The defining feature of juggling was to amaze and deceive through dexterous manipulation—which should remind the reader of Alfred Gell's discussion of enchantment, explored at the end of the previous chapter.

Many commentators were prompted to pass bleak judgment on the moral implications of such entertainments, especially as they increased in popularity; one author, writing in 1820, mused that "our whole race may be divided into the jugglers and the juggled...the major part of mankind love deception so much, that they reward liberally those who impose the best upon their senses and cheat them of their understanding, in the most specious and plausible manner."[30] Yet Hazlitt did not dismiss Samee's skill only because it was useless, or even because it was a kind of trickery. He also had another, more nuanced argument to make: that "mechanical dexterity is confined to doing some one particular thing, which you can repeat as often as you please, in which you know whether you succeed or fail." Skill, he thought, is an all or nothing affair, objective rather than subjective, and which, with practice, becomes nearly automatic. It is nothing like genius. Nothing, for example, like the works of Hazlitt's idol, eighteenth-century portraitist and history painter Joshua Reynolds, with "his grace, his grandeur, his blandness of *gusto*," his ineffable power to capture the "soft suffusion of the soul." In comparison to such achievements, the accomplishments of the Indian juggler, as impressive as they might be, seem almost inhuman. "Certain movements and impressions of the hand and eye," Hazlitt explains, "having been repeated together an infinite number of times are unconsciously but unavoidably cemented into closer and closer union; the limbs require little more than to be put in motion for them to follow a regular track with ease and certainty; so that mere intention of the will acts mathematically, like touching the spring of a machine." The juggler is like a robot, with its predictable routines. He may execute his feats of skill very well, but he can only do so repetitiously. Perhaps if you handed him a fifth ball, Ramo Samee would be all at sea. Hazlitt conflates skill and mechanical certainty into one and the same thing, opposing both to true artistic invention.

It is no coincidence that just as Van Kempelen's chess-playing automaton was a Turk, Hazlitt's juggler was an Indian. One of the commonest and most pernicious habits of nineteenth-century racism was to portray non-Western subjects as something less than fully human. Arindam Dutta has noted the occasion on which Richard Burton, the great nineteenth-century traveler, captain of the East India Company, and translator of *1001 Arabian Nights,* described the typical "Hindoo" in the following terms in the course of relating his journey through the Sindh valley:

> How timidly he appears at the door! How deferential he slides in, salaams, looks deprecating, and at last is induced to sit down! Might not he be considered a novel kind of automaton, into which you transfer your minds and thoughts—a curious piece of human mechanism in the shape of a creature endowed with all things but a self?[31]

Such a repulsive sentiment is reminiscent of the attitude taken to British factory operatives; the difference was that while a British mechanic could be improved, the Indian's lack of humanity was typically viewed as a permanent condition. Ironically it was their masterful skill, the extraordinary elegance of their motions, that constituted the best evidence on this point:

The weak and delicate frame of the Hindu is accompanied with an acuteness of external sense, particularly of touch, which is altogether unrivalled, and the flexibility of his fingers is equally remarkable. The hand of the Hindu, therefore constitutes an organ, adapted to the finest operations of the loom in a degree which is almost, or altogether, peculiar to himself...The hand of an Indian cookwench will be more delicate than that of an European beauty.[32]

So we read in James Mill's *History of India* (1817), which is not necessarily unusual in its racism for the period, but which is exemplary in its fusion of derision about the uninventive character of Indian artisans and admiration for the elegance of their movements. This would become the default position for subsequent representations of Indian craft, most importantly at the Great Exhibition.[33] The formula was to praise the skill of a craftsman, at the same time denying that it had any mental basis at all; at best, it could be ascribed to unconscious impulse, a "multitudinous variety of ornamental conceptions, the bringing forth of which [is] a spontaneous effort."[34] Such ideas were not necessarily limited to non-European artisans, or even to living beings. Heinrich Wilhelm von Kleist, a German contemporary of Hazlitt's, made much the same argument as the English essayist in his 1810 essay "On the Marionette Theatre." A puppet, he wrote, could achieve a naturalness and lack of self-consciousness that no human performer ever could. In this respect, knowledge and naturalness of motion were diametrically opposed: "as thought grows dimmer and weaker, grace emerges more brilliantly and decisively."[35]

Just as, for Hazlitt, Ramo Samee's superhuman dexterity bespoke his subhuman soul, and for Kleist, a nonhuman actor might be the most elegant performer of all, Indian artisans were routinely described as having brought various crafts (especially textile manufacture) "to an exquisite degree of perfection," but only because of their inadequate humanity. Mill framed both the strengths and weaknesses of Indian craft in terms of that culture's putative primitiveness, placing it in direct temporal sequence before the stage of civilization. Thus, for example, he granted that Indians artisans had an impressive talent for copying, but took this very skill as further evidence of their uncivilized status:

As the talent of the Hindus for accurate imitation, both in the manual and in some of the refined arts, has excited much attention; and has been sometimes regarded as no mean proof of ingenuity and mental culture, it is necessary to remark, that there are few things by which the rude state of society is more uniformly characterized. It is in reality the natural precursor of the age of invention; and disappears, or at least ceases to make a conspicuous figure, when the nobler faculty of creation comes into play.[36]

What Indian craftsmen lacked was not "mere mechanical facility," in which they were adept, but "those faculties of the mind that conduce to that species of judgment called Taste"; the result was that even "in the best of Indian examples the details will not bear looking at...there is an absence of glaring faults, but no one feature of beauty."[37] Similarly dismissive comments in this period were frequently made about other non-European cultures, even the Chinese, who were revered for their technical prowess as well as their craftsmanship. Nonetheless, while China's artisans were considered superior to India's, they were similarly thought to be possessed of "considerable dexterity and facility [in] performance" but completely lacking in the arts of design and representation: "In examining the painted porcelain of this singular people, one is almost led to imagine that their artists have been debarred the sight of the objects which they attempt to represent."[38]

Mill also designated other aspects of Indian craft as signs of an undeveloped civilization, even those which might have been seen as strengths: artisans' dependence on a very limited number of crude tools (two or three, for a task that "with us a hundred tools would be employed"); their itinerant work habits, which meant that they could not rely on a well-equipped shop; and even certain points of "mechanical" excellence, such as the consistent sharpness of cut in architectural carving.[39] All of these traits could well have been seen positively—as signs of flexibility and mastery—and the so-called company paintings made on commission by Indian painters for British East India Company officials often present craftspeople in an attitude of placid autonomy, with only a few tools scattered around them as they ply their trades (Figures 3.2 and 3.3). But in Mill's view, this could only be interpreted as a poverty of means, the endemic malady of a culture immune to the

Figure 3.2   "A woman embroidering." Leaf from an album of fifty-three drawings depicting occupations, Lucknow, ca. 1815–1820. V&A: AL.7970:25. © Victoria and Albert Museum, London.

Figure 3.3 "A tinner of kitchen utensils." Leaf from an album of fifty-three drawings depicting occupations, Lucknow, ca. 1815–1820. V&A: AL.7970:42. © Victoria and Albert Museum, London.

instinct of self-improvement. The implication was clear: if craft skill is best embodied in these primitive artisans, then craft itself is equally static and resistant to forward change. From the nineteenth century to the present day, this single idea has been expressed in both positive and negative terms. Some Victorian design reformers, including figures of the stature of Owen Jones and Richard Redgrave, found in the "instinctive" designs of India an aesthetic superiority to the products of the mechanized factory.[40] On the other hand, the Indian artisan's supposed inability to work from design drawings, or otherwise undertake a task outside traditional areas of competence, was seen as a grievous limitation. Curator Caspar Purdon Clarke (later director of the South Kensington Museum) claimed in the late nineteenth century that "it would be unwise to hamper [an Indian builder] with large detailed drawings, and indeed, a drawing of a facade strictly to scale would greatly puzzle him."[41] Either way, it was assumed (and too often, still is) that the Indian craftsman's instinctive state is one of stasis.

However the supposedly natural quality of craft was assessed in nineteenth-century accounts, the very supposition of its naturalness settled it firmly within the province of the "Other"—displacing it both in space and time, either into the past or an unchanging, mystically tinged ever-present. (Here we might think of the work of Johannes Fabian, who has critiqued the modern discourse of comparative anthropology for tacitly postulating different temporalities for different cultures: "there is no knowledge of the Other which is not also a temporal, historical, a political act.")[42] Again and again, writers brought home the lesson of this distinction between progressive design and regressive craft, often comparing "savage" craftsmen with uneducated British mechanics. One critic, writing just in advance of the Great Exhibition of 1851, was moved to particularly eloquent bigotry on this point:

> The savage who tattoos his flesh, is a painter; the barbarian who ornaments his club with carvings, is a sculptor; the Red Indian who constructs his wigwam, is an architect; and even the cannibal who sings in triumph while his enemy is burning at the stake, may be called a musician. These are the wild shapes in which the passion for painting, sculpture, architecture, and music primitively developed themselves; and in proportion as these arts have advanced from the primitive state, we find man advanced in civilization and intelligence...Nor is the disparity between the untutored daub of a New Zealand artist, and the divine impressions of the great Italian master, much greater than that which may be observed between the industrial products of a people who employ the rudest kind of labour, and those who call into requisition the highest skill and intelligence.[43]

As we have already seen, writers like Hazlitt and Kleist used mechanical bodies (automata and puppets) as metaphorical exemplars of manual dexterity; they represented an ideal that a flesh and blood body could only approximate. The less self-conscious the person, the better artisan he or she would be. This is an excellent example of a nineteenth-century idea with a powerful twentieth-century inheritance. For example, in the *mingei* theory of Soetsu Yanagi and his associates, including potters Bernard Leach and Shoji Hamada, the "unknown craftsman" of Korea occupied the same position as the Indian craftsman for earlier British writers. For Yanagi, the peasant potter at work was not a fully aware modern subject, but this lack of consciousness is exactly what imbued the work with a kind of essential truth, which a more cosmopolitan maker (that is, a maker more knowledgeable of the scientific principles of the craft) could never achieve.[44] This is just one instance of theorists seeing in craft a meditative state of "no-mind," as if the artisan were a hollow vessel into which ancient skills flowed, only to be poured out anew. Walter Benjamin, too, accepted this idea of the artisan and therefore placed craft at the center of his imagined world of premodern oral tradition. Storytelling is "an artisan form of communication," as he put it. A weaver silently working in the workshop, plying a shuttle back and forth, seemed to him a perfect receptacle for ancient narratives: "The more self-forgetful the listener is, the more deeply is what he listens to impressed upon his memory. When the rhythm of work has seized him, he listens to the tales in such a way that the gift of retelling them comes to him all by itself. This, then, is the nature of the web in which the gift of storytelling is cradled."[45]

Even contemporary accounts of skill, as positive as they may be, tend to resort to the notion that execution must be done without thinking too much about it, lest the "flow" or "stroke" be spoiled.[46] This is yet another instance of the forceful invention of craft as a new category, for it was not always this way. Prior to the early nineteenth century, workmanship was usually considered a very conscious, and even self-conscious, endeavor. A 1757 dictionary, for example, described the activities of the artificer, artisan, or mechanic as "the arts which keep the mass of the people in useful action, and their minds engaged upon inventions beneficial to the whole community: and this is the grand preservative against that barbarism and brutality which ever attend an indolent and inactive stupidity."[47] The shift from such a attitude, in which the artisan's mental powers are taken for granted, to the later view that craft is all in the hands and not in the mind, could not be more stark.

STATE OF NATURE

One way of following this shifting attitude to skillful bodies at work is to consider the usage of the term "artificial" during this period. Like craft itself, this was a word in the midst of change. For many centuries, it had been used primarily to designate something fabricated by human hands ("made by mannes witte," as one sixteenth-century text put it, or "by art, not produced naturally, or in the common course of things," in one mid-eighteenth-century dictionary).[48] In cabinets of curiosities, *artificialia* were collected alongside *naturalia*—between them, these two categories and their occasional hybridizations (a partly carved, highly figured stone or horn, for example) covered the entire possible range of physical artifacts.[49] Artificial could also mean something unusually well made (as could the word "curious"). A piece of metalwork, for example, could be described as "extremely artificial" as an expression of admiration. And finally, the word artificial could mean contrived or imitative, as in an affected manner of speaking. In the realm of objects, this might be applied to a glass or ceramic object repaired "so artificially [that] one cannot perceive it was ever broken," or in the creation of an "artificial stone." (This latter phrase is a good example of the flexible meaning of the word, because it could also be used to designate a dressed stone for use in masonry.)[50] This last use of "artificial" to signify simulation became increasingly common in the middle of the eighteenth century, and is of course the primary meaning of the word today.

Political philosopher Edmund Burke's 1756 book *A Vindication of Natural Society* was both emblematic and influential in this semantic shift. Like much of Burke's writing, the text was something of a diatribe, an attack on what he called "artificial society," by which he meant the excessive incursion of institutions into human affairs. Among the specific instances of artificiality he singled out for criticism were the division of people into political groups or factions, the erection of elaborate religious systems that interfered with direct worship of the divine, and the growth of technologies for torture and warfare. He saw all of these developments as maladies of the modern age, as forces that divorce people from their rightful natural state. For Burke, these artificial systems were false and pernicious, but he was unusual in making this judgment. His contemporaries more often used the word to convey the same self-consciously modern meaning, but in a neutral or positive sense. "By the term artificial," one typical definition of the 1750s reads, "is here intended the Exercise and Progress of the *peculiar Genius* and inventive Powers of the Individuals in a State, considered in their *private* Capacity."[51] A more personal, and equally affirmative, use of the word can be seen in John Barnard's *Present for an Apprentice,* written just after the author completed a short stint as mayor of London. Barnard advises his youthful readers to adopt an "artificial insensibility" in regard to the passions, that is, a studied restraint with respect to "fear, anger, sorrow, or any concern whatever."[52] In this usage we see the equation of artificiality in the self with quasi-mechanical control.

If we return to the mechanisms explored in chapters one and two, organizational management and discursive explication, both of which controlled craft skill through abstract or institutional means, we can readily see that this repertoire was "artificial" in the early modern sense. This is another of the displacements involved in the invention of modern craft. While in previous centuries workmanship had been seen as the province of artificiality, gradually it was rendered "natural," unconscious, and thereby subsumed within comparatively powerful artificial structures alien to its interests and workings. This is, again, a distinctively modern idea about craft that has remained influential to the present day. Craft is readily presumed to be direct, forthright, honest, authentic, undisguised, organic, integrated. These are all positive terms, of course, but when seen in the light of early modern discourse about artisans both at home and abroad, we can see that these associations have their origin in an ugly discourse of asymmetrical power relations of class and imperialism. Even the most laudatory portraits of artisans were grounded in the presumption that they were special cases. Think again of Longfellow's village blacksmith, standing under his spreading chestnut tree, who "earns whate'er he can/And looks the whole world in the face/For he owes not any man" (see chapter two). In the imagination of the time, this was the characteristic picture of the modern craftsman: admirable, yes, but standing somehow outside "the whole world," detached from the economic bonds that made it go round.[53] This modern caricature of the artisan is potent because it masks marginalization through idealization. It has been all too easy for even the most fervent champions of craft to fall into the trap.

So pervasive was the modern tendency to place craft outside of artificial modernity, in both space and time, that by the nineteenth century the British artisan had become something of a conundrum. Already in 1820 John Sidney Taylor, one of the principal movers behind the London Mechanics' Institute only a few years later, was arguing that craft could only thrive in a state of primitive society. The savage's existence, he wrote in terms reminiscent of Rousseau, is "poetic" and characterized by "vigorous impulse [in] the ordinary occupations of his life."

> Not so the artisan in a civilised community; he is cut off from Nature; the fountain of his most healthful sensations is dried up; his sedentary, monotonous toil produces relaxation and infirmity; he becomes inert, sullen, and querulous, and has recourse to debauching pleasures in order to procure that excitement, which is so much the darling object of human pursuit.[54]

Taylor's solution was not universal regression to savagery, of course, but rather its opposite: artistic cultivation. Marching to the drumbeat of improvement, the workforce would eventually arrive at a fully scientific and artistic state, leaving its roots in craft behind. Yet this was always a conflicted position, for it involved respect for what was being lost, and a desire to preserve its remnants in a quasi-museological condition. As we will see in this book's final chapter, it was only a short leap of the imagination from the wholesale embrace of "artificial" means to the Arts and Crafts movement's opposite impulse to celebrate and preserve the "naturalness" of artisanal work. The generation of the 1820s and 1830s, who constructed the narrative in which craft was primitivized, sought to ameliorate that condition.

John Ruskin was the first to invert this thinking. He agreed with authors like Taylor that the essence of craft was "savagery," and also that craft was located in the past. The difference was that while Taylor regarded this savage state as irretrievable, Ruskin adopted the more quixotic objective of reinstating savagery within modern culture. Though in his case gothic Venice served as the model, his contemporaries were similarly moved to preserve Indian craft in its undisturbed primordial state. As Bernard Cohn wrote in his contribution to the seminal volume of essays *The Invention of Tradition,* imperial authorities in India "believed that Indian arts and crafts had entered a period of sharp decline in the face of western technology and machine-made products, hence their arts and crafts had to be collected, preserved, and placed in museums."[55] Yet while craft may have been *discursively* positioned as savage or natural, both at home and abroad, in *practice* it retained its ability not only to make things "artificially," to imitate. To discover this submerged region of artificial craft practice, we need to redirect our attention from the types of work the Arts and Crafts reformers would prize—textiles, furniture, metalwork, and ceramics—and instead look at activities in which imitation, rather than expression, was the presiding logic.

REPLICATION AND THE INDUSTRIAL ARTISAN

Here we run headlong into a definitional question about craft. Today the term is often used in a way that implies it necessarily involves individual creativity. This was the value sacred to Ruskin and Morris, and lay at the heart of the twentieth-century studio craft movement as well.[56] But there is another way of looking at the question. Art historian Rachel Weiss has recently argued that imitation rather than expression lies at the heart of artisanal work:

> The replica is, in a way, the realm of pure craft. It is a vehicle par excellence for bravura displays of craftsmanship since, for one thing, its success is measured by the closeness of its resemblance. The mimetic object has no identity of its own, no proper content or meaning beyond that of what it reproduces, and so the means by which it is made takes on added significance. Its objectness, its materiality, its form absorb the force that would otherwise arise from its "content."[57]

Weiss immediately follows this observation by noting that "these assertions, taken too generally, might be precarious." Maybe so; but she is definitely on to something. If you had to establish who was the most skilled among a group of glassblowers, how would you proceed? You probably would not ask all of them to invent their own objects, because then you would be testing their design aptitude, not their skill in making. It would be much better to take an existing work—a goblet, let's say—and ask each glassblower to create an exact copy of it (Figure 3.4). None would succeed completely. Every handmade copy will vary in some way, however slightly, from its model. But you could say that the person who made the *closest* approximation of the original goblet possessed the highest level of relevant skill. This is not to say, incidentally, that you would have therefore identified the best glassblower. That of course depends on what one means by "best." The quality of a craftsperson might indeed involve artistic as well as technical ability, or perhaps knowledge of a diverse repertoire of skills, and hence greater adaptability. So in finding the best copyist, you would not necessarily have found the best artisan, only the most technically skilled. As Weiss observes, this exercise would focus attention exclusively on materiality and away from content, which is effectively "given" in the form of the original.

All of this points to a little noticed and perhaps troubling aspect of craft: in its purest technical form, it is the opposite of creativity. It is premised upon the *absence* of originality. Craft in this limited, technical sense is "artificial" in the same sense as a paste gemstone: mimetic, standing in relation to something outside itself. This line of thinking yields an understanding that radically differs from the individualist, expressive convictions inherited

Figure 3.4   Goblet. Enameled glass. Collected as ca. 1770, but now thought to be a forgery. V&A: C.123–1927. © Victoria and Albert Museum, London.

from the Arts and Crafts era. It suggests that we should instead view craft as a limited, hard-won, and potentially derivative matter of approximation. As Barry Schwabsky has recently observed, craft can often be a matter of making a "good enough" object—close enough to serve some externally mandated or previously established threshold of quality or functionality, and no better.[58] Even if it would be ideally embodied in an exact replica, real-life processes are always more or less distant from a prescriptive model.

Yet craft's imitative character can also be powerfully generative. The design reformers of the mid-nineteenth century understood this, and put copying at the heart of their didactic regimens of training. Richard Redgrave, an early director of the South Kensington Museum (a designer of papier-mâché items, among other goods), wrote early in his career that "All those who have arrived at excellence have done so by beginning more or less with laboured and careful imitation." This was even truer of what Redgrave called the "ornamentist" than the fine artist, because "much of the beauty of his work depends upon mere skill of execution."[59] Yet at the same time, he insisted that "mere imitation" should never be confused with true mastery. (It is striking, by the way, how often the word "mere" was placed before such words as imitation and execution. That short modifier did a great deal of unspoken work in putting craft in its marginalized place.) Indeed, imitation and repetition were a plague upon the aesthetic landscape, wrought by machines and unthinking artisans alike:

> The mere mechanical production of ornament...the continual machine repetitions of small portions to form a whole—of segmental compartments—of alternating series, whether by blocks, the lathe, moulds, stenciling, electrotyping, or any other of the multiplying means used for that purpose, whereby the labour of the skilled hand is superseded and replaced by the dull uniformity of the machine. How opposite is this to the unending variety of nature's works!...Art, thus mechanically working, sickens us with the sameness of a tame and disgusting monotony.[60]

Redgrave's view of imitation, then, was that it is "only a means, not an end."[61] On the one hand, he saw it as the basis of artisanal prowess, the means by which mastery could be attained. On the other hand, he saw mimesis as a state to be transcended through the application of principles of design. This modern idea about craft, which frames the copyist's skill as foundationally important but also as the work of an intellectually dead hand, has been powerfully influential ever since. We can find it, for example, in the value the great British craft theorist David Pye (to whom I return at greater length in chapter four) placed on "free" workmanship because of the "diversity" it engendered. He saw this as a fundamentally human, non-artificial, antimechanical quality. The accumulated effect of many inadvertent variations enlivens a handmade product, and equally, their absence deadens a mass-produced one.[62] Here Pye echoes not only Redgrave's ideas, but also those of Hazlitt and Kleist. Visual and tactile diversity arises not out of expression, but through slight departures from a thoroughly internalized norm. So it is precisely in craftsmen's inability to repeat that the human quality of their work becomes most evident. Craft's great strength, as well as its fatal weakness, is that it cannot play a theme without variation.

Until the end of the eighteenth century, however, the presumption that craft was largely a matter of copying was taken for granted. Variation from a norm was seen as a mark of poor quality, not human affect, creativity, or individuality. The scenario imagined earlier, in which glassblowers copy a given goblet design, was in fact the normal practice of Murano hot shops for centuries. The same can be said of silversmiths or potters producing runs of more or less identical teapots day after day, and furniture makers creating sets of eight or twelve side chairs with two armchairs to match, each with exactly the same ornament. Neither the master carver, who created a model chair for journeymen to copy (Figure 3.5), nor the eventual client would have taken any pleasure in the degree to which chairs within the set differed from one another. Craft involves duplication in other ways, too. We easily miss the fact that any symmetrical object is already a copy—the left side has to match the right, and if it doesn't then we have reason to suspect that the workmanship is poor. Early design drawings often depict only half of an object, because all concerned assumed the skilled artisan executing the work would be able to replicate the form once, as drawn, and then again in reverse. Within guild-sanctioned workshop practice, copying was also the means by which skills were learned, as when an apprentice mimicked the works of a master. While Redgrave saw this as a purely educative process to be left behind at the appropriate moment, artisans in earlier centuries continued to make copies at all levels of mastery.

Figure 3.5   Side chair, Philadelphia, ca. 1769. Mahogany. Attributed to the shop of Benjamin Randolph. Chipstone Foundation 1997.17. This chair is marked "I" on an inside rail, suggesting it is the pattern chair for a set.

Only with the formation of modern craft did hand skill come to be seen as the domain of the "one off." Previously, replication was the core business of artisanal practice.

It would be easy, but very wrong, to assume that artisans' traditional role as copyists was superseded by machines, which after all do a much better job of repeating the same task over and over. In fact, however, the nineteenth century was also a time in which skilled imitation and repetition achieved unprecedented importance—paradoxically, due to the very mass production technologies that threatened to displace them. Craft operations were crucial for the industrial revolution, in ways historians often miss. First, in most areas of production, automated machines were used only in the initial stage of the manufacturing process. Finishing was generally done by hand, so that even very large factories continued to depend on repetitive handwork to complete supposedly machine-produced articles. In chapter one, I mentioned this dynamic in the case of carving. Machines could be used to rough out a form in wood, but could not achieve any detail. The same is true for lace, which was machine manufactured in large factories in the nineteenth century, but finished by supposedly "unskilled" women and girls.[63] A more surprising example is the making of interchangeable parts for guns, an innovation associated with Eli Whitney, among other improvers, that is often described as a landmark in the history of automation. Yet as David Hounshell has noted, although replicating lathes were used to create wooden stocks and metal components, these parts actually required hand finishing to make them smooth and functional. A report delivered to the British Parliament in 1853, based on observation of the American gun industry, noted that while a machine-made rifle could be made as well as one by hand, "it would have to be finished by hand; the quality would depend entirely upon the finish after it came from the machine...Whenever we want great perfection of parts we must do it by hand labour."[64]

A second way artisans continued to work at the heart of manufacturing is essentially the opposite of the first: prior to the stage of machining the article, rather than after. Patterns and prototypes, which could be replicated through casting or other processes, are an understudied but vital instance of industrial craft. As Sarah Fayen Scarlett has recently explained, the fabrication of cast metal objects such as stoves and machine tool parts depended on the skills of pattern carvers, a situation that (as she writes) "flies in the face of our commonly assumed separation of traditional crafts from industrial production, an instinct that may be especially pronounced in the case of iron foundries, whose fiery furnaces and molten metal have become quintessential symbols of industry writ large."[65] In this multistage craft, a wooden pattern was carved on the basis of a drawing (*see* Figure 3.6; an existing object, for example, a cast iron component, could also be used as the pattern). This model was then used to make a negative mold, in which the final object was destined to be cast in iron or some other metal. This is a good example of the way a mass production system can increase the importance of craft skill rather than diminishing it, for the quality of thousands of products could be dependent of the execution of a single handcrafted wooden model. A great deal of value was riding on these carved patterns, much more than any handmade commodity circulating in the marketplace.

Similarly, prototypes, though they do not have quite as direct a relationship to the final product, have long been crucial in the process of inventing and adapting designs, and remain so to the present day. In the eighteenth century, it was common for improvers to make or commission a small working model of a machine to test its operating principles, and carefully wrought prototypes have remained central to stylistic and technical innovation ever since.[66] The automotive industry has only recently abandoned the practice of developing new cars with full-scale clay models, which in turn are usually based on small-scale prototypes in other materials like cardboard or plastic. Unlike design drawings, three-dimensional modeling requires workshop space, tools, and artisanal skills, and the material and techniques used to create the prototype will always have an influence on the finished design. Patterns and prototypes are not copies, strictly speaking, but they are mimetic objects, in which craft skill is tested not on the basis of originality, but by its ability to approximate an external ideal.

A third area of craft's ongoing vitality in the era of mass production is in the operation and maintenance of machine tools, defined by John McHale as "generalized tools to make tools, which are used to manufacture the prime movers and the mass production machinery itself."[67] As mentioned in chapter one, these drivers of industrialization were typically

Figure 3.6   Cope & Timmins, lock plate pattern, nineteenth century. Carved wood. V&A: W.14–2001. © Victoria and Albert Museum, London.

handcrafted to begin with, and they typically required considerable skill not only to operate, but to keep in working order.[68] Anyone who has visited a historic site devoted to nineteenth-century industry, such as Ironbridge in Shropshire or Sturbridge Village in Massachusetts, will be struck by its intensely artisanal character. Not only tools like lathes, drill presses, and looms but also power sources, like steam engines, water mills, and blast furnaces: all were made using long-established crafts of blacksmithing, carpentry, and masonry. Keeping production going was also a job for artisans. In a sense the repair of these large-scale machines and even small bench tools was another imitative craft, in that the goal was to restore the tool to its original, or at least its working condition. This is a particularly elusive topic for the historian, because repair was (even more than other aspects of industrial craft) taken for granted in its own day. This is a subspecies of a more general problem in craft history, well described by Thomas Schlereth twenty years ago but that has not changed much since: "Often in the fetish we make of finished things or the hero worship we accord individual artisans, we forget that in pre-industrial times crafts-men often spent as much (or more) time repairing objects for clients as making them."[69]

It is still all too rare for historians to attend to repair rather than making from scratch. A fascinating exception is the essay "On a Particular Kind of Love and the Specificity of Soviet Production," by anthropologist Sergei Alasheev, which provides a compelling account of machine operatives in a Soviet ball bearing factory. According to Alasheev, despite their horrendous working conditions (unbearable noise, inadequate materials, low pay), these men identified strongly with their tools, partly because they were so old and unreliable. This meant that each had to develop an intimacy with his machine, doing endless ad hoc repairs to keep it working. Alasheev notes that the workers never traded stations with one another, and perhaps could not, so bespoke was each machine as a result of many years of patching and fixing.[70] Nineteenth-century operatives doubtless had the same personalized relationship to their tools, a relationship founded in what historian of technology Robert C. Allen calls "local learning," defined as "studying existing practice in an effort to modify it." This mentality led to the invention of tools fundamental to the progress of the industrial revolution, like the spinning jenny, invented by handloom weaver James Hargreaves in the 1760s. As Allen notes, the jenny, which permitted the operator to simultaneously spin from many spindles of cotton, "clearly mimicked the actions of a spinner and wheel, but on an expanded scale."[71] The same adaptive process occurs in an ad hoc repair, when a tool's functionality is replaced, despite the fact that its original parts cannot be.

In these three areas of industrial craft—finishing, prototyping, and tooling—there is a thorough interdependence of hand and automated processes. Modern craft exists in this impure state more often than not. The great historian of the British industrial classes, Raphael Samuel, noticed this over fifty years ago—"Formerly the skill of the artisan was expended on the objects produced; now it is expended on the machines, tools, and materials to produce them."[72] Among the greatest failings of modern craft historians has been their neglect of this vast terrain of second-order workmanship.

THE REPRODUCTIVE CONTINUUM

Yet another neglected instance of such hybridity is the artisanal manufacture of copies of works of art. Handmade replicas lay right at the heart of didactic and commercial aesthetic culture in the nineteenth century. Most were made of plaster, and it is this material I would like to explore in depth, but it is worth noting that reproductions were also realized in wax (at the celebrated emporia of Madame Tussauds and Mrs. Salmon) and in papier-mâché, discussed in the previous chapter as a novel material. Manufacturer and promoter Charles Bielefeld expounded on the superiority of this material for making casts of antique sculpture: "how perishable and fragile is a plaster-cast! How cumbrously heavy! How difficult of transport!" A papier-mâché copy, he wrote, could be made "with perfect truth and fidelity, its weight it scarcely one sixth that of plaster, and its liability to fracture less than that of stone, marble or wood."[73]

Electroforming—an application of the technology of electroplating, in which a base metal is gilded with silver in an electrically charged chemical bath, to the casting of an entire object—was another new means of making copies. It was normally conducted at a smaller scale, more appropriate for decorative domestic goods, but some firms produced large-scale "electrotypes" (exact copies) of sculptures, such as the pioneer in the field, Elkington and

Figure 3.7 Alexandre Gueyton, casket, 1851. Oxidized silver and silver gilt, set with rubies and half pearls. V&A: 155–1852. © Victoria and Albert Museum, London.

Co., with shops in London and Birmingham; Giovanni Franchi and Son; and the German firm of H. Geiss.[74] Once fabricated, an electrotype needed to be finished or "worked down" by hand, not unlike a gun part.[75] It is not surprising, though, that like rubber and the other "plastic" media of the time, electrotyping was seen as a viable replacement for craft rather than an extension of it. This was made explicit through the copying of notable feats of skill past and present—a cup by Renaissance master Benvenuto Cellini, for example, or specimens by contemporary silversmiths. When the South Kensington Museum purchased a Gothic Revival casket by French craftsman Alexandre Gueyton, which had been awarded a medal at the Great Exhibition for its quality of execution (not its design, which was found excessively architectural given its small scale), it promptly commissioned an electrotype copy from Elkington's at about one-fifth of the price of the original (Figures 3.7 and 3.8). Yet the two caskets were considered equally valuable as objects of study—their forms, after all, were identical. While Gueyton's casket was obviously precious and unique, it was also anchored in the past, both in terms of its style and its manner of making. The Elkington copy by contrast was thoroughly modern, a demonstration of technology's astonishing reproductive powers. What was admirable in the Frenchman's original could be ascribed to him alone; the copy attested to an achievement of a broader nature, a cultural rather than individual achievement. (Interesting, a South Kensington Museum catalogue of its

Figure 3.8 Elkington & Co., casket, 1854. Electrotype reproduction of the Alexandre Gueyton casket shown in fig. 8. Copper, silvered and oxidized. V&A: REPRO.1854D-40. © Victoria and Albert Museum, London.

collection of electrotypes paused to note that publishing original works of art would be useful in "guarding against spurious imitations which are now executed with the greatest ingenuity and skill." Clearly, some kinds of copying were considered better than others.)[76]

Electrotyping has often been compared to photography, partly due to a coincidence of timing—the two processes were invented just on either side of 1840—but also because both were ways of producing a duplicate of unprecedented fidelity through artificial means. Electrotypes and photography, along with other techniques like plaster casts, were both means of gathering together the world in the form of the copy. Together, they initiated one of modernity's most conspicuous features, the pervasiveness of simulacra within the field of experience (Figure 3.9).[77] There are numerous ways of approaching this topic, but here I want to focus on the question of *indexicality*—a semiotic term that designates a sign with some direct physical relationship to its referent—for example, a footprint on the beach that captures the impression of the foot that made it.[78] All crafted objects are indexical to the extent that they reveal the process of their own making. Photographs and plaster casts are double indexes: of the things they represent and the technique used to create them, which is, of course, much more involved than stepping in wet sand. These two types of indexicality have a dynamic relation to one another, as is evident from the fact that making a natural-looking

Figure 3.9   Retail showroom of Elkington & Co., Birmingham, 1904. V&A Metalwork Department, photography files.

photograph or a very accurate cast requires quite a lot of skill. This paradox is inherent in any mimetic process, and was already recognized in the eighteenth century, even before the emergence of modern reproductive technologies. Diderot puzzled over the value of illusion in painting (not an indexical process, granted, but the line of thinking is relevant), and noticed that skillful painters seem to erase the marks of their own craft. In the words of art historian Marian Hobson, he observed that "if the view is transparent, it must tend to annul its own process of production, the very *faire* [making] which brought it into being. *Faire* does not mediate between the subject of the picture and the spectator, but strives to cancel itself."[79] This self-effacing function is still more powerful and confounding in photography and casting. Both involve a truth effect, which verisimilitude is to some extent an automatic outcome of the process, and to some extent a matter of contrivance. The more skilled the artisan, the more likely it is his or her skill will be taken as "merely" mechanical.

When it comes to photography, this dynamic has been well studied; since the influential writings of Susan Sontag in the 1970s, many theorists have addressed the medium's characteristic blurring of automatic and authorial effects.[80] It is indeed fascinating how this artificial technology has come to completely transform our understanding of the world around us. So skilled have photographers become at restaging reality that we often find their surrogates more persuasive than the things they represent. The degree of artfulness may vary, but it is present to some extent in every photo. There would appear to be an absolute difference between documentary images, which seem to flatly transcribe the world, and obviously styled images that depart from "natural" ways of seeing. But in practice the distinction is impossible to maintain. In examining even the most banal newspaper snapshot, one soon notices the subtle narrative effects of exposure, crop, color, and development. Conversely, there is a nagging facticity at the heart of the most artfully composed and processed art photo.

The thicket of photographic authorship may seem even more tangled today than it did in the past, thanks to digital manipulation, but matters were already plenty complicated in the nineteenth century. For one thing, photographic images were usually encountered indirectly, through the mediating craft of wood engraving. This refinement of woodblock printing, in which a dense block was carved on its end grain, was invented in the late eighteenth century as a technique for mass distribution of drawings and paintings. It had a brief moment of creative autonomy early in the century, exemplified by the playful vignettes of Thomas Bewick (the subject of a recent, lovingly detailed biography by Jenny Uglow).[81] But it only became commonplace from the 1840s, thanks to its usefulness in transcribing photographs (see Figure 4.1). As Gerry Beegan has shown, wood engraving rapidly became "mechanical" under the pressure to accurately mimic: "Harnessed to photographic technologies, engravers and draughtsmen became producers of facsimile work, copiers rather than interpreters of images," and the small shops that initially pursued the craft were replaced by dispersed outwork systems, much like the furniture making trade discussed in chapter one.[82] This is another skilled trade to add to the roster of modern crafts that deflected attention away from themselves.

Like an electrotype, a photograph, or a photographically based wood engraving, a plaster cast presented itself to the nineteenth-century viewer as a indexical object, a true representation, but it was actually the product of careful manipulation. Of course there is one big difference among these sorts of copy: while a photo captures a spatial view and compresses it into a two-dimensional plane, electrotypes and casts transcribe discrete objects exactly, retaining their three-dimensionality. This makes them seem more neutral than a photo; and it is true that they offer less room for maneuver. Yet this apparently self-evident character is deceptive. Like a photographic snapshot, a cast is a frozen moment in time. It captures the original at only one moment (Figure 3.10). This temporal fixity can be quite dramatic, as in a death mask, or relatively inconsequential, as in an architectural cast—though here too the factor of temporal specificity may suddenly become crucial if the original building is drastically eroded or destroyed. More pertinent for my purposes, a plaster cast is like a photograph in that it indexes not one, but two realities: the original, and the process of making of the copy, prioritizing the former over the latter.

Plaster casts, like electrotypes, were didactic in their intention. Great works of European architecture and sculpture were copied so that students could copy them again in drawings. The origins of this practice lay in fine art academies, which had long kept casts for the use of students, but the craft expanded rapidly in eighteenth-century Italy as a result of the Grand Tour. Miniature and full-scale plaster casts were sold to aristocratic tourists, alongside architectural models in cork and hand-carved copies of sculpture in marble (some

Figure 3.10   Domenico Brucciani & Co., plaster cast of Thomas Carlyle's hands (after a sculpture by Sir Joseph Edgar Boehm). Plaster. V&A: REPRO.1892–1897. © Victoria and Albert Museum, London.

masquerading as originals). When brought back to England, France, Germany, Scandinavia, or elsewhere in Northern Europe, these copies functioned doubly as decorative specimens and objects of study.[83] In America, far distant from the acknowledged centers of culture, they were seen as a way for an unlettered public to be "illuminated by the great and ancient ideals of art in foreign lands."[84] Yet in the reception of these supremely aestheticized and explanatory objects, most of the artisans who actually made copies disappeared from view. There were prominent exceptions—John Cheere, who produced sculptures in both stone and lead in his workshop, or Benjamin and Robert Shout, who offered an extensive catalogue of plaster casts depicting historical and popular subjects, much in the manner of ceramic manufactories.[85] But as the statuary business grew from a modest trade to a grandiose artisanal industry, authorship remained firmly attached to the figure of the sculptor rather than the artisan. Much of the plaster cast industry was based in Italy itself, in order to serve the tourist market, and artisans there were treated with xenophobia and condescension: "the Italian image-venders, whom we encounter daily on our streets, holding out a Washington or a Venus, an appealing to us to 'buy—very fine!'"[86]

In this respect, the making of sculptural copies prefigures the equally disdained production of kitsch figurines sold at tourist sites today. Yet plaster casts were also carried out at a massive scale, akin to civil engineering. Making a copy of the magnitude of the ones displayed in the Cast Courts of the South Kensington Museum (now the V&A), which opened in 1873—the entirety of Trajan's Column (so large that it is cut into two to fit into the building), or the façade known as the Pórtico da Gloria, from the gothic cathedral Santiago de Compostela in Spain—was no easy matter (Figure 3.11). Only a handful of firms were capable of the feat, notably that of Italian expatriate Domenico Brucciani, who moved to London in the 1830s, exhibited his casts as specimens of technical excellence at the Great Exhibition, and by 1861 was operating a workshop with twenty-five artisans.[87] When Brucciani and his team created a large-scale architectural cast like the Pórtico da Gloria, the main challenge was to take an accurate mold off the original, a process that necessitated detailed piece molding, especially if the object to be cast featured deep undercutting. (Contemporary plaster casting is done with a flexible molding material such as silicone rubber. In the nineteenth century, clay was used, until the invention of seamless gelatin molds by cast maker Giovanni Franchi—also a pioneer in electrotyping. This technique made it possible to create larger, more volumetric forms in a single piece.[88]) There were many other considerations as well. The original had to be carefully covered with thin foils to protect its surface, and after the molds were made in sections, they had to be joined and patched to create a seamless whole. Finally, a surface treatment was applied to imitate the original's coloration. Again, the procedure was understood at the time as comparable to photography. Casting projects like the one at Santiago de Compostela, carried out by Brucciani in 1866, were sometimes paired with a photographic documentation campaign. At South Kensington, the plaster casts and photos were displayed alongside one another, as well as with electrotypes and less well-known types of copy such as "fictile ivories" (plaster casts dipped in stearine), in what Malcolm Baker has called a "reproductive continuum."[89] Interested visitors and art school lecturers could even reproduce the experience of the reproductions by ordering photographic prints or plaster casts from the museum's Department of Science and Art.

As this implicit comparison between different indexical processes suggests, the overwhelming tendency in the nineteenth century was to treat casts as if they were direct transmissions of an original; any original contribution by a set of human hands specific to the copying medium itself was most unwelcome. The fidelity of the cast was valued, not its craftsmanship, even though the former was entirely dependent on the latter. It is for this reason that *surmoulage* or "after-casting" was so disdained. In this practice, a cast was taken off another cast rather than an original. Because of the logistical difficulty of gaining direct access to antique works and the expense of keeping large collections of molds on hand, there was a strong motivation to create such copies of copies. The phenomenon was widespread already in the eighteenth century and became only more common over time. This infuriated connoisseurs and museum professionals. Though they cited concerns about loss of surface detail, it is clear that what really bothered them was the gap between the copy and its referent that the intervening copy seemed to constitute.[90]

A similar problem arose in the context of fabricating new sculptures. Modern ateliers were prolific as never before, serving the period's huge enthusiasm for public monuments and new display opportunities afforded by museums and international expositions. To meet the demand, artists became increasingly dependent on plaster casts. For the most successful

Figure 3.11   Domenico Brucciani & Co., plaster cast of the Pórtico da Gloria, Santiago de Compostela, 1866. Plaster. V&A: REPRO.1866–1850. © Victoria and Albert Museum, London.

neoclassical sculptors of the time, figures like Antonio Canova, Francis Chantrey, Hiram Powers, and Bertel Thorvaldsen, casts served an important mediatory role, capturing the marks of the master's hands so they could be reproduced by a team of assistants. The sculptor would first make a quick sketch (*bozzetto*), and then either a more finished small-scale maquette or a full-scale model in clay. This autograph work was then used as the basis for a plaster cast, which was then remade again (sometimes more than once) in marble, through a process that would at the time have been seen as eminently "mechanical"—transferred through the use of a pointing machine, and then carved roughly to shape by assistants. The sculptor would then intervene again, applying a finish or skin, much as a painter might leave the drapery and landscape background of a portrait to others and fill in the head and hands. Sometimes the plaster cast was embedded with shallow knobs to assist in the pointing. Because these projected just off the surface, the marble copy was slightly larger than the plaster (and, of course, the clay original), giving the master sculptor a thin layer to carve in order to achieve the final surface.

The mediatory plaster casts themselves had unclear status. On one hand, given that the unfired clay maquettes were typically destroyed, the casts were as close as one could get to the sculptor's original conception, and they were normally retained by the studio (partly so that subsequent versions of the work could be made, if the occasion arose; see Figure 3.12).

Figure 3.12   Sir Francis Chantrey, maquette for a statue of Reginald Heber, Bishop of Calcutta, ca. 1827. Unfired clay. V&A: A.29–1933. © Victoria and Albert Museum, London.

Some sculptors, like Chantrey, displayed their casts in their ateliers or in private galleries, describing them with the appropriately uncertain terminology: "original models."[91] Of course they were not originals, only copies—neither handmade prototypes nor finished artworks. So other sculptors tended to treat their casts merely as mechanical aids, instead drawing attention to their modeling and carving skills. As Martina Droth notes, "by thus underplaying the manual engagement of the hand, the artist's work was presented not so much as a physical carving-out of form than as a quasi-conceptual process: the imprint of thought, the application of inspiring touches."[92] Canova, for example, emphasized his abilities in rendering the delicate texture of flesh and cloth, prompting what one art historian calls a "cult of the surface" around his work (Figure 3.13).[93] Already in the late eighteenth century, this led to a hierarchical arrangement in what might be called the sculpture industry, in which some sculptors were recognized as authorial geniuses, while others worked "mechanically" and in obscurity—despite the fact that they did most of the work. Matthew Craske has framed this division in terms of class, writing that while leading sculptors enjoyed a privileged relationship with aristocratic and political elites: "this relationship [was] denied the 'workman' producer, whose involvement in the mechanical grind of 'facture' placed him at a considerable disadvantage in his dealings not only with aristocratic, but

Figure 3.13   Hugh Douglas Hamilton, *Antonio Canova in his Studio with Henry Tresham and a Plaster Cast for Cupid and Psyche*, 1788–1791. Pastel on paper. V&A: E.406–1998. © Victoria and Albert Museum, London.

also with wider 'polite' society."[94] Here is yet another case where artisans effaced themselves by means of their own imitative craft.

Rather like nineteenth-century museums, sculptors and their clients were unsure how to treat the plaster cast: was it to be considered interchangeable with its original or a distinctly inferior object? In later years, this question was settled in favor of the latter point of view. The vast majority of Victorian plaster casts were destroyed in the early twentieth century; the V&A's collection is a rare survival, and even in this case there was a close call in 1928, when prominent architect Reginald Blomfeld recommended that the architectural casts should be discarded, as by then they seemed "unworthy to the Museum, [and] actually injurious to students."[95] Even as they fell from favor as teaching tools, casts stopped being used within sculpture workshops, as more immediate techniques like direct carving and assemblage became the norm—reflecting the twentieth-century art world's overwhelming preference for unique originals. Thus the currency of plaster casts, in both educational and exhibitionary contexts, lasted little more than a century. Yet in that time they had been emblematic objects of modern craft. Like so many artisanal contributions to the nineteenth century's ideas of progress, they were the products of extraordinary, even unprecedented skill, the greatest feats of plasterwork ever attempted. Yet the specificity of their making was of little interest to observers at the time. It was even, to some extent, an inconvenience. Plaster casts were all about directing attention away from themselves: backward to the history of art and architecture, to an absent original, or else, in the manner of a prototype, ahead to a subsequent stage along a chain of reproduction. The more well made they were, the more effectively they performed this work of redirection, the harder they were to see as craft at all.

ANALOGUE PRACTICE

In the crafted copy, then, skill hides in plain sight. The handmade replica anchors an expansive structure of value, in which the opposing ideals of indexicality and originality are set into a dialectical relation.[96] In recent years, this strategy has been front and center in the art world, all the more potent because of the mediated distribution through images of what was already a reproduction. Consider for example *Sphinx*, British artist Marc Quinn's imagining of Kate Moss twisted into the contorted positions of a yoga master (Figure 3.14). The work and its many subsequent versions are achieved through casting in plaster, in this case directly from a live (super)model.[97] Once he had created molds of Moss's head and each of her limbs, Quinn was able to assemble the casts of her body parts into various configurations—exploiting the section-by-section, collage-like composition that has always been a part of making plaster casts, though that is rarely so dramatically evident in the finished object. This composite body was then cast in bronze, which is painted white (suggesting marble or precious metal without actually imitating it; improbably enough, a later version called *Siren* was fabricated in eighteen carat gold). With their Buddha-like seated postures and echo of a multi-armed Hindu diety, the sculptures wryly capture the truism that celebrities are the twenty-first century's spiritual icons. The unsettling distortions of Moss's body, which leave her impassive, beatific face undisturbed, also convey the idea that she was an impossible object to begin with. Thanks to photographic burnishing, a super-model like Moss is an unattainable ideal; there is even a suggestion here of the nineteenth-century idea that casts and photographs operate in more or less the same territory.[98] As the artist puts it, the work is "a portrait of an image, and the way that image is sculpted and twisted by our collective desire."[99]

Quinn's work is deft in its investigation of these themes, but when you see one of the sculptures in person, you almost have to remind yourself to think about its conceptual content. You're too busy being amazed by the craftsmanship, just as when you visit the Cast Courts at the Victoria and Albert Museum your first reaction is not generally to think about the scrambled history of art and architecture presented to you, but rather the amazing scale and hyperrealism of the copies. While Quinn's sculptures are vividly contemporary, in sheer productive terms they are strongly reminiscent of nineteenth-century sculpture. He initiated the Kate Moss series in 2006 and has created numerous variations since, repeating and adapting the figure like an academic nineteenth-century sculptor. And like Chantrey or Canova, Quinn realizes his work with the help of numerous specialized assistants, though in his case this is not conducted in his own atelier but outsourced to London-based fabrication firms like MDM Props and AB Foundry. These same companies also produce theater sets, retail fixtures, museum exhibitions, and historical restorations; like Italian cast maker Brucciani, their talents can be put to a range of uses, from the commercial to the artistic.

Quinn's portraits of Kate Moss, then, could be considered a bookend to the history of modern sculpture that began with the rise and fall of the plaster cast. They mark a decline that is also a return—the decline of the unique original, made by the artist's own hands, as

Figure 3.14   Marc Quinn, *Sphinx*, 2005.
Painted bronze. Photo: Stephen White.
Courtesy White Cube.

the dominant model of art making, and a return to the more potent but conflicted tactics of distributed authorship.

Nor is Quinn alone in his investigations of historical sculpting techniques. Many other artists have turned to the complex processes of prototyping and copying within the studio, often using plaster casts as part of the process. Some, notably Rachel Whiteread, are interested in the quality of plaster as a medium in its own right, but for most it is a means to an end. Tony Cragg uses plaster models, as well as ones made in plywood and polyurethane, to realize monumental sculptural forms that hover somewhere between figuration and abstraction. Like Quinn, he relies on a large workforce to do this, though in Cragg's case the assistants are not outsourced, but based in his own workshop in Wuppertal, Germany. Recently, his process has involved creating stacks built out of profiled planks, which can be modulated into one another through hand carving (Figure 3.15). Interestingly, this process echoes works made right at the beginning of his career, in which found objects (for example, studio detritus) might be stacked or otherwise assembled into a geometrical shape, like a cube, or a representational image. He developed this approach into the body of work for which he was, until recently, best known—sculptural pictures of a Union Jack, a figure, or a map, all rendered in bits of found plastic rubbish. After a few years of exploring this postmodernist repertoire, he felt it had become repetitive. He describes the itinerant experience of making them—alighting at one museum after another, in one city after another, gathering material and making the pieces as he went—as initially exciting and ultimately a bore. So he decided

Figure 3.15 The studio of Tony Cragg, 2009. Courtesy of the artist.

to return to the studio and to invest in more traditional means of sculptural production, particularly metal casting using plaster molds. His first experiments with this technique were already monumental: large-scale versions of everyday objects, such as a mortar and pestle or a set of abstracted chemical flasks, which referred back to the transformative powers of alchemy.[100] Gradually, working from this base, he developed the much more involved procedures of stacking and carving that he uses today, which give him the flexibility to "build, unbuild and rebuild" as he invents a form. With these techniques, he can create complex curvilinear shapes with internal channels and voids, which would be impossible to realize through conventional direct carving (Figure 3.16).[101] Cragg does rely on digital renderings to establish the profile for each component—"we'd be stupid not to use the best tools for the job, I don't want to be silly about it"—and he relies on a digital technician to do this work for him. But he does not regard the computer as a creative design tool. Far from it:

> A computer can't make decisions. You can give it a job—make a spoon. And it will make one spoon, ten spoons, a million spoons. It could fill the universe with spoons and it wouldn't make a bit of difference, because the computer doesn't care... digitalizing everything is a kind of way of accelerating entropy. It's too easy, it slips through everything.

Cragg here voices opposition to any treatment of materiality as if it were a frictionless affair completely subject to technology, or, for that matter, to the will of the maker. On the

Figure 3.16   Tony Cragg, *Hamlet*, 2009. Wood. Courtesy of the artist and the Lisson Gallery.

contrary, the difficulty of achieving his forms is a big part of their attraction, both for Cragg himself and for his public. While he would not necessarily call himself a craftsman, and is quite suspicious of any romantic associations his sculptures' "handmade" qualities might carry, there is nonetheless something deeply artisanal in his approach. More often than not, this has to do with analogue replications and translations—the extensions and alterations that occur as one of his hand drawings is transformed into a digital rendering, and then into a three-dimensional prototype, and finally into a monumental cast metal sculpture that yet retains some of the gestural quality of the original drawing. Cragg finds his forms by reflecting on every step of this process, and the work of many hands that occurs along the way, and revisiting this terrain of production over and over again. He often finds himself stepping back from a finished sculpture and the preparatory studies made for it and reconsidering. "At the end of it, you are left with the thought about what would have been it would have been a completely different result," he says. "And that can be the essence of the next work. The path not taken can be the next project."

At the far end of the spectrum from Cragg's exploratory form finding, which treats materiality as a fluid terrain, we find an even more thickly populated terrain: the realm of the handmade copy, an idiom in which the concept of analogue process is applied much more literally and prescriptively. While this type of work refers more explicitly to a Duchampian, conceptual tradition of art, it is actually no less craft intensive than Cragg's process. An early and particularly effective example, made long before Quinn persuaded Moss to submit to being molded in plaster, is Vija Celmins' sculpture *To Fix the Image in Memory* (1977–1982), for which she cast eleven stones in bronze and then painted them to match the originals (Figure 3.17). So fine is Celmins's handiwork that it is impossible to tell when examining the work which are the real rocks and which the fakes. This has a rather befuddling effect. The viewer's initial reaction is certainly to be amazed, but it's a very different kind of response from the one incited by Cragg's feats of making. Not only do these humble rocks lack visual dynamism and imaginative form; it is not even clear which ones are the products of great skill and effort and which are just natural stones. You want to appreciate the craftsmanship, but you literally don't know where to look for it.

Many artists since have created handmade replicas in a similar spirit, not usually placing them in direct relation to an original, as Celmins did, but rather duplicating objects so everyday that their verisimilitude can be easily assessed. These reproductions recall Rachel Weiss's idea that imitation is the purest form of craft, and they draw their aesthetic and conceptual potency directly from that source. Often the effect is to monumentalize that which is previously overlooked, as in Yoshihiro Suda's carved and painted sculptures of weeds, which are inserted into the marginal spaces of museums, Robert Gober's handprinted copies of newspapers, which turn the headlines of any given day into concrete poetry, or Wilfrid Almendra's handcrafted tools, "charged with an optimism and a consideration that we rarely come across these days," at least according to his gallery.[102] Other artists revisit the *vanitas* tradition of still life, using the fixity of the crafted copy as a way to arrest the flow of time: Ugo Rondinone's handpainted metal fruits, or Charles Ray's perfect copy of a crashed automobile, complete

Figure 3.17   Vija Celmins, *To Fix the Object in Memory,* 1977–1982. Stones and painted bronze, eleven pairs. Museum of Modern Art, New York, 679.2005.

with intricately made casts of every scrap of twisted metal and upholstery, and even the trash that was in the car's rear trunk. There are the psychologically resonant uses of casts by Janine Antoni, who created self-portraits in chocolate and soap, and then licked and washed them in an exercise of alternately painful and pleasurable narcissism; Tom Friedman, a maestro of tedium who has made exact, hand-folded copies of crumpled office paper; Mike Nelson, who recreates real-world spaces, duplicating them by hand and joining them into walkthrough labyrinths; and Urs Fischer, who has revived the tradition of grand-manner baroque sculpture in his full-scale wax model of Giambologna's *Rape of the Sabines,* then burned it down like a giant candle, so that it cascades to the floor in drips and rivulets—a powerful image of art history going up in smoke. And then there are artists who use handmade replicas to explicitly draw attention to disregarded forms of labor, such as Susan Collis, who uses inlay and embroidery to fashion preternaturally accurate replicas of the desiderata of art installation, such as paint-spattered tarps, stepladders, and dropcloths, or the Swiss partnership Peter Fischli and David Weiss, who have completely recreated their own studio (complete with pizza boxes and other studio trash) in carved and painted polyurethane, or Sam Durant, who has commissioned a Chinese porcelain factory to make copies of injection molded plastic chairs (also typically made in China, but globally omnipresent). In this case no casting was made; all the work is done by hand, from scratch. But the monochrome glazes and softly molded edges of Durant's chairs evoke the quality of cast plastic, and even the faux basket weave upholstery on the back is reproduced faithfully in a delicate lattice of clay. In this case, craft has been used to faithfully duplicate an object that was already a simulacrum, a copy of a copy that never had an original. So where is the real thing here? Perhaps, Durant suggests, only in the specific interlinked circumstances of production, in which he (as an American artist employing Chinese artisans) has enmeshed himself. So much is implied by his titles for the chairs, which include the name of every person who contributed to their manufacture, "to ensure," as Durant notes, "that this information will never disappear as they circulate in the art world" (Plate 10).[103]

All of these handmade copies, and the legion of other instances of the strategy in contemporary art, mark a post-postmodern relation to authorship, which is not so much a matter of paralytic doubt (the much-discussed "death of the author" has little purchase on these works) as it is an active exploration, which might be poetic, psychological, or political. All of these possibilities are opened up by the intersection of craft and indexicality. The process of remaking something, unlike Duchampian appropriation, takes time as well as skill. The fact of extreme duration—a theme emphasized in many of the works mentioned earlier—allows the artist to claim an existing piece of the world without yielding fully to its productive reality. Craft here stands in as an assertion of will, a refusal to remain passive in the face of mass-produced commodities. For some artists (such as Gober and Durant), the transposition of one material to another acts as political commentary; in other cases, the simple fact of the effort involved in making the copy is enough to create a rupture in the fabric of commodity exchange. Strangely enough, by chaining themselves to the principle of imitation, these artists create a free space for invention. As Fischli has noted, "'Duchamp's [ready-mades] could revert back to everyday life at any point in time. Our objects can't do that; they're only there to be contemplated…They are, to put it simply, freed from the slavery of their utility.'"[104]

The vitality and flexibility of this artistic strategy is exemplified by French artist Isabelle Cornaro, who looks back to the nineteenth century for inspiration, and beyond. She too uses casting techniques, and for her these refer not only to plaster casts but also to the astonishing grotesques of sixteenth-century French potter Bernard Palissy. Festooned with every manner of lizard, frog, shell, and fern, these half-millennium-old ceramics exhibit awesome technical mastery, and are replete with spiritual associations grounded in process (for Palissy, life casting was infused with divine overtones because of its similarity to the fossil making God conducted through the geological actions of the earth).[105] It is ironic that these intensely naturalistic works should be so inspirational for Cornaro, for as she says, her own interest lies primarily in the "denaturalization" of given aesthetic categories. "What we call a 'minimal' black line on a piece of paper," she writes, "may arise from a totally metaphoric and 'figurative' process; or a casted heap of kitsch objects may be the result of a purely nominalist gesture and thus be quite 'abstract.'"[106]

Instead of medium specificity, then, Cornaro explores media mutability, transformations that cross the apparent gaps between one discrete process and another. In two related series entitled *Moulages sur le Vif (Vides Poches)* and *Homonymes,* the two indexical processes of photography and plaster casting are brought face to face with the found objects they reproduce (Plate 11 and Figure 3.18). Cornaro skips like a stone between these three object-states, subjecting each in turn to the same scenographic vision. Within this motion, the act of copying provides a stable ground in what would otherwise be a vertiginous viewing experience. There is more than an echo here of Joseph Kosuth's famous Conceptual art work *One and Three*

Figure 3.18   Isabelle Cornaro, *Homonymes*, 2010. Grey plaster cast. Casting by Pierre Imbertèche.

Chairs (1965), which consists of an actual chair, a photo of a chair, and a dictionary definition of the word chair. That work aspired to the condition of an ontological proposition—a philosophical meditation about the nature of being. What Cornaro brings to this well-laid table is an additional reflection on process. The replication of the "original" objects, either in somber gray plaster or as a large-format digital scan, dramatically abstracts them, turning them into a still-life sculpture like one might find atop a tomb, or into a nearly abstract, flat composition. Her choices of title are revealing. *Homonymes* speaks for itself, but the punning subtitle of the photographic works resists translation: *Moulage sur le Vif* means "life moulding," but also implies a speculative process; *Vide Poche* literally means "empty pocket," but also is an idiomatic term for a valet tray of the kind left on a hallstand to collect keys, coins, and the like. These double meanings capture the simultaneity of absence and casual presence in the works, which are at once a faithful transcription of the original objects' faux casual arrangement and an erasure of their physicality. The three-dimensional *Homonymes,* rendered in gray plaster, similarly restate their originals while also turning them into ghostly traces, monumentalizing an entirely provisional arrangement. Unlike Quinn, or for that matter the sculptors of Canova's generation, in this case it is the original that seems lacking, requiring the compositional force achieved through the process of replication.

Like the work of Quinn, Celmins, Collis, and the other art world examples described previously, Cornaro's sculptures can be described as analogue practice in a double sense, both as things that are handmade (not digital) and as copies, which approximate the world outside the work (in the manner of a literary analogy, but in material terms). Her "flatbed" compositions explicitly claim not only the ceramics of Palissy and the Conceptual art of Kosuth as precedents, but also the assemblage-based combines of Robert Rauschenberg.[107] The crucial difference is that Rauschenberg simply incorporated the detritus of everyday life in his work, while Cornaro processes it through a more arcane set of skills—skills the viewer can't really miss, given that they are contrasted directly with one another. In this respect, she is using the handmade copy as one way to reinscribe the line between life and art, a line both permeable and resistant, with craft assuming the frictional, transformative, neo-alchemical role with which we are now familiar.

IN AND OUT OF TOUCH

If analogue practice is a matter of partial resistance to the flow of commodities through our lives, then one of the things it is undoubtedly resisting is the all-pervasive fluidity of the digital. When artists make accurate replicas by hand, they are asking us to look more carefully, prompting us to evaluate what we see instead of letting experience wash right over us, as it so often does these days. Of course, that impulse to slow down our perceptions is not limited to the confined precincts of the art world. The handmade copy may be an unusually explicit case, but it only emphasizes what we already know: craft stands in tacit opposition to the rapid-fire movement of contemporary life, especially life online, which presents us with an unending precession of vicarious, often shallow, experiences. Similarly for structures of making; as I have argued throughout this book, craft performs a vital facilitating role within modern structures of dispersed authorship, which is enabled by the appropriation and displacement of skills. But it also constantly applies a brake to distributive movement. In this sense too, craft is intrinsically analogue (as opposed to digital). Its physicality is irreducible, and while it can be translated through casts or other mechanical means, that process will always retain its own specificity.

So what value does craft retain in an environment conditioned by the hyperreal? Is it just a matter of getting in the way, an obstacle course that impedes the otherwise irresistible flow of information? That is one way it is often described, especially by DIY "craftivists" who believe that slow and local are the way to go. There is an undeniable logic to this argument. Craft demands proximity—the material to the maker, the tool to the work—and this spatial consideration applies its own sort of friction. But to count too heavily on such immediacy is to construct a conception of craft premised upon its own eventual failure (much like the machine-breaking protests carried out by the Luddites of the 1810s).[108] Digitization is too sweeping in its effects to be ameliorated by simply digging in and sitting tight. It transforms and speeds up not only the flow of information, but also the production of material things and their subsequent movement. It inaugurates a completely new spatial logic. If the analogue operates along sequences of discrete vectors, coherent if not quite predictable, then digital space is haphazard, structured around arbitrary leaps. Analogue motion is like walking, while digital movement is more like teleportation.[109] We are all familiar with this experience of constant displacement through browsing the web or engaging in a social network like Facebook. But the same dynamic also occurs in the context of production. With the help of digital technology, commodities are more and more easily synthesized from components built in disparate places, ideas formulated in different contexts. Objects are increasingly brought into being through disconnection, not despite it. The frictional effects of craft, if conceived merely as stoppages in this system, could only ever be provisional anyway. They would soon be circumvented.

So craft does indeed need to integrate itself with digital means—the two are not incompatible. This is not to give up on the idea that the analogue is opposed to the digital; in fact, insofar as opposition is the beginning of any dialectical train of thought, the mutual antagonism of these categories is exactly why it is so interesting to see how they interact. Yet new forms of practice will inevitably be forged through the synthesis of the analogue and the digital themselves. The first scholar to argue persuasively for such a triangulating maneuver was Malcolm McCullough, in his 1996 book *Abstracting Craft: The Practiced Digital Hand,* and he did so in somewhat surprising terms. McCullough contended that hand skills were central to computer-assisted design and would become dramatically more so over time. Simple point-and-click motions, he predicted, might become the basis of a haptically rich craft practice. He was of course aware that using a standard computer mouse is hardly similar to wielding a traditional craft tool, but he nonetheless thought that it was the first step toward a brave new world of digital craft process: "we can begin to develop a provisional sensibility based on what we have, and wait for eventual developments in touch technology to remove our remaining reservations."[110]

McCullough's book was written over fifteen years ago. Today, with the benefit of hindsight, his optimism seems to have been at least somewhat misplaced. One never knows what the future will hold, but the promise of completely computer-based craftsmanship seems to remain a distant prospect. It is true that there have been a number of experiments in which objects are achieved, directly or indirectly, with haptic tools—digital hammers, interactive software that exploits touchscreen and motion sensor technology, and so on. Other projects claim to document a craft-like attitude to digital tooling, such as the British Crafts Council's exhibition Labcraft (2010). But so far, none of this research seems to meet a real need. Rather than being dictated by external demand or the inherent logic of the new tools, the motivation seems to be mostly about finding an ongoing home for craft (or perhaps more accurately, university craft departments) in unfriendly terrain. This contemporary "digital craft" is uncomfortably reminiscent of the "designer-craftsman" phenomenon of the 1950s, when studio craft movement advocates argued that industrial designers should involve them in the process of creating prototypes for mass production.[111] Those claims fell largely on deaf ears, and the same seems to be true today. Corporations may require skilled workers to develop their product lines, but they seem eminently capable of training and directing those workers on their own terms. There's nothing wrong with the

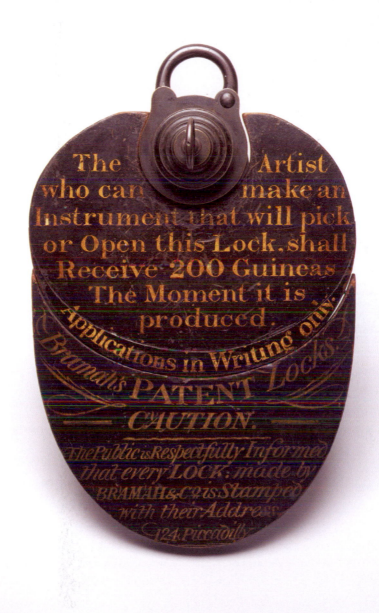

Plate 1. Challenge Board for Bramah Padlock, 1801. © Science Museum/Science & Society Picture Library.

Plate 2.   Robert Adam (designer), Matthew Boulton (mount maker), and Mayhew and Ince (cabinetmakers), with earlier *pietra dura* plaques by Baccio Cappelli, the Kimbolton Cabinet, 1771–1776. Mahogany and oak, with marquetry in satinwood and rosewood, pietra dura plaques and ormolu (gilt-bronze) mounts. W.43–1949. © Victoria and Albert Museum, London.

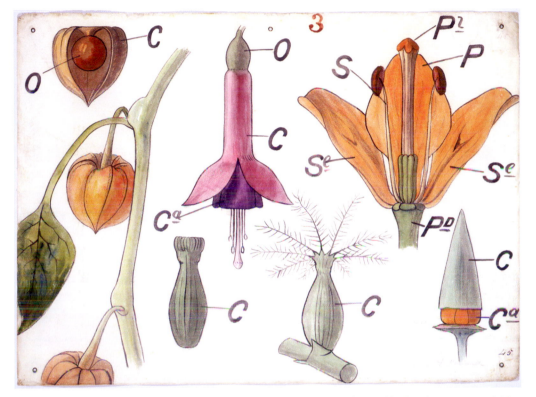

Plate 3. Christopher Dresser, botanical drawing, ca. 1855. Watercolor and bodycolor on paper, laid on canvas. V&A: 3968. © Victoria and Albert Museum, London.

Plate 4.   Grinling Gibbons, carved lace cravat, ca. 1690. Limewood, with raised and openwork carving.
V&A: W.181:1–1928. © Victoria and Albert Museum, London

Plate 5.   Alexander McQueen (designer) and Paul Ferguson (modeler), Grinling Gibbons gold-heeled show boot, 2010. Embossed leather, cast resin, gold paint. Image courtesy of the Alexander McQueen Archive.

Plate 6.   Bow Porcelain Factory, vase, ca. 1758–1760. Soft-paste porcelain with enamels. V&A: C.980–1924. © Victoria and Albert Museum, London.

Plate 7. Jennens and Bettridge, sidechair, ca. 1850. Japanned and painted wood, with papier mâché and mother-of-pearl. W.3B/1, 2–1929. © Victoria and Albert Museum, London.

Plate 8.   Joris Laarman Lab, *Heatwave Radiator,* 2003. Reinforced polyconcrete and plumbing parts. Photograph by Bas Helbers.

Plate 9.   Hella Jongerius, Chicle Delft jug, 2009. Delftware jug, natural latex (chicle).
Photo: Roel Van Tour.

Plate 10.　Sam Durant, *Unique Mono-Block Resin Chairs, Built at Jiao Zhi Studio, Xiamen, China, Produced by Ye Xing You with Craftspeople Xu Fu Fa and Chen Zhong Liang. Kang Youteng, Project manager and Liason,* 2006. Porcelain. Image courtesy of the artist and Blum & Poe, Los Angeles, CA.

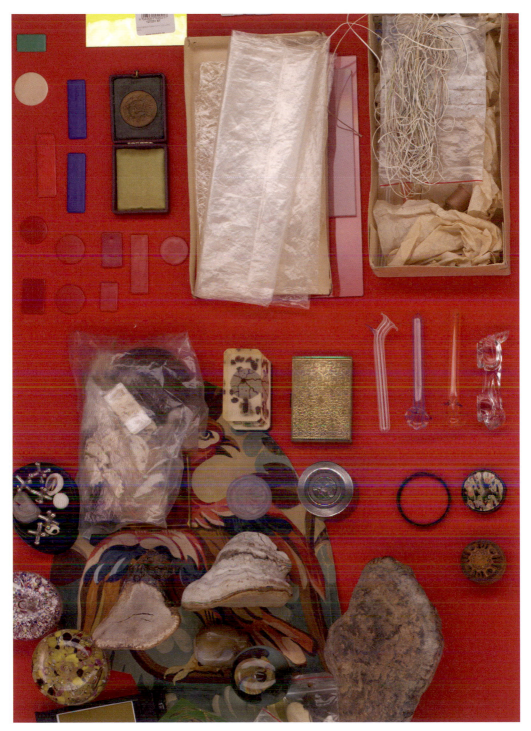

Plate 11.   Isabelle Cornaro, *Moulage sur le Vif (Vide Poche)*, 2009. Pigment print on Rag Paper. Scan and printing by Studio Bordas.

Plate 12. Jeroen Verhoeven, *Cinderella Table,* 2004–2007. Birch plywood, 57 layers. (c) Demakersvan courtesy of the artist and Blain|Southern Gallery.

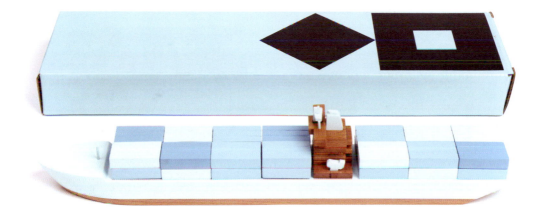

Plate 13.   PostlerFerguson for Papafoxtrot, *Wooden Giants* toys, 2011. Image courtesy of PostlerFerguson.

Plate 14.   James Sharples, Trade Emblem of the Amalgamated Society of Engineers, Machinists, Millwrights, Smiths and Pattern Makers, 1852. Engraved by George Greatbatch. Colored engraving. Trades Union Congress, London / The Bridgeman Art Library.

Plate 15. Janie Terrero, embroidered handkerchief, 1912. Made in Holloway Prison. Museum of London.

Plate 16. Part of a flounce made at the Convent of the Poor Clares, Kenmare, ca. 1886. Needle lace. Collected by Alan Summerly Cole to demonstrate technique; the left edge is unfinished, so that the parchment used to construct the pattern is still present. V&A: T.17–1913. © Victoria and Albert Museum, London.

impulse to find new uses for traditional knowledge, but it should not distract us from the fact that, like it or not, we simply don't need to understand digitization in the established terms of craft. After all, as "extensions of man," to use Marshall McLuhan's famous phrase, computers are valuable because they are so completely detached from the body. Physical strength, hard-won somatic skills, human scale: usually these are simply not relevant in digital design. That is exactly why it is so powerfully transformative.

And yet digital instruments have their own limits. They do not yield the nuanced control or satisfaction that even the simplest hand tool provides, and that has a constraining effect on the product. Powerful evidence of this, ironically, is the depressing stylistic homogeneity of digital craft objects, which tend to be limited to a vocabulary of topological layers, accumulated blocks, and point-to-point "morphs." One exception that proves the rule is Geoffrey Mann's *Shine*, which exploits a defect of 3D scanning technology. Because it uses a laser, the tool is unable to create an accurate scan of a reflective surface. The result, when applied to a Victorian silver candelabrum, is a spiky form that traces the uncertainty of the tool itself (Figure 3.19). Mann has cleverly found a way to turn the "dumbness" of rapid prototyping against itself to create a spectacular object. For the most part, however, the restricted material palette of rapid prototyping and its kindred processes are simply unsatisfying: insipid masses of fused powder or deposited resin, or else cartoon cutout slabs of

Figure 3.19   Geoffrey Mann, *Shine* candelabrum (from the *Natural Occurrence* series), 2010. Bronze cast, silver plating. Manufactured at Powderhall Bronze Foundry. Photography by Nick Moss.

laser cut metal or wood. These objects are even more devoid of human affect than the mass-produced goods that drove the early design reformers to distraction. An optimist might well say: just wait. The rapid-prototyping equipment of the future will change all that. Maybe so; but for the moment, the promise lies in handcraft as an intelligent partner of digital design, not the fusion of the two categories into one another. It is striking that this partnership tends to operate best when it adopts the same dynamics found in early modern production. Earlier in the chapter, before turning to the subject of the handmade replica, I enumerated several of these: hand finishing, the making of tools, prototyping, and repair. I believe these are still the principal ways craft and computer-based design can find common ground; in this way, the rich history of industrial craft can be updated for the twenty-first century.

This argument will come as no surprise to those who follow contemporary design, which has been picking its way along the rich seam between the analogue and the digital for years. Just as is the case for handmade replicas in contemporary art, instances of hand/machine hybrid objects are legion. In these cases, computers are not treated as if they were craft tools; rather, digital and analogue processes are joined together as separate stages within a making process. Jeroen Verhoeven's *Cinderella* tables in plywood and marble are carved with a digitally guided router, but require hand finishing by skilled artisans—just like rifle butts made on early replicating lathes (Plate 12). In this case, the machine precedes the hand, but that polarity is reversed in Front Design's *Sketch* furniture, which relies on motion-capture and rapid prototyping technology to translate drawings made quickly in mid air into solid chairs and tables.[112] It could fairly be objected that examples like these are exceptions and have nothing to do with realistic production scenarios—these flashy demonstrations of hybrid technique have little chance of entry into the consumer market. But analogue/digital partnerships are becoming more and more common in less spectacular registers of the design world, too.

Take for example a set of painted wooden toys, designed by the London firm Postler-Ferguson (Plate 13). The formal simplicity and charming palette of sky blues evokes the playthings of times gone by—one is put in mind, here, of Roland Barthes's loving description, in his book *Mythologies,* of the wooden toys of his own youth:

> Wood removes, from all the forms which it supports, the wounding quality of angles which are too sharp, the chemical coldness of metal. When the child handles it and knocks it, it neither vibrates nor grates, it has a sound at once muffled and sharp. It is a familiar and poetic substance, which does not sever the child from close contact with the tree, the table, the floor. Wood does not wound or break down; it does not shatter, it wears out, it can last a long time, live with the child, alter little by little the relations between the object and the hand…Wood makes essential objects, objects for all time.[113]

PostlerFerguson's toys conjure such nostalgic thoughts, but they are thoroughly contemporary nonetheless. They are based on the enormous pieces of infrastructure that keep the global economy going: satellite dishes, drilling platforms, oil tankers, power plants, wind turbines, and cargo ships stacked with containers. The designers have a history of hybridizing old and new: among their past projects are computer-designed architecture based on traditional Islamic patterns, hyper-realistic guns made from folded paper, and lamps based on marine buoys. For their toy series, entitled *Wooden Giants,* PostlerFerguson adopted a similar approach. They wanted to reduce the world's most massive pieces of technology to a tabletop scale so they could be manipulated by a child. The motto of the line is "play with today"—an idea that resonates with another, less poetic aspect of Barthes's discussion of toys as "reduced copies of human objects, as if in the eyes of the public the child was, all told, nothing but a smaller man, a homunculus to whom must be supplied objects of his own size."[114] For an adult trained in the history of art and design, the project is rich with historical resonance: LeCorbusier's aestheticization of grain towers and steam ships; Bernd and Hilla Becher's photographs of water towers, blast furnaces, and mining equipment. But their ambition was not so much to aestheticize this alien technology, which so few of us actually encounter in day-to-day life; nor was it explicitly political—these toys are meant to be factual rather than critical. But the designers did aim to humanize this massively scaled technology and to make it seem available to rethinking. As Martin Postler puts it, "this stuff didn't appear from heaven. And it all can change."[115]

Producing the toys was a process of many steps. PostlerFerguson first created digital models of each component, then translated them into paper models by hand, then rapid prototyped them using a CNC (computer-driven) router. It was at this point that they involved Guan Yi, a fabrication firm located in Shenzhen, China. That may seem like a standard bit of outsourcing, but their choice was not based on cheapness—as one is perhaps too quick to assume when a factory in the Far East is involved—but rather trust: "our whole venture is built on personal relationships and familiarity."[116] Though Postler-Ferguson is familiar with the manufacturing processes that will ultimately be used at Guan Yi to make the toys, the company depends greatly on the expertise of the fabricators to guide them in selecting forms appropriate to the tooling involved. Once the designs have been finalized, they are put into production—a largely mechanized process until the hand-finishing stage, which depends on the skills of fabricators and painters. Finally the products are shipped to England, on a container ship just like the ones depicted in the toys, and sold under the brand name Papafoxtrot (taken from the phonetic alphabet used by radio signalers—PF, of course, being the initials of the designers).

It is not easy to locate craft in this narrative of production. Certainly, it is a relevant consideration at the finishing stage—and the high quality of the toys is testament to this. Would it also be right to see the initial stages of design and prototyping as craft-like, given the amount of care and materials-based knowledge involved? And what about the aesthetics of the objects, which simulate antique, handmade toys produced in quite a different manner? Does this make them craft, or only craft-like? Rather than adopting an absolutist position on such questions of status and authenticity, it is better to think of craft as a flexible variable within production. Ian Ferguson describes the digital models and 3D printers used in making the toys as a "physical mirror" that allows the designers and makers to produce identical results at more or less the same time, halfway around the world. Despite the high level of mediation this entails, Ferguson feels the result is a more artisanal design process because the prototype can be tooled and retooled continuously. This is "craft knowledge at a distance," an authorial structure he likens to choreography rather than dancing.[117]

The other arena in which PostlerFerguson exploits the power of craft, of course, is in the image of the product. Just as in the eighteenth and nineteenth centuries, craft today is discursive as well as physical. Indeed, craft's potency as image has always rivaled (and often outweighed) its importance as a way of actually getting things done. And the rhetorical power of the analogue is stronger now than ever. PostlerFerguson is hardly alone in drawing upon the rich cultural memory associated with handwork to sell its products. At least its toys do require the contributions of skilled makers; many companies align themselves with artisanal values on much thinner pretexts. Jeep advertises one of its new vehicles, which is of course entirely mass produced, as "imagined, drawn, carved, stamped, hewn, and forged here in America." Camper sells its shoes under the motto "Extraordinary Crafts." Jack Daniels emphasizes the traditional skills that supposedly go into its whiskey: "there's much more to our handcrafted oak barrels than meets the eye." In Britain, you can get "fresh handmade cosmetics" from a company called Lush. The aesthetic ranges from hipster to old-timer, macho to girly, but the message is much the same. Craft is good for you, and we're selling.

It's no coincidence that these promotional campaigns have come along at the same time as the best-selling book by mechanic and latter day antimodernist Matthew Crawford, *Shop Craft as Soul Craft*. (In the United Kingdom, the title was changed to the more prosaic *The Case for Working With Your Hands*.) Crawford's book is based on his own experience of hating the "corporate doublespeak" he found at a K Street lobbying office and finding true happiness in a motorcycle repair shop. Crawford presents today's white-collar worker as someone asked daily to engage in deception, a victim of the pervasive evils of corporate abstraction and "learned irresponsibility."[118] His remedy is a day's (or better, a life's) honest labor. The sturdy mechanic, unlike the demoralized knowledge worker, grasps his own responsibilities by the scruff of the neck. No doubt Crawford would find PostlerFerguson's toys objectionable on numerous counts. They are "intellectual" (a term he disdains, like most contemporary conservatives), witty, and self-referential. They are made through an indirect process that would offend his moral claims about authentic labor. And to an extent he would be right: these little wooden playthings are indeed compromised, lacking the autonomy he has adopted as a life value. They are unapologetically branded. They inhabit the system of global capitalism rather than seeking to escape it. But that is exactly why they seem a promising sign of craft's future. For Crawford's autonomy is entirely illusory. It seems only fair to point out that he would never be able to repair motorcycles if corporations weren't making them in the first place. Harley-Davidson and Yamaha employ plenty of white-collar workers, many of them in advertising. The same goes for the manufacturers who make and sell the tools he uses every day, and of course for Penguin, one of the largest trade publishers in the United States, the company that gets his book into people's hands. Crawford's simple convictions about workmanship (so close, ironically, to the rhetoric Jeep uses to sell its cars) blind him to the way that making always relates to larger systems.

In chapter one, I discussed outsourcing as a problematic that lies at the heart of craft history. It is a means by which artisans have long been subjected to control and exploitation, a situation that grows apace with each passing day. But the answer is not to simply ignore or run away from the phenomenon. Rather, we must engage the question of displaced authorship and distributed labor head on. If contemporary designers are guided by a sufficient ethical compass (a big "if," I grant), then they can treat the outsourcing of skill as a creative, adaptive technique. In this context, we might see craft as a supplementary connective tissue—what Jacques Derrida called a *passe-partout*—that frames and connects different levels of practice from the object-based to the social.[119] Outsourcing can thus be conceptualized as a "machine" in its own right, a mechanical process involving both physical and social dynamics. Imitative, artificial, and inauthentic as it may be, craft remains one of the driving motors of this vast social network. Designers like PostlerFerguson operate in the same sphere as "black market" knockoffs of branded commodities: the handbags, garments, electronics, appliances, sports equipment, and other goods copied by anonymous hands the world over. The makers of such debased products, like so many others in the history of modern craft, are made invisible through their own labor. PostlerFerguson's toys do comment on this condition, through allusion to their own infrastructural preconditions, but they make no attempt to break out of it entirely. On the contrary, they literally make a game out of it. The message is that craft skill must take its place among many other countervailing factors: the mass distribution of goods (as well as authorship), the use of digital technologies as a way of vaulting over time and space, the dominance of images over substance. Many other artists and designers are finding a place for craft in all of this, too, but the ones to watch are those who see clearly that its value is only contingent—that it requires a considerable amount of buttressing to have a significant effect. While the digital does depend, ultimately, on the analogue, the contrary is true as well.

This chapter began with the story of an inarticulate craftsman—someone who tried to speak for himself but found that others were happy to speak for him. Still today, craft's voice can be heard within a cacophony of competing interests, but only rarely does it come through loud and clear. One must strain to hear it: to detect its presence in a hand-made copy, to ferret out a concealed story of skilled production, to notice it lurking in the background of a building, garment, product, or image. When all is said and done, craft is indeed tacit. And though generations of reformers have been dismayed by the idea, and many continue to be so today, craft at its best can indeed be altogether unthinking. That is one of the most thought-provoking things about it. We must continue to defend it from the modern presumption that it needs "improvement"—through the addition of theory, or art, or more latterly, the power of the digital. Craft can sometimes be purely a matter of rote execution—as the example of direct copying attests. Equally it can find itself intermingled with discourse of all kinds, whether ethical, aesthetic, or technological. To that extent, it is important to resist the allure of reductive accounts like Crawford's, which echo the long-ago ideal of the village blacksmith standing proudly but ineffectually outside of modernity. But conversely, to believe that craft finds its value *only* through integration with concepts beyond itself—that the much-lauded union of practice and theory is required to redeem it—is to do it an equally great disservice. Since the moment of its invention, and across the two centuries of progress since, craft has always been a way of executing other people's intentions. Yet it has remained a complex domain of integrated knowledge in its own right. To see it as a living part of a larger mechanical system, sometimes supportive, sometimes transformative, is to understand this double nature.

NOTES

1. The Andersonian Institution evolved into the present-day University of Strathclyde and was also the institution where notorious factory apologist Andrew Ure taught (see below). The London Mechanics' Institute would be renamed the Birkbeck Literary and Scientific Institution in 1866, and is now Birkbeck College.
2. "Public Meeting, For the Establishment of the London Mechanics' Institute," *Mechanics Magazine* no. 12 (November 15, 1823): 177–191; 179.
3. On Brougham's involvement in mechanics' institutions, see Celina Fox, *The Arts of Industry in the Age of Enlightenment* (New Haven, CT: Yale University Press, 2009), pp. 461–462.
4. "Institutions for Instruction of Mechanics: Proposals for a London Mechanics Institute," *Mechanics Magazine* no. 7 (October 11, 1823): 99–102; 100.
5. John Johnson, "The Cause of the Independence of London Journeymen," *Mechanics Magazine* no. 14 (November 29, 1823): 220–221; John Johnson, "Plan to Erect an Iron Tunnel Under the Thames," *Mechanics Magazine* no. 17 (December 20, 1823): 258–261.
6. "Public Meeting," p. 180.
7. Ibid., pp. 187–188.
8. Ibid., pp. 189–190.
9. Tom Telltruth, "London Mechanics' Institution: Observations of the Late Meeting," *Mechanics Magazine* no. 13 (November 22, 1823): 195–198; 196–198.
10. Mabel Tylecote, "The Manchester Mechanics' Institution, 1824–1850," in *Artisan to Graduate: Essays to Commemorate the Foundation in 1824 of the Manchester Mechanics' Institute*, ed. D.S.L. Cardwell (Manchester: Manchester University Press, 1974), p. 65.
11. "The Factory Child," in *Selections from the Writings of the Late John Sidney Taylor* (London: C. Gilpin, 1843), p. 64. Taylor, an abolitionist, was also one of many to draw comparisons between black slaves in the American colonies and the oppressed "white slaves" of the British working class.
12. Hiram, "Extraordinary Machine Pointed out to the Notice of the Institution," *Mechanics Magazine* no. 14 (November 29, 1823): 212–213; 213.
13. *Machinery: Its Tendency, Viewed Particularly in Reference to the Working Classes, by an Artizan* (London: Charles Fox, 1843), p. 15.
14. Joseph Bizup, *Manufacturing Culture: Vindications of Early Victorian Industry* (Charlottesville: University of Virginia Press, 2003), pp. 19–20.
15. Jennifer Karnes Alexander, *The Mantra of Efficiency: From Waterwheel to Social Control* (Baltimore, MD: Johns Hopkins University Press, 2008), p. 35.

16. Quoted in Bizup, *Manufacturing Culture,* p. 30.

17. Robert Owen, "To the Superintendents of Machines," in *A New View of Society: Or Essays on the Principle of the Formation of Human Character* (London: Cadell and Davies, 1813), p. 64.

18. For an explicit contrast between "the man of feeling, the man of science, and the man of execution"—the latter being, of course, the artisan—see James Henry, "The Nature and Use of Beauty," *The Crayon* 3/1 (January 1856): 1–4; 1.

19. "On the Importance of Practical Information: In a Letter from a Correspondent" (January 24, 1822), reprinted in *The Technical Repository,* ed. Thomas Gill (London: R. Watts, 1822), p. 183.

20. Thomas Sprat, *The History of the Royal-Society of London, for the Improving of General Knowledge* (London: J. Martyn, 1667), p. 397.

21. Manchester Mechanics' Institution Annual Report (1828), p. 23; quoted in Tylecote, "The Manchester Mechanics' Institution," p. 55.

22. "Sir Jonah to the Apprentices of the Universe," *The Apprentice* no. 1 (February 3, 1844): 1. This journal was a supplement to *The Artizan,* which aimed at an older and more expert audience of "masters."

23. The same rhetoric is evident in engineering handbooks of the period, such as John Nicholson's *The Operative Mechanic and British Machinist* (London: Knight and Lacey, 1825), dedicated to George Birkbeck. "The advanced state of science," Nicholson wrote, "animate those who for many years have compared theory with practice to come forward in the hope of being able to offer something in aid of the common cause" (p. 2).

24. "The Second Annual Exhibition of the Bookbinders' Finishers' Association," *Journal of Design and Manufactures* (1849): 129.

25. Gordon W. Roderick and Michael D. Stephens, *Education and Industry in the Nineteenth Century: The English Disease?* (London: Longman, 1978), p. 54. For an examination of the situation in France, where a two-tiered system of elite Conservatoire and more vocational Ecoles made the distinction between theoretical and practical training even more explicit, see James Edmonson, *From Mecanicien to Ingenieur: Technical Education and the Machine Building Industry in Nineteenth-Century France* (New York: Garland, 1987).

26. W. J. Fox, "Lectures to the Working Classes," *The Apprentice* no. 27 (May 25, 1844): 129.

27. William Hazlitt, "The Indian Jugglers," in *Table-Talk: Essays in Men and Manners,* vol. 1 (1821–1822).

28. Degrand's Boston Weekly Report of Public Sales and Arrivals, vol. 1, no. 23 (Oct. 2, 1819): 4. Samee purportedly earned between twenty-five and thirty pounds per week, a huge amount at the time, according to the possibly exaggerated account given in "Life in London: The Sword and Snake Swallower," *The Red Republican* 1/1 (June 22, 1850): 6.

29. Johann Beckman, *History of Inventions and Discoveries,* vol. 3, trans. William Johnston (London: J. Bell, 1797), p. 282.

30. J. Frederick Lake Williams, *An Historical Account of Inventions and Discoveries in those Arts and Sciences, which are of Utility or Ornament to Man,* vol. 2 (London: T. and J. Allman, 1820), pp. 329, 331.

31. Burton quoted in Dutta, *Bureaucracy of Beauty,* p. 191.

32. James Mill, *The History of British India* (London: Baldwin, Cradock, and Joy, 1817), p. 342.

33. Grace Moore, *Dickens and Empire: Discourses of Class, Race and Colonialism in the Works of Charles Dickens* (Burlington, VT: Ashgate, 2004), p. 5; Deepali Dewan, "The Body at Work: Colonial Art Education and the Figure of the 'Native Craftsman,'" in *Confronting the Body: The Politics of Physicality in Colonial and Post-Colonial India,* ed. James H. Mills and Satadru Sen (London: Anthem Press, 2004).

34. "Studies in Furniture Design: Hindoo-Indian," *The Decorator and Furnisher* 2/2 (May 1883): 46.

35 Heinrich Wilhelm von Kleist, "On the Marionette Theatre" (1810), trans. Idris Parry. Online at: http://southerncrossreview.org/9/kleist.htm [accessed 30 October 2012].

36. Mill, *The History of British India,* p. 359.

37. Ralph Nicholson Wornum, "The Exhibition as a Lesson on Taste," *The Art Journal Illustrated Catalogue: The Industry of All Nations* (London: G. Virtue, 1851) pp. 1, 6–7.

38. George Richardson Porter, *A Treatise on the Origin, Progressive Improvement, and Present State of the Manufacture of Porcelain and Glass* (London: Longman, Rees, Orme, Brown and Green, 1832), p. 112.

39. Mill, *The History of India,* pp. 353–355.

40. Lara Kriegel, *Grand Designs: Labor, Empire, and the Museum in Victorian Culture* (Durham, NC: Duke University Press, 2007), p. 142.

41. Quoted in Arindam Dutta, *The Bureaucracy of Beauty: Design in the Age of its Global Reproducibility* (New York: Routledge, 2007), p. 88.

42. Johannes Fabian, *Time and the Other: How Anthropology Makes Its Object* (New York: Columbia University Press, 1983), p. 1.

43. Philoponos, *The great exhibition of 1851, or, The wealth of the world in its workshops: comparing the relative skill of the manufacturers, designers, and artisans of England with that of France, Belgium, Prussia, and other continental states* (London: Edward Churton, 1850), pp. 16–17.

44. Soetsu Yanagi, *The Unknown Craftsman: A Japanese Insight into Beauty,* adapted by Bernard Leach (Tokyo: Kodansha, 1972). For a critique of Yanagi's discussion of Korean craftsmen, see Kim Brandt, *Kingdom of Beauty: Mingei and the Politics of Folk Art In Japan* (Durham, NC: Duke University Press, 2007), and Yuko Kikuchi, *Japanese Modernisation and Mingei Theory: Cultural Nationalism and Oriental Orientalism* (London: Routledge Curzon, 2004).

45. Walter Benjamin, "The Storyteller: Reflections on the Works of Nikolai Leskov" (1936), sections 8–9. Reprinted in *Illuminations,* trans. Harry Zohn, ed. Hannah Arendt (New York: Schocken Books, 1968). See also Esther Leslie, "Walter Benjamin: Traces of Craft," *Journal of Design History* 11/1 (1998): 5–13.

46. See Peter Dormer, "The Ideal World of Vermeer's Little Lacemaker," in *Design After Modernism,* ed. John Thackera (London: Thames and Hudson, 1988); Mihaly Czikszentmihalyi and Isabella Selega Czikszentmihalyi, *Optimal Experience: Psychological Studies of Flow in Consciousness* (Cambridge, UK: Cambridge University Press, 1990).

47. Malachy Postlethwayt, *The Universal Dictionary of Trade and Commerce,* translated and adapted from the work of Jacques Savary des Brûlons (London: John and Paul Knapton, 1757), p. 116.

48. Christopher Langon, *A Very Brefe Treatise, orderly declaring the Principal Partes of Phisick,* 1547 (cited in *Oxford English Dictionary* entry for "artificial"); Ephraim Chambers, *Cyclopaedia: or, an Universal Dictionary of Arts and Sciences* (London: printed for D. Midwinter et al., 1738).

49. For more on period conceptions of *naturalia* and *artificialia,* see Lorraine Daston and Katharine Park, *Wonders and the Order of Nature* (Cambridge, MA: Zone Books, 1998).

50. For the example of repair, see Postlethwayt, *The Universal Dictionary of Trade and Commerce,* p. 198. For contrasting usages of "artificial stone," see Chambers, *Cyclopaedia,* and the 1736 English translation of Palladio's *Four Books of Architecture.* An instructive range of technical usage is found in William Salmon's comprehensive craft manual *Polygraphice* (London: Printed for A. and J. Churchill and J. Nicholson, 1701), which applies the term "artificial" to chemical and mineral preparations, blended wine, imitation topaz, sapphire and other gems, and metal alloys.

51. Josiah Tucker, *Instructions for Travellers* (Dublin: William Watson, 1758), p. 21. A similar usage is found in John Campbell's *Political Survey of Britain* (London: printed for the author, 1774): "Artificial Expedients, for facilitating the Progress of national Improvements, of infinite Utility" (p. 225).

52. John Barnard, *A Present for an Apprentice* (Glasgow: John Gilmour, 1750; earliest edition 1740), p. 80.

53. I have elsewhere described this detached positioning of the craftsman according to the socio-poetic theory of the pastoral. See *Thinking through Craft* (Oxford: Berg Publishers/V&A Publishing, 2007), ch. 4.

54. John Sidney Taylor, "Influence of the Fine Arts" (1820), in *Selections from the Writings of the Late John Sidney Taylor* (London: C. Gilpin, 1843), p. 57.

55. Bernard S. Cohn, "Representing Authority in Victorian India," in *The Invention of Tradition,* ed. Eric Hobsbawm and Terence Ranger (Cambridge: Cambridge University Press, 1984), p. 183.

56. On this point, see Glenn Adamson, "Gatherings: Creating the Studio Craft Movement," in *Crafting Modernism: Midcentury American Art and Design,* ed. Jeannine Fallino (New York: Museum of Arts and Design, 2011).

57. Rachel Weiss, "Between the Material World and the Ghosts of Dreams: An Argument about Craft in los Carpinteros," *The Journal of Modern Craft* 1/2 (Summer 2008): 255–270; 258.

58. Barry Schwabsky, "Good Enough Objects," *The Nation* (October 11, 2010): 34–36.

59. Richard Redgrave, "Importance of the Study of Botany to the Ornamentist," *Journal of Design* (1849): 147–151, 178–185; 150.

60. Ibid., p. 178.

61. Ibid.

62. David Pye, *The Nature and Art of Workmanship* (Cambridge: Cambridge University Press, 1968).

63. Elaine Freedgood, "Fine Fingers: Victorian Handmade Lace and Utopian Consumption," *Victorian Studies* (Summer 2003): 625–647; 628.

64. Joseph Whitworth, *Report on Small Arms* (1853), quoted in David A. Hounshell, *From the American System to Mass Production, 1800–1932* (Baltimore, MD: Johns Hopkins University Press, 1984), p. 23.

65. Sarah Fayen Scarlett, "The Craft of Industrial Patternmaking," *Journal of Modern Craft* 4/1 (March 2011): 27–48.

66. See Larry Stewart, "A Meaning for Machines: Modernity, Utility, and the Eighteenth-Century British Public," *Journal of Modern History* 70/2 (June 1998): 259–294.

67. John McHale, *The Future of the Future* (New York: George Braziller, 1969), pp. 40–41. See also Samuel Smiles, *Industrial Biography: Iron Workers and Tool Makers* (London: John Murray, 1863), excerpted in Adamson, *The Craft Reader.*

68. For a sensitive discussion of the craft skills involved in machinists' work, see Craig Heron, "The Crisis of the Craftsman: Hamilton's Metal Workers in the Early Twentieth Century," *Labour/Le Travail* 6 (Autumn 1980): 7–48.

69. Thomas J. Schlereth, *Cultural History and Material Culture: Everyday Life, Landscapes, Museums* (Charleston: University of Virginia Press, 1990), p. 114.

70. Sergei Alasheev, "On a Particular Kind of Love and the Specificity of Soviet Production," in *Management and Industry in Russia,* ed. Simon Clarke (Cheltenham: Edward Elgar, 1995); excerpted in Adamson, *The Craft Reader.*

71. Robert C. Allen, "The Industrial Revolution in Miniature: The Spinning Jenny in Britain, France, and India," *The Journal of Economic History* 69/4 (December 2009): 901–927; 905.

72. Raphael Samuel, "Class and Classlessness," *Universities and Left Review* 6 (Spring 1959): 44–50; 48. See also Samuel, "The Workshop of the World: Steam Power and Hand Technology in Mid-Victorian Britain," *History Workshop Journal* 3 (Spring 1977), excerpted in Adamson, *The Craft Reader.*

73. Charles Frederick Bielefeld, *On the Use of the Improved Papier-Mache in Furniture, in the Interior Decorations of Buildings, and in Works of Art* (London: J. Rickerby, ca. 1842), p. 11.

74. Alexander Parkes, who developed the process of electroforming at Elkington and Co., was a quintessential example of the Victorian improver. He also refined the process of vulcanizing rubber and invented the first semi-synthetic heat-formed plastic (Parkesine). His father, curiously enough, was a lock manufacturer. For Geiss, see "Bronzed Zinc Statuary," *Art-Journal* 5 (1853): 178.

75. See Frederick J. F. Wilson, *Stereotyping and Electrotyping* (London: Wyman's and Sons, 1880).

76. *Inventory of the Electrotype Reproductions of Objects of Art* (London: South Kensington Museum, 1869), p. v.

77. The key point of reference here is Jean Baudrillard, "The Precession of Simulacra," in *Simulacra and Simulations* (Ann Arbor: University of Michigan Press, 1994 [orig. pub. 1981]); but for correctives to Baudrillard's totalizing view, see Hillel Schwartz, *The Culture of the Copy* (Cambridge, MA: MIT Press, 1998), and Marcus Boon, *In Praise of Copying* (Cambridge, MA: Harvard University Press, 2010).

78. The semiotic theory of the index was first developed by Charles Sanders Pierce, with later development by Ferdinand de Saussure, Roland Barthes, and Rosalind Krauss. For a recent discussion, see Mary Ann Doane, "Indexicality: Trace and Sign: Introduction," *Differences* 18/1 (2007): 1–6.

79. Marian Hobson, *The Object of Art: The Theory of Illusion in Eighteenth-Century France* (Cambridge: Cambridge University Press, 1982), p. 70.

80. Susan Sontag, *On Photography* (New York: Farrar, Straus and Giroux, 1977); Roland Barthes, *Camera Lucida* (New York: Hill and Wang, 1981 [orig. pub. 1980]); Abigail Solomon-Godeau, *Photography at the Dock* (Minneapolis: University of Minnesota Press, 1994).

81. Jenny Uglow, *Nature's Engraver: A Life of Thomas Bewick* (London: Faber and Faber, 2007).

82. Gerry Beegan, "The Mechanization of the Image: Facsimile, Photography, and Fragmentation in Nineteenth-Century Wood Engraving," *Journal of Design History* 8/4 (1995): 257–274; 257. An early historian of the trade noted, "it cannot be too strongly stressed that the engravers of the last century were for all the world mere 'Form-schneider' [form cutters], only their equipment was vastly fuller. They copied pen-drawings in facsimile, and what little chance they had for brain-work or originality entered, was where they had to translate washes or tints into the hard uncompromising medium of line…" Douglas Percy Bliss, *A History of Wood-Engraving* (London: Spring Books, 1928; 1964 ed.), p. 197. See also Kriegel, *Grand Designs,* p. 46.

83. Peter Connor, "Cast Collecting in the Nineteenth Century: Scholarship, Aesthetics, Connoisseurship," in *Rediscovering Hellenism: The Hellenic Inheritance and the English Imagination,* ed. G. W. Clarke (Cambridge: Cambridge University Press, 1989). The French national collection of casts was initiated by Gothic Revival architect Viollet-le-Duc and opened in the Trocadero in 1882. See *Monumental: Revue Scientifique et Technique des Monuments Historiques* (Paris: Centre des Monuments Nationaux, 2007).

84. Eugene Benson, "Art-Progress in America," *The Art Review* 1/2 (September 1870): 1–2; 1.

85. My thanks to Greg Sullivan for his comments on statuary makers in this period.

86. "Italian versus English Character," *The Crayon* 7/1 (January 1860): 7–14; 8.

87. Connor, "Cast Collecting in the Nineteenth Century," p. 209; Peter Malone, "How the Smiths Made a Living," in *Plaster Casts: Making, Collecting and Displaying from Classical Antiquity to the Present,* ed. Rune Frederiksen and Eckart Marchand (Berlin: De Gruyter, 2010), p. 165. For more on Brucciani, see Malcolm Baker, "The Establishment of a Masterpiece: The Cast of the Pórtico de la Gloria in the South Kensington Museum, London, in the 1870s," in *Actas Simposio Internacional sobre O Pórtico da Gloria e a Arte do Seu Tempo* (Galicia, Spain: Gráfico Galaico, 1991).

88. "Giovanni Ferdinando Franchi," *Mapping the Practice and Profession of Sculpture in Britain and Ireland 1851–1951,* University of Glasgow History of Art and HATII, online database 2011.

89. Malcolm Baker, "The Reproductive Continuum: Plaster Casts, Paper Mosaics, and Photographs as Complementary Modes of Reproduction in the Nineteenth-Century Museum," in Frederiksen and Marchand, eds., *Plaster Casts.*

90. Charlotte Schreiber, "'Moulded from the Best Originals of Rome': Eighteenth-Century Production and Trade of Plaster Casts after Antique Sculpture in Germany," in Frederiksen and Marchand, eds., *Plaster Casts.*

91. Matthew Greg Sullivan, "Chantrey and the Original Models," in Frederiksen and Marchand, eds., *Plaster Casts,* p. 302.

92. Martina Droth, "The Ethics of Making: Craft and English Sculptural Aesthetics, c. 1851–1900," *Journal of Design History* 17/3 (2004): 221–235; 224. Droth goes on to argue that an increasingly craft-based attitude to the making of so-called New Sculpture in late nineteenth-century England, parallel to the activities of the Arts and Crafts movement, paved the way for direct carving and other hand processes in the twentieth century.

93. Johannes Myssok, "Modern Sculpture in the Making: Antonio Canova and Plaster Casts" in Frederiksen and Marchand, eds., *Plaster Casts,* pp. 278–281.

94. Matthew Craske, "The Politics of Modelling in Late-Eighteenth-Century London," unpublished paper, delivered at the conference "At Cross Purposes? Design History and Art History," Courtauld Institute, London, October 2011. Craske shows that in some cases, particularly in large-scale architectural statuary, sculptors even outsourced the making of their commissions, taking no direct part in the making, but claimed authorship nonetheless—an interesting anticipation of practices in sculpture today.

95. Reginald Blomfeld, "Architectural Exhibits and a Note on the Cast Courts of the Museum," memorandum, Jan. 28, 1928. Archive of Art and Design, MA/46/I/2. My thanks go to Marjorie Trusted for this reference and for access to a range of other publications and research materials on plaster casts.

96. The canonical text on indexicality in the context of contemporary art is Rosalind Krauss, "Notes on the Index, Part 1" *October* 3 (Spring 1977): 68–81. I depart from Krauss in two respects: first, in emphasizing the skill required to fabricate an indexical work; and second, in seeing indexicality as a rudder to be used in navigating the postdisciplinary condition, rather than as an anchor for medium specificity (thanks to its "sheer physical presence"), as she did.

97. Stephen Feeke, *Second Skin: Historical Life Casting and Contemporary Sculpture* (Leeds: Henry Moore Institute, 2002).

98. A photo-based precedent for Quinn's portraits can be found in Jean Paul Goude's *Grace Jones Revised and Updated* (1978), which presents the pop star assuming a superhuman arabesque pose. Goude photographed Jones multiple times, cut the photos into fragments, and joined them together into the impossible image. See *So Far So Goude* (New York: Assouline, 2006); and Glenn Adamson and Jane Pavitt, eds., *Postmodernism: Style and Subversion 1970 to 1990* (London: V&A Publications, 2011).

99. Quoted in Charlotte Higgins, "Meet Kate Moss—Distorted," *Guardian* (April 12, 2006.

100. Patrick Elliott, *Tony Cragg: Sculptures and Drawings* (Edinburgh: National Galleries of Scotland, 2011), p. 112.

101. All quotations from Tony Cragg are taken from an interview conducted on August 3, 2011.

102. Gallery website for Bugada and Cargnel, www.bugadacargnel.com/en/pages/artistes.php?name=18492&page=portfolio&categ=63#, accessed July 1, 2011.

103. Sam Durant, "Porcelain Chairs," 2009. www.samdurant.com/porcelain-chairs, accessed January 2, 2012.

104. David Fischli quoted in Robert Fleck, *David Fischli, Peter Weiss* (New York: Phaidon, 2005), p. 22.

105. Neil Kamil, *Fortress of the Soul: Violence, Metaphysics, and Material Life in the Huguenots' New World, 1517–1751* (Baltimore, MD: Johns Hopkins University Press, 2005).

106. Isabelle Cornaro, personal communication with the author, June 24, 2010.

107. Leo Steinberg, "*The Flatbed Picture Plane,*" from *Other Criteria: Confrontations with Twentieth Century Art* (Chicago: University of Chicago Press, 2007 [orig. pub. 1972]).

108. For a contemporary discussion of Luddism and its legacy, see Ele Carpenter, "Coal Powered Craft: A Past for the Future," *Journal of Modern Craft* 4/2 (July 2011): 147–160.

109. I owe this analogy to graphic designer Peter Saville, who mentioned it in an interview conducted October 19, 2010. The idea of cultural teleportation is perhaps best modeled in terms of Riemann space, as explored by Gilles Deleuze and Felix Guattari, *Capitalism and Schizophrena, vol. 2: A Thousand Plateaus,* trans. Brian Massumi (London: Continuum, 2004 [orig. pub. 1980]).

110. Malcolm McCullough, *Abstracting Craft: The Practiced Digital Hand* (Cambridge, MA: MIT Press, 1996), p. 26.

111. See Glenn Adamson, "Serious Business: Designer-Craftsmen in Postwar California," in *California Design, 1930–1965: Living in A Modern Way,* ed. Wendy Kaplan (Los Angeles: LACMA, 2011).

112. The process is viewable online at: www.designfront.org/category.php?id=81&product=92.

113. Roland Barthes, *Mythologies,* trans. Jonathan Cape (Paris: Editions de Seuil, 1957; trans. 1972), pp. 54–55.

114. Ibid., p. 53.

115. Author's interview with PostlerFerguson (Martin Postler and Ian Ferguson), July 14, 2011.

116. The connection with Guan Yi came through Herman Cheung, a Shenzhen-based prototyping entrepreneur whom the designers have known for some time (he has introduced them to Chinese clients, for example). Cheung is the third partner in the Papafoxtrot business.

117. Author's interview with PostlerFerguson.

118. Matthew Crawford, *Shop Craft as Soul Craft: An Inquiry into the Value of Work* (New York: Penguin, 2009), p. 138ff.

119. Jacques Derrida, *The Truth in Painting,* trans. Geoff Bennington and Ian McLeod (Chicago: University of Chicago Press, 1987 [orig. pub. 1978]).

4   MEMORY

William Morris liked to tell a story, one remembered from his youth. At the age of seventeen, he had been taken by his mother to the Great Exhibition in Hyde Park (Figure 4.1). It was, at least potentially, one of the great encounters of the century: the young man who would, in time, reshape the world of design by his inspiring example, visiting what was arguably the most important design event that had ever occurred. So what happened?

Morris refused to go in. He found the Crystal Palace "wonderfully ugly." Rather than walk amongst the crowds and gawp at the modern spectacle on show, he preferred to sit outside and wait. Was he simply being a petulant adolescent? Perhaps. But later in life, Morris remained proud of his reaction, and it certainly was a sign of things to come. He spent his career attacking the modern engineering the Exhibition's steel-and-glass building exemplified. The technologically driven production of his own time seemed to him a "horrible and restless nightmare," and he never did come to grips with plate glass windows—to him, they simply seemed to let in too much light.[1] He preferred the dimmer, color-splashed illumination afforded by stained glass. Once a journalist asked Morris why he was so conspicuously unconcerned with contemporary life. You might have expected him to deny the charge. But instead he responded, "What is there in modern life for the man who seeks beauty? Nothing. You know it quite well... The age is ugly—to find anything beautiful we must look 'before and after.'"[2]

It was just this sort of thing weaver Anni Albers was thinking of when she observed that craft is "often no more than a romantic attempt to recall a *temps perdu,* a result of an attitude rather than a procedure."[3] Though she meant to be dismissive, she had put her finger on something big. In my previous book *Thinking Through Craft,* I devoted a chapter to the concept of the pastoral—a literary mode of classical origin in which removal from the centers of power is felt to provide objectivity and hence a basis for critical observation. This distancing is both spatial, in the sense that pastoral texts are typically set outside of cities (their emblematic figure is the shepherd, or *pastore,* from which we derive the term) and also located, figuratively anyway, in the past. Modern craft has routinely adopted this pastoral stance. It tends to be found in marginal geographies, which are seen as repositories of long-established, unbroken tradition; and it is often carried out in a spirit of revival, in which case the past serves as an armature on which to build a better present. Whether rediscovered or created, craft tends to be "conservative," in the positive sense of the term. Like any pastoral maneuver, it is a way of holding on to fragile values.

342.   VIEW OF THE GRAND ENTRANCE TO THE EXHIBITION.

Figure 4.1   *View of the Grand Entrance to the Exhibition*, 1851 (published later). Wood engraving. V&A: S.2340–2009. © Victoria and Albert Museum, London.

In this final chapter, I would like to expand on this dimension of modern craft. In particular, I want to examine in detail its tendency to orient itself toward the past, rather than to the present (or, for that matter, the future). This idea, that craft inherently looks back over its own shoulder, is perhaps the most perplexing aspect of its invention. Why did Morris, the first great advocate for craft, feel the need to describe it as something that had already vanished—a paradise lost that needed regaining? He addressed this matter, repeatedly, and in no uncertain terms:

> The latter half of the eighteenth century saw the beginning of the last epoch of production that the world has known, that of the automatic machine which supersedes hand-labour, and turns the workman who was once a handicraftsman helped by tools, and next a part of a machine, into a tender of machines.[4]

On the face of it, Morris seems simply to have been in the wrong. As I have shown throughout this book, skilled artisans had a large measure of responsibility in giving shape to modernity. Even taking into account Morris's aesthetic predilections, which may have blinded him to the craftsmanship that lay behind Victorian material culture, and his political leanings, which led him to reject all factory labor, skilled or not, as inherently exploitative, there were still thousands upon thousands of craftspeople active in Britain whose workshops would have pleased even the most idealistic eye. Indeed, he himself relied on many of those workshops to execute his pattern designs and the other objects produced by his decorating firm, Morris, Marshall, Faulkner & Co. He did carry out some crafts under his own roof: stained glass, tapestry weaving, and dyeing (he was dissatisfied with the dyestuffs used in contemporary textile production and undertook a remarkable campaign to master the use of natural colorants).[5] But he outsourced most of the other production jobs to skilled workers at companies like the Wilton Carpet Works, silk weaver Nicholson and Co., wallpaper printers Jeffrey and Co., and various independent cabinet-makers in Manchester; high-quality pot glass for windows, and ceramic tiles that could be decorated with hand painting, were brought in from outside firms, too (Figure 4.2). Given this wide experience, why did Morris say that craft stood at the very threshold of death's door and was incompatible with industry?

It is true that when craft was invented, it was constructed as an inferior category. As I have shown in the preceding chapters, craftsmen's hands were increasingly manipulated by others; craft knowledge was thoroughly explained, so that it was robbed of its former mystery; and craft itself was represented as merely mechanical, a matter of execution rather than principle. None of that, though, should necessarily have given rise to the idea that craft had actually melted away as a result of industrialism. It is worth dwelling on just how strange this assumption was—and still is, for it is so engrained in modern thought that we have a difficult time viewing craft history in any other way. The narrative of loss, typically accompanied by a plaintive cry for preservation and/ or revival, is the norm from which any other story about craft must depart. It is truly amazing that every generation can tell itself the same thing as if the idea were a new one—that it is witnessing the disappearance of craft forever, and therefore has a unique responsibility to save it, rather as one might be obliged to save an endangered species of animal. This feeling goes back even further than Morris and the Arts and Crafts

Figure 4.2   William Morris for Morris, Marshall, Faulkner & Co., *Daisy* tile, designed 1862. Hand-painted tin-glazed earthenware. V&A: C.58–1931. © Victoria and Albert Museum, London.

movement. All the way back in 1829, Thomas Carlyle had written, "on every hand, the living artisan is driven from his workshop to make room for the speedier, inanimate one. The shuttle drops from the fingers of the weaver and falls into iron fingers that ply it faster."[6] A century later, in 1923, George Sturt wrote of the craft of the wheelwright, which had remained intact since the days of the Canterbury Tales (or so he believed) but seemed to be vanishing from the face of the earth.[7] And today, organizations like the Heritage Crafts Association devote themselves to preventing the loss of traditional crafts skills, haunted by the day in each trade "when the last craftsperson stops working."[8] The problem is always that of imminent disappearance, and the solution is always to go back to the past.

Two hundred years, then, in which craft has been constantly shadowed by the sense of an ending. Given the persistence of this narrative of crisis, it would be easy enough to disparage it as alarmist, and even to view it as a counterproductive undermining of craft's ongoing vitality. Certainly, at the least, we should be suspicious. Obviously craft is not going away as a result of modernity; as I hope to have demonstrated by now, craft is itself a modern invention. How, then, to understand the ongoing sense of loss? One reaction might simply be to ignore it—to insist that craft need not look backward. This would mean framing craft as a powerful driver of progressive change in its own right. Although that has been a minority view in modern times, there is plenty of precedent for it, and as is probably clear by now, it is a view I endorse wholeheartedly. But embracing craft's potential for the future does not necessarily mean disregarding its relation with the past. There is much to learn from the rich tradition of describing craft as a disappearing act. Indeed, it leads us back to the most powerful, and paradoxical, idea about craft that has come down to us from the nineteenth century: craft was invented *as an absence*. It came into being as a figure of cancellation, an "X" marking a spot that never existed in the first place.

This Proustian image of craft, as a memory that haunts the present, is an inextricable aspect of its extraordinary cultural power. When craft was invented, it was defined as inferior, passive, and limited. Yet it was also understood to be deeply necessary, and not just in a practical sense. Like the involuntary memories of a dimly remembered childhood that trouble Marcel in *Remembrance of Things Past,* craft simultaneously gives shape to our desire for continuity and reminds us of the actual, tragic discontinuity of our experience. If it is firmly set in a position of servitude to the rest of modern culture, that is partly because it is indeed providing a crucial service: the task of memory work. It is a means of processing unsettled matters in history, always as that history is imagined from the perspective of the present. Understanding this phenomenon requires the techniques of the psychoanalyst as well as those of the historian. Rather than trying to evaluate the success or failure of the craft movements that have flourished since the nineteenth century, then, I aim in this chapter to view them (sympathetically, like any good therapist) as a set of cultural symptoms—an understandable response to the crisis of modernity.

CRAFT AS MEMORY WORK

There is a term for the experience of loss I am trying to describe and the memory work that arises from it. The word is *trauma,* etymologically derived from the Greek for "wound." Though it is normally understood as a psychological condition (and that is how I am using it here), the concept of trauma was originally based on medical observation of the body. When flesh is traumatized—pierced, burned, subjected to a blow, or otherwise seriously harmed—the effects are more than local. The whole body reacts, the single wound producing an effect of general destabilization. Trauma is not the wound itself, but the dispersion of the original rupture through the total entity. Psychoanalysts of Sigmund Freud's generation adopted this as a metaphor to describe the way an especially upsetting event could affect the psychic makeup of a patient.[9] Unlike bodily trauma, where the wound is usually evident, the origin of a psychological disturbance might well be difficult to locate. Partly this is because the symptoms themselves arise as a way of concealing the original event from the conscious mind. Ruth Leys, the finest of contemporary trauma theorists, notes that for Freud, "trauma was an experience that immersed the victim in the traumatic scene so profoundly that it precluded the kind of [distance] necessary for cognitive knowledge of what had happened."[10] The result is a fragmentation of the subject, an inability to grasp the traumatic scene in its totality. It can only be dealt with piecemeal, in ways the patient is unaware of, treating the psychic wound without ever fully healing it. Such traumatic response provides a degree of comfort, but it also shields the subject from ever confronting the underlying, unresolved conflict.

There is an old joke in which a little girl says, "my memory is what I forget with."[11] Here we come to the parallel between traumatic response and craft revival: both are reactions to a kind of rupture, or tear, within a fabric; and both operate by reframing the past, and partly by obscuring it. The otherwise inexplicable narrative of craft's disappearance becomes completely comprehensible when it is understood as an ongoing response to modernity, which, in the words of one theorist of collective memory, "irreversibly fractured particular *milieux de mémoire* that had remained intact for generations."[12] The eruption of the industrial revolution was no doubt traumatic, and generations of revival have clearly not banished its destabilizing effects. Three characteristic symptoms of trauma in particular seem deeply inscribed in the history of craft revival: repetitive behavior, false memories, and flashbacks. All of these find clear cognates in the Arts and Crafts movement and its later derivatives, and are key to understanding its function as memory work. They are palliatives for the shifts associated with modernity, cures that obscure in order to heal.

Let's first take the example of repetitive behavior, a symptom in which, as Freud put it, the traumatized subject reproduces the original distressing event "not as a memory but as an action; he *repeats* it, without, of course, knowing that he repeats it."[13] This compulsive activity affords a constant distraction that prevents the subject from having to encounter the memory of the trauma, which is too disturbing to fully integrate back into consciousness. The traumatic event might return in fragments—the particular actions that are repeated may be telltale clues to the source of the trauma, in fact—but never as a whole.[14] This sort of distracted, repetitive experience is a key part of modern craft, hence the common emphasis on the pleasures of unthinking "flow" (see chapter three). The haptic, rhythmic quality of artisanal work resides exactly in the arena where Leys sees traumatic response occurring: "bodily memories of skills, habits, reflex actions, and classically conditioned responses that lie outside verbal-semantic-linguistic representation."[15] Craft is carried out through repetitive somatic movements, as in hammering up a metal sheet into a volume, wedging clay, throwing a pot, smoothing a board with a plane, or plying a shuttle at a loom (Figure 4.3). These gestures—and significant, not the more abrupt but equally skilled movements used by artisans, like annealing, quenching, and riveting—have thoroughly penetrated the modern symbolic consciousness.[16]

Given that the experience of modernity is so disjunctive, it is no wonder that the rhythmic quality of craft seems so comforting. And equally, it has always seemed an exemplary case of the fragility of memory in the face of modern disruptive forces. As we saw in chapter two, it is not reducible to language or other forms of transcription. Once lost, a skill is lost forever. And so it must be "revived," literally brought back to life—though like Frankenstein's Monster, it will only come back in unnatural form. In this respect craft resembles oral tradition. Its cultural value depends on a sense of continuity. It is no coincidence that the syntactical structures of craft and storytelling are closely parallel. Both have internal repetitive forms that aid in the act of recall. Reciting an extensive epic poem, for example, is greatly aided by a

Figure 4.3   Eugene Deutsch throwing a pot, ca. 1948. Courtesy of Nancy Kalis.

composition based on theme and variation. Craft techniques tend to operate in this way too. They are formulaic and mnemonic. As Walter Benjamin noticed, their very forms create the impression of something being remembered.[17] But we also need to recognize in this repetition a form of concealment. One speaks of "losing oneself" when immersed in a skilled task. Repetition is, in this context, precisely a means of forestalling an encounter with the self—a way of maintaining dissociation between the present and the disruptive past.

A second type of traumatic symptom is the "screen memory," an alternative reconstruction of the past experienced as true recollection. Like any form of personal mythology, such a fictional belief can incorporate a patient's unconscious desires, and at its core it marks the search for a "real" or "original" identity. This quest for authenticity is of course a phantom, as identity is always in formation. The desire for a coherent account of the self nonetheless structures memory, and the traumatized subject is no exception in this regard.[18] As the phrase implies, a screen memory deflects access to the traumatic scene by presenting a false image in its place, one more in keeping with the subject's sense of internal coherence. So it is a particular form of self-deceptive amnesia.[19] Yet the "screening" action involved, ironically, is also a means of protecting the memory of the trauma itself, because the repression of it serves as a means of preservation: "sealed off from other memories, they remain intact indefinitely."[20] In other words, the trauma is protected from the interpretive action of the conscious mind, affording it a kind of power and autonomy. Ironically, in order for memory to create the impression of stasis, it must be extremely dynamic, because this is the only way for it to cope with the fact of continuous change. As the great historian Raphael Samuel put it, "memory is inherently revisionist and never more chameleon than when it appears to stay the same."[21]

The metaphor of the screen memory is particularly valuable as a way of understanding modern craft revivalism. It helps us understand, first, why industry looms as an absolute force, which can only be seen as destructive to craft's purposes. And to put it the other way round, the narrative of craft's disappearance serves as an ongoing testament to industry's unquestioned power. This is why, for the most part, industrial artisans have been invisible to craft historians and practitioners, Morris included; they are screened from view by the desire for a simple story of loss. Second, the metaphor of the screen memory is a great tool to understand why people derive deep feelings of authenticity from profoundly fictional situations. Regional "vernacular" craft traditions are invariably modern inventions, to some degree. They are fashioned according to the needs of the present day, and the objects produced in these circumstances acquire potent totemic value. The Freudian term for this process is *cathexis,* which he defined as "a sum of psychic energy, which occupies or invests objects." The mind works through its desires and fears partly through fixation on cathected objects.[22] To perform this memory work effectively, however, the objects in question must seem completely independent from such needs. Even to point out the constructed nature of a putatively traditional craft, much less to exploit it for financial gain, can come across as an act of violence against it. That is because such a response reminds us of the trauma of modernity, which the tradition is, again, meant to screen.

A third type of traumatic response is the flashback. This is another type of repetition, but rather than a rhythmic or obsessive experience, it is a sudden and dramatic return of the past. Leys describes the flashback as a "mimetic" experience, "a situation of unconscious identification with, or 'primary repression' of, the traumatic scene."[23] It provides the patient a moment of dissociation from the present self. This severs the temporal continuity of the subject, so that the moment of trauma cannot be reintegrated into a coherent narrative. Interestingly, Freud thought that a therapist could reverse the polarity of the flashback, staging a "mimetic" reenactment within the course of treatment. This would expose the site of the original trauma, making it available for analysis: "the compulsion to repeat forces the analytic process to deal with a traumatic past as and in the form of a present scenario."[24] What lay behind this method was Freud's theory of *Nachträglichkeit* or deferred action (though a more literal translation might be "afterwards-ness"), which held that psychic reactions could occur long after the events that prompted them. The mimetic approach to treating traumatic disorder seeks to exploit this nonlinearity of psychic experience. Together the analyst and the patient can deal with a disturbance as if it were happening in the present moment. An obvious example of such a flashback in the nineteenth century is medievalism; this is just one example of the craft movement's propensity to reenact the past. Any instance of such revivalism is a "narrative fragmentation" (in the words of trauma theorist Richard J. McNally) that marks a dissociation from the present.[25]

All three of these "symptoms" can be found throughout craft revivals from the nineteenth century to the present day. Let's begin with an early emblematic example: A.W.N. Pugin's book *Contrasts* (1836). In this foundational text of the Gothic Revival, Pugin's method was simple—so simple that his biographer, Rosemary Hill, has described the result as "morally and literally black and white."[26] He placed images of medieval and modern architecture alongside one another, always to the "great disadvantage" of the latter. In one particularly charged example, the western front of St. Mary Overie Cathedral in Southwark, London, which had been built in the fourteenth century but had recently been destroyed, was contrasted to its replacement, a much plainer though still nominally "gothic" triple archway that was one of many recent restorations and replacements carried out by architect George Gwilt, Jr. In the illustration of this contrast, a heap of rubble lies pitifully at the foot of the new design, with a sign above it reading "old materials for sale." Cross-sections drawn by Pugin show how rich ornament has given way to a blank slate.

In juxtapositions like this one, Pugin no doubt felt he was condemning his contemporaries much more effectively than he could in words. Reading *Contrasts* through the lens of psychoanalytic theory, however, we can also see that he was dissociating himself from the present day in more than conscious terms. In a telling passage of the preface, he noted, "I am well aware that the sentiments I have expressed in this work are but little suited to the taste and opinions of the age in which we live: by a vast number they will be received with ridicule, and, by some, considered as the result of a heated imagination."[27] Pugin was proud of being out of time. His representations of medieval structures were certainly based on careful study; by the standard of the day, they could even be considered archaeological.

But this does not change the fact that his use of that past was chiefly a stick with which to beat the present, and, as Hill has shown, Pugin was (for reasons both psychological and spiritual) deeply dedicated to an idea of himself as stuck in the wrong century. As he placed one barefaced modern structure after another directly next to its decorated precedent, he was restaging a sense of loss over and over again. The most well-known page of *Contrasts* shows a generic "Catholic Town in 1440" and "the same town in 1840" (Figure 4.4). The medieval village is unified, not only stylistically through its Perpendicular Gothic architecture, but also through the list of buildings given below—a catechism of saints' names and religious imagery interrupted only by the solitary "Guild Hall." Four hundred years later, there is cacophony. The scene may not strike twenty-first-century eyes as particularly alarming, but to Pugin it was disturbing in the extreme. Its lack of stylistic harmony is a sign of cultural disaster, further demonstrated by signs of disorder: a "new jail," a lunatic asylum, the proximity of the parsonage to the "pleasure grounds," which we are meant to see as a den of iniquity. There is also a thorough atomization of every walk of life, from systems of belief (there are separate provisions for Unitarians, Baptists, Quakers, etc.) to production, with works for gas and iron separated from the "Socialist Hall of Science"—a lamentable gulf between the site of manufacturing and the site where knowledge is produced, leading to a politicization of science itself. Pugin wants to undo this complexity and separation through the mechanism of historical return, a fantasy of unity restored.

It may seem odd to insist that Pugin's technique in *Contrasts* is akin to an unconscious psychological symptom, given how explicit he is in his rejection of the present. Indeed, his attacks were pointed and carried out with considerable wit. A wonderful page of satirical advertisements included in the book skewers the new institutions that subjected builders to control. Professional architects offer "a large assortment of rejected designs, selling considerably under prime cost," while at the "Mechanicks Institute" one can hear "a lecture on a new designing machine capable of making 1000 changes with the same art of ornaments, by a composition maker." But for all of his sharp-sighted critique, Pugin was blind to the fictional qualities of his ideal medieval world, which (matters of architectural form apart) had very little to do with historical fact and everything to do with creating a negative image of the present. He had absorbed the ideas of modernity thoroughly, such that they structured his every argument. He may have systematically cancelled them out, but they were still the constitutive element in his thought. "I feel acutely the fallen condition of the arts," Pugin wrote, "when each new invention, each new proceeding seems only to plunge them deeper in degradation. I wish to pluck from the age the mask of superior attainments so falsely assumed, and I am anxious to direct the attention of all back to the real merit of past and better days."[28] But he was the one doing the masking. In the particularities of architecture, as in the case of St. Mary Overie, Pugin presented the modern day simply in terms of absence. At this level of detail, one could learn from the past, restore the great times of gothic ornament and the deep spiritual feelings they expressed. But when it came to the general view, there was no way to dispel the modern world and all its complexities. It is for this reason, perhaps, that his juxtaposition of two towns, four centuries apart,

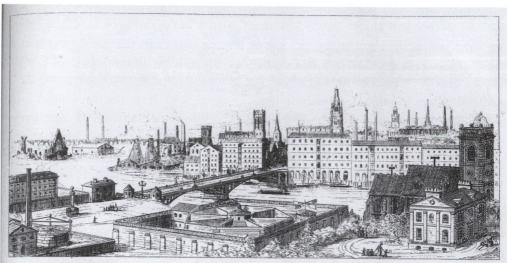

THE SAME TOWN IN 1840

1. St. Michaels Tower, rebuilt in 1750. 2. New Parsonage House & Pleasure Grounds. 3. The New Jail. 4. Gas Works. 5. Lunatic Asylum. 6. Iron Works & Ruins of St Maries Abbey. 7. Mt Evans Chapel. 8. Baptist Chapel. 9. Unitarian Chapel. 10. New Church. 11. New Town Hall & Concert Room. 12. Wesleyan Centenary Chapel. 13. New Christian Society. 14. Quakers Meeting. 15. Socialist Hall of Science.

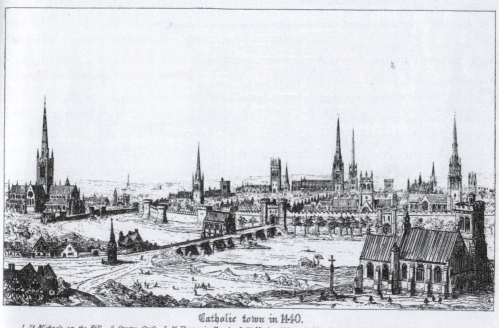

Catholic town in 1440.

1. St Michaels on the Hill. 2. Queens Crofs. 3. St Thomas's Chapel. 4. St Maries Abbey. 5. All Saints. 6. St Johns. 7. St Peters. 8. St Alkmunds. 9. St Maries. 10. St Edmunds. 11. Grey Friars. 12. St Cuthberts. 13. Guild hall. 14. Trinity. 15. St Olaves. 16. St Botolphs.

Figure 4.4 A.W.N. Pugin, comparative images of a town in 1440 and the same town in 1840, from *Contrasts* (1836).

needed to be generic, a Nowheresville masquerading as everywhere. Had he tried to render a specific town back into its medieval equivalent, it would have become all too clear that what he really was after was total erasure.

Despite his prescriptive tone, then, Pugin's idea of the present was ultimately structured around its own impossibility, a unified mental landscape forged from disjunctive temporality. The power of his *Contrasts,* and of craft revivalism in general, is that it offers both an alternative modernity (as Tom Crook has called it) and an alternative *to* modernity.[29] These two things are of course incommensurable—one seeks to transform the present, and the other to escape it entirely. One is concrete and the other fictitious, but each constantly assumes the guise of the other. The psychoanalytic theory I have reviewed here helps us to understand why that contradiction is so useful: it prevents us from having to confront the reality of modernity, permitting us instead the option of distracting ourselves from it, hiding it from view, and, crucially, *re-scripting* it. This memory work is escapist, but not only that; it also describes modern experience in such a way that it can be critically engaged. The point cannot be overstressed: the memory work performed by craft revival is not simply avoidant, nor in any way to be disdained. Not only has it had important practical consequences to do with preservation (of architecture, skills, and communities). It is also a profoundly human response to modernity, which is deeply antagonistic to memory itself.[30] Long before the advent of Google and Wikipedia, modern technology was already gradually superseding the need to store things in the mind, and modern narratives were casting doubt on the accuracy of human recollection. Henceforth memory was not to be trusted. The Freudian theory I have been using here—the whole idea of psychic trauma, for that matter—is quintessentially modern in this regard, as is the genre of professional history, which assigns itself the job of systematically correcting less formal accounts of the past (a category into which the book you are reading falls comfortably).[31] Modernity prioritizes the new. But as a consequence, remembering itself comes to seem more and more an act of resistance, as all that is solid melts into air and capitalism wreaks its creative destruction upon us all. This is so even when the memories involved are false ones. Seen in this light, understanding craft as symptomatic of traumatic response is not condescending (even if setting myself up as an "analyst," as I have done here, may suggest that). It is, rather, to understand why craft needed to be invented in the first place.

DISMANTLING RUSKIN

Understanding the motivations that undergirded modern craft revival, however, should not dissuade us from trying to move past its contradictions. Slavoj Žižek once wrote that "the essence of trauma is that it is too horrible to be remembered, to be integrated into our symbolic universe. All we have to do is to mark repeatedly the trauma as such."[32] But in the case of modern craft, we can do better than this. We can look to craft theory and practice alike not only as traumatic symptoms, but also as akin to the act of psychoanalysis itself. For Freud, the analyst's "primary goal was to help patients remember and then work through traumatic occurrences from the past that continued to disturb them in the present," to induce a response to the events "which they had not been able to achieve earlier on, when such a response was appropriate and should have occurred."[33] In a sense, we still have the same problem on our hands that the Victorian revivalists faced. Craft is still a means of responding to the conditions of modernity. It took on its meaning within that framework, and it retains this identity today. But with two centuries of modern craft behind us, we have the opportunity to avoid the traps of manipulation and idealism that usually beset that endeavor. Our own era is just as potentially traumatic and disruptive as the time of the industrial revolution. And craft remains intimately bound up with these ongoing transformations. To understand this present moment, however, we must move past the options left to us by figures like John Ruskin and William Morris. We cannot continue to simply re-revive the strategies of the nineteenth century, gamely staging one flashback after another. Nor can we simply roll back the years.

So what to do? Here we might find some consolation in the notion that even traumatic events of the scale of mass warfare can have some salutary effects. As Jenny Elkins writes, "they are overwhelming but they are also a revelation. They strip away the diverse commonly accepted meanings by which we lead our lives in our various communities. They reveal the contingency of the social order and in some cases how it conceals its own impossibility."[34] We do need to take some forms of craft out from behind the screen, but we can still try to understand how craft functions in relation to memory—hopefully helping us to undo some of the hierarchical, repressive aspects of modernity while retaining its spirit of invention. I return to that project in more detail later in the chapter, but first, now that we are prepared with a set of analytical tools for understanding how craft, modernity, and memory relate to one another, I want to turn again to the ideas that emerged around modern craft in the mid-nineteenth century. We have already seen the unstated contradictions at the heart of Pugin's *Contrasts*. Now we can examine the even more influential figures of Ruskin and Morris and try to build a revisionist account of their thinking that might be useful for the present day.

This is a tall order, so I'll begin by enlisting a craft theorist who has already begun the work: David Pye. A British woodworker and writer, active primarily in the 1960s and 1970s, Pye is best known for his distinction between the "workmanship of risk" and the "workmanship of certainty"—a dichotomy that seems to map neatly onto the difference between craft and industry. That is almost, but not quite, correct. It would be better to say that making processes can always be located somewhere between complete risk and complete certainty (hardly ever at those frontiers). Craft is not a term Pye tended to use much—he disliked its ideological overtones—but if we had to locate craft somewhere on his sliding scale of workmanship, we would probably want to put it right in the middle, an ideal and intelligent balance between risk and certainty.[35] To paraphrase an example that Pye gives himself, one can cut a piece of paper in many ways: by tearing it abruptly; by folding and then tearing it (in which case it forms its own "jig" or guide); burnishing the edge of that fold and then tearing it, to reduce the material's tendency to render the tear inexact; cutting it with a knife; cutting it using a pair of scissors, which are self-guiding (the blade acts as a jig); using a single-blade cutter (or "guillotine"); or, eventually, opening up a paper mill and mass producing sheets by the thousands.[36] Along this continuum there is diminishing risk, and increasing certainty, bought at the price of increased time and tooling. Somewhere down the line (probably in the vicinity of careful folding and scissoring) one has arrived at what most people mean by craft (Figure 4.5). But Pye's point was a different one. He wanted to show us that *every* process is susceptible to degrees of risk and certainty, from the artisan's bench to the largest of factories; and, moreover, that those varying degrees of predictability could be consciously intermixed and mingled, producing different results.

So skilled workmanship, for Pye, is the opposite to how it is usually presented under the rubric of modern craft. It can exist within all forms of production; it is not a category separated from industry. It is an interweaving of both technical and practical knowledge, the work of head and hands acting in concert, an intelligent process rather than an unconscious or instinctive matter of execution. Though he wrote over forty years ago, Pye's thinking is surprisingly compatible with the world of postdisciplinary production, in which the

Figure 4.5   T. Hunter, cut paper work, 1786. Vellum. V&A: E.116–1928.
© Victoria and Albert Museum, London.

categories of modern craft no longer hold and hierarchies are all up for grabs. To be sure, he was not much of a cultural theorist. Pye always grounded his claims in the technical nuances of workmanship, and that can occasionally make him seem myopic. (He did say that the workmanship of risk produces a humanistic "diversity" in the environment, but that rather abstract claim is his only serious argument about the broader cultural effects of craft.) Even so, he is an outstandingly useful guide in our attempt to escape the legacy or, as he called it, the "dogma," of the Arts and Crafts movement.

Edward S. Cooke, Jr. has written that twentieth-century craft revivals were carried out under the "long shadow" of Ruskin and Morris, which effectively "precludes both the notion of a professional industrial designer who works with a team to develop prototypes and then plans or orchestrates manufacture as well as the concept of a craft object existing as a commercial commodity with recursive meanings."[37] Pye could not have been more explicit in his attempt to demolish this tradition. In *The Nature and Art of Workmanship*—the same book that presents the argument about risk and certainty—he included a chapter entitled "Critique of 'On the Nature of Gothic'" in which he thoroughly dismantled John Ruskin's foundational text of craft revival. Curiously, this chapter is not very well known. It has even been possible for many writers to borrow equally from the Ruskin-Morris tradition and from Pye, as if there were not a vivid contradiction between the two. Yet Pye's critique of Ruskin sits within the historiography of modern craft like a depth charge, exploding the logic of the craft movement right at its spiritual center:

> The deficiencies of the Arts and Crafts movement can only be understood if it is realized that it did not originate in ideas about workmanship at all. Indeed it never developed anything approaching a rational theory of workmanship, but merely a collection of prejudices which are still preventing useful thought to this day... Ruskin did injustice to Victorian workmanship and to the men who produced it, whom he called slaves; and he influenced William Morris to cause yet more harm. Between them they diverted the attention of educated people from what was good in the workmanship of their own time, encouraged them to despise it, and so hastened its eventual decline.[38]

This is strong stuff; Pye is claiming that, far from being the saviors of good workmanship, Ruskin and Morris were guilty of contributing to its destruction (so even Pye was not immune from the narrative of disappearance). What led him to this bracing accusation?

As always with Pye, the devil was in the details. He pointed out that, first, Ruskin had confused craft with ornament, as, for example, in his claim that a Gothic cathedral, "every jot and tittle" of it, was completely suffused with the "individual fire" of the creative workman. To this, Pye deftly counters: "you cannot get individual fire into plain walling or the cylindrical shaft of a column." Ruskin had isolated the least functional aspects of the cathedral and pretended that in these details were contained all there was to making the whole: "he writes as though building were ornament."[39] This slippage between craft and the decorative—two concepts that are by no means interchangeable, as completely functional things can be made by hand and highly ornamental things through mass production—is one of the most influential displacements in Arts and Crafts ideology. It tacitly cedes the majority of production, anything efficiently structural or functional, to industry, implying that craft can have no part in it. As Pye rightly says, that was simply to drive a wedge between craft and "the practical necessities of life," identifying it only with "what is inessential."[40]

A second problem Pye finds in "On the Nature of Gothic" concerns the concept of "perfect finish," which to Ruskin was the dead surface presented by the vast majority of Victorian material culture. Morris similarly distinguished between "true finish," which bore the irregular marks of handwork, and "trade finish," which in its over-perfection spoke only of the subjugation of the worker.[41] Because they believed in vital, "savage" workmanship, Ruskin and Morris both thought that a flawlessly made object must necessarily be a sign of dehumanization. As Ruskin put it, "no good work whatever can be perfect, and the demand for perfection is always a misunderstanding of the ends of art." Pye flatly contradicts this assertion: "every carver knows that it is not so, and in a trade like joinery or cabinet-making countless examples demonstrate that it has never been so." Craft can indeed be highly regulated. This is the whole point of attaining skills, developing a repertoire of specialized tooling, and all the other refinements that constitute the history of trades. In fact, as we have seen, given the limitations of machines in the nineteenth century, perfection of surface was *only* achievable through handwork. Why did Ruskin and Morris commit this gratuitous error? Pye's answer is perceptive: their aesthetic preference for imperfection really has to do with questions of authorship. "Perfect finish" is to be rejected because it implies that the workman is executing someone else's design. Irregularity is desirable because it gives proof of on-the-job improvisation. "Choose whether you will pay for the lovely form or the perfect finish," demands Ruskin, "and choose at the same moment whether you will make the worker a man or a grindstone." Again Pye demurs, pointing out that a joiner might well work to his own drawing rather than another's and produce the same result: "how is the workman more enslaved by working 'perfectly' from another man's drawing than he is by working from his own?"[42] But what Ruskin really is saying when he expresses his aesthetic preference for an unregulated surface is that craftspeople should be free from regulation itself—free from any outside dictates upon their work.

And here we come to the core dilemma of Ruskin's formulation of craft. His arguments in *The Stones of Venice* seem to promote the ideals of handwork, but they actually systematically rule out any possibility for its integration itself with modernity. Here is Pye again:

> In [Ruskin's] day the greater part of manufacture was directed to the strictly practical ends of making such things as bricks, tiles, slates, boards, castings, rails, forgings, ships, machinery, vehicles, warehouses, docks, roads, tools, factories, mills, agricultural implements. Where in all that is the workman to do his inventing unless the clock is put back a hundred years?[43]

Of course, putting the clock back is exactly what Ruskin thought he was trying to do. But just like Pugin in *Contrasts,* he had absorbed the definitional structures of modern craft, as we have seen them outlined in the previous chapters, and simply inverted them. He reframed its supposed limitations as virtues. The irregularity and "savagery" the mechanics' institutes sought to correct became positive characteristics.[44] Similarly, he called malevolent any use of craft his contemporaries would have regarded as appropriate, not just skillful hand finishing and working to the designs of others, but also making copies by hand ("never encourage imitation or copying of any kind").[45] In Ruskin's mind, the industrial artisan was simply a contradiction in terms. He pretended that a high level of skill was completely incompatible with machine production, when in fact it is crucial. At the core of his dissociative thinking was an identification of craft with impracticality and imperfection. By setting the standard for handwork firmly in the distant past, he made it impossible to conceive any practical means of integrating it in the present.

In contrast to Ruskin, Pye spent relatively little time in taking apart William Morris, though he did bristle at the great reformer's tendency to pretend that things were made by machine when they were manifestly not. In response to Morris's claim, in the essay "The Revival of Handicraft" (1888), that "the making beautifully all kinds of ordinary things, carts, gates, fences, boats, bowls…has gone," Pye offered another of his characteristically blunt rejoinders: "[that] was untrue then, and was still untrue fifty years or so afterwards." He was more incensed still by Morris's sweeping condemnation of Victorian goods as shoddy—this was what Pye had in mind when he wrote that Arts and Crafts rhetoric had actually hastened the decline of skilled workmanship by underestimating its important role in contemporary production. It moved him to particularly poetic dissent: "many ordinary things of that age have survived to ours, and by them Morris's untruth stands condemned."[46] Extending Pye's discussion, we might observe that Morris, like Ruskin, prized the unthinking "flow" of craft and disdained any form of copying. A skilled weaver, he wrote, "was thinking least of his materials, when he was wrapped up in the invention of his design and the beauty of its hues." In times of "degradation of the art," by contrast, weavers thought too much. They "spent time and pains to make, for instance, woven silk look like printed paper and so forth."[47] Of course we can draw many other parallels between Ruskin and Morris, but all of them would lead us to the same conclusion: both men absorbed the modern idea of craft established in the early nineteenth century and simply inverted its priorities. Their attempt was to free artisans, but in fact they left the terms by which they were subjugated intact. Their image of craft is essentially negative, in the sense of a photographic negative: they looked at the world of skill around them and were attracted to everything they did not see.

The incidence of what I have called "screen memory" was particularly central to Morris's imagination, underpinning not only his politics of labor and his craft production, but also his very perception of the world around him. In moving prose, he described his tendency to imagine, as he traveled through the countryside of England, a landscape that had long disappeared from the earth, replacing each sight with its lost (and to him, always superior) equivalent:

Not seldom I please myself with trying to realize the face of mediæval England...the villages just where they are now (except for those that have nothing but the church left to tell of them), but better and more populous; their churches, some big and handsome, some small and curious, but all crowded with altars and furniture, and gay with pictures and ornament; the many religious houses, with their glorious architecture; the beautiful manor-houses, some of them castles once, and survivals from an earlier period; some new and elegant; some out of all proportion small for the importance of their lords. How strange it would be to us if we could be landed in fourteenth-century England.[48]

In this passage, a verbal equivalent to the pictorial veiling we saw in Pugin's *Contrasts*, Morris describes himself mentally redressing the whole landscape, as if preparing a vast set for the filming of a period drama. As with Pugin, the real Middle Ages have little place in his vision. Both repainted what are often called the Dark Ages in unremittingly glowing tones. But it is the act of screening itself that is of interest here; and this urge to recast the present on the model of the past is everywhere in Morris's work. He imagined factories as medieval workshops surrounded by gardens, and even human bodies as literally reformed: "straight-limbed, strongly knit, expressive of countenance."[49] This optic, that of a regressive but critical utopianism, is best exemplified by his novel *News from Nowhere,* with its

Figure 4.6   William Morris's Kelmscott Manor, as shown in the frontispiece for *News from Nowhere* (1893).

introductory incantation in the conditional voice—"If I could but see it! If I could but see it!"—and its imaginary eradication of the signs of industry: "The soap-works with their smoke-vomiting chimneys were gone; the engineer's works gone; the lead-works gone; and no sound of riveting and hammering came down the west wind from Thorneycroft's."[50] As design critic Deyan Sudjic noticed many years ago, there is something terrifying in the way Morris scrubbed away the mess of modernity: "He was no totalitarian, but in the Phnom Penh of Year Zero, there is a hideous echo of *News From Nowhere*."[51] This is probably putting things too strongly. But at a minimum, as Morris's biographer Fiona McCarthy writes, his text is profoundly disorienting, and meant to be so: "Where are we and when is it? This is and is not England."[52]

UNITED AND INDUSTRIOUS

So far, I have been somewhat inexact about the nature of the trauma Ruskin, Morris, and the other craft revivalists internalized. Of course, there is some reason to be vague. As with any traumatic response, the whole point of the amnesiac qualities and screening functions associated with craft was to deflect and disguise. There were many elements to the disquiet Ruskin and Morris felt, some of which they were able to formulate clearly (though, as we have seen through Pye's critique, even these statements were shadowed by blindness). The core of it, though—the thing they could really not bear to see—was that craftsmen, far from being the enemies of modernity, were not only produced within it, but were also among its most influential protagonists. Throughout this book, I have discussed the ways in which craft, once it had been invented as a discrete category, became the instrumental "other" to modern progress. Its various self-effacements disguised a crucial contribution to the linked projects of improvement, industrialism, and imperialism. Discussion of this contribution may have been missing from Arts and Crafts discourse, but that does not mean it was absent from nineteenth-century thinking altogether. On the contrary: it is possible to find examples in which craft was positioned not as a repository of the past, but an active driver of the present, into the future.

One such case is that of the Amalgamated Society of Engineers (ASE). This was just the sort of organization Arts and Crafts advocates either ignored or actively criticized. Though Morris was a committed socialist, his opinion of organized labor was a damning one: "the Trades Unions, founded for the advancement of the working class as a class, have already become conservative and obstructive bodies, wielded by the middle-class politicians for party purposes."[53] For him, the established unions were part of the system rather than the solution. Partly for this reason, though the ASE features preeminently in historians' accounts of nineteenth-century labor politics, it finds no place in existing craft histories. Yet in its own day, there was no larger or more powerful institution fighting for the interests of artisans. In the divergence between the principles of this organization and those that animated the Arts and Crafts movement can be found a disconnection that has haunted modern craft to this day. Founded in 1851, the year of the Great Exhibition, the ASE was the world's first super-union. It was composed of more than 120 previously existing trade societies, including Manchester's largest, the Journeymen Steam Engine Makers', Machine Makers' and Millwrights' Friendly Society (founded in 1826 and nicknamed the Old Mechanics). Among the nearly twelve thousand artisans the ASE could claim as members by the end of its first year of operation were smiths, turners, pattern makers, millwrights, mechanical draughtsmen, brass finishers, and coppersmiths, machine makers, and shipwrights. For the most part, these were the new artisans of the nineteenth century, rather than practitioners of long-established skills. Indeed, from the moment of its inception, the Society was understood as something new, marking a new phase in labor politics. "The leading idea," according to a history issued on the organization's fiftieth anniversary, "was a very simple one; namely, the welding together of the local and sectional societies of the engineering trade into one organization, dominated by one policy, controlled by one executive authority."[54]

The premise was straightforward enough. By banding together, skilled laborers could exert greater pressure on their managers and employers. Each paid only modest membership dues, but the influence of the union as a whole was enormous. Mistreated workers at a factory in Birmingham could threaten to instigate a general strike affecting trade in Manchester, Liverpool, and London—which would lead to pressure on the offending Birmingham manufacturer to resolve the dispute. Of course, capitalists had long operated within just such networks and had reaped great advantages in economies of scale. By moving production from place to place and relying on extended supply chains, they could keep wages, material costs, and other outlays as low as possible. So the idea of banding together in a single, large-scale union could be considered an instance of fighting fire with fire, a mirroring of the employers' practices. Yet so novel was the idea of labor "amalgamation" that there was serious debate about its legality. Management argued it should be seen as a form of "conspiracy or illegal and malicious combination," a charge the ASE's lawyers vigorously contested.[55] In this, anyway, they were successful. The Society was not broken up by the government, and it remained the principal union in the British engineering trades (broadly construed) for seventy years, until it was absorbed into an even larger union in 1920.

Pioneering labor historians Sidney and Frances Webb pointed to the ASE as the exemplary "new model" trade union of the 1850s. Partly this novelty was a matter of scale and organization, but it was also a difference in philosophy. Unlike the more radical movements that had emerged earlier in the century, such as the Chartists, or the socialists of Morris's circle, they "[laid] aside all projects of social revolution," instead embracing the idea that they should work within the existing system while trying to ameliorate the worst abuses of the capitalist managerial classes.[56] Opinion varies among more recent historians as to the accuracy of the Webbs' view: was large-scale organization the critical element in evolving industrial labor relations, resulting in more effective representation for the workers? Or was it, as Marxists inclined to emphasize working-class culture (notably E. P. Thompson, a sympathetic biographer of William Morris) tend to believe, a constraint on the radical potential that had been contained in informal alliances and solidarities?[57] For the purpose of our discussion, which focuses on the conceptualization of craft rather than its actual political fortunes, it is not necessary to take sides in this debate. The important thing is that organizations like the ASE were crucial in formalizing modern perceptions of industrial craft. First of all, the trade unions' objectives were unrelated to questions of aesthetics, marking a great divergence between their concerns and those of the craft revivalists. They concentrated on more logistical issues. They were staunchly opposed to piecework pay systems, for example, which tended to drive down wages and also to demand greater work rate over time. (Though it lacked the pseudo-rationalist element of "scientific management," piecework might be considered a forerunner of twentieth-century Taylorism.) The Society also fought wage cuts in times of economic distress, when employers tended to try to cover their losses by lowering wage bills. And it advocated limiting the maximum number of working hours per day to nine (and once this was widely accepted, to eight).

These points were not in any way divisive among workers. But another issue proved more controversial. This was the effort to clearly demarcate skilled artisans, like those represented by the ASE, from unskilled laborers and apprentices. As we saw in chapter one, it was clearly in the interest of management to subdivide labor so that lower-skilled, lower-paid workers could execute the majority of tasks. Just as clearly, it was in the interest of the skilled workforce to prevent such "degrading." In practice, this meant the construction of an elite echelon of artisans with a distinct set of interests, which were directly opposed to those of unskilled workers. This "labor aristocracy," explicitly differentiated by craft skill (and tacitly by gender, for it was an entirely male domain), was demarcated from other workers. As one journeyman engineer put it in 1873, "Between the artisan and the unskilled labourer a gulf is fixed... The artisan creed with regard to the labourers is that the latter are an inferior class and that they should be made to know and [be] kept in their place."[58] Skilled workers had made this argument for years as a means of protecting their status, but it was made official by the ASE—installed in the union rules and embraced as an unquestioned principle. This "spirit of exclusiveness," as the Webbs called it, had important consequences in terms of the definition of the skilled worker.[59] According to the organization, a trained artisan was not to be confused with the unthinking, mechanical laborer so often described by modern improvers. Rather, he was comparable to "the physician who holds a diploma, or the author who is protected by copyright."[60]

Sure enough, in the organization's first year of existence, a controversy about labor hierarchy erupted in Oldham, just northeast of Manchester, at the firm of Hibbert, Platt and Sons, one of the largest machine manufacturers in the world. Ironically, the dispute centered on the use of "self-acting machines" to make other machines. This had allowed the company to hire a large number of unskilled (and nonunionized) workers paid on piecework rates. The factory's skilled workforce tendered a demand that the unskilled laborers be removed. In reply, the firm locked them out. At first, everything went according to plan: within a month of the confrontation in Oldham, more than thirty-five hundred skilled artisans were on strike or locked out in London and Manchester. The Society's coffers were too low to fight on for more than a few months, and eventually management got the better of the dispute, forcing the artisans back to work on relatively unfavorable terms.

Nonetheless, an important point had been made. The ASE was a force to be reckoned with, and it was fighting not for the rights of all workers—as the socialists then gathering strength in Europe were—but on the side of the skilled alone.

Thus, as feminist historian Cynthia Cockburn once put it, "for any socialist movement concerned with unity in the working class, the skilled craftsman is [a] problem."[61] This uncomfortable fact was one of the great separations between Morris's thinking and that of the artisan activists of his own day. But it was certainly not the only one. Indeed, the ASE stood against everything the Arts and Crafts movement would come to believe in. Rather than the quasi-sacred principle of joy in labor, the ASE espoused a goal that was perhaps less lofty, but more important to the artisans themselves: economic prosperity. The Society championed the idea of artisanship as a respectable profession, rather than a free amateur pursuit, and there seems to have been little expectation among its ranks that their own work even *should* be pleasurable. One looks in vain for any mention of that issue in the organization's rhetoric. Indeed, the constant emphasis on limiting shift hours suggests that work was considered a burden, not a joy. Instead, the objective was to get skill recognized and justly compensated. Ruskin's chastising voice is audible in the background: "I think it is pay that you want, not work."[62]

The ASE also provides a vivid contrast with the Arts and Crafts movement with regard to the questions of memory I have been examining in this chapter. It positioned itself as an instrument of progress, rather than an obstacle or alternative to modernity's onward march. The Society's spokesmen voiced no despair about the present or future state of the artisanal trades they represented or their relevance in contemporary life. Despite conflicts like the one at Oldham, they were confident that the skills of their members, far from being superseded by machines, were becoming ever more important, ever more in demand, with the expansion of industry. Other crafts, like hand sewing, might fall away, but this would only make the skills of the machinist even more crucial:

> Look at the ceaseless progress of invention in the application of machinery to perform the tasks which before were regarded as fit only for the more delicate mechanism of the human hand; the sewing machine, for instance, to take a recent case. Look where you will, in short, you will find facts that will teach you that there need be no apprehension but that there will be a largely increasing demand for engineering work for many a year to come.[63]

ASE leaders talked constantly of the organization as an instrument of forward motion, and even claimed that their constituency of skilled workers was *more* progressive than the capitalist factory owners who opposed them. "The workmen of the nineteenth century are as a body quiet, at least in this country, orderly and reasonable. But who [can] say as much for the other side?" they asked. "The progress and enlightenment of a hundred years seem to have produced a very small modicum of reformation amongst employers as a class."[64] Far from requiring improvement, as was implied by the employers, the machinists were model citizens: "the most skilful of the trade, the best conducted of the trade, the most moral and useful of the trade."[65] At a labor demonstration held in London in 1867, one speaker expounded on the theme: skilled workers were not the problem, an obstreperous class to be swept aside by modernity; thanks to their own self-reliance, they were the driving force of progress. The transcript, published under the ASE's imprint, records the words of one mechanic after another proclaiming the virtues of the skilled artisan:

> Self-reliance, that reason-animating, heart-stirring, soul-inspiring quality (applause), which whispers to a man, no matter whether he be the tailor in the garret, the shoemaker in the cellar, the engineer at the lathe, the weaver at the loom, the bricklayer or mason on the scaffolding, self-reliance whispers into the deepest recesses of his soul, in gladdening tones, and says, look up! There is a better and happier future before you! (Loud cheers.)[66]

These speeches contrast starkly to that delivered in 1823 by John Johnson—the submissive, inarticulate whitesmith we encountered at the beginning of chapter three. The trade unions had fully absorbed the lessons of the Mechanics' Institutes set up in a previous generation, with the difference that now they had no interest in being helped by their superiors. In this new context, skilled workers presented themselves as dedicated to the cause of self-improvement, but certainly not in need of assistance.

In all these ways, they might have leapt straight from the pages of Samuel Smiles's *Self-Help,* the hugely popular guide to modern life published in 1859. Smiles's breathlessly sententious book preached happiness through hard work. He held up for admiration great figures in the history of craft like Benvenuto Cellini, Bernard Palissy, Johann Böttger, and Josiah Wedgwood, who earned their place in his pantheon of engineers, scientists, and fine artists not only for their ingenuity but also for their "intelligent hands," their manual skill: "the skill that comes by labour, application, and experience."[67] In short, Smiles espoused a capitalist model of individualism in which every man was completely self-reliant. Institutions could, at most, "leave him free to develop himself and improve his individual condition."[68] Craft was central to this social project. As one of Smiles's many acolytes, Francis Chilton-Young, would put it some years later in his how-to book *Every Man His Own Mechanic,* "how can men [best] help themselves? By learning to use their hands as well as their head!"[69] Smiles's devotion to individualism and self-education was so extreme that he even cast doubt on institutions devoted to fostering personal development, including the mechanics' institutes of the day, which he claimed had never produced a truly great mechanic or inventor. He also dismissed the idea that British industrial success was a matter of technological sophistication: "it is not tools that make the workman, but the trained skill and perseverance of the man himself."[70]

Smiles's message was embraced wholeheartedly by figures associated with the ASE, but it always sat uneasily with the organization's devotion to collective action. The tension existed even before the society's founding. As early as 1850, when Smiles was just beginning to lecture about "self help," one of the ASE's founders, John "Rise and Shine"

Rowlinson (a leader of the Old Mechanics and veteran of labor strikes in Bolton), aligned himself with the idea that "self-help was the most valuable of all helps" even as he called for the introduction of "associated labour."[71] And here, we touch on a similarity between the trade unionists and the Arts and Crafts advocates: though their outlooks on the problem were very different, both ran headlong into one of the characteristic problems of modernity, the conflict between collectivity and individualism. Ruskin and Morris sought to resolve this dilemma by reverting to a time before it had emerged (or so they believed). They adopted as their template the medieval artisan working in a communitarian context, perhaps on a joint endeavor like a cathedral or tapestry, who nonetheless expressed himself in completely personal (albeit unself-conscious) form. For the artisans of the ASE, this solution had no appeal, for they considered themselves quintessentially modern. Accordingly, they sought solutions that were not aesthetic but structural. They worked together to raise the bargaining power and status of skilled artisans, not in order to depart from a capitalist conception of individuality, but on the contrary, to build a framework in which each workman could do as Smiles urged: advance his own interests as effectively as possible.

This pairing of two contrary goals—self-reliance and collectivity—was expressed visually in the ASE's official emblem, designed in 1851 by an ironworker and self-taught artist named James Sharples, who came from Bury, another satellite town of Manchester (Plate 14). He had responded to a public competition to create the emblem, and won the prize—five pounds. As the company's fiftieth anniversary history put it, "most people will agree that he was not overpaid."[72] The emblem he conceived is complicated and richly allegorical. Its dominant figures are two workmen in contemporary dress, being bestowed wreaths by an angel. They offer their services to two figures representing War and Peace. On either side are two further illustrative figures in classical garb, one breaking a single stick over his knee and the other failing to break a bundle of sticks, or fasces. This image, drawn ultimately from Aesop's fables, is intended to convey the idea that there is strength in unity (the fasces was adopted by the ancient Romans to symbolize this principle and would of course be used in the 1920s and 1930s by the Italian Fascists—hence the name).[73] All of this activity is staged atop a temple-cum-factory shown in cross-section. The structure is divided into six separate compartments, each showing one of the trades represented by the union. The vignettes are not too different from the illustrations of Diderot's *Encyclopedia* a century earlier, but here they are connected to the wider world of industry, suggested by a sailing ship to the right and a train to the left, with a factory issuing smoke in the background. The overall impression given by the emblem is one of a complex system set completely in order. At the bottom runs the didactic slogan "Be United and Industrious," a remarkably concise encapsulation of the twin virtues of amalgamation and self-reliance. The emblem's message is that the two could be bound together in one symbolic system through the culture of craftsmanship.

As it happens, Sharples's story was among the many inspiring biographies Smiles related in his book *Self-Help*. Rather as Sequoyah was adopted by reformers as an instance of the ideal Native American (see chapter three), the blacksmith-turned-artist served as an example of the self-improving impulse in action. After relating an anecdote about the young Sharples drawing out plans for industrial boilers on the floor of his home in chalk— he was working as a rivet boy at the time, and was supposedly inspired by the process of laying out the machines in the factory—Smiles told his readers how the young man taught himself painting and then steel engraving. This last skill Sharples developed expressly to produce a print, based on one of his own paintings, entitled *The Forge* (Figure 4.7). The image is indeed unusual (if not unique), a representation of a Victorian industrial workshop by an artisan who actually worked in one. Perhaps most striking is its detailed specificity. Though Sharples said he did not mean to represent any particular foundry, but rather a general impression of one, he carefully renders the architecture of the space, the world of tools it contains, and the dress and bearing of the workers. It is so marvelously explicit that one could easily imagine using it as a visual aid to explain the operations of the modern foundry. This is not to say that it is lacking in artistic license. Like Joseph Wright of Derby, who painted the same subject several decades earlier (see Figures 2.8 and 2.9), he exploits the dramatic light effect of the forge and heroizes the figures—particularly the two men straining to maneuver a long, heavy pipe into the furnace, and another who crouches in the foreground, preparing the next workpiece to be hoisted into place on a chain. The two pictures differ greatly, however, in their representation of labor itself. While Wright offers

Figure 4.7   James Sharples, *The Forge*, 1859. Steel engraving. British Museum PD 1865–6–10–25.

us a staunchly independent forge master, whose relations are primarily those of family, Sharples gives us a scene of professional interdependency, in which labor is clearly divided into discrete tasks according to skill level. This hierarchy is spelled out in a progression from left to right: first, a younger figure, perhaps an apprentice, who stokes the forge fire; then the two foundrymen with the pipe; and finally, the shop foreman who directs the activity by pointing into the background and whose long experience is subtly indicated by the worn leather apron he wears.

The Forge, then, uses the tools of visual narrative to convey the same themes as Sharples's ASE emblem: all workers are in their rightful place, according to their skill. The print also upholds the virtue of orderly craftsmanship in its careful material execution. It was the first engraving Sharples had ever made, and he trained himself on the job during his leisure time—with the result that it took several years to complete. This was a subject of great interest to Smiles, who quoted the artist's own account of making the engraving at length:

> With the engraving I made but very slow progress, owing to the difficulties I experienced from not possessing proper tools. I then determined to try to make some that would suit my purpose, and after several failures I succeeded in making many that I have used in the course of my engraving. I was also greatly at a loss for want of a proper magnifying glass, and part of the plate was executed with no other assistance of this sort than what my father's spectacles afforded, though I afterwards succeeded in obtaining a proper magnifier, which was of the utmost use to me . . . I had neither advice nor assistance from any one in finishing the plate. If, therefore, the work possess any merit, I can claim it as my own; and if in its accomplishment I have contributed to show what can be done by persevering industry and determination, it is all the honour I wish to lay claim to.[74]

Though Sharples did benefit from the various forms of education aimed at artisans at the time—he took courses at the local mechanics' institute and consulted instructional literature on anatomy, perspective, and other subject—Smiles de-emphasizes the fact, using the artist's own words to present himself as a model of self-edification, teaching himself the "fine arts" through trial and error, elevating himself from ironmonger to artist. His workmanlike approach to self-improvement, while remarkable, has nothing to do with genius. The implication is that any reader of *Self-Help* could do the same.

The image making of James Sharples, like that of the Amalgamated Society of Engineers in general, suggests the extent to which modern ideas about craft had permeated the ranks of skilled artisans by the mid-nineteenth century. They understood themselves as a community of sorts, tied together by mutual dependencies and their own common interests, and fought against the opposing interests of management. Yet the ASE's rhetoric, both verbal and visual, was drawn entirely from the conceptual framework built around modern craft in the early part of the century. The organization did resist exploitation, of course, but it also accepted, and even agitated for, a structure of work in which some forms of labor were seen as superior to others. Its embrace of the principle of self-help was entirely consistent with this hierarchical view. The ASE also embraced the explicit, didactic language of the Victorian improver—mystery plays no role in its approach—and its members also seem to have taken for granted the idea their own work should be seen as mechanical, rather than expressive. Sharples's print of *The Forge* exemplifies all these ideas: a triumph of the artist's own mechanical skill applied to the job of explication, which depicts a harmonious workplace built around a strict chain of command.

AFFECTIVE RELATIONS

Sharples and his fellow industrial workers did not base their collective identity on tradition. They sought to ally themselves with the cause of progress, and certainly did not see themselves as repositories of memory, in need of protection from the forces of change. How different in all these respects is Sharples's representation of a forge from yet another treatment of the same subject, made just a few years later by Benjamin Creswick (Figure 4.8). Another self-taught artist from the ranks of industrial artisans, Creswick had been a knife grinder working in Sheffield until he encountered the Museum of the Guild of St. George in nearby Walkley. Like the mechanics' institutes of the day, this institution dedicated itself to the educational uplift of the artisanal classes. And like the ASE, it was meant to be funded through contributions from each its members. Ruskin formed the Guild not to prepare workmen for modern industry, however, but rather to rescue them from it. As he put it, "The mountain home of the Museum at Walkley was originally chosen not to keep the collection out of smoke, but expressly to beguile the artisan out of it."[75] In addition to the museum, which was its most concrete outcome, the Guild (founded in 1871) also was intended to function as a cooperative farm and a utopian community. Ruskin's plan was to acquire unused land and "make it fruitful." There the Guild members would live cooperatively and self-sufficiently. All work would be done by hand—no steam engines or sewing machines allowed. The museum, meanwhile, would provide a sort of spiritual center. As Robert Hewison has written, "Agriculture and the ownership of museums may at first seem odd functions to be carried out by a single society, but the land and the museum collection are the polarities of Ruskin's unified scheme. In between, at least in theory, lay an elaborate social organization, a society that would present a radical alternative to the structure of the contemporary world."[76] This combined ethical and aesthetic separatism was an important precedent for subsequent rural Arts and Crafts experiments, notably C. R. Ashbee's Guild of Handicraft and Ethel and Godfrey Blount's Haslemere Peasant Industries in Britain, and many comparable communities elsewhere.

As its medieval name implies, the Guild of St. George was an attempt to escape from the modern world into the past, and predictably that quixotic goal remained elusive. Guild members were inspired by Ruskin's rhetoric, but most found the organization's impracticality frustrating to say the least—one member, the unfortunate Egbert Rydings, lost two thousand pounds trying to operate an "old Corn Mill" according to traditional methods.[77] Tellingly, the most lasting success was the museum in Walkley, a temple to past glories hung with numerous images of Venice (some by Ruskin himself) and other Gothic Revival

Figure 4.8 Benjamin Creswick, *The Forge,* 1870s. Terra cotta. Collection of the Guild of St. George, Museums Sheffield.

images. There was little in the way of art from the nineteenth century apart from that of J.M.W. Turner, whom Ruskin had famous and vigorously championed.[78] The sculptor Creswick had first come to the museum as a visitor, but soon found himself under the great critic's wing. As he learned to model and carve, he concentrated on images of labor, including his own craft of knife grinding (he created an allegorical frieze on the subject for the façade of the Worshipful Company of Cutlers in Sheffield), and a portrait of Longfellow's blacksmith standing "under a spreading chestnut tree."[79] Creswick's forge, acquired by Ruskin for the Guild, is modeled by hand in terra cotta—much more immediate and expressive than Sharples's chosen medium of steel engraving. The setting, too, could not be more different from Sharples's carefully observed modern foundry. The outmoded hammer and anvil work is given little context to ground it in place and time apart from the rustic dress of the smiths, one of whom sports a beard in the manner of an ancient philosopher. We could be in any time, really—apart from the present. A gaggle of small children, to the left, shield themselves from the heat and noise, just as in Wright's late eighteenth-century forge paintings.

Perhaps Creswick was simply following precedent in including these children; but he might also have been thinking of another of Ruskin's teachings: that every workplace should be run along the lines of a family household, based on bonds of affection, rather than as a system premised on the flow of capital. His most well-known formulation of this idea was his manifesto *Unto This Last,* which first appeared as a series of articles in 1860–1861 and was republished in book form in 1862. The text was intended mainly as a riposte to the emergent science of political economy, as it was called in the nineteenth century. Ruskin was not circumspect in his choice of enemies, vigorously attacking the leading contemporary economic theorists such as David Ricardo and John Stuart Mill, whose writings on wages and trade were influential at the time and have remained so since. What infuriated Ruskin was their contention that individual profit seeking and collective prosperity could be reconciled (the same principle that underpinned the politics and imagery of the ASE). Against this, he insisted that the individual pursuit of wealth was a zero-sum game. "The art of becoming 'rich,' in the common sense, is not absolutely nor finally the art of accumulating much money for ourselves, but also of contriving that our neighbours shall have less."[80] From any economic point of view, he was wrong about this, and Ricardo and Mill were right. Within a multiparty system of exchange, your neighbor's money might well be crucial to your own investment. Ruskin seems to have missed the most elementary law of capitalism: given sufficient growth, competition and mutual gain are indeed not only compatible, but mutually reinforcing.

But Ruskin was not writing from an economic point of view. He may not have understood the general principles of wealth, any more than he grasped the physical realities of making (as we saw previously in the chapter). He did, however, have profound insights into the experience of working and being worked for:

> No man ever knew, or can know, what will be the ultimate result to himself, or to others, of any given line of conduct. But every man may know, and most of us do know, what is a just and unjust act...I have said balances of justice, meaning, in the term justice, to include affection,—such affection as one man owes to another. All right relations between master and operative, and all their best interests, ultimately depend on these.[81]

Again and again in *Unto This Last,* Ruskin returns to the idea of affection as the key to social justice—a concept he seems to have adapted from the medieval concept of fealty, or allegiance.[82] He insists that all economic relations should have an emotional or "passionate" basis. This of course runs counter to our expectations about professional conduct in modern life. We know that an employer and a worker have responsibilities to one another; but we rely on contracts and regulatory laws to enforce them. Conversely, we have all experienced the building of friendships within a workplace, but our tendency is to regard these sympathies as extraneous to our jobs. Ruskin wanted us to invert this way of thinking and to consider our business relationships in the same way we regard our familial obligations. "Supposing the master of a manufactory saw it right, or were by any chance obliged, to place his own son in the position of an ordinary workman," he wrote. "As he would then treat his son, he is bound always to treat every one of his men. This is the only effective, true, or practical rule which can be given on this point of political economy."[83] This metaphor, that of the happy family, was the means by which he sought to resolve the conflict between individualism and the collective that beset nineteenth-century conceptions of production.

A decade later, in his *Fors Clavigera,* a series of open letters addressed to the workers of Britain, he wrote with genuine humor but also withering sarcasm about the failure of political economy to calculate human values into its equations:

> You might [be] tempted to ask…"What things are useful, and what are not?" And as Mr. Mill does not know, nor any other Political Economist going—and as they therefore particularly wish nobody to ask them—it is convenient to say, instead of "useful things," "utilities fixed and embodied in material objects," because that sounds so very like complete and satisfactory information, that one is ashamed, after getting it, to ask for any more.[84]

Ruskin's message about the real value of production—that it should be judged not in terms of practical "utility" but only on the basis of the social relations that arise from it—may have been simplistic in comparison to the analytical feats of contemporaneous political economy. But it was also, in a positive sense, simple: easy to grasp and hold on to. As Edith Hope Scott put it in 1931, "the lever by which Karl Marx has moved the world was logic. Ruskin's call was a cry of compassion."[85] Though William Morris was a disciple of both figures, he worried that he would never fully understand *Das Kapital,* while he could sign on unhesitatingly to Ruskin's passionate ethical defense of the worker. Some decades later, when Mahatma Gandhi encountered *Unto This Last,* it so stirred him that he was unable to sleep. He immediately translated it into Gujarati, hoping it might serve as a template for social relations in a postcolonial India. It later was translated back into English, in a beautifully concise paraphrase that for the contemporary reader may be something of an improvement on the original.[86]

Today, in an atmosphere of general anxiety about the workings of the economy, it is not surprising that Ruskin's concept of affection should have a renewed appeal. When we conceive of wealth in individualistic, asocial terms we are not only being possessive; we are also, inadvertently, being possessed. Yet we should also be aware of the limitations of the idea of affection. It sounds attractive as a principle, but how can it actually be implemented, given the workings of economy and power? In practice, Ruskin and Morris were unable to answer this question, and so ended up in a position of indignant retreat from modernity. In the contrast I have been drawing between the Amalgamated Society of Engineers and the Guild of St. George, Sharples and Creswick, the industrial artisan and the traditional craftsman, we seem to be faced with a seemingly intractable choice. On one hand, we have a mechanical view of craft, which more or less accepts its position as an instrument of large-scale economic forces. Within this framework, artisans conceived of their interests not in terms of affection, but the reductive concerns of utility and capital. On the alternative path charted by Ruskin and Morris, craft was valued for its anticapitalist and expressive potential and its capability to support an imaginary continuity, a line of invented tradition cast backward into history. Such a "selective tradition," even if it pretends to an oppositional stance, conforms to the analysis made by Raymond Williams: "always the selectivity is the point; the way in which from a whole possible area of past and present, certain meanings and practices are chosen for emphasis, certain other meanings are neglected and excluded."[87] Though Williams was critiquing the dominant or "hegemonic" culture of capitalism, Arts and Crafts ideology—which inverted the value system of modern craft—was equally selective, by virtue of reinscribing that dominant system in reverse. Despite their antithetical nature, the two positions I have outlined here presented themselves as progressive, but both were, in truth, fundamentally conservative (craft's usual valence within modern thought). The industrial artisans of the ASE embraced the narrative of improvement that was attached to modern industry, but they saw craft skill as a bulwark against radicalism, a way to distinguish workers within a hierarchy. The nascent Arts and Crafts movement, by contrast, conceived itself as egalitarian and politically progressive—emblematized by Ruskin's call for affective relations and Morris's socialism—but it was tied down by tradition, an anchor moored in the past.[88]

STITCHES IN TIME

This false choice of modern craft, between present and past, complicity and detachment, is a discursive trap. Only by traversing that dialectic can craft be a powerful agent of change, both morally and economically. This requires the full realization of its potential for memory work. Earlier in the chapter, I suggested that we might be able to understand craft not as a negative symptom of traumatic experience, but as a positive working through, much like the act of psychoanalysis itself. Too often craft is treated as a static remnant of times gone by, or a mechanical execution of the imperatives of larger economic forces. Instead we should embrace it as a dynamic cultural force in which claims to cultural memory (like those made by Ruskin and Morris) are intermingled with more active, self-consciously modern, and therefore potentially disruptive impulses (like those espoused by the ASE). Craft's relation to time is complex—rather like a novel set in times past, but written in the authorial present. When the potential of this temporal structure is realized, craft can be a powerful mediator between the present and the past, and therefore between the individual and the collective. Artisans forge objects of memory that allow us to articulate the relations between these diametrically opposed poles. In short, modern craft is potent not in spite of its temporal impurity, but because of it. Its dynamic relation to memory provides a framework in which traumatic experiences can be processed, forms from the past renewed, questions of agency brought to the fore, and new possibilities explored, all at once.

I would now like to pursue this theme through reference to Maurice Halbwachs, a French sociologist who wrote in the 1920s and 1930s before he was murdered by the Nazis at the Buchenwald concentration camp. Under the influence of Freud, Halbwachs formulated a counterintuitive but nonetheless influential theory of memory. Beginning from the simple observations that all remembering happens in the present, and that memories nearly always involve other people, he argued that *all* memory was collective. That is, despite the fact that it feels interior, individual, and retrospective, recollection is in fact a powerful psychological tool for building relationships with others, in the "now." According to Halbwachs, every time you call a moment to mind you are actually using the raw material of the past to act on the present, as surely as a potter makes a drinking vessel from clay. Aware that this argument might seem improbable, he used a lovely and rather convincing example to get his point across:

> Our agreement with those about us is so complete that we vibrate in unison, ignorant of the real source of the vibrations. How often do we present, as deeply held convictions, thoughts borrowed from a newspaper, book or conversation? They respond so well to our way of seeing things that we are surprised to discover that their author is someone other than our self.[89]

For Halbwachs, all memory worked like this. In recalling something from the past, he thought, we are actually only reestablishing our link to those we care about. As memory diverges from history, it acquires an illusory but potent authenticity.[90] Forgetting, conversely, can be seen as the result of social alienation, a separation of the individual from the group. This already adds to our understanding of craft as a response to the trauma of modernity, because we can see that the oft-cited fear of the loss of skills is actually not (or not only) a simple call for preservation, but rather an expression of a broader anxiety about isolating, fragmentary experience; furthermore, the amnesiac repetition of the anxiety is a way of tacitly insisting on that idea of fragmentation. As discussed earlier, modernity is in itself destructive of the sense of continuity, both across time and within social relations. Jeffrey Olick has written that:

> contemporary societies have separated memory from the continuity of social reproduction; memory is now a matter of explicit signs, not of implicit meanings. Our only recourse has been to represent and invent what we can no longer spontaneously experience.[91]

But modernity has no existence outside of human relations; it is constantly produced by our interactions with one another. Halbwachs conceptualized memory in a way that reflected this dynamic process. His might even be called a proto-postmodernist stance, in that he did not conceive of modernity as a progressive improvement over the past, or a radical departure from it, but rather a constantly transforming rearrangement of existing cultural material. Many art historians and anthropologists in the 1980s and since have particularized this insight further, drawing particular attention to monuments and museums as *loci* for collective memory.[92] But it is not only in conspicuous and explicit moments of commemoration that the collective psyche impinges on, and is in turn formed by, individual recollection. That same mutuality is pervasive even in the most seemingly trivial, everyday act of recall. Though we are usually unaware of it, the reason we remember one thing and not another has only to do with our present needs and desires, which are entirely conditioned by our relations with people around us. The crucial corollary is that if we *are* aware of this dynamic, then we can use the cultural material embedded in memory as a tool to shape the present.

Now, it may initially seem that craft revival is a way of doing just this. By employing a gothic or vernacular style from the past, we can continue to live in the present while simultaneously asserting difference from it—or so the thinking goes. Certainly, revivalism provided a way to understand objects as connective, not only to the past but to others in the present. Pugin, Ruskin, and Morris, all in their own ways, built communities around themselves, activated through acts of recollection and repetition. Yet there is a crucial limitation in this approach. As we have seen, "revival" is a very particular kind of memory work, which has to do with masking unsettling truths rather than drawing attention to them. As the word implies, revival betrays an impossible desire to bring the past back to life in unaltered form. Ideally, the revivalist would like to reconstruct contemporary society along the lines of the past, as if building a church to a set of long-lost architectural plans. This aspiration denies the fact of social change, and in turn, the realities of present-day social difference. For this reason the strategy has been useful within nationalist movements of various kinds.[93] As Halbwachs wrote: "When it considers its own past, [a] group feels strongly that it has remained the same and become conscious of its identity through time."[94] But any use of memory that involves a claim of simple identity between a present community and the past must necessarily be an act of falsification.

The question, then, is not whether the past can be revived (it can't), but what new social forms are brought into being through the act of remembering. Arts and Crafts endeavors tended to assume the integrity of the group—the very thing that should be challenged—and thereby created communities based upon disconnection and retreat. Ruskin's Guild of St. George again affords a resonant example. Though very little craftwork was conducted under the auspices of the Guild itself, it did generate a spinoff in the form of the Ruskin Linen Industry, led by a woman with the delightful name of Marion Twelves. After reading *Fors Clavigera,* Twelves became an unswerving disciple of Ruskin and devoted herself to reviving the arts of spinning and lace making by hand. She went so far as to acquire Irish flax, antique spinning wheels, and a dilapidated loom so old no one involved in the workshop knew how to operate or even assemble it. Supposedly it was restored to working condition only through reference to paintings by the Renaissance painter Giotto, which showed a similar loom in use. This was a textbook example of fashioning the self along the lines of an imagined past. H. D. Rawnsley, another follower of Ruskin (he had gone so far as to turn to the priesthood under his influence) was prompted to an enthusiastic flight of rhetoric on the occasion:

> Little enough could the great Florentine, as he designed or worked with his own hands at the weaver's panel in his splendid Duomo tower, have imagined that, centuries after, his stone picture of an Italian home-industry would come to the aid of Norse peasants in a far-off Westmoreland vale, and be the means of giving a new lease of life to a dead industry in British homes.

For Rawnsley, Twelves and her colleagues seemed a throwback in the best possible sense. Their evocation of a dead art drew on deeply buried cultural instinct, which was literally running through their veins:

> The art was in their blood and the generations of those who had been mistresses of "the divine spiral" had left an inheritance of aptitude, that in a surprisingly short time enabled them to spin thread fine enough for chalice veils and soft and delicate enough for a princess's apparel.[95]

In Arts and Crafts endeavors like this one, the objective may seem to be the "reintroduction of a dead art" (as Rawnsley put it).[96] But actually, their project was motivated by a desire to systematically forget the present. In their search for authenticity, Twelves and her colleagues rejected modern materials, tools, and knowledge. They even imagined themselves as serving a thirteenth-century clientele—churches to buy chalice veils, princesses to buy lace apparel. Tellingly, Twelves adopted the Guild of St. George's emblem as the symbol for her own exercise in screen memory. Used with Ruskin's permission, it was a medieval-styled rose accompanied by the motto "to-day." Evidently neither she nor he could see the irony.

It is no coincidence that the Guild's most concrete outcome was in the field of needlework, for it is the textile crafts that seem most submerged in the warm bath of memory. Even today, such activities as knitting, embroidery, and appliqué are, as Joanne Turney writes, "embedded [in] a language of loss and an idealistic and rural past."[97] This set of associations was no less powerful in the nineteenth century. Textiles were automated much more extensively than other artisanal trades, and though hand needlework was by no means a rarity, it was often taken as anachronistic. As a result, it served as a convenient shorthand for the past. The link between tradition and textiles was also grounded in attitudes toward gender difference. Victorian women were understood as the guardians of what Halbwachs would call the collective memory: repositories of stable, upright, moral values. By retaining their roots in the familial past, women compensated for the more dynamic, perhaps ethically compromised, but emphatically modern lives of their husbands. When, in the late nineteenth century, histories of needlework began to be written for the first time, the texts reflected this set of gender associations. Samplers, upholstery, quilts, caskets, and other examples of needlework (not to mention delicate constructions of cut paper, shells, quillwork, and other materials) had long been made as "domestic accomplishments" by young women as a way of proving their refinement—a practice latterly embraced by feminists as an undervalued legacy, a submerged history of feminine creativity invisible to mainstream art history.[98]

In the Victorian period, authors such as Mrs. Bury Palliser and Mrs. Beeton (as their noms de plume imply, they published as wives as well as experts) were already noticing the value of this past. They described domestic needlework as a thread that connected virtuous women in an unbroken chain, all the way back to Eve. Almost needless to say, like all crafts, it was described as a tradition under threat. In Mrs. Beeton's words, "Knitting has never entirely quitted the hands of English and German ladies; indeed, among all good housewives of any civilised country it is reckoned an indispensable accomplishment...[yet] of the rudiments of this useful art many ladies are at present ignorant."[99] Writers routinely criticized machine-made textiles as pale shadows of their handmade equivalents: "At one glance, a cultured eye detects and ignores the work of the soulless machine. That slight irregularity which always proceeds from whatever is wrought, even under the worst conditions, by man or woman, is precious in any handsome fabric."[100] Antique examples that predated the deleterious effects of industry were accorded pride of place, and contemporary makers were encouraged to attend to these examples closely.

After Mrs. Bury Palliser published her authoritative history of lace, many other collectors and writers followed in her wake, constructing a romanticized "age of homespun" out of the "personal relics of ancestors and talismans of a nostalgically remembered past."[101] By the end of the century, there was a widespread antiquarian interest in textiles, strongly charged with a sense of moral uplift. It is hardly surprising to encounter, in one catalogue of samplers compiled by antiquarian Marcus Bourne Huish, an example wrought by John Ruskin's own grandmother, Catherine Tweedall (also spelled Tweddale), in 1775 (Figure 4.9). The sampler features a typical homiletic verse of the eighteenth century:

> She who from Heaven expects to Gain her end
> Must by her own efforts her self befriend
> The wretch who ne'er exceeds a faint desire

Figure 4.9   Catherine Tweedall, sampler, 1775. As reproduced in Marcus B[ourne] Huish, *Samplers and Tapestry Embroideries* (London: Fine Art Society/Longmans, Green, 1900), plate X.

Goes not half way to what she would acquire
She that to virtues high rewards would rise
Must run ye race before she win ye prize

Ironically, the sentiment expressed in this short doggerel is more compatible with competitive capitalism than Ruskin's consensual, affective worldview. But that did not prevent Huish from observing sanctimoniously that "the verse was probably often read by her renowned grandson, and may perchance have spurred his determination to strive in the race in which he won so 'high a reward.'"[102] As this example suggests, needlework readily served as a potent symbol within narratives of familial continuity, much like the ones Ruskin tirelessly promoted. And in this respect, Marion Twelves's work at Ruskin Linen, with its imaginative connections back to the thirteenth century, does indeed seem the perfect material emanation of the great reformer's ideas.

Yet, as we all know, families can be dysfunctional too. Behind the gracious veil of antiquarianism and the sweet music of well-tempered gender relations lay a story of exploitation and distress. After all, the vast majority of women making textiles by hand in the nineteenth century were not doing so as amateurs, but rather as supposedly "unskilled" workers in sweatshops or as low-paid outworkers. These artisans were completely excluded from the "labor aristocracy" and its representative organizations, like the ASE.[103] Not until the very end of the century, and only after tragedies like the Triangle Shirtwaist Factory fire in New York City (1911), did women even begin to find a formal voice in the labor movement. In the meantime, they worked at long hours for little compensation, most likely in combination with the completely unpaid domestic labor of housekeeping, child care, laundry, mending, and cooking. As early feminist sociologist Harriet Martineau put it in 1837, "the condition of the female working classes is such that if its sufferings were but made known, emotions of horror and shame would tremble through the whole of society . . . the lot of the needlewoman [is] almost equally dreadful, from the fashionable milliner down to the humble stocking-darner."[104] In an important article about Victorian lace production, Elaine Freedgood pointed out that popular books on handmade textiles, which celebrated their history and quality, functioned as a screen that obscured this unpleasant reality from view: "a bulwark—albeit a phantasmatic one—against the moral, physical, and aesthetic depredations of industrialization."[105] This is yet another instance of that most characteristic tendency of modern craft. Skilled handwork not only serves to efface its own reality, but is valued for that very service. Freedgood puts it beautifully: skilled hands "make useful symbols around which cultural wishes can accrue because they are both psychically manageable and representationally malleable."[106] Yet as she also suggests, it was not in the protected precincts of craft revival that this malleability was most potent, but rather in situations where needlework was less explicitly freighted with symbolic meaning. Where craft was still a viable economic project—which is to say, those situations that the Arts and Crafts reformers tended to ignore or despise—its potential to cathect the collective memory was brought face to face with modern transformations ranging from the political to the technological to the aesthetic.

In late nineteenth-century England, the lace industry was strictly divided by gender. Machine-produced examples were made mainly by men in factories, while the handmade lace so praised by authors of the time was typically produced by women as piecework in the home. This means of gaining income accorded with another widely shared assumption about gender, in which women were presumed to have an innate affinity for small-scale manual tasks, including not only crafts like sewing but also other dexterous, precise jobs like piano playing and typing.[107] Such tasks, and the principles of bodily control they were thought to require, were inculcated in girls from a young age, an artificial training that pretended to gender-based naturalness (Figure 4.10). Even so, historian Sonya Rose emphasizes, "Whatever women's supposed 'natural' talents, such as 'nimble fingers,' it was their identity as cheap workers that brought them to mind as an appropriate source of labor."[108] Even in the midst of such egregious exploitation, the cultural memory associated with textiles was put to work. Let's take, as an exemplary case, the lace industry that flourished in Ireland from the 1850s to the end of the century. This is not necessarily the example that springs to mind when one thinks of late nineteenth-century Irish craft. Rather, one thinks of the Celtic Revival—Ireland's answer to the gothic taste—that bespoke a deep-seated romantic nationalism. Irish craft reformers produced stained glass, silverwork, stone carvings, and embroideries, all of which featured a semi-invented indigenous vocabulary of native saints, interlace and knotwork, and rounded medieval script.[109] As Nicola Gordon Bowe notes, this syncretic style was both organic and scholarly in nature. Ireland "had no industrial revolution to react against; in common with other impoverished, agriculturally based nations seeking Home Rule and vernacular expression, the roots of the culture and identity she sought to establish, and the growing spirit of national consciousness, were given substance by archaeological, philological and antiquarian research."[110] This gave the Irish version of the Arts and Crafts movement a somewhat different character than its British antecedents; both the imagery and the political motivations were unique. But structurally, this regional craft revival operated on the premise of cultural continuity we have seen in Pugin, Ruskin, and Morris. Its symbolic repertoire was deployed as a way of reimagining the present, but its claims rested on essentialist claims about national identity, which depended upon a narrative of continuity.

The lace industry is a very different case. It was not a symbolic affair, but quite literally a matter of life and death. And though the makers involved had recourse to the past, they laid no claim to unbroken tradition. Though lacework had been practiced in Ireland historically, mainly as a domestic craft, modern production centers only emerged in the mid-nineteenth century, and their products were based not on Irish precursors. The industry was at first a commercial endeavor, transplanted from England to the city of Limerick by a capitalist improver named Charles Walker. From humble beginnings—a few English workers imported to teach the locals—lace making gained ground quickly. By 1844, about seventeen hundred women worked in the craft in the city, mostly producing tambour lace (chain stitch done with a needle on an open net stretched over a rigid circle). As a historian of the industry notes, Walker toured the country before he settled on Limerick, choosing it

How a Class should *not* Sit.

Figure 4.10   Helen Brietzcke, "How a Class Should *Not* Sit," from Helen Brietzcke and Emily Rooper, *Collective Lessons in Plain Needlework and Knitting: For Use in Elementary Schools* (London: Swan Sonnenschein, 1885).

on the basis of "the large population of unemployed females providing cheap labour."[111] In this respect, at least, the factories founded there were a precursor of things to come. For the real story of the lace industry begins with the Great Potato Famine, which began in 1847. This horrific catastrophe, made even worse by mismanagement and outright negligence by the British then governing the country, led to widespread starvation and mass emigration. Of the various philanthropic schemes implemented to ameliorate the effects of the disaster, among the most successful were the lace workshops established across the country. Unlike Walker's factories, these were charitable rather than commercial in nature. Most were located in convents, or under their jurisdiction.

One of the most striking features of Irish lacework from the post-famine period is the fact that it was closely based on antique models from continental Europe—especially Italy and France. Unlike other contemporaneous revivals of the craft (like the one in Burano, an island outside Venice), this was not a cultural reclamation project drawing on local history. As one writer put it in the 1880s, "the lace industry of Ireland is the successor to no ancient school, nor can Erin boast of any laces of her own invention."[112] The value of the work was rooted not in a narrative of continuity or revival, or even originality, but rather sheer productive technique. Incredibly, these poor Irish girls were able to emulate professionally made baroque lace (the same type that inspired Grinling Gibbons's carved cravat, discussed in chapter one) so closely that even for specialists today, it can be difficult to tell the difference on casual inspection.[113] Especially in its early years, this was a trade that depended largely on copying, not originality. One of the most successful centers to emerge at mid-century was

Youghal, in County Cork, where lace making began in 1852, immediately at the end of the famine. The impetus was a single piece of old Italian lace in the collection of the local convent. According to a later Victorian chronicler, when Mother Mary Anne Smith, one of the nuns resident there, found the fragment, "immediately the thought struck her that if she could only reproduce the stitches and make lace trimmings and the like, the work would prove a remunerative one."[114] Her instinct proved correct. Eventually over fifty girls and women were at work in the Youghal convent, many of them providing the sole income for their families. There were similar stories at other convents. Over time, each center acquired a distinctive style and repertoire, based to some extent on the antique laces that had initially acted as the inspiration for their work. Sometimes historic pattern books or detailed photographs provided the models instead, but in every case the design was rooted in some non-Irish historical precedent. Marion Twelves and her colleagues at the Ruskin Linen Industry might have fancied themselves to be directly engaging with history when they based their loom reconstruction on a Giotto painting; but replicating a forbiddingly complex piece of baroque needle lace stitch by stitch was another order of analogue practice entirely.

To grasp what it meant to copy a piece of historic lace, it is necessary to understand something of the technical aspects of the craft.[115] The word "painstaking" is often applied to feats of copying, but there can be few undertakings for which it is more apt. There are several ways of making lace, which can be divided into pillow or bobbin lace (in which the threads are wound around one another as they are held in tension by pins and weights); crochet (done with a slender hook); and needle or point lace, which as its name implies is done through hand stitching. The last of these, which is capable of astounding intricacy and variation, was impossible to convincingly duplicate by machine, and it was the type most widely practiced in Ireland at this date because it made the most of the inexpensive labor of the local populace. To make lace with a needle and thread, a pattern is first laid down as a drawing—perhaps on an open net (usually machine made at this date), or else a stiff parchment. Having traced out the design, workers would stitch along the lines in cotton or linen thread, making up the substance of the lace itself. In some processes, they built up volume atop this foundation through repeated, tightly packed stitches; in others the pattern was left flat. Once the design was executed, the supporting net or parchment might be cut away by hand using a tiny pair of scissors, which would produce an open-work "guipure." Alternatively, in a similar cutwork technique associated particularly with Carrickmacross, the pattern is made by stitching through a layer of muslin laid over a net and then cutting away parts of the muslin while leaving the underlying net intact. Another important type was embroidered lace, associated with Limerick, in which case the pattern is executed directly in stitch work onto a machine-woven net, with no subsequent cutting. In all of these variants, needle lace was precision work, and extremely time-consuming; it might take a skilled worker a full day to produce a square of finished lace one half inch on a side. To produce a full piece—a bridal veil or even a single flounce (a decorative band hung from a skirt)—might require months of work. Accordingly the job was usually split up among the young women in the workroom. This was division of labor, but not in the sense usually conveyed by that phrase. The workers were all performing the same task side by side, and would finally make up the piece from their many separate fragments. This meant that the self-expressive diversity prized by Ruskin and Morris (or, for that matter, David Pye) had to be suppressed: if the lace was to be consistent, it could not betray the individuality of each maker. Every pair of hands had to ply the thread at the same tension and execute the stitches with the same number of threads per inch.

Thus Irish lace production, despite the fact that it was skill-intensive and virtually free of mechanization, was nonetheless a very modern craft. It was regulated, involved exact copying, and was carried out by thoroughly subjugated workers. Though the industry was crucial in providing these women's livelihoods, it exacted a horrendous toll on them too. They were prone to blindness and manual disability after years of this minutely detailed work. But this did not stop British observers from celebrating the charitable achievements of the Irish lace industry. The wearing of their expensive products was considered a philanthropic, even a patriotic act; as design historian Janice Helland rightly says, "the discrepant space between the consumer who purchased the lace and the women who made it remained gigantic."[116] In the years after the famine, it was possible for an aristocratic lady to wear literally years worth of other women's labor on her body and congratulate herself for her charitable impulses in doing so.

Furthermore, because it was not valued as a remnant of a traditional craft, Irish lace could be readily subjected to all the modernizing aesthetic imperatives of design reform, with which we are now so familiar from other instances of craft improvement. Alan Summerly Cole—son of Henry Cole, the founder of the South Kensington Museum—is the key figure here. An authority on historic laces, he undertook a series of trips to Ireland in the 1880s, sponsored by the Science and Art Department of the museum. Appointed the head of a government committee charged with improving the commercial prospect of the industry, he laid out his goals explicitly. This was not to be a revivalist enterprise but rather one based on a firmly contemporary footing, not dependent upon the "evanescent and uncertain fancy of consumers for something 'quaint and original' or to a sentimental desire for what is rather detrimentally called a 'National Production.'"[117] With this principle in mind, Cole visited the various centers; offered his own "clinical discourse" on the techniques involved; took notes on the most promising workers (such as the "daughter of a boots at the hotel" in Killarney, "whose work seemed to have originality and character"), who might be taught drawing and elevated to the job of pattern making, much as in the South Kensington system (see chapter one); and everywhere propounded the benefits of good design.[118] Despite its antique roots, Cole noted, lace was a supremely fashionable product and subject to vicissitudes in taste. He saw this as a good thing, because rapid change constantly refreshed the market. Despite this early embrace of the principle of planned obsolescence, he applied his father's objective principles consistently, advocating that all young lace makers be trained in draftsmanship, promoting the careful study of historic examples (or photographs thereof), and also encouraging new designs through prizes, art school training, and publication. Cole collected examples of the best Irish work (see Plate 16). He championed talented designers such as Michael Hayes, a product of the South Kensington system who created a wide range of patterns for Irish workers to follow, including those at the convent in Youghal (Figure 4.11). These conformed to Cole's description of a successful design, which required consistency of vision, an overall "artistic plan" that was organic in its logic:

> The usual ideas are—let us make a pattern, and then somehow, by squeezing or expanding, by dropping out a bit here or adding a bit there, fit it into a shape…This wholly unworthy ignorance has to be rooted out wherever it is to be met with.[119]

Cole himself conceded that the process of involving professional designers was not without difficulties, because of the gulf lying between them and the makers who would execute their ideas: "unfortunately Mr. Hayes did not know much, if anything, concerning the method of making lace, and further than this, when the lace makers got the pattern, they

Figure 4.11   Michael Hayes (designer), part of a flounce, ca. 1886. Made at the Presentation Convent, Youghal. Needle lace. © Victoria and Albert Museum, London.

were more or less staggered by its complexity."[120] But in the long run it would be worth it. The designer, kept abreast of the latest fashions and working on sound principles, could form an alliance with the comparatively ignorant but highly skilled Irish lace makers to realize a commercially successful product.

Until the early twentieth century, when lace went out of fashion due to broader shifts in taste, this was indeed a successful formula, at least in commercial terms.[121] Many more artisans were employed within this exploitative industry than in the various Arts and Crafts-inspired embroidery workshops active at the time. In retrospect, reformers' ideology seems to have blinded them to the fact of exploitation in the industry. For all the wondrous quality of the products, this lace production should be seen as compounding the tragedy of the famine, subjecting an already victimized people to long years of drudgery and physical pain. To some extent, this hard labor was to their benefit, given that grinding poverty or even starvation was the alternative. But obviously the "collective" this particular memory work called into existence was very far from utopian. When we look at Irish lace from this period, in all its beauty, variety, and intricacy, we must necessarily do so with mixed feelings. And the same goes for any modern craft objects made under economic duress, which tend to act as a palliative to the conscience of people who purchase them. We are ethically obligated to see such works as both exploitative and expressive—not necessarily expressive of the individual makers' sensibilities, but rather of truths more moving and poignant than any one person's artistic vision. Craft history must acknowledge the fact that the "collective memory" artisans enact is not necessarily their own.

The case of Irish lace is fascinating because of its makers' combination of extreme skill and equally extreme lack of agency. In seeing how memory manifests itself in crafted form, despite (or even because of) appalling circumstances, we can see how it serves to process trauma not only in a symbolic way but also in eminently practical terms. This is a further complexity in the way craft articulates collective memory. Though it is often explicitly ideological, it can also be a pragmatic coping mechanism. Throughout the history of modern craft, these two kinds of working through intermingle, often to the extent that it can be difficult to distinguish them from one another. As memory work, craft is at once fiction and fact, both a symbolic gloss on tradition and a tactical usage of the past, which establishes itself in real economic and material terms.

A further example of this temporal complexity, in which the variables of agency, skill, history, and trauma are again involved but in a completely different configuration, can be found in another story about stitches: the sewn objects made by suffragettes during their campaign to win women the vote. This, the last historic case study I want to examine, brings us finally out of the nineteenth century and into the early twentieth. That leap traverses the height and incipient decline of the Arts and Crafts movement, and so brings us to a time when craft was explicitly politicized but also increasingly uncertain. The quixotic program of the craft reformers had, by 1900, already begun to founder in a sea of failed projects and (even worse) successful commercialization. Companies like Liberty, Heals, and L. and J. G. Stickley, and even faux utopian communities like the Roycrofters, promoted the Arts and Crafts style without adhering strictly to the movement's tenets of self-expression and irregular workmanship. William Morris died in 1896. Had he lived to see the first decade of the twentieth century, he would have been horrified to observe that the Arts and Crafts movement was achieving prominence and influence through exactly the sort of organization, automation, and "trade finish" he had so loathed. For many, the conclusion was that one had to choose between economic vitality and spiritual integrity. But as we have seen in the case of the Irish lace makers, the symbolic uses of craft could also be put to other, more practical uses. The suffragettes realized this. They handled the tools of publicity with great expertise, and needlework was one of their primary instruments. This is a powerful example of collective memory deployed to radical ends through the material means of craft.

Thanks to pioneering research by design historian Lisa Tickner, the specifics of suffragette craft are well understood. Their primary handmade medium was the protest banner, carried aloft in procession through the streets of London and other cities. The marches were carefully composed stagecraft, designed to convey through sheer numbers the fact that obtaining rights for women was not merely the preoccupation of a lunatic fringe. The events were also calculated to make an impression at second hand, through photographic reproduction. Large-scale banners were critical to this strategy, and a good deal of thought went into their design and making. As Tickner points out, there was an important precedent for the suffragettes' signs in hand-painted trade union banners, which had become extremely popular in the 1890s.[122] These were mainly produced by a single London manufactory (owned by George Tutill) and tended to have complex allegorical imagery, not too dissimilar from James Sharples's emblem for the Amalgamated Society of Engineers (see Figure 4.8). They tended to be expensive and enormous. The suffragettes' banners were something different. Decorated in embroidery or fabric appliqué rather than paint, they referred to the long history of women's stitching. They were made collectively. The banners' imagery tended toward the medieval, an iconography intended to convey a quasi-religious moral uprightness. Mary Lowndes, a painter working in the Artists' Suffrage League, was the most active and thoughtful of the banner makers, inspired by what Tickner describes as "a particular reading of courtly chivalry compounded of Victorian medievalism and nineteenth-century feminism."[123] When Lowndes wrote a short manifesto about banner production in 1909, she laid out their function in no uncertain terms as a kind of memory work, which drew on female mythology of the deep past but was engaged in direct present-day conflict: "In all the ages it has been women's part to make the banners, if not to carry them... The divers colours of needlework, handwrought, are coming into play again, and now for the first time in history to illumine woman's own adventure."[124] Lowndes's most ambitious project was a series of vertical banners celebrating great women of the past, from the ancient British queen Boadicea to painter Angelica Kaufmann, actress Sarah Siddons, and astronomer Caroline Herschel. These designs, which emulated medieval field banners in their simplicity and use of clearly legible crests, are also a direct precedent for Judy Chicago's monumental feminist art installation *The Dinner Party*, made decades later.

The politicization of craft in the service of the suffragette cause reached its apogee with the movement's escalation in tactics, beginning in 1908. A campaign of orchestrated vandalism, notably the smashing of shop windows, led to the imprisonment of many suffragettes, including the movement's leader, Emmeline Pankhurst. Once in jail, the women continued their protest by the only means available. They broke their cell windows and then went on hunger strikes. By starving themselves, perhaps to death, they planned to further raise consciousness for their cause. Prison authorities responded to this remarkable declaration of intent by force-feeding the women, a harrowing experience that might involve a rubber tube inserted into the nose or a steel gag that held the mouth open. This was trauma of a very nonabstract nature. Suffragettes turned again to textile crafts as a way of marking the experience of the hunger strikes. A banner made in 1910 commemorated eighty women who had undergone the ordeal. Each was named in a rectangle of linen, all framed by bands in the movement's symbolic colors of purple, white, and green.[125] A more personal object was made by Janie Terrero, a fifty-four-year-old woman from Essex incarcerated in 1912, initially for smashing the window of an Oxford Street engineering shop.[126] After two stints in jail, both involving hunger strikes and force-feeding, she collected signatures of the women who had been imprisoned alongside her and added their names to her own in chain stitch (Plate 15). The piece also features the movement's colors, as well as the slogan of the Women's Social and Political Union "Deeds Not Words"—an apt testament to the importance of craft, as well as direct protest, in the suffragettes' thinking. Terrero's work is particularly affecting, resonating as it does with the long history of women's samplers being collected by antiquarians at the time, but turning this sentimentalized format to militant ends. The handkerchief's central motif—a wreath of flowers in WSPU colors, tied with a bow at the bottom—finds a vivid counterpart in the stark cell bars stitched in at the top. In a very modern touch, she appended a promotional postcard of Emmeline Pankhurst and her daughter at the bottom of the cloth.

Suffragette crafts, including Terrero's handkerchief, occupy a prominent position in feminist narratives of cultural memory. In her influential book, *The Subversive Stitch* (1984), which laid out a sociopolitical history of embroidery for the first time, Rozsika Parker wrote of the handkerchief as an inversion of marginalization, noting that Terrero and her compatriots "signed their names in the very medium which was considered proof of their frailty, and justification for their subjugation."[127] Even as she held up women's crafts for admiration, Parker never forgot the oppressive circumstances in which those objects were made. Cultural stereotypes of femininity are often enacted through the making and mythology of needlework, and Parker saw clearly that the craft could itself be a tool of oppression. But she also saw it as containing the potential for liberation and resistance, precisely because of its categorization as craft: "Paradoxically, while embroidery was employed to inculcate femininity in women, it also enabled them to negotiate the constraints of femininity."[128] More recently Maureen Daly Goggin, in an essay-length study of the Terrero handkerchief, has echoed this view, seeing in the object an "identity performance" that anchors the historian's attempts to reconstruct the experience of a militant feminist past. Goggin writes eloquently of the disappearance of past subjectivity:

> Like grasping a handful of water, identity seeps through the fingers, evaporates and escapes precisely because it is not a *thing* but an ongoing series of performances that always exceed and are constrained by a given moment.[129]

For Goggin, the handkerchief serves to interrupt this dissipation, materializing Terrero's identity in a manner that is both explicit (in that it registers as protest art) and tacit (in referring back to the long history of women's work). Most of all, Goggin makes clear that the handkerchief is an invitation to ongoing memory work. Around this single square of cotton she recreates a whole society of women in solidarity with one another, tracking down the biography of each suffragette whose names are stitched into the cloth, and re-imagining the traumatic experiences they had undergone. This one craft object—again, precisely because of its tacit qualities—is a repository of suggestion, so richly encoded that it can fuel numerous interpretations: "the range of latent possibilities is great, and is there for scholars and others to mine under different circumstances and different purposes... the handkerchief is situated in a social web that connects us, and other knowing observers, to these women and to Terrero."[130]

This "web"—not only suffragette crafts themselves, but also the historic textiles that inspired them, and their subsequent memorializations—constitutes an imagined, cross-temporal community that would not otherwise exist. Ruskin's grandmother Catherine Tweedall, early textile historians such as Mrs. Bury Palliser and Mrs. Beeton, poverty-stricken Irish girls, the imprisoned radical Janie Terrero, and historians such as Freedberg, Tickner, Parker, and Goggin: all these women actually have little in common beyond their gender. They are separated, each from the other, by massive gulfs of cultural history. But in feminist practice, it is possible to construct a sense of solidarity across these gaps of time and space through the materialization of memory. No less than Ruskin's medievalism, this is an imaginative projection, but, as Halbwachs suggested, it is one constructed purposefully to deal with the "now," whenever that now might be. From a feminist perspective, craft is a telescoping, transhistorical optic, a commemoration of a commemoration of a commemoration—a series I am conscious of extending here. At every stage of this historical procession, craft serves as a means to articulate the present: remembering marks a departure from precedent as well as a continuity. In fashioning their stitches and their texts, feminists have been mindful of the past, but certainly do not advocate a return to it. On the contrary, they have all been concerned to mark a traumatic site, both in literal terms (the proximate memory of self-starvation and force-feeding, in Terrero's case) and, in a more general sense, the lack of agency that arises from gender inequality.

As theorist Rita Felski has argued, femininity can be understood as a negative construction, a "space of non-identity rather than identity, heterogeneity and otherness rather than the will to truth." Feminist discourse, in turn, is not to be understood as the celebratory embrace of a stable identity (or even a palette of multiple identities) but rather "the unending process of generating questions and critical interpretations of gender."[131] With this principle in mind, one might even argue that Terrero, whose relation to craft was only in passing and hardly even skilled, is a better role model than Pugin, Ruskin, or Morris. Her use of stitchery to mark her own immediate personal past was "affective," to be sure, but it was not an attempt to revive some past ideal. Her act of embroidery involved no effacement of the present, no "screen" of the kind we encounter in *Contrasts* or *News From Nowhere.* Terrero did not treat the past as a solution, but simply as a vocabulary with which she could articulate her own present-day identity.

IN MEMORIAM

Feminists have pioneered the understanding of craft as an active tool of memory work, but the application of that idea is certainly not limited to considerations of gender. Contemporary practitioners of all kinds have explored craft as a way of expressing identities, both marginal and hegemonic. A prominent example can be found in architecture. It has become almost a cliché to place the fragmentary remains of a destroyed building within an exquisitely handcrafted framework, as David Chipperfield has done for the Neues Museum in Berlin (which was mostly destroyed by bombing in World War II). So commonplace is the strategy that its familiarity has itself become important. Like the repeated returns to stitchery we observed in the case of the suffragettes, laying claim to identity through craft in this way has become an incantatory, self-reinforcing phenomenon, a tradition in its own right that gains force with each iteration, even as it proliferates across multiple seams of difference.

An interesting variant on this strategy is seen in the work of artist Aya Haidar, who has made a group of embroidered photographs entitled *Recollections: Seamstress Series* that show various sites in war-torn Beirut. One of these images shows the side of a modernist housing block, which is pockmarked by bullet holes. Each impact has been picked out or "ornamented" with a tight clutch of brightly colored stitches (Figure 4.12). Though born and raised in Britain, Haidar is of Lebanese extraction and these works are a way for her to engage with that personal history. She explicitly locates her work within the feminist practice of "bringing the domestic into a discursive platform."[132] Haidar is also a sort of specialist in the use of craft as a response to traumatic experience, having worked previously as a leader of youth workshops for refugees from conflict countries such as Somalia. She learned through interacting with these children that craft could be a means of coping with the past, a means of expression that might serve when language fails or feels inadequate to experience. From refugee families Haidar has also learned that craft can be, as she says, "a way of creating a normal." For a parent who has lost her home, and perhaps more than one family member, making something for a child by hand can be a powerful means of reasserting a sense of care and control, even if it just a doll made out of bits of plastic bags and tent fabric.

Figure 4.12   Aya Haidar, Recollections (Seamstress series) VII, 2011. Embroidery on printed linen. Courtesy of the artist and Bischoff Weiss Gallery.

Haidar has taken inspiration from these experiences when creating her *Recollections* images. At first, they seem like straightforward examples of the feminist strategy described earlier: marking a site of trauma through the patient, durational process of craft. Yet in Haidar's case, the simplicity of the gesture is overlaid with several further layers of complexity. First of all, the setting is generic. There is no indication in the work (and indeed, Haidar herself does not know) where in Beirut this particular piece of damaged architecture might be: "this building is everywhere." This lack of specificity is matched by the photographic quality of the work, which is saturated and painterly, conveying the sense of collective rather than individual experience. This could be the setting of a dream (or nightmare) rather than a particular urban space. Of course it is a real building—the indexicality of the photographic medium guarantees this—but the image operates on the level of generality. This is true not only in spatial terms, but also in the emotional weight given to the durational act of stitching. Sewing allows Haidar to imaginatively occupy her own familial past in Lebanon. Like many young artists, she was taught to sew by her grandmother, and therefore associates the medium with the idea of generational continuity: "with every passing of the thread I feel a connection to that person." This is a very personal matter, but even an uninformed viewer can grasp the fact that memory work is happening here. As in a suffragette banner, the stitches can be read clearly as marking commitment and care, even for those who are ignorant about Lebanon's recent history of warfare. Haidar sees craft's nonlinguistic character not as a limitation, but as its great promise to communicate. Finally, we might note the way her stitches function simultaneously as ornament and as bindings. There is nothing strictly functional about them, but conceptually they act as "colored bandages," gestures that simultaneously denote the site of a wound and heal it. If the building is anthropomorphized into a traumatized body, then craft also acts in a double capacity, both as a forensic description of violence and as the means of working through it.

Haidar's work is an unusually clear, almost didactic instance of craft serving in this dialectical manner, as both symptom and treatment.[133] Yet this dynamic can also be observed in many other usages of craft right across the culture, well outside the boundaries of the art world, and from margin to center. I'd like to conclude now with a pair of examples that highlights this diversity and the ongoing importance of craft as memory work within a culture. Both are statements of British identity, and both involved skillful stitching organized within a collective. Yet in many ways they could not be more different. Exhibit A is another quilt, made in Wandsworth Prison (on the other side of London from Holloway, where Janie Terrero was locked up; see Figure 4.13). It is the product of a social outreach project called Fine Cell Work, which trains prisoners to sew and then sells their work, returning some of the profits to the makers. The initiative helps the inmates to fill long hours of solitude, hopefully resulting in a better-adjusted prison population more likely to be rehabilitated upon release. It also results in objects that are almost unbearably moving. The one in question was commissioned by the V&A for a recent exhibition on the history of British quilting and patchwork, and is now in the museum's collection.[134] It is conceived as a group self-portrait. One of the prisoners (all the participants remain anonymous in consideration of the victims of their crimes) had the idea of laying out the quilt in a diagram depicting the architectural footprint of the prison itself, and this floor plan has been filled with content determined by the individual contributors. The motifs range from protestations of innocence—"I didn't do it guv! Honest!!"—to the everyday material culture of the jail. Together they amount to a closely observed picture of day-to-day life at Wandsworth.

The most affecting "cells" of the quilt are those that speak to temporality itself, either literally (a stitched clock, or the words "time moves slowly") or through heart-breaking implication—a pair of hanging legs and the phrase "I can't take it anymore." The soul-crushing reality of time's passage, as much as thread and fabric, seems to be the true medium in which the quilt is made. There is no doubting the emotional power of the object; it is something to cry in front of.[135] And yet the quilt is also a commodity, and to some degree an advertisement. Whether placed on view at a press conference, hung in an art gallery, or reproduced in the pages of this book, it serves to raise awareness not only about prisoners and their lives, but also about Fine Cell Work itself, which must necessarily engage in all the promotional techniques of contemporary commerce in order to perform its stated objective. This is a good example of the two strands of nineteenth-century craft discourse bound together in a single contemporary object. The quilt is equal parts affective memory work and pragmatic advocacy.

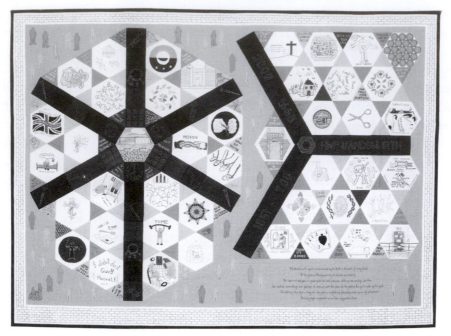

Figure 4.13   Quilt, 2010. Made by anonymous prisoners at HMP Wandsworth under the direction of Fine Cell Work. V&A: T.27–1020. © Victoria and Albert Museum, London.

Exhibit B was made only a few miles away, but worlds apart: the bridal gown made for the royal wedding in April 2011 (Figure 4.14). Designed by Sarah Burton—who took over as the head of the fashion house of Alexander McQueen after his tragic suicide—the dress features lacework made by the Royal School of Needlework (founded 1872), now based at Hampton Court Palace. The lace is largely executed in the Carrickmacross appliqué technique described earlier. No commentator has (to my knowledge) connected the garment with the tragic historical circumstances in which this craft "tradition" first emerged. Yet the reference to Ireland is certainly one aspect of an explicit and multilayered evocation of the British past. As one fashion journalist wrote on the day of the wedding, the dress

> recalled Queen Victoria's decision in 1840 that her bridal gown should promote the nation's skills, while the classic and graceful lines could have been inspired by both the modernist Princess Margaret, who in 1960 also married in Westminster Abbey, and the more romantic style of Princess Grace, whose wedding had taken place four years earlier. The latter reference could be also be seen as a very sensitive and sympathetic homage to Diana, Princess of Wales, who had had an instant rapport with the former Hollywood film star and saw her as a style icon.[136]

With its Victorian corset understructure and bustle (common features of McQueen's dressmaking), and paired with a Cartier tiara dating from 1936 (a loan from the

Figure 4.14   The Duchess of Cambridge, 2011. The royal wedding bridal gown was designed by Sarah Burton and made at the Royal School of Needlework. Getty Images.

queen), the dress is a veritable palimpsest of cultural history, a mainstream version of the cascading associations we saw in the feminist embrace of Terrero's handwork. But as the previous passage suggests, in this case all the lines converge at one inevitable reference point: the previous royal wedding in 1981, when Diana Spencer, not Kate Middleton, was the leading dramatic persona. Few people watching the royal wedding of 2011 could have been unaware of this precedent thirty years earlier. Equally present in the minds of spectators was the protracted tragic aftermath of Diana's marriage to Prince Charles, culminating in her death in a car accident and an immediate public outpouring of grief that was strange in its intensity. Indeed, not since the seemingly atavistic paroxysm of mourning for Diana in 1997 had London seen a public display of emotion on the scale that attended Middleton's wedding to Prince William. The dress, then, functioned as the locus for a giant spectacle of national sentiment and sentimentalism, but also as a marker of past sorrow and present-day healing (almost the lifting of a curse). There is no denying that the dress, just like the Wandsworth quilt, is eminently capable of moving adults to tears. Among its many messages was the idea that British craftsmanship apparently thrives after all, despite two centuries of dire warnings about its imminent demise. Anyone thinking that craft is threatened in the twenty-first century might find consolation in the thought that Middleton's dress could only ever have been handmade.

It is important that we subject objects like the quilt and the dress to the critical criteria I have been pursuing throughout this chapter—criteria rooted in the theories of Freud and Halbwachs and the tactics of feminist theory. This may seem unwarranted; after all, these are not works of contemporary fine art. At a stretch, the Wandsworth quilt might perhaps be classed as "outsider art"—the creative work of prisoners is frequently described that way—though there was clearly a good deal of institutional involvement in its making. Middleton's dress, meanwhile, is the epitome of insider fashion. These are not realms where we necessarily look for critical reflection. Yet they should not be exempted from analysis. If craft remains pervasive within modern production, as I have argued throughout this book, then it is surely incumbent on us to assess its effects no matter where it appears, not just in the confined precincts of the art world. Indeed, the task of evaluating objects like the quilt and the dress dramatically illustrates the fact that criticism itself is always situated in wider belief systems (a fact art critics don't always dwell on). What you think of self-help programs for prisoners and televised royal weddings will surely be affected by your politics. But understanding the role of craft in these two objects is not just a matter of testing them against one's own ideological inclinations. It is also, less judgmentally, to understand the mechanics of a handmade object and its representations. So how might we read these two cases in light of the discussion of memory I have outlined in this chapter?

In so many ways, these two works of hand stitching seem to be diametric opposites. The Wandsworth quilt is a representation of life at the troubled lower reaches of society; the royal wedding dress the crowning pinnacle of a (surprisingly intact) class system. The quilt was made by men at society's periphery, who must remain unnamed—even Fine Cell Work's promotional videos present the prisoners in dark shadow. The dress was worn by a woman when the eyes of the world were on her (24 million people in the United Kingdom alone), at the center of an extravagantly staged celebration of power and prestige. And yet both of these objects take temporality itself as their content and articulate that subject principally through craft. It is striking that in public discourse, both objects tend to be presented in statistical terms, as if something were being proven. Fine Cell Work estimates that the prisoners working with the organization commit as much as four hundred thousand hours to their stitching annually, while the workers of the Royal School of Embroidery (according to one press report) "had to wash their hands every thirty minutes to keep the lace and threads pristine, and renew the needles every three hours, to keep them sharp," applying "minute stitches every two to three millimeters."[137] These are all just numbers. But the consumption of time itself that they are intended to convey is intrinsic to the objects' emotive power. While these two works of craft may inhabit poles apart in terms of the social register, both exemplify memory work as it is realized through the sustained, skilled labor of many hands.

Moreover, the temporal qualities of these two objects are remarkably complex in relation to individual and collective identity. The Wandsworth quilt is, as I have said, a group self-portrait. It expresses personal feelings, some of them deeply painful, within a framework of collective identity—a collective not of the members' own choosing, in which individuality itself is eroded through multiple techniques of control. Both in its form, built of individual cells, and its making, the execution of many thousands of stitches by many hands, the quilt establishes a powerful sense of truth through accumulation. It is, paradoxically, a collective attempt to arrest the erosion of individuality. Middleton's dress, by contrast, is a highly individualistic object—interpreted by most observers as an expression of the bride's sense of fashion, her personal elegance—yet it also speaks for the entirety of the British public, and even serves as a key motif within their collective narrative of national loss and renewed hope. No less than Haidar's embroidered bullet holes, the lace on this dress both inscribes and expiates a national trauma. One might well say that this narrative is completely fraudulent: that the fixation on young women like Kate Middleton (or for that matter, Diana Spencer) as convenient surrogates for collective identity is reactionary, a function of spectacle culture that fights against decades of feminist progress. Yet feminist theory is the best way to grapple with that fact: it helps us how to see how this symbolic object serves to tie together multiple strands of memory into a new and powerful configuration, enacted through the binding agency of craft.

These two concluding examples—the quilt and the dress—amply demonstrate the fact that craft is just as potent as ever, if not more so, thanks to modern social technologies such as museum exhibitions and television broadcasts. In this chapter I have focused on craft as a response to traumatic experience; but I hope I have not conveyed the impression that this is its only role in modern and postmodern culture. The situations that I have described—lace makers living in the shadow of the famine, Janie Terrero thinking back on her own harrowing imprisonment, Aya Haidar marking the scars of recent war, a group of anonymous men stitching their way through years of confinement, and the instinctive turn to craft as a national symbol—are all exceptional. These instances, in their very different ways, all stand apart from the general condition of craft. To be sure, handwork has a place in everyday life of any kind, not only in the wake of tragedy. By focusing on craft's importance in these extreme circumstances, however, I hope to have shown how very crucial it is, and how much potency can attach to it under certain conditions.

The year 1750 is a long time ago, and 1850 and 1900 may not seem that much closer. But many of the problems people of those times confronted are unfinished business (Plate 16). We still have to deal with the quintessentially modern conflict between individuality and collectivity and a pervasive sense of disconnection with the past. Craft has long been an indispensable means of working through these issues, and remains so today. Yet this does not require that we revert to a spirit of revival or preservation, as if stasis were the best we could hope for. It is an ironic legacy of the modern invention of craft that it still today has a reputation for weakness and fragility—that is, after all, exactly how the factory owners and improvers wanted it to seem. As I hope to have shown, this is a completely inaccurate assessment. In reality, craft remains one of the most effective means of materializing belief, of transforming the world around us, and less positively, of controlling the lives of others. Without understanding the way it operates—the way the variables of time, skill, and symbolism are embedded in the fabric of a well-made thing—we are liable to simply fall under its spell. We might well be tempted to allow craft to "enchant" us (to use Alfred Gell's term one last time). But ideally, a critic, historian, theorist, or practitioner of craft should aspire to more than this. Speaking of craft should never be a matter of simple advocacy. On the contrary, we have good reason to be skeptical. We have been told often enough that craft is threatened. But the truth is that craft can be so powerful, so convincing, that we will gladly stand helpless before it. And as with any form of power, it is crucial that we try to understand it, if only so that it might be reinvented—not just once, but again and again.

NOTES

1. William Morris, *Gothic Architecture: A Lecture for the Arts and Crafts Exhibition Society* (Hammersmith: Kelmscott Press, 1893). The story about the Crystal Palace can be found in *Art Journal Easter Annual* (1899): 1.

2. William Morris quoted in Imogen Hart, *Arts and Crafts Objects* (Manchester: Manchester University Press, 2010), p. 122.

3. Anni Albers, "Handweaving Today: Textile Work at Black Mountain College," *The Weaver* 6/1 (January/February 1941): 3–7: 3.

4. William Morris, "The Revival of Handicraft." Originally published in the *Fortnightly Review* (November 1888).

5. With the exception of preliminary experiments, even dyeing was carried out mainly at the industrial works of Thomas Wardle in Leek. So even when Morris was dissatisfied with contemporary production, he found it necessary to reform it from the inside. Charles Harvey and Jon Press, *William Morris: Design and Enterprise in Victorian Britain* (Manchester: Manchester University Press, 1991), pp. 97–98.

6. Thomas Carlyle, "The Mechanical Age," in *Signs of the Times* (1829).

7. George Sturt, *The Wheelwright's Shop* (Cambridge: Cambridge University Press, 1923).

8. Robin Wood, "Technology and Hand Skill in Craft and Industry," *Journal of Modern Craft* 4/2 (July 2011): 193–202; 197. Wood, the founder of the Heritage Crafts Association, rightly points out that it is in this moment of imminent disappearance when the craft is transformed into "heritage," but not while it is a viable economic concern.

9. On the development of trauma theory by Freud and other early psychoanalysts, see Paul Lerner and Mark S. Micale, *Traumatic Pasts: History, Psychiatry and Trauma in the Modern Age 1870–1930* (Cambridge: Cambridge University Press, 2001). Though it is somewhat tangential to my use of this body of thought, it is not coincidental that trauma theory emerged exactly at the same time as the Arts and Craft movement; both were reflections of a newly introspective stage in thinking about modernity.

10. Ruth Leys, *Trauma: A Genealogy* (Chicago: University of Chicago Press, 2000), p. 9.

11. Donald A. Laird and Eleanor C. Laird, *Techniques for Efficient Remembering* (New York: McGraw Hill, 1960), p. 101.

12. David Gross, *Lost Time: On Remembering and Forgetting in Late Modern Culture* (Amherst: University of Massachusetts Press, 2000), p. 102. Gross cites the Gothic Revival and the Arts

and Crafts movement as "reprisings of memory" that sought to cope with this destruction (p. 106).

13. Sigmund Freud, "Remembering, Repeating and Working-Through: Further Recommendations on the Technique of Psychoanalysis," in *Standard Edition of the Complete Psychological Works of Sigmund Freud,* trans. James Strachey (London: Hogarth Press, 1955), p. 150.

14. "In young children," for example, "repetitive play may occur in which themes or aspects of the trauma are expressed." Philip A. Saigh and J. Douglas Bremner, *Post-traumatic Stress Disorder: A Comprehensive Text* (Boston: Allyn and Bacon 1999), p. 9.

15. Leys, *Trauma,* p. 7.

16. For a discussion of gesture in craft practice, see Patricia Ribault, "Tradition in Question: Glassblowing in Murano, Tunisia and Afghanistan," *Journal of Modern Craft* 3/2 (July 2010): 209–223.

17. Walter Benjamin, "The Storyteller," in *Illuminations* (New York: Schocken, 1969). See also Esther Leslie, "Walter Benjamin: Traces of Craft," *Journal of Design History* 11/1 (1998), excerpted in Glenn Adamson, *The Craft Reader* (Oxford; Berg Publishers, 2010); Walter Ong, *Orality and Literacy: The Technology of the Word* (New York: Methuen, 1982), p. 178. Katharine Hodgkin and Susannah Radstone usefully distinguish between traumatic memory and oral tradition, the former "interposing the disruptions of memory between the event and its representations," the latter engaging in "disruptions [that] are intrinsic to memory itself (which distorts, conflates, masks, omits)." Hodgkin and Radstone, eds., *Contested Pasts: The Politics of Memory* (London: Routledge, 2003), p. 6.

18. Leys, *Trauma,* p. 11.

19. Bruce M. Ross, *Remembering the Personal Past: Descriptions of Autobiographical Memory* (Oxford: Oxford University Press, 1991), p. 47ff.

20. Richard J. McNally, *Remembering Trauma* (Cambridge, MA: Harvard University Press, 2003), p. 160.

21. Raphael Samuel, *Theatres of Memory* (London: Verso, 1994), p. x.

22. Sigmund Freud, *Studies in Hysteria* (London: Hogarth Press, 1895).

23. Leys, *Trauma,* p. 36.

24. Linda Belau and Petar Ramadanovic, eds., *Topologies of Trauma: Essays on the Limit of Knowledge and Memory* (New York: Other Press, 2002), p. xvi.

25. McNally, *Remembering Trauma,* p. 135.

26. Rosemary Hill, *God's Architect* (London: Penguin, 2007), p. 153.

27. A.W.N. Pugin, *Contrasts: A Parallel between the Noble Edifices of the Fourteenth and Fifteenth Centuries, and Similar Buildings of the Present Day, Shewing the Present Decay of Taste* (London: Author, 1836), pp. iii, iv.

28. Ibid., p. 35.

29. Tom Crook, "Craft and the Dialogics of Modernity: The Arts and Crafts Movement in Late-Victorian and Edwardian England," *Journal of Modern Craft* 2/1 (March 2009): 17–32. The present chapter owes a great deal to Crook's explanation of the Arts and Crafts movement as a "dialogical" phenomenon, in which oppositions are not dialectically resolved but instead "remain in play, in an ongoing dynamic of struggle and provocation" (p. 20).

30. Both Ruskin and Morris were early and influential advocates of architectural preservation. See Andrea Elizabeth Donovan, *William Morris and the Society for the Protection of Ancient Buildings* (New York: Routledge, 2008).

31. Gross, *Lost Time,* pp. 25–35. See also T. J. Jackson Lears, *No Place of Grace: Antimodernism and the Transformation of American Culture 1880–1920* (Chicago: University of Chicago Press, 1994).

32. Slavoj Žižek, *For They Know Not What They Do: Enjoyment as a Political Factor* (London: Verso, 1991), pp. 272–273.

33. Gross, *Lost Time,* p. 42.

34. Jenny Elkins, *Trauma and the Memory of Politics* (Cambridge: Cambridge University Press, 2003).

35. For an earlier reading of Pye's discussion of risk and certainty, see Christopher Frayling and Helen Snowdon, "Skill: A Word to Start an Argument," *Crafts* 56 (May/June 1982): 19–21.

36. David Pye, *The Nature and Art of Workmanship* (Cambridge: Cambridge University Press, 1968), pp. 18–19. See the excerpts included in Adamson, *The Craft Reader.*

37. Edward S. Cooke, Jr., "The Long Shadow of William Morris: Paradigmatic Problems of Twentieth-Century American Furniture," in *American Furniture 2003* (Milwaukee, WI: Chipstone Foundation/University Press of New England, 2003), as excerpted in Adamson, *The Craft Reader,* p. 228.

38. Pye, *The Nature and Art of Workmanship,* pp. 62, 66.

39. Ibid., p. 62.

40. Ibid., pp. 66–67.

41. William Morris, "A Factory As It Might Be, part III," *Justice* (June 28, 1884): 2.

42. Pye, *The Nature and Art of Workmanship,* p. 64.

43. Ibid., pp. 65–66.

44. Predictably, Ruskin dismissed Mechanics' Institution-style lecturing as mere entertainment, "fire-worky-downy-curry-and-strawberry-ice-and-milk-punch-altogether" in his wonderful description. "To get the knowledge it has cost a man half his life to gather, first sweetened up to make it palatable, and then kneaded up into the smallest possible pills, and to swallow it homeopathically and be wise—that is the passionate desire and hope of the multitude at the present day." Quoted in *Odd-Fellows Magazine* [Manchester] (January 1876): 309.

45. Ruskin, quoted in Pye, *The Nature and Art of Workmanship,* p. 65. It should be noted that Ruskin did make an exception for "preserving record of great works," and in fact employed people to do just that, including social reformer Octavia Hill. In this exceptional case, he adopted the opposite policy: "how difficult it is, to tell any man not to 'improve' his copy! All one's little character and life goes into the minute preferences which are shown in the copy. In one's own feeble sort, it must be prettier than the original, or it is dead." Ruskin, letter to Charles Eliot Norton, April 11, 1874; quoted in Catherine W. Morley, *John Ruskin: Late Work 1870–1890, The Museum and Guild of St. George: An Educational Experiment* (New York: Garland, 1984), p. 153.

46. Pye, *The Nature and Art of Workmanship,* pp. 66–67.

47. William Morris, *Textile Fabrics: A Lecture Delivered in the Lecture Room of the Exhibition* (London: William Clowes, 1884).

48. William Morris, "The Hopes of Civilization," originally published in Morris, *Signs of Change* (1888).

49. William Morris, "A Factory As It Might Be, part I," *Justice* (May 17, 1884): 2; William Morris, "How We Live and How We Might Live," *Commonweal* (1887), introduction.

50. William Morris, *News from Nowhere, or, An Epoch of Rest, Being Some Chapters from a Utopian Romance* (London: Reeves and Turner, 1891), ch. 1. On the concept of critical utopianism, see Fredric Jameson, *Archaeologies of the Future: The Desire Called Utopia and Other Science Fictions* (London: Verso, 1995); and Marianne Hirsch and Leo Spitzer, "Generations of Nostalgia," in *Contested Pasts: The Politics of Memory,* ed. Katharine Hodgkin and Susannah Radstone (London: Routledge, 2003), p. 83.

51. Deyan Sudjic, "Papering Over the Cracks," *The Guardian* (May 3, 1996): 6.

52. Fiona McCarthy, *William Morris* (London: Faber and Faber, 1994), p. 585.

53. William Morris, "Art Under Plutocracy," lecture delivered November 7, 1883.

54. George N. Barnes, *Amalgamated Society of Engineers: Jubilee Souvenir* (London: ASE, 1901), p. 11. Bishopsgate Library.

55. "Important to Trade Societies," loose clipping, 1851. Howell Ephemera 77/6, Bishopsgate Library.

56. Sidney Webb, Frances Potter Webb, and Robert Alexander Peddie, *The History of Trade Unionism* (London: Longmans, Green and Co., 1902 [orig. pub. 1894]), p. 162.

57. E. P. Thompson, *The Making of the English Working Class* (Harmondsworth: Penguin, 1968 [orig. pub. 1963]). For a useful historiographical overview of this debate, see Jonathan Zeitlin, "From Labour History to the History of Industrial Relations," *Economic History Review* 40/2 (May 1987): 159–184. For a recent analysis of Marx's discussion of the medieval artisan, contrasting his more pragmatic approach to the idealism of Morris, see John Roberts, "Labour, Emancipation and the Critique of Craft Skill," *Journal of Modern Craft* 5/2 (July 2012): 137–148.

58. Thomas Wright, *Our New Masters* (London: Strahan & Co., 1873), quoted in Raphael Samuel, "Class and Classlessness," *Universities and Left Review* 6 (Spring 1959): 44–50; 48. See also Maxine Berg, ed. *Technology and Toil in Nineteenth Century Britain* (London: CSE Books, 1979), p. 11; and A. J. Reid, "Intelligent Artisans and Aristocrats of Labour: The Essays of Thomas Wright," in *The Working Class in Modern British History: Essays in Honour of Henry Pelling,* ed. J. Winter (Cambridge: Cambridge University Press, 1983), pp. 171–186.

59. Webb, Webb, and Peddie, *The History of Trade Unionism,* p. 200.

60. *Rules of the Amalgamated Societies of Engineers* (London: Thomas Poulter and Sons, 1890), p. 8. Bishopsgate Library.

61. Cynthia Cockburn, "The Material of Male Power," *Feminist Review* 9 (October 1981): 41–58; 41. See also Jonathan Zeitlin, "Craft Control and Division of Labor: Engineers 1890–1920," *Cambridge Journal of Economics* 3/3 (1979): 263–274.

62. John Ruskin, *Fors Clavigera* II (February 1871).

63. E. Vansittart Neale, *Prize Essay on the Best Means of Employing the Surplus Funds of the Amalgamated Society of Engineers, &c., in Associative or Other Productive Objects* (London: ASE, 1855), p. 8. Bishopsgate Library.

64. *Full and Authentic Report of the Speeches Delivered at the Great Demonstration of Trade Societies, in Exeter Hall, London, on Thursday, 21st February, 1867* (London: Amalgamated Society of Engineers, 1867), p. 3. Bishopsgate Library.

65. William Newton in *Full and Authentic Report,* p. 14.

66. *Full and Authentic Report,* pp. 24, 29.

67. Samuel Smiles, *Self-Help* (London: 1859), ch. 2, 3.

68. Ibid., ch. 1.

69. Francis Chilton-Young, *Every Man His Own Mechanic* (London: Ward, Lock and Co., 1880), p. 4. My thanks to Stephen Knott for this reference.

70. Smiles, *Self-Help,* ch. 5.

71. John Rowlinson, "Mr. Rowlinson's Tour," *The Trades' Advocate, and Herald of Progress* (July 20, 1850): 29.

72. Barnes, *Amalgamated Society of Engineers: Jubilee Souvenir,* p. 49.

73. The ASE also used the similar slogan "united we stand—divided we fall." *Rules of the Amalgamated Societies of Engineers,* p. 5.

74. Smiles, *Self-Help,* ch. 6.

75. John Ruskin, letter to the *Times* (March 6, 1883), in *John Ruskin: Works,* vol. 30 (New York: Longman, Green, and Co., 1907), p. 317.

76. Robert Hewison, *Art and Society: Ruskin in Sheffield 1876* (London: Guild of St. George/ Brentham Press, 1979), p. 7.

77. Morley, *John Ruskin: Late Work,* pp. 225–226.

78. A set of annotated historic photographs of the Museum of St. George, which shows the original location of Creswick's relief sculpture, is available online at: www.ruskinatwalkley.org.

79. *Arts and Crafts Society: Catalogue of the First Exhibition* (London: Chiswick Press, 1888), pp. 132–133.

80. John Ruskin, *Unto This Last* (London: Cornhill, 1862), part II.

81. Ibid., part I.

82. In early modern England, all interdependent economic relations—like those between a landowner and a tenant—would have been understood as a sort of "friendship." See Keith Wrightson, *English Society, 1580–1680* (London: Routledge, 1993).

83. Ruskin, *Unto This Last,* part I.

84. John Ruskin, *Fors Clavigera* IV (April 1, 1871).

85. Edith Hope Scott, *Ruskin's Guild of St. George* (London: Methuen, 1931), p. viii.

86. Mohandas K. Gandhi, *Unto This Last,* translated by Valji Govindji Desai (Ahmedabad: Jitendra T. Desai, Navajivan Mudranalaya, 1956); available online at: en.wikisource.org/wiki/ Unto_This_Last_-_M._K._Gandhi. My thanks to Alice Motard of Raven Row Gallery for this citation and for discussions about the text.

87. Raymond Williams, *Culture and Materialism: Selected Essays* (London: Verso, 1995 [orig. pub. 1980]), p. 44.

88. The same dichotomy can be observed in Ruskin's descriptions of his political beliefs, which ranged from declaring that he was a "Tory of the old school" to his self-perception as a communist, "'reddest also of the red." Quoted in Hewison, *Art and Society,* p. 13.

89. Maurice Halbwachs, "Individual Memory and Collective Memory," undated [before 1940], in Maurice Halbwachs, *The Collective Memory* (New York: Harper and Row, 1980), pp. 44–45.

90. Ana Douglass and Thomas A. Vogler, *Witness and Memory: The Discourse of Trauma* (New York: Routledge, 2003), pp. 18–19.

91. Jeffrey K. Olick, *States of Memory: Continuities, Conflicts, and Transformations in National Retrospection* (Durham, NC: Duke University Press, 2003), p. 3. See also Paul Connerton, *How Modernity Forgets* (Cambridge: Cambridge University Press, 2009).

92. Suzanne Küchler and Walter Melion, *Images of Memory: On Representation and Forgetting* (Washington, DC: Smithsonian Institution Press, 1991); Andreas Huyssen, *Twilight Memories: Marking Time in a Culture of Amnesia* (New York: Routledge, 1995); Erika Doss, *Memorial Mania: Public Feeling in America* (Chicago: University of Chicago Press, 2010).

93. Benedict Anderson, *Imagined Communities: Reflections on The Origins and Spread of Nationalism* (London: Verso, 1983); Pierre Nora, "Between Memory and History: Les Lieux de Mémoire," *Representations* 26 (Spring 1989): 7–25; Raphael Samuel, *Theatres of Memory, Parts 1 and 2* (London: Verso, 1995, 1998).

94. Halbwachs quoted in Ross, *Remembering the Personal Past*, p. 152.

95. H. D. Rawnsley, *Ruskin and the English Lakes* (London: Macmillan, 1901), pp. 140–142. See also Scott, *Ruskin's Guild of St. George*, p. 10ff.

96. Ibid., p. 136.

97. Joanne Turney, *The Culture of Knitting* (Oxford: Berg Publishers, 2009), p. 49. See also Sabrina Gschwandtner, "Knitting Is...," *Journal of Modern Craft* 1/2 (July 2008): 271–278; Maria Elena Buszek, ed., *Extra/Ordinary: Craft and Contemporary Art* (Durham, NC: Duke University Press, 2011).

98. The keystone of this literature is Rozsika Parker, *The Subversive Stitch: Embroidery and the Making of the Feminine* (London: Women's Press, 1984). For further bibliography and discussion, see Glenn Adamson, *Thinking through Craft* (Oxford: Berg Publishers, 2007), p. 155ff.

99. Mrs. [Isabella Mary] Beeton, *Mrs. Beeton's Book of Needlework* (London: Ward Lock and Tyler, 1870), p. 289; see also Mrs. Bury Palliser, *History of Lace* (London: Sampson, Low & Son & Marston, 1865).

100. Hester M. Poole, "Lace at the Columbian Exposition," *Decorator and Furnisher* 22/6 (September 1893): 219–221; 219.

101. Susan P. Schoelwer, *Connecticut Needlework: Women, Art and Family 1740–1840* (Hartford: Connecticut Historical Society, 2010).

102. Marcus B[ourne] Huish, *Samplers and Tapestry Embroideries* (London: Fine Art Society/Longmans, Green, 1900), plate X.

103. On conservative gender politics in the nineteenth-century labor movement, see Anna Clark, *The Struggle for the Breeches: Gender and the Making of the British Working Class* (Berkeley: University of California Press, 1995); and Sonya O. Rose, "Gender Antagonism and Class Conflict: Exclusionary Strategies of Male Trade Unionists in Nineteenth-Century Britain," *Social History* 13 (1988): 191–208. On the growth of female employment in the textile trades

and other industries, see Maxine Berg, "What Difference Did Women's Work Make to the Industrial Revolution?" *History Workshop Journal* 35 (1993): 22–44.

104. Harriet Martineau, *Society in America,* vol. 2 (Paris: A. and W. Galignani, 1837), p. 178.

105. Elaine Freedgood, "'Fine Fingers': Victorian Handmade Lace and Utopian Consumption," *Victorian Studies* (Summer 2003): 625–647; 628.

106. Ibid., p. 642.

107. Juliette Kristensen, "A Crafty Woman's Touch: A Phenomenology of Embroidery, Piano Playing and Typing," unpublished lecture, Design/Body/Sense conference, Kingston University, 2007.

108. Sonya O. Rose, *Limited Livelihoods: Gender and Class in Nineteenth-Century England* (London: Routledge, 1992), p. 103. See also Joyce Burnette, *Gender, Work and Wages in Industrial Revolution Britain* (Cambridge: Cambridge University Press, 2008).

109. For an overview of Irish "romantic nationalism" alongside comparable movements in Scandinavia, Hungary, and elsewhere, see Wendy Kaplan, *The Arts and Crafts Movement in Europe and America: Design for the Modern World 1880–1920* (Los Angeles: LACMA, 2004).

110. Nicola Gordon Bowe, "The Irish Arts and Crafts Movement," *Irish Arts Review Yearbook* (1990/1991): 172–185; 175.

111. Nellie Ó Cléirigh and Veronica Rowe, *Limerick Lace: A Social History and A Maker's Manual* (Gerrards Cross: Colin Smythe, 1995), p. 12.

112. Mabel F. Robinson, "Irish Lace," *Art Journal* 50 (1887): 145. The Burano Lace School was set up in 1872, also for charitable reasons, as a way of replacing income from the declining local fishing industry.

113. Interview with Clare Browne, V&A, August 30, 2011. My thanks to Clare for her kind assistance with technical and interpretive points regarding the history of Irish lace.

114. James Coleman, "Youghal Convent and Youghal Lace," *Irish Monthly* 24/281 (November 1896): 587–593; 591.

115. An excellent overview is Patricia Wardle, *Victorian Lace* (London: Jenkins, 1968). See chapter 5 passim on Irish lace.

116. Janice Helland, "Caprices of Fashion: Handmade Lace in Ireland 1883–1907," *Textile History* 39/2 (November 2008): 193–222; 213. For more on lace making as a reform activity, see Sarah Archer, "Craft, Class, and Acculturation at the Greenwich House Settlement," *Journal of Modern Craft* 4/3 (Nov. 2011): 231–250.

117. Alan Summerly Cole, *A Renascence of the Irish Art of Lace-Making* (London: Chapman and Hall, 1888), p. 37.

118. Alan Summerly Cole, *Irish Lace: Report Upon Visit to Convents, Classes and Schools…* (London: Eyre and Spottiswoode, 1887), p. 1; Cole, *Irish Lace: Report on his Visit to Lace Making Centers* (April 1889), National Art Library (V&A), 43.C.80, p. 2.

119. Alan Summerly Cole, *Lecture on Designing Patterns for Various Irish Laces* (April 1889), National Art Library (V&A), 43.C.81, p. 11.

120. Alan Summerly Cole quoted in "Two Forgotten Talents of Limerick Lace: Michael Hayes and Eileen O'Donohue," *Irish Arts Review Yearbook* 15 (1999): 61–70; 64.

121. Helland, "Caprices of Fashion," p. 195.

122. Lisa Tickner, *The Spectacle of Women: Imagery of the Suffrage Campaign, 1907–14* (Chicago: University of Chicago Press, 1988), p. 62. My thanks to Hans Liu for his research assistance on the suffragette movement and its craft activities.

123. Tickner, *The Spectacle of Women,* p. 58.

124. Mary Lowndes, "On Banners and Banner-Making," *Englishwoman* (September 1909), reprinted in Tickner, *The Spectacle of Women,* p. 262.

125. The banner, like Terrero's handkerchief, is now in the Museum of London.

126. For Terrero's biography, see Roger Fulford, *Votes for Women: The Story of a Struggle* (London: Faber and Faber, 1957), p. 250; Elizabeth Crawford, *The Women's Suffrage Movement: A Reference Guide 1866–1928* (London: UCL Press, 1999), p. 684.

127. Rozsika Parker, *The Subversive Stitch: Embroidery and the Making of the Feminine* (London: Women's Press, 1984), p. 201.

128. Parker, *The Subversive Stitch,* p. xx.

129. Maureen Daly Goggin, "Fabricating Identity: Janie Terrero's 1912 Embroidered English Suffrage Signature Handkerchief," in *Women and Things, 1750–1950: Gendered Material Strategies,* ed. Maureen Daly Goggin and Beth Fowkes Tobin (Burlington, VT: Ashgate, 2009), p. 19.

130. Ibid., p. 33.

131. Rita Felski, *Doing Time: Feminist Theory and Postmodern Culture* (New York: New York University Press, 2000), pp. 184, 195. Here Felski echoes the groundbreaking work of earlier feminist scholars, notably Judith Butler's *Gender Trouble* (New York: Routledge, 1990).

132. All quotes from Aya Haidar are taken from an interview conducted on September 13, 2011.

133. For a parallel discussion of craft as both symptom and treatment, see Julia Bryan-Wilson, "The AIDS Quilt: Craft Remains," the 2010 Peter Dormer lecture. Online at: www.rca.ac.uk/Default.aspx?ContentID = 504060.

134. *Quilts 1700–2010* was curated by Sue Prichard and was open at the V&A from March 20 to July 4, 2010.

135. See James Elkins, *Pictures and Tears: A History of People Who Have Cried in Front of Paintings* (New York: Routledge, 2001).

136. Hilary Alexander, "Kate Middleton Wedding Dress is Sarah Burton for Alexander McQueen," *Telegraph* (April 29, 2011).

137. "That Dress...," *Daily Mail* (May 2, 2011).

INDEX

Italics indicate illustrations.